Oleksandr Pankieiev (ed.)

Narratives of the Russo-Ukrainian War
A Look Within and Without

With a foreword by Natalia Khanenko-Friesen

Ukrainian Voices

Collected by Andreas Umland

60   Josef Wallmannsberger (ed.)
        Executing Renaissances
        The Poetological Nation of Ukraine
        ISBN 978-3-8382-1741-3

61   Pavlo Kazarin
        The Wild West of Eastern Europe
        A Ukrainian Guide on Breaking
        Free from Empire
        Translated from the Ukrainian
        by Dominique Hoffman
        ISBN 978-3-8382-1842-7

62   Ernest Gyidel
        Ukrainian Public Nationalism in the General Government
        The Case of Krakivski Visti, 1940–1944
        With a foreword by David R. Marples
        ISBN 978-3-8382-1865-6

63   Olexander Hryb
        Understanding Contemporary Russian Militarism
        From Revolutionary to New Generation Warfare
        With a foreword by Mark Laity
        ISBN 978-3-8382-1927-1

64   Orysia Hrudka, Bohdan Ben
        Dark Days, Determined People
        Stories from Ukraine under Siege
        With a foreword by Myroslav Marynovych
        ISBN 978-3-8382-1958-5

The book series "Ukrainian Voices" publishes English- and German-language monographs, edited volumes, document collections, and anthologies of articles authored and composed by Ukrainian politicians, intellectuals, activists, officials, researchers, and diplomats. The series' aim is to introduce Western and other audiences to Ukrainian explorations, deliberations and interpretations of historic and current, domestic, and international affairs. The purpose of these books is to make non-Ukrainian readers familiar with how some prominent Ukrainians approach, view and assess their country's development and position in the world. The series was founded, and the volumes are collected by Andreas Umland, Dr. phil. (FU Berlin), Ph. D. (Cambridge), Associate Professor of Politics at the Kyiv-Mohyla Academy and an Analyst in the Stockholm Centre for Eastern European Studies at the Swedish Institute of International Affairs.

Oleksandr Pankieiev (ed.)

NARRATIVES OF THE RUSSO-UKRAINIAN WAR

A Look Within and Without

With a foreword by Natalia Khanenko-Friesen

Bibliographic information published by the Deutsche Nationalbibliothek
Die Deutsche Nationalbibliothek lists this publication in the Deutsche Nationalbibliografie; detailed bibliographic data are available on the Internet at http://dnb.d-nb.de.

Bibliografische Information der Deutschen Nationalbibliothek
Die Deutsche Nationalbibliothek verzeichnet diese Publikation in der Deutschen Nationalbibliografie; detaillierte bibliografische Daten sind im Internet über http://dnb.d-nb.de abrufbar.

ISBN (Print): 978-3-8382-1964-6
ISBN (E-Book [PDF]): 978-3-8382-7964-0
© *ibidem*-Verlag, Hannover • Stuttgart 2025
All rights reserved.

No part of this publication may be reproduced, stored in or introduced into a retrieval system, or transmitted, in any form, or by any means (electronic, mechanical, photocopying, recording or otherwise) without the prior written permission of the publisher. Any person who commits any unauthorized act in relation to this publication may be liable to criminal prosecution and civil claims for damages.

Alle Rechte vorbehalten. Das Werk einschließlich aller seiner Teile ist urheberrechtlich geschützt. Jede Verwertung außerhalb der engen Grenzen des Urheberrechtsgesetzes ist ohne Zustimmung des Verlages unzulässig und strafbar. Dies gilt insbesondere für Vervielfältigungen, Übersetzungen, Mikroverfilmungen und elektronische Speicherformen sowie die Einspeicherung und Verarbeitung in elektronischen Systemen.

Printed in the United States of America

Contents

Authors, sorted alphabetically ix

Foreword — The war that will change the world: Russia's invasion of Ukraine and why we need to care
Natalia Khanenko-Friesen xi

Introduction — Assessing the Russo-Ukrainian war: Are we reading the signs correctly now?
Oleksandr Pankieiev 1

Acknowledgments 14

1 The signs were there for all to see, but we did not read them right
Bo Petersson 15

2 Four false narratives of Russia's war in Ukraine
Davis Daycock 21

3 Ukrainians have crossed the threshold of fear: They're fighting for victory
Mykola Bielieskov 29

4 "We are all on the front lines now": Baltic states' solidarity with Ukraine
Dovilė Budrytė 39

5 The fallacy of "Russian culture" in Ukraine
Hiroaki Kuromiya 49

6 Contradicting Putin: Ukrainians and Russians are not "one people"
Nataliya Shpylova-Saeed 55

7 "Never again" vs. "We can repeat it": Russians will pay any price to restore the glory of Soviet victory in WW II
Oleksii Polegkyi 63

8 Putin's dehumanizing discourses and the power of Ukrainian resistance and resilience
Cynthia Nielsen 71

v

9 Explaining the "Westsplainers": Can a Western scholar be an authority on Central and Eastern Europe?
Aliaksei Kazharski 79

10 The fall of Lysychansk and the fate of the Donbas
Hiroaki Kuromiya 87

11 Russian foreign policy and the origins of the "Russian World"
Oleksii Polegkyi and Dmytro Bushuyev 97

12 To be or not to be: Attitudes of Ukrainian society about gender equality and diversity after Russia's invasion
Tamara Martsenyuk 105

13 Russia's war against Ukraine: Empires don't die overnight
Serhii Plokhy 113

14 Ukraine must restore control over its sovereign territory
Mariia Zolkina 119

15 Ukrainians forced into fighting an asymmetrical war, getting good at it
Mykola Bielieskov 127

16 What we are seeing now in Ukrainian society is grassroots Ukrainization
Olexiy Haran 137

17 I hope that Ukrainians will encourage new voices in Poland
Elżbieta Kwiecińska 147

18 After Russia's departure from great power status, the world will once again become bi-polar
Alexander Motyl 157

19 Participation of lgbtq+ people in the war effort cannot be ignored
Maryna Shevtsova 167

20 The West either deals with Mr. Putin now on our own terms or later on his terms
Michael Bociurkiw 177

21 In the EU, Ukraine is perceived as "the eastern edge of Western Europe"
Peter Vermeersch 187

22 Russia has failed to subordinate Ukraine
Alexander Vindman 195

23 Russia's disinformation goes nuclear
Polina Sinovets, Khrystyna Holynska, and John V. Parachini 209

24 Russo-Ukrainian war is a clash between two national armies and two global world views
Agnieszka Legucka 219

25 Ukrainian universities engaged in war effort beyond expectations
Serhiy Kvit 227

26 Ukrainian refugees are gradually finding their place in Irish society
Donnacha Ó Beacháin 235

27 More than a year into the escalated war finds Ukraine with a stronger voice in Western media
Marta Dyczok 243

28 Equipping Ukraine for the long haul: Some initial thoughts
Frank Ledwidge 253

29 Russians are going into Ukraine to kill Ukrainians and to be killed
Marci Shore 263

30 Russia's undue influence on Western scholars and scholarship
Hiroaki Kuromiya 267

31 We value Canada's support of Ukraine's future membership in NATO
Yuliya Kovaliv 273

32 Kremlin plans on a long-term engagement, on a long war
Bo Petersson 279

33 Russians cannot perpetuate their myth of Russia if they lose control over Ukraine
Jade McGlynn 285

34 UK can become a special platform for rebuilding Ukraine
Andrii Zharikov 293

35 Ukrainians need to win the war as quickly as possible
Mychailo Wynnyckyj 301

36 Losing intellectuals on the front lines is a disaster for Ukrainian culture
Iryna Tsilyk 313

37 Sanctions are indirectly sowing divisions among Russians
Margarita Balmaceda 321

38 Evil must be called evil
Yevhenia Podobna 327

39 Russia selectively and deceptively manipulates Western media and public discourses
Vitaly Chernetsky 345

40 Commitments to Ukraine in Budapest Memorandum are legally binding
Mariana Budjeryn 355

41 The field isn't "Slavic studies" at all — it should be called "Russian propaganda studies" — and a few exceptions only confirm the rule
Ewa Thompson 365

42 Time is on Ukraine's side in this war
Mitchell Orenstein 371

43 Invasion of Ukraine has proved to be a disastrous decision
Rajan Menon 379

Index of Names 389

Authors, sorted alphabetically

Margarita Balmaceda	321
Mykola Bielieskov	29, 127
Michael Bociurkiw	177
Mariana Budjeryn	355
Dovilė Budrytė	39
Dmytro Bushuyev	97
Vitaly Chernetsky	345
Davis Daycock	21
Marta Dyczok	243
Olexiy Haran	130
Khrystyna Holynska	209
Aliaksei Kazharski	79
Natalia Khanenko-Friesen	xi
Yuliya Kovaliv	262
Hiroaki Kuromiya	49, 87, 267
Serhiy Kvit	227
Elżbieta Kwiecińska	147
Frank Ledwidge	253
Agnieszka Legucka	219
Tamara Martsenyuk	105
Jade McGlynn	285
Rajan Menon	379
Alexander Motyl	157
Cynthia Nielsen	71
Donnacha Ó Beacháin	235
Mitchell Orenstein	371
Oleksandr Pankieiev	1
John Parachini	199
Bo Petersson	15, 279
Serhii Plokhy	113
Yevhenia Podobna	327
Oleksii Polegkyi	63, 97
Maryna Shevtsova	167
Marci Shore	263
Nataliya Shpylova-Saeed	55
Polina Sinovets	209
Ewa Thompson	365
Iryna Tsilyk	313
Peter Vermeersch	187
Alexander Vindman	195
Mychailo Wynnyckyj	301
Andrii Zharikov	293
Mariia Zolkina	119

Foreword

The war that will change the world: Russia's invasion of Ukraine and why we need to care

In your hands you have an unusual collection of essays. No doubt you have been following expert discussions about the Russian war in Ukraine, which resumed with new force in 2022 after some eight years of continued fighting in parts of Eastern Ukraine that were occupied by Russian troops in 2014. Depending on your positionality, background, academic, and general interests, you most likely have selected commentators and analysts whose take on this escalated invasion you value and whose line of thought speaks to you the most. Perhaps this book aligns with the opinions of your preferred experts. Perhaps you may find here new rationale and arguments that invite you to reconsider your currently held understandings of what has been happening in Ukraine, Europe, and the world since the pivotal year of 2022.

I wish this book would never had to have been put together. I wish the world was not witnessing this war, which many are rightly worried about, concerned about the directions it has taken thus far and where events could go next. I most certainly wish that Ukraine was not invaded by its neighbour, neither in 2022 nor in 2014. It has long been clear that Russia's invasion of Ukraine is more than a regional conflict—so many other domino pieces of fragile global peace and security began to fall at the very moment when Russian tanks advanced deep into Ukrainian territory with the goal of capturing Kyiv, Ukraine's capital, on 24 February 2022.

I belong to the category of people who were raised on the liberal values and ideas of the late 20th and early 21st centuries that advanced a powerful and convincing line of reasoning: *democracy, liberty, and respect for international order will prevail*. So much work was done toward these aspirational goals. After the horrors and genocides of the Second World War, so many nations and states invested themselves into rebuilding Europe and the world as a shared political space where peace would rule, never imagining there would be a return to large-scale military actions and brutality. So much good work was done by various nations around the world toward meaningful memorialization of WW II, commemoration of its largest tragedies, the genocides, nuclear bombing, mass murders, and other losses that the war brought upon peoples and nations. In particular, the work that was done in what today is the EU toward reconciliation, redress, and atonement—directed at rebuilding relationships between and within states that once had fought on different sides of the front lines—appeared to be very successful. Similarly, so did the work that the world did jointly to establish an international network of organizations called upon to oversee and govern global affairs in the post-WW II context and later in the post-Cold War times. All this created a sense for so many of us that global peace is indeed a possibility, that humanity learned its lesson from the wars, and that the world is at the point of realizing that large-scale worldwide conflicts are in our past.

In contrast, there have been other powerful voices—the one of Margaret MacMillan, for example—who have been warning us not to fall for this illusory vision of the future. In her book *The Rhyme of History: Lessons of the Great War*, published in 2013 just prior to Russia's illegal annexation of Crimea in 2014, MacMillan revisits two historical periods, comparing the global state of affairs at the onset of WW I and the global context in which the world has found itself on the eve of the Great War's 100th anniversary (MacMillan 2013). There are too many parallels and similar developments, she insists—in global politics, economy, technology, and means of communication—to be ignored by us, the contemporaries. Lulled by our own imagined inconceivability of returning to the most brutal pages of human history, we continued to believe that such mass violence is no longer possible, given that humanity has "progressed" so much after what it had seen and lived through in the two world wars.

MacMillan cautioned us that the hundredth anniversary since the onset of WW I should make us think more critically about the future, because there are so many parallels between the way global affairs and global politics unfolded just on the eve of 1914 and now. Like these days, just prior to WW I the world witnessed accelerated growth and development, with breathtaking technological innovations that upended long-established statuses quo in the economic, political, cultural, and social contexts of the day. Electricity was taking over, railroads were being built, manufacturing and new global corporations were constantly growing, mass migrations were occurring, new and radical cultural ideas (for example, psychoanalysis) and political ideologies were emerging, human rights movements were expanding, and "the predatory ideologies of fascism and Soviet communism" were taking root (2013: 6).

Fast forward to the early 21st century. The recent global disruptions of the 1990s—i.e., the collapse of Communism in Europe, the Balkan wars, the genocides in Srebrenica and Rwanda—were in the past, however recent. Meanwhile, although the start of the new century was unquestionably affected by the terrorist attack on the United States on 11 September 2001, its first decade is now recognized as being a relatively peaceful period, during which only several regional interstate military conflicts stood out on the basis of losses, depth, and extension of the conflict: Eritrea–Ethiopia, India–Pakistan war, and Iraq versus the United States and its allies (Harbom and Wallensteen 2010, 61).

Whether still lingering or recuperating from these and other conflicts, the world moved on and began to embrace new technological advancements reaching into every corner of human life and (almost) every corner of the planet. The 21st century has brought about novel and dramatic shifts in the organization of our increasingly globalized lives, forcing millions to leave their homelands in search of better prospects for their families elsewhere. New technologies offered novel opportunities for operating our economies, making and saving our monies, making and raising our children, and communicating with each other across the globe. The rise of corporations, infused with ever-changing and adapting AI technologies, offered unprecedented opportunities for use but also for abuse of informational flows, directly feeding into the spread of disinformation, hybrid warfares, and leading to brazen violations of international law and world order.

In the political domain, another important development has taken place: a gradual change in the very nature and distribution of global power. The rise of Communist China to the position of a new and powerful global leader, and its growing influence on world affairs, has added another layer of complexity in today's historical context. Alexander Motyl, whose article is included in this collection, offers further insights into how distant historical context can illuminate today's circumstances. One important thing that we learned from the Cold War, Motyl asserts, is that bi-polar systems are less conducive to wars than multi-polar systems (ch. 18). With China reaching new heights and Russia trying to retain its sense of relevance, now with the help of the war in Ukraine, the global system is once again being redrawn—just like in the early 20th century, becoming multi-polar and more fraught with tension.

In the 2010s, democracy made big strides toward peace building in the world; so it was felt, yet we the citizens of the world started witnessing many unsettling developments, including rising global tensions and the arrival of various powerful far-right ideologies and political movements that put down roots around the world, and alarmingly so, within its democratic fold. As counter-actions, we have seen the impressive mobilization of various grassroots resistance movements that became political movements over a short period of time. We have been witnessing the phenomenal growth of media and communication technologies that accelerate the spread of radical ideologies and conspiracy theories. To our chagrin, the same technologies gave birth to very expedient means of undermining truth telling and trustworthy information sharing, and thus we have been watching, with much worry, the impact that novel and powerful disinformation wars have on our national and international political institutions, our communities, and our allies.

Within the same decade, in 2014 an act of inter-state military aggression took place on the territory of Ukraine, and as time went by, the impact of this violation of an international order was felt deeper and deeper, and on global scale. In the early spring of 2014, exploiting the political upheaval in Ukraine—when the entire nation was caught up in active protests against the rule of President Viktor Yanukovych's repressive, anti-European government—and having just wrapped up hosting the Olympic games in Sochi, President Vladimir Putin swiftly and cunningly moved Russian troops into Crimea. Within mere days, the peninsula was occupied by uniformed "green men" without any identifiable insignia, and within two weeks Ukraine's Crimean Autonomous Republic was illegally annexed to the Russian Federation in a staged referendum that was criticized by the international community as fake. Not until 2022 would most of the world begin to comprehend and see the full repercussions of the illegal annexation of Crimea, finally understanding that de facto it was the beginning of a new, protracted, and on many counts highly dangerous "non-regional" war that in 2024 marked its tenth year.

In comparison to various "regional" wars and military conflicts that have affected other parts of the globe, Russia's occupation of Ukraine in 2014 and its recent effort to accelerate the military takeover of Ukraine have a profound potential to change the course of global history. Russia's attack on Ukraine has undermined and challenged global peace, security, and international law. Motyl, as mentioned earlier, sees this war as an imminent boost to the establishment of a much-preferred bi-polar system within the framework of global relations, where the main competitors remain China and the US with its allies. Whatever time it might take, and whatever outcome the current war will have, the scholar expects the resistance so many nations around the globe have displayed towards Russia in response to its open aggressive military invasion of Ukraine to cause Russia to lose its position of global leader. Emerging new juxtapositions will change the balance of global powers.

Realization by observers of the war's neocolonial nature also has been growing, along with an understanding of its global implications. There is a comprehension now that the war is directly informed by Russia's neocolonial appetite, which aims to annihilate Ukraine as a state and reabsorb the Ukrainian territory as its own. In the present volume, this argument is revisited in various ways by Oleksii Polegkyi (7, 11), Dmytro Bushuyev (11), Cynthia Nielsen (8), Peter Vermeersch (21), Bo Petersson (1, 32), and other contributors.

Serhii Plokhy (13) sees the eruption of this war as the death throes of Russia's imperial legacy — as the final phase, however slow and painful it might be, of disintegration of the lingering (neo)totalitarianism that had continued to define Russia as an autocratic state after the collapse of the USSR and led to the establishment of the repressed and state-controlled social, political, and cultural landscape in Russian society.

Another outcome of the war is Europe's growing sense of solidarity with Ukraine as a part of the European cultural and political space — described here in chapters by Dovilė Budrytė (4), Elżbieta Kwiecińska (17), Donnacha Ó Beacháin (26), and Andrii Zharikov (34). Despite differences in how various European states expressed and offered their support to Ukraine, we have also seen significant mobilization around NATO, making the alliance stronger and more relevant than it has been for a long time. Repercussions of the Russo-Ukrainian war expand beyond the European level, as under its pressure nations around the world — and in particular, those far away from Europe — are drawn into alliances based either on pre-existing political and economic ties with Russia or a lack of understanding of history and what led to the genocidal Russian invasion of Ukraine.

An important for Ukraine and globally felt impact of the war concerns re-imagination of the place of Ukraine and Ukrainians within global history. The long-overdue realization is growing that Ukrainians are a different people from the Russians—a topic addressed in extended ways in contributions to this volume by Hiroaki Kuromiya (5, 10, 30), Nataliya Shpylova-Saeed (6), Agnieszka Legucka (24), and others. Another large and looming topic of discussion—calls for reassessment of Western systems of reference and framing when it comes to understanding Ukraine, Russia, and their long-term unequal relationship over many centuries—is informed by arguments put forward here by Aliaksei Kazharski (9), Jade McGlynn (33), Vitaly Chernetsky (39), and others.

From the vantage point of today, as I write these words in late spring 2024, much has changed in how political and cultural analysts have been discussing the war over the last two years. The presented collection of essays and interviews offers readers an opportunity: (a) to revisit and re-examine the pivotal moments and aspects of the ongoing Russian war in Ukraine since its escalation in 2022 and the beginning of the full-scale invasion; and (b) to explore key takeaways and analytical interpretations, developed and employed in real time, by scholars, policymakers, and political analysts from both within and without Ukraine. The book, therefore, is an invitation to engage with experts and follow the evolving international discourse on the events and outcomes of Russia's invasion of Ukraine, which reached its tenth year in 2024.

To highlight the evolution of the analytical discourse since February 2022, the articles here are placed in the chronological order in which they appeared. The table of contents will give you a sense of how the topics evolved and shifted over time and what was of concern to the analysts and to Ukraine at any given moment in the war. The contributors represent a broad spectrum of scholars with diverse academic training and different cultural backgrounds, research interests, citizenship, and national belonging. The submissions were originally published in *Forum for Ukrainian Studies* (ukrainian-studies.ca)—the prime analytical platform that the Canadian Institute of Ukrainian Studies (cius.ca) has been publishing since 2016. As the online newsmagazine of our Contemporary Ukraine Studies Program, *Forum* has justifiably earned a strong international reputation, and as the CIUS director I am proud to state that this stellar collection of thought-provoking analyses, delivered by globally recognized experts, is a direct outcome of our work at the institute, focused on providing international audiences with academically sound and analytically valid interpretations of global affairs that have Ukraine at their core.

Debates on how to properly name Russia's ten years of military aggression against Ukraine are still ongoing. In English, it has come to be referred to as the *Russo-Ukrainian war*. Some continue to operate with the term "Russian war *against* Ukraine," aiming to maintain emphasis on the fact that this war was started by the Russian Federation and that calling it the "war in Ukraine" or the "Ukraine/Ukrainian war" is unacceptable. Most recently, the Ukrainians favour an apt phrase, *velyka viina* (great war), reminding outsiders of the very existential threat that this war poses to Ukraine. It is, after all, a war in which a large neighbour nation, once the core of a former empire, then a totalitarian regime, and now an autocratic state—in support of the ambition of its autocratic leader to regain his country's neocolonial dominance in the world and restore a centuries-long repressive hold over its neighbour—invaded its neighbour state, intending to fully reabsorb it. To accomplish this, Russia is now actively and openly perpetuating a large-scale genocidal war against Ukraine, illegally appropriating its lands, destroying its resources, torturing those who resist, abducting and indoctrinating children, and aiming to eradicate the very essence of its people, their culture, history, identity, memory, and language.

Of all the points raised and addressed in this collection, one persistent note continues to resonate in me. It is a kind of question that many commentators have been grappling with when tasked with providing empirically grounded and analytically sound commentary on Russia's ongoing efforts to decimate Ukraine as a nation, a people, and a state. *How do we in the 21st century respond to the new, large-scale neocolonial war at the heart of Europe as analysts, commentators, and human beings?* How could such an unthinkable idea—to cancel an entire nation by means of extermination and distraction—even be conceivable after the crimes and genocides of WW II? What vocabulary can help us to deliver on our professional obligation and enable us to effectively tackle this task of explaining what is happening in Ukraine, without undermining our expert credibility but also without suspending our own subjectivities?

I found a passage from Marci Shore's interview (29) with the editor of this volume, Oleksandr Pankieiev, so powerful when she shares the story of her Yale professor Tony Judt contemplating the fate of Europe in the 20th century. Precisely these words of his struck me, as they struck Shore: "We are unwise to laugh too quickly at those who describe the world as a conflict between good and evil. If you can't use the word 'evil,' you have a real problem thinking about what happened in the world." This invitation—to follow our deeply felt and implicitly experienced inner truths when it comes to comprehending the scope and purpose of Russia's war in Ukraine—is redemptive, as the evil that is being committed by Russia on the territory of Ukraine these days is not even masked or covered up; on the contrary, it is quite bare, Shore states, and propagandized as the desirable, even holy, course of action.

The future is still ahead of us as we endeavour to imagine and predict the outcomes of this war and its broader impact on the world. One thing is clear, though: to successfully resolve the current immense tensions that have pervaded the globe in recent years, any state using war and human extermination as a geopolitical tool for self-advancement should be compelled to leave the political stage of world affairs as a key international player. I invite you to read the essays included in this volume to better understand the role and place of Ukraine in this existential struggle for the global good.

Natalia Khanenko-Friesen
Director, Canadian Institute of Ukrainian Studies
Huculak Chair in Ukrainian Culture and Ethnography
Faculty of Arts, University of Alberta

Edmonton, June 2024

Works cited

Harbom, Lotta, and Peter Wallensteen. 2010. "Patterns of major armed conflicts, 2000–2009." Appendix 2A. *SIPRI Yearbook 2010: Armaments, Disarmament and International Security*. https://www.sipri.org/sites/default/files/SIPRIYB201002A.pdf.

MacMillan, Margaret. 2013. *The Rhyme of History: Lessons of the Great War*. The Brookings Essay. Brookings Institution Press, 14 December 2013. http://csweb.brookings.edu/content/research/essays/2013/rhyme-of-history.html.

INTRODUCTION

Assessing the Russo-Ukrainian war: Are we reading the signs correctly now?

Oleksandr Pankieiev

July 2024

> Oleksandr Pankieiev is the editor-in-chief of *Forum for Ukrainian Studies,* the online analytical magazine of the Contemporary Ukraine Studies Program at the Canadian Institute of Ukrainian Studies, University of Alberta. With a Candidate of Sciences (PhD equiv.) degree in history from the National Academy of Sciences of Ukraine's Hrushevsky Institute of Ukrainian Archaeography and Source Studies, his main research interests include the history of Steppe Ukraine (Southern Ukraine) and Russia-Ukraine relations. He also pursues research in the fields of ethnography, propaganda, digital humanities, and Ukrainian Canadian diaspora studies. Pankieiev is the author of historical sourcebooks, edited collections, and numerous articles on related topics.

The Russo-Ukrainian war, which started in 2014 and escalated on 24 February 2022, has massive implications for the world-order architecture that can be traced and observed in many aspects of everyday life on all continents. The most severe and sinister consequences of the war are borne by Ukraine. For one more time in its history, it has become the epicentre of war—the biggest conflict in Europe since WW II.

As the Kremlin's war on Ukraine progressed to the full-scale invasion, many initiatives throughout the world were set up or reoriented their focus to examine more closely the rapidly changing situation. Nuanced analytical information about Russia's war against Ukraine was needed from a variety of angles: defence, humanitarian aid, history, identities, international relations, media landscape, firsthand testimony, etc.

Published since 2016 under the auspices of the Contemporary Ukraine Studies Program at CIUS (cius.ca), the online analytical and scholarly magazine *Forum for Ukrainian Studies* (ukrainian-studies.ca) has allowed experts, practitioners, and academics to discuss, explore, reflect upon, develop, and transform international understanding of contemporary Ukraine. More recently, *Forum* has also launched new projects with the aim of better understanding and informing the world about the Russo-Ukrainian war from an analytical and scholarly approach. Being housed at CIUS, which has almost 50 years of experience and expertise in w holistic research of Ukraine, has helped the *Forum* team to navigate many complex questions. Significantly, the institute's own history is also a part of the global story of Ukraine's struggle for recognition. For a long time, émigré communities in the European, North and South American, and Australian diaspora were virtually the only place where the concept of Ukraine was preserved, nurtured, and continued to be researched.

In 1976, when CIUS was established at the University of Alberta, the Soviet Union was well into yet another campaign to curtail re-emerging tentative but also powerful signs of Ukrainian identity. In 1972 alone, several hundred dissidents, cultural figures, and scholars in the Ukrainian SSR were arrested or fired — under the pretext of combating "anti-Soviet activities" and "bourgeois nationalism" but in reality fearing the Ukrainian identity movement that had burgeoned in the 1960s, partially as a result of the Khrushchev Thaw. This wave of repressions also deliberately targeted many historians whose topics of research were deemed dangerous to the imposed, pervasive, and largely false Soviet/Russian interpretation of Ukrainian history. Only institutions abroad, like the Ukrainian Free University (Vienna, Prague, and Munich), the Harvard Ukrainian Research Institute, and CIUS (Edmonton and Toronto), as well as individual scholars at other universities, could conduct research on Ukraine in those years, and for this determined and increasingly compelling activity they were also targeted with discreditation efforts by the KGB (Kohut 2024). Gravely handicapped by centuries-long persecution, rapacious genocide, and statelessness, Ukraine remained invisible to the outside world, a terribly disadvantageous situation, perpetuated by the almost complete lack of awareness or demand for knowledge about it. The academic fields of Slavic, East European, Soviet, or Russian studies subsumed Ukraine's culture-history in their "grand narrative" frameworks, where Ukrainian existence was not acknowledged and did not have an authentic voice. In this colonial vacuum, "Does Ukraine have a history?" was actually posited as a legitimate question, which then demanded to be addressed unequivocally (Von Hagen 1995).

Ukraine regaining its state independence in 1991 allowed it to start researching and writing its own history. But Russia viewed this as a departure from its "zone of influence." The 2004 democratic Orange Revolution, which rejected the rigged presidential election that had brought in Viktor Yanukovych, a candidate with a pro-Russian agenda, was interpreted in Russia as a direct threat to Vladimir Putin's attempts to consolidate his power and influence over the former republics of the Soviet Union. The clear pro-democratic trajectory of Ukrainians and their desire for closer integration with the European Union did not sit well with Russia, either. In 2013, the Euromaidan erupted in protest against Yanukovych's decision to abandon an Association Agreement with the EU and instead turn to the Russia-led Eurasian Economic Union, contrary to the people's will. The Revolution of Dignity started when Yanukovych tried to violently remove the protesters from the Kyiv city centre; by 20 February 2014 around a hundred were killed, and President Yanukovych abdicated and fled the country. Russia used this very moment to invade Ukraine, as on the same day covert Russian forces began the illegal seizure of Ukraine's Autonomous Republic of Crimea. Later that year, using hybrid warfare tactics Russia also occupied numerous districts of Donetsk and Luhansk oblasts.

All this time, there was a demand for information about Ukraine as never before. Still, narratives about the war in Ukraine were dominated by Russian propaganda, which framed it as a "Ukrainian crisis." It was a clear indication to us at CIUS, particularly in the Contemporary Ukraine Studies Program under the direction of historian Volodymyr Kravchenko, that new initiatives were acutely needed in order to combat misrepresentations of Ukraine in media and professional circles and to mobilize recent academic knowledge that had been developed in Ukraine, at institutions abroad, and by individual scholars.

Thus, in response to the escalated invasion *Forum* launched the Media Monitoring Service (MMS). This project produces weekly media reports that examine Ukraine's portrayal in North American media and identifies misconceptions and disinformation about Ukraine that have been disseminated, consciously or not, by reputable outlets, often those with a large readership.

An unanticipated albeit uniquely valuable benefit from the MMS has been its replenishment of *Forum*'s pool of potential contributors by highlighting the op-eds of renowned experts on Ukraine, the region, and the war; the *Forum* editorial team can then nimbly adjust its publication strategy as appropriate, inviting selected authors to address relevant theoretical and factual issues in more detail in the form of short essays and interviews. The diversity of professional backgrounds of the contributors in the present collected volume not only gives greater depth to our understanding of the events of the Russo-Ukrainian war from its start in 2014 to its current escalated invasion stage but also puts it in the broader context of the preceding events and theoretical concepts that dominated the political, economic, and cultural field and precipitated the war. The voices included in this collection are representatives of academia, analysts who work with different think tanks, diplomatic practitioners, former military officers, journalists, writers, and film directors. These authors come from Ukraine and other countries, which helps us to understand their positions from perspectives both within and without.

This volume presents a selected collection of essays and interviews from among those published by *Forum for Ukrainian Studies* during the first two years of Russia's full-scale invasion of Ukraine. The materials not included in this collection are also of high value, and we encourage readers to visit the *Forum* website (ukrainian-studies.ca) and find them there. The first text in this collection was published on 7 March 2022, almost immediately after the escalated invasion began, and the last one was released on 15 February 2024. All the essays and interviews in the book are presented chronologically, putting them in the larger context of the events that unfolded within Ukraine and outside of its borders and contributing to the redefinition of many perceived ideas—most of all to a reconceptualization of the fundamental principles of global order. We trust that in this new format, these texts will continue to help readers to understand and analyze the overarching narratives and discourses that have been produced around or influenced by those events at particular moments.

Many of the essays and interviews speak to each other and tackle the same sets of questions. In some cases, we intentionally asked the same (or slightly rephrased) questions of different experts, seeking to comprehend how understandings of Ukraine as an actor have shifted in various discourses and scholarly fields throughout the full-scale invasion. Some questions may seem provocative, but we encourage you to persevere and read the whole book in order to maximize appreciation and benefit from its unique format.

At the start of Russia's escalated invasion, there was a moment when many presumed experts were puzzled and shocked by the fact that they hadn't seen it coming. Bo Petersson's essay title captures the prevailing mood of that time among Western experts who had studied Russia and Ukraine in their respective fields for decades: "The signs were there for all to see, but we did not read them right" (ch. 1). Olexiy Haran mentions in his interview (16) that in 2014 "very few experts […] anticipated the annexation of Crimea because it was so irrational" and that in 2022 "it seemed irrational for Putin to start a full-scale invasion and try to conquer Kyiv"— but we all know that he did. A number of essays and interviews in this volume tackle the question of why the escalation happened and how those "rational" and "irrational" causes have been reinterpreted over the two years of the escalated invasion.

In his essay, Prague-based Aliaksei Kazharski (9) asks whether Western experts have been well-informed or had enough expertise to comment on Ukraine. He deals with the "Westsplaining" and "Westsplainer" phenomena. In late February 2022, the vast majority of scholars and experts who were providing explanations of the historical and geopolitical causes that precipitated Russia's escalated invasion of Ukraine had no background in Ukrainian studies. Kazharski and some other authors point out that the problem with those commentators is their Russo-centric interpretation of both past and contemporary events. In her interview (41), Ewa Thompson argues that the root of the problem is that Slavic studies in North American academia have been dominated by scholars trained in Russian studies, who mostly came directly from Russia and occupied key academic positions at leading universities in the US. She mentions, moreover, the generations of students who have been trained in the traditions of Russian historiography. Teaching courses about Ukraine's history, culture, and literature can change the situation. Vitaly Chernetsky (39) asserts that decolonization of the curriculum is crucial to changing the overall academic field. Chernetsky and Thompson describe the theoretical complexity of decolonization in the context of the specific historical and cultural relations between Russia and Ukraine. Chernetsky deconstructs the notions of postcolonialism and postmodernism, explaining their place in the cultural spaces of both countries that were constructed after the fall of the Soviet Union. He also examines the cancellation of Russia's participation and demotion of its cultural status in the West, which have become points of action and discussion, and how Russians respond by framing themselves as the victims.

In one of three essays contributing to this volume, Hiroaki Kuromiya examines "distinct Russian culture" and argues that it is a tool of cultural appropriation and colonial expansion (5). The language of literature doesn't define its belonging, and the Russian language of writing doesn't justify equating it with Russian culture outside the Russian Federation. He explains that "Ukraine has Ukrainian culture, not a 'distinctive Russian culture,' even when it is written and expressed in the Russian language." Kuromiya concludes his essay by explaining how Rus' and Russia are different. Nataliya Shpylova-Saeed's essay (6) examines Russian mnemonic constructs which foster the idea that Ukrainians and Russians are "one people" and Ukraine's "(r)evolutionary" departure from the shared memorial space that Russia has forced on Ukraine. That is why, according to Shpylova-Saeed, the war against Ukraine is another forceful attempt to Russify Ukraine. In his essay about the fall of Lysychansk (10), Kuromiya says that Putin has mercy neither for Ukrainians nor for his own people or soldiers. In his desire to achieve the goal of subjugating Ukraine, the Russian president doesn't care about casualties on either side.

Oleksii Polegkyi's essay (7) examines one of the cornerstones of Russia's memory politics, which it has used to project its power within its borders, on its neighbours, and far abroad. Russia's public and political spheres are defined and shaped by its mythicized interpretations of World War II and the cult of victory that emerged from those interpretations. Russian propaganda has amplified and twisted those interpretations to such a degree that the Kremlin used them to justify its aggression against Ukraine. Cynthia Nielsen's essay (8) posits that Putin's and Stalin's regimes are alike in their views and violent attitudes toward Ukraine. She also points out that Russia's imperial discourses—in contrast to those that dominated in Europe, regarding the colonized as exotic others— did not construct the view of Ukraine and Ukrainians as the Other but instead promoted the view that Ukrainians and Russians are the same people.

Russia's war against Ukraine is also about Putin's "misreading of history," as Serhii Plokhy opines in his interview (13), but it is also the sign of another process. Plokhy is convinced that what we see indicates an extended decline of the empire, which started in WW I and is still happening today. The Russo-Ukrainian war is also symbolic of Putin's failure to recognize that Ukraine's democratic trajectory is not a plot against Russia orchestrated by the West but an authentic European cultural-historical tradition possessed by Ukraine long before modern institutions such as the European Union were created.

Davis Daycock's essay (2) deconstructs the justifications that President Putin employed to start the invasion. The problem of NATO's "expansion," alleged "genocide" and oppression of the Russian-speaking population in Ukraine, and the denial of Ukraine's statehood and labelling of Ukrainians as "fascists" were the main narratives that Russia used to justify its aggression. All of them, Daycock shows, are false and manipulative.

Russia also justifies its war against Ukraine as part of preserving and protecting the *russkii mir* "Russian World" as the space that goes beyond its borders. A review of the "Russian World" as an integral component of modern Russia's political and ideological concept is provided by Oleksii Polegkyi and Dmytro Bushuyev in their essay (11). They identify three elements of the "Russian World" that are at the foundation of its experience: the Russian Orthodox Church, common historical memory, and "heartless technocrat[s]" that execute any command without questioning—for instance, Russian soldiers who kill Ukrainians and frame it as them "just trying to do their job."

The escalated invasion has affected people in Ukraine many different ways. Ukrainian society has shown incredible resistance and adaptivity to wartime's new realities and hardships. The war has also ushered in a new era, where identities are constituted more sharply, and attitudes and worldviews are undergoing rapid transformation. Many texts in this collection address how the war impacts Ukrainian society and its extraordinary capacity for resilience.

On the one hand, Haran reminds us in his interview that Ukraine's internationally admired resilience did not appear overnight on 24 February 2022 and should not be surprising. He says that the "distinctive nation-building trends" in Ukrainian society date far back even before 1991. On the other hand, Mychailo Wynnyckyj admits in his interview (35) that Ukrainian society has indeed undergone massive changes since the full-scale invasion. First of all, the invasion has shattered the myth of the "cleft nation"; instead,

Wynnyckyj uses the metaphor of a *beehive* to describe how Ukrainian society functions. It is not often hierarchical in how it functions, and it has many instances of situational leadership—in contrast to how it is in Russia. (Haran also points out that Ukrainians have an inherent distrust of institutions.) Wynnyckyj also asserts that it is no longer relevant to analyze processes in Ukraine through the prism of oligarchy, as the war has undermined their financial positions and, therefore, their ability to exercise power.

The question of women in the Armed Forces of Ukraine and LGBTQ are discussed in the essay by Tamara Martsenyuk (12). She observes that women are now more visible in the armed forces, and also that acceptance and support for partnerships for same-sex couples have increased in Ukrainian society. The interview with Maryna Shevtsova (19) provides further details on the issues of women's and LGBTQ rights in Ukraine in the past decade and developments in this field since the beginning of the escalated invasion. Serhiy Kvit (25) discusses how the war has affected universities, their role in the resistance, future reconstruction, and rebuilding of Ukraine, as well as possible challenges that Ukraine might face due to the mass migration of refugees and displaced people from the country.

The interview with Iryna Tsilyk (36), a writer and filmmaker, examines how the war has affected the cultural scene in Ukraine. The fact that many Ukrainian artists have been directly affected by the war, some of them taking up arms to protect their country, is reflected in the cultural products that are now being produced in Ukraine. War poetry is what Tsilyk singles out as a powerful example that conveys the essence of the time and its experience. But the broader tragedy of this time is that the war has also taken the lives of many talents, and those who have fallen won't produce anything anymore. Tsilyk confesses that she thinks the war was not avoidable. The war accelerated metamorphoses in Ukrainian society that were happening in Ukraine in the first thirty years of independence.

In her interview, Yevhenia Podobna (38) describes in detail her observations of the transformations in Ukraine's media landscape. As a professional journalist, she speaks from first-hand experience. She challenges the "standard of pluralism" that Western media try to uphold in their reporting of Russia's war against Ukraine. In her opinion, it stimulates the spread of "terrorist ideas and lies" in many cases. On the positive side, she acknowledges that many Western journalists are now reporting about Ukraine while being in the country and seeing the war with their own eyes. Podobna has also been actively involved in collecting war testimonies, which she defines as "anthropological journalism." She shares her practical and methodological experiences of working with eyewitnesses to the war. The role of media is further discussed in other texts in this collection. In her interview Marta Dyczok (27) scrutinizes Russia's weaponization of media and its use of propaganda in preparation for the full-scale invasion. The narratives that Russia produces find willing audiences around the globe. She draws attention to the fact that the effectiveness of the Kremlin's propaganda is often associated with long-existing, assiduously cultivated, and overly mythologized beliefs about Russian culture in some regions of the world, especially the countries of the Global South. The fact that Ukraine is not presented as an sovereign nation with historical agency in university courses in the US and Canada is a crucial factor in Russia's chauvinistic vision of Ukraine often being accepted without question. Dyczok also shares how the media has been functioning in Ukraine under wartime conditions, recognizing that Ukraine has improved its position in the RSF World Press Freedom Index.

The essay by Polina Sinovets, Khrystyna Holynska, and John Parachini (23) deals with cases of Russia's fake propaganda about nuclear threats from Ukraine. In its propaganda messages, Russia often accuses Ukraine of working to regain its nuclear status, aiming to frame Ukraine as a real threat and justify its invasion. Agnieszka Legucka speaks about "*matryoshka*-style" Russian disinformation in her interview (24) and that Russia has broadened the geography of its disinformation campaigns. Legucka observes that the messages spread by the Kremlin now are not pro-Russian but rather anti-Ukrainian.

Jade McGlynn instead tackles the question of propaganda inside Russia (33). She argues that Russia's external propaganda succeeds inside the country because it resonates with the pre-existing system of worldview beliefs that most ordinary Russians uphold. McGlynn points out that this is not the problem of one person, and Putin's departure probably won't be a solution to end the war. She also contemplates the role of Russia's opposition groups and their varying stances on Ukrainian issues and the war.

Alexander Motyl discusses the "collective Putin" phenomenon (18), using the term to identify both ordinary Russians who have absorbed all the values fed to them by Putin during his reign and elite figures who have shown unvarying support for him for several years. But Motyl conjectures that now the "collective Putin" is much weaker, especially in Moscow and St. Petersburg. He points out that the elites in Russia are fractured, and if there is an opportune moment, they will definitely use it to get rid of Putin and save themselves.

Mitchell Orenstein opines (42) that the sanctions on Russia are doing their work, slowly eroding the support that Putin has enjoyed so far, even if there are no visible signs of dissent now. Margarita Balmaceda (37) also has a similar view toward determining the effectiveness of sanctions. While it is indirect and they cannot stop the war now, in the long run they could recalibrate the decisions of the elite and wobble their loyalty to Putin.

Canadian journalist Michael Bociurkiw is concerned about Ukraine's ability to get diplomatic messages to the outside world. He believes that the Ukrainian diaspora can be very instrumental, and that at the time of his interview (20) the interest of Western media in Ukraine was noticeably more visible. As a global affairs analyst, Bociurkiw gives his perspective on the slowness of Western partners in providing promised and needed ammunition to Ukraine, particularly the crucial air defence systems. But he also underscores the unique nature of this war, where "victory depends more on technology and tactics than on men on the front lines."

Several interviews and essays in this volume focus on the full-scale invasion, specifically from the perspective of military studies. Mykola Bielieskov provides an overview of the first few months of the escalated military aggression from the tactical, operational, and strategic aspects (3). He explains why Russia underperformed and why Ukraine managed to succeed in defending Kyiv. However, he also warns that Russia learned the lessons and will review its tactics. Bielieskov admits that Ukrainian grassroots efforts to allocate resources to combat needs at the front are unprecedented and even, in some cases, bypass the state's capabilities.

In his interview, Alexander Vindman argues that the US and the West could do more to help Ukraine (22). He declares that Russia needs to lose the war if we want to preserve the rules-based international system. This interview was conducted during a heavy battle in Bakhmut. He argues that Bakhmut has little strategic significance and that staying there wouldn't play out in Ukraine's favour if Ukraine wanted to proceed with a counteroffensive. He also thinks that further Western support will be questioned if the fighting extends through 2024.

In his essay, Frank Ledwidge (28) also brings up the war continuing beyond 2024, stating that Ukraine needs to be armed and equipped for the long haul in order to face Russia's threats even after the war is over. He provides a detailed overview of what military equipment Ukraine would require to withstand the growing pressure on the battlefield.

Some essays and interviews focus on acts of solidarity, empathy, and help that Ukraine has received from different countries and communities around the globe. Dovilė Budrytė explains (4) why the Baltic states feel a deep connection to Ukraine and are among the most devoted supporters and helpers of Ukraine. The traumatic experience of shared memories of the Soviet Union provides a deep connection and understanding of the existential threat that Ukraine is facing now. The help that the Baltic states have provided ranges from advocacy on behave of Ukraine on the world stage to the supply of lethal weapons from the first days of the war.

In her interview, Elżbieta Kwiecińska (17) reveals that at the start of the full-scale invasion, she had become actively involved in different volunteering initiatives to help Ukrainians who arrived in Poland fleeing the war. As an academic, she also observed how the universities in Poland responded to the growing interest in understanding the Russo-Ukrainian war as a phenomenon. Kwiecińska tackles the issues of decolonization and "Westsplainers" in addressing Ukraine.

The case of Ireland's support is examined in detailed in the interview with Donnacha Ó Beacháin (26). Despite the geographical distance and different historical circumstances, Ireland finds many similarities with Ukraine in its experience of colonialism, which has contributed to Ireland's reasoning behind helping Ukraine and Ukrainians. He considers whether a Good Friday Agreement scenario of ending the Russo-Ukrainian War is applicable. He also addresses other important questions about changes in the geopolitical environment of the EU.

The UK's response to Russia's escalated invasion is addressed in an interview with Andrii Zharikov (34). One of the strongest backers of Ukraine, the UK has similarities in past historical experience that have also shaped positive attitudes toward Ukraine and Ukrainians. But this time, it is particularly the memories of WW II that have been at the core of the UK's drive to help Ukraine. Because the UK has hosted about 200,000 displaced Ukrainians, Zharikov also evaluates immigration policies that address challenges associated with the influx of Ukrainians in the country.

The Ambassador of Ukraine to Canada, Yuliya Kovaliv, discusses in her interview (31) Canada's response to Russia's escalated invasion of Ukraine, ranging from supplying military equipment to providing financial aid that assists in stabilizing Ukraine's economy, which has been dramatically affected by the war. Kovaliv singles out the importance of the training that Canada has provided to around 30,000 Ukrainian soldiers since 2015, which proved to be pivotal in the first months of the full-scale invasion. Canada is also one of the first countries to legislate the seizure of Russian assets in favour of Ukraine.

The interview with Peter Vermeersch (21) addresses a broader range of questions regarding the transformation of knowledge and perceptions about Ukraine in the EU. Vermeersch acknowledges that Ukraine is no longer perceived in Brussels as something remote and unknown but rather a country on the "eastern edge of Western Europe." Nevertheless, there are still many factors and obstacles, both Internet and external, that Ukraine is likely to face on its way to becoming an EU member. Vermeersch compares the Russo-Ukrainian war with the Yugoslav Wars, concluding that the main difference is that the "Russian invasion of Ukraine is not simply a sort of identity fight but Putin's decision to start that fight and present it as one about identity."

Mariia Zolkina (14) analyzes the narratives that Russia spreads in the Global South in her interview. She says that Russia is exploiting the existing anti-American sentiment in the countries of the Global South, portraying Ukraine as being totally controlled by Washington; however, Ukraine is simultaneously presented as having many similarities with Russia. Zolkina explains that Ukraine needs to strengthen its political and cultural cooperation with the countries of the Global South. Meanwhile, Russia uses the region's food vulnerability to manipulate its reaction and subsequent vote in the UN on questions concerning Ukraine.

The Russo-Ukrainian war has challenged the confidence in the power of international organizations, international law, and overall world security infrastructure that were created in the aftermath of WW II and after the collapse of the Soviet Union viewed as unshakable. Many experts in this book scrutinize the reaction of those organizations to the breach of fundamental security principles that those organizations serve to guarantee and protect. In the interview with Mariana Budjeryn (40), she acknowledges that the inadequacy of global power structures has been evident for a very long time, but she also conveys that we cannot dismiss their importance. She underscores that every legal document, if you want to get something from it, needs to be worked on to leverage its potential. In the case of the Budapest Memorandum, it didn't produce meaningful cooperation, due to both internal processes in Ukraine and the ignorance of Ukraine's concerns by the Western signing parties of the memorandum. But Budjeryn concludes that the historical significance of the memorandum is undeniable for that historical time, and we cannot disregard it.

Many of the contributors in this volume contemplate how the war will end and what should be done to prevent Russia's possible future aggression. Rajan Menon (43) suggests that the ideal scenario for Ukraine is to regain all its territories and join NATO. He predicts some obstacles, however, that may be in Ukraine's way to achieving those goals. The first one is that Ukraine's Western partners are still cautious about provoking Russia, and some view the liberation of Crimea as a dangerous move that could lead to escalation. Nevertheless, Menon is convinced that Ukraine's future security is in the West.

This introduction can hardly provide a comprehensive overview of all the questions and topics that are covered by the authors in this book. And of course the war is still ongoing, taking the lives of innocent people in Ukraine and continuing to reshape the world order. In sum, as Marci Shore says in her interview (29), "It's now very clear that there is no such thing as the End of History," and we should not be "skeptic[al] about the existence of evil" in this world.

Works cited

Kohut, Andriy. 2024. "Operation 'Pharisees': KGB 'Active Measures' and the Holodomor." Panel presentation at the 28th Annual World Convention of the Association for the Study of Nationalities, Session 7, 17 May 2024.

Von Hagen, Mark. 1995. "Does Ukraine have a history?" *Slavic Review* 54, no. 3 (1995): 658–73. https://doi.org/10.2307/2501741.

Acknowledgments

This book would not have been possible without the assistance that I received throughout my work on it. The editorial team members of *Forum for Ukrainian Studies* contributed immensely to its production. First, I want to thank CIUS editor Ksenia Maryniak for her excellent professional language editing of all the texts collected in this volume—and the majority of those published on the *Forum* website. The layout and index of this book are also Ksenia's work. Editorial assistant Kevin Theriault provided tremendous support as well. He helped to coordinate and arrange many of the interviews, conducted one interview himself, and assisted with preparing the transcripts.

Ostap Kushnir, during his tenure as the 2022/23 Kolasky Distinguished Visiting Fellow for the Study of Contemporary Ukraine at CIUS, conducted many of the *Forum* interviews that are included in this collection. The numerous discussions I had with him were very thought-provoking and helped to shape the angles of some of the topics addressed in this volume. Other interviews were done by CIUS community relations coordinator and Kule Ukrainian Canadian Studies Centre director Jars Balan, Natalia Khanenko-Friesen in her capacity as KUCSC senior researcher, and Artem Mamadzhanov, a graduate student under the University of Alberta's Disrupted Ukrainian Students and Scholars initiative.

My thanks also go to CIUS director Natalia Khanenko-Friesen for her eloquent "Foreword," which adds a valuable overall context and perspective to the selected contributions. Last but not least, I am grateful to colleagues and friends at CIUS, who provided a supportive and encouraging environment that was also crucial to the creation of this book.

CHAPTER 1

The signs were there for all to see, but we did not read them right

Bo Petersson

Essay published 7 March 2022

> Bo Petersson is a professor of political science at Malmö University (Sweden), where he is one of the founders of the research platform Russia, Ukraine, and the Caucasus Regional Research (RUCARR). He is also during 2022/24 a researcher at Södertörn University, Stockholm. His special areas of interest include legitimacy, authoritarianism, national identity, and political myth, and he has throughout his academic career specialized in Russian and post-Soviet politics. He is, inter alia, the author of *The Putin Predicament: Problems of Legitimacy and Succession in Russia* (2021), *National Self-Images and Regional Identities in Russia* (2001; 2nd edn 2018), and *Stories about Strangers* (2006).

When the Putin regime launched its all-out attack on Ukraine on 24 February 2022, I was almost as shocked as everybody else, although I have followed Russian politics professionally for almost four decades. The barbarity, the naked and brutish force that Putin unleashed, was something that I had not expected to see. Even as the military build-up along the Ukrainian borders progressed since November 2021, I believed that Putin would stick to the modus operandi that had been his characteristic during his more than twenty years in power. Along with many other international analysts of Russian politics, I thought that he would continue to be cautious and pragmatic, advance his positions where he could, but go for small, incremental steps and take limited, carefully calculated risks in a "salami tactics" way. It was ruthless of course, but rationally so. This was how he had behaved when he, as prime minister under the nominal president Dmitry Medvedev, occupied Abkhazia and South Ossetia in 2008, then, as president again, annexed Crimea and involved Russia in warfare in the Donbas in 2014 and launched aggressive military operations in Syria in 2015.

As of 24 February, that careful strategy of the judoist is all gone. Now, still as a committed judoist but disgracefully stripped of his black belt, he seems to have thrown all rationality overboard. Seated at one of his giant marble or mahogany tables, with a motionless, deadpan look on his face, he issues commands to his underlings, to his clique of yes-men in the National Security Council and other bodies. All these old men of his own age surrounding him seem to be driven by the same ideological force, by the same uncompromising hatred against Ukraine and the West. They really seem to believe what they are talking about when they refer to the "imminent threat to Russian security and sovereignty" posed by the USA and NATO through Ukraine. They seem to believe in the absurd lies that Ukraine is ruled by neo-Nazis and is on the verge of acquiring nuclear weapons. Inside that group of greying men, everybody seems to think the same, and they are living proof of the devastating effects of what Irving Janis once called groupthink (Janis 1983). In a group where no dissent is allowed, the quality of decisions taken tends to be dismal and even disastrous.

So how did it come to this? How did we come to the point where all Western expertise was so thoroughly taken aback by the developments? To be quite honest, we should not have been very surprised, because the signs were there for all to see, but we did not read them correctly. Already at his Munich speech in 2007 (Putin 2007), Putin depicted the USA as Russia's main enemy, and on all occasions that he could he brought up his favoured narrative that the United States had promised Russia never to expand NATO and bring it closer to Russia's borders. This unsubstantiated claim was brought up as a mantra so often that the Russian leader may have started to believe in it himself. Ever since the Maidan Revolution in 2014, which drove the then president from Ukraine and paved the way for a new president to be elected, the Russian president kept repeating that this development amounted to an unconstitutional coup, that the Ukrainian government was dominated by neo-Nazis, and that Russians and Ukrainians were in essence were the same people. All together, this added up to Russia's self-proclaimed right to intervene in Ukrainian domestic affairs. However, Putin repeated those grievances so often that they seemed to amount to an obligatory litany, the ranting of a bitter aging man who could scarcely be taken seriously anymore, since he had always been talking like that.

How wrong we were. And indeed, not for the first time did Putin prove us all wrong. By way of example, the overall international expert opinion was deceived by Putin's repeated assurances that he would never ever change the Russian Constitution of 1993, which stipulates the Russian President as its chief guarantor. Putin lied about this so many times that pundits across the world believed that he was sincere, till the day in early 2020 when he suddenly initiated constitutional amendments that for all practical purposes enabled him to cling to the presidency for the rest of his life.

Conversely, when Putin in his rantings repeated how Russia had been deceived by the West, how the rightful president of Ukraine had been unlawfully toppled in a coup instigated by the West, and how all these measures had the ulterior aim of bringing destruction and havoc to Russia, few were inclined to believe that the man was not only repeating his mantra but outlining a program of action. Alas, had we only taken his words for it, then instead of choosing to believe his lies about his loyalty to the Constitution, precautionary actions could have been taken. Perhaps then Ukraine's accession to NATO would have been accelerated, and then the country would not have been doomed to take on Russia's aggression all alone. If more of us so-called experts had only "cried 'wolf'" a little more often and decidedly louder, then maybe the Western political community would have taken appropriate action.

The signs were indeed there, and they were amassing continuously. One of the most clear-cut signs was evident for all to see in Putin's address to the Federal Assembly on 1 March 2018 (Putin 2018), when he triumphantly introduced new generations of hypersonic missile technology to the deputies of the assembly and to the world. In this and other speeches at that time, Putin displayed a new assertiveness and aggressiveness with respect to the West, and he signalled very clearly his belief that Russia had now gained the upper hand over the United States in the global arms race. This was certainly helped along by the fact that the USA was led by the Trump administration at the time, which meant that for all practical purposes America had abdicated its leading role in the world and was intent on giving Putin and Russia all that they wanted. Putin gleefully commented that the USA would no doubt try to imitate the new cutting-edge arms technology but by that time Russia would already have developed an even smarter generation of arms technology. In October 2020, at his annual appearance at the Valdai Club Putin was already expressing himself in such ominous words that the cataclysm of February 2022 could have been anticipated, had we as analysts only taken them seriously: "I would like to tell those who are still waiting for Russia's strength to gradually wane: the only thing we are worried about is catching a cold at your funeral" (Kremlin 2020).

I could perhaps try to boast that I had seen these signs and that I even wrote about them in my book The Putin Predicament that was published in October 2021 (Petersson 2021), and indeed it included a chapter about Putin's increasing assertiveness in the global arena and in Russia's competition with the United States. I observed the chilly harshness of tone and how it had hardened gradually ever since Putin's "return" to presidential power in 2012. Like so many others, I observed how Putin's domestic popularity had risen sky-high after the annexation of Crimea and the beginning of the war against Ukraine in 2014, and how his approval rates stayed at the 80-plus level for four years after the annexation as the effect of the so-called "Crimean consensus" in Russian politics. My dismal error, however, was downgrading the importance of these signs. I falsely believed that the increased assertiveness in relation to the West was plain verbosity and that it was of less importance than factors such as Putin's increasing age and listlessness, his lack of strength and visibility in dealing with the covid-19 pandemic (Blackburn and Petersson 2021), and the obvious ways in which his deteriorating charisma was eclipsed by the radiance and communication skills of his unrelenting and courageous critic, Alexei Navalny, who appealed to the younger urban generations to an extent that Putin could only dream about.

All in all, the analysis about Putin's accelerating weakness at home was correct, but, sadly, the conclusion was wrong. Like so many other experts out there, I could read the signs but not the overall pattern that they formed. The proper conclusion to draw would have been that it was precisely this domestic weakness that made Putin so dangerous. The president needed decisive and ruthless action in order to be able to reverse his receding popularity curves. Putin needed a new achievement that surpassed even the Crimean consensus, and he went for it by means that were totally out of previous proportions. Speculations abound that he is unwell and that his ill health has prompted him to take the kind of action that he has been mulling over for many years now. Living in his echo chamber of like-minded yes-men, he seems to have become more and more convinced that his personal writing of history is the correct one. Had we, the members of the expert community out there, only taken him more seriously during all these years, then maybe the present situation would not have been as disastrous as it is now. Again, if only we had cried "Wolf!" more often.

Works cited

Blackburn, Matthew, and Bo Petersson. 2021. "Parade, plebiscite, pandemic: Legitimation efforts in Putin's fourth term." *Post-Soviet Affairs* 38 (4): 293–311. https://doi.org/10.1080/1060586X.2021.2020575.

Janis, Irving. 1983. *Groupthink*. Boston: Houghton Mifflin.

Kremlin. 2020. "Zasedanie diskussionnogo kluba 'Valdai.'" Presidential Executive Office, 22 October 2020. http://kremlin.ru/events/president/news/64261.

Petersson, Bo. 2021. *The Putin Predicament: Problems of Legitimacy and Succession in Russia*. Stuttgart: Ibidem.

Putin, Vladimir. 2018. "Poslanie Prezidenta Federal'nomu Sobraniiu." Presidential Executive Office, 1 March 2018. http://kremlin.ru/events/president/news/56957.

— — —. 2007. "Speech and the following discussion at the Munich Conference on Security Policy." Presidential Executive Office, 10 February 2007. http://en.kremlin.ru/events/president/transcripts/24034.

CHAPTER 2

Four false narratives of Russia's war in Ukraine

Davis Daycock
Essay published 9 April 2022

> Davis Daycock is a specialist in Soviet and East European studies and a Senior Scholar at the University of Manitoba, Winnipeg. He obtained his PhD in government studies, with a specialty in Soviet and East European studies, at the London School of Economics and has taught political theory, comparative government, and Soviet studies at the University of Manitoba since 1966, as well as courses in Ukrainian government and politics, Ukrainian history, and Ukrainian political economy.

Summing up her impression of Russian President Vladimir Putin, former US Secretary of State Condoleezza Rice once said that there was a five percent chance that "he is crazy." Perhaps she was on to something, although her estimate was somewhat on the low side. We might find him easier to understand if he really was just "crazy." Putin unquestionably shows traits of a sociopath, but we need more than that to account for his decision to invade Ukraine.

Let us start with what we know for sure. Putin is a backstreet bully from St. Petersburg who made a career as a KGB thug. He is a man with a distorted and malevolent view of history and his place in it. He has made it abundantly clear that he does not accept the post-1991 world. His vision is of a Russia restored to its imperial splendour and a Russia which returns to its long-standing role as the "prison of nations." He will pursue this dream with all the means at his disposal. However, we have misjudged him. He is not the careful, patient adversary with justifiable objectives, the chess player who deserves our respect. He is a poker player who relies on bluff and lies. He is, moreover, without any kind of empathy for the victims of his ambitions. He accepts no moral or legal restraints on his methods.

This is not a hopeful starting point for any negotiation to end the Russo-Ukrainian war. Before we find the correct balance between relying on credible confrontation and negotiation, we must clear away the misunderstandings that exist about Putin's motives and objectives. We must therefore confront and counter four pervasive false narratives that cloud our perspective on Russia's war in Ukraine.

First false narrative

The Reason for Putin's decision to invade Ukraine can be traced to mistakes and wrong-headed "imperialist" ambitions on the part of NATO. These commitments were broken despite the West's promises when the Soviet Union broke up – not to expand the alliance into the territory of former Soviet republics and Warsaw Pact countries. Expansion of NATO has betrayed Russia's legitimate security concerns.

This interpretation is President Putin's central contention. The decision by the Ukrainian government to seek inclusion in NATO and the EU was, so he says, an intolerable threat to Russian security. Few buy into this argument, whether partly or wholly, and too many in the West still do. But the argument is false.

On the question of NATO expansion, no promises or guarantees were ever formally made. We can never be sure if there were informal oral promises. The fact that in 2014 the Soviet President, Mikhail Gorbachev, denied that such assurances were ever mentioned or that the subject was ever raised with him, casts serious doubt on the Russians' allegation that they were ever given. As Gorbachev said: "The topic of NATO expansion was not discussed at all and it wasn't brought up in those years. I say this with full responsibility. Not a single East European country raised the issue, not even after the Warsaw Pact ceased to exist in 1991. Western leaders didn't bring it up either."

Anyway, if there were informal assurances, they became redundant after formal undertakings were concluded between Russia and NATO—especially the 1997 "Founding Act on Mutual Relations, Cooperation and Security," which makes clear that Russia accepted that expansion of the alliance posed no security risks to Russia and that "NATO and Russia do not consider one another adversaries."Russia also undertook formally, in the Budapest Memorandum of 1994 and in the Treaty of Friendship and Co-operation with Ukraine in 1997, to guarantee the sovereignty and territorial integrity of Ukraine.

The small, even token, presence of NATO in the Baltic countries and the generally low profile and weakness of NATO's capabilities throughout Europe show the consistently defensive posture of the alliance. In fact, the perceived weakness and lack of resolve on the part of NATO have probably played a part in Putin's decision to attack Ukraine by highlighting not a growing threat posed by NATO but rather its fecklessness. Such a perception is no doubt reinforced by the overall impression of the weakness and "decadence" of the West. In fact, the driving force for NATO expansion has come not from the alliance but from countries that are themselves anxious to join. This pressure has actually been somewhat resisted by NATO. Bids from Ukraine and Georgia for fast-tracking their membership were not successful, and their applications have remained on the table for years. Meanwhile, the new East European NATO partners are looking for safeguards against Russian aggression and possible renewed Russian domination.

So, are we really to believe that an all-out war was provoked just because at some point in the future Ukraine may join NATO? From the evidence of his statements and actions, the real reason for Russia's hatred of NATO is clear enough. For Putin, it simply represents the principal obstacle to the reconstruction of his Greater Russia, not a "security" threat in any other way.

Second false narrative

Ukraine is oppressing ethnic Russians and Russian-speaking Ukrainians through a campaign of Ukrainization and "genocide." The Donetsk and Luhansk so-called People's Republics are under a murderous assault by Ukraine, and they need help from Russia to resist Ukrainian aggression against Russophones.

Again, some in the West accept this argument, in whole or in part. In reality, however, tensions around language issues have been consistently exaggerated and exploited by Putin and his apologists. The 1991 referendum on Ukraine's independence after the collapse of the Soviet Union was supported by an overwhelming majority of Russian-speaking Ukrainians. This was true everywhere in the country. Even in Crimea, where Russophones comprised the overwhelming majority, more than half voted for independence for Ukraine. Russian and other minority language rights are guaranteed by Article 10 of the Constitution of Ukraine. Russian speakers are not oppressed. Ukrainian has been designated as the "state language," which in no way prevents the use of Russian or penalizes people for speaking Russian. Many in Ukraine understand Russian and the language is widely used.

On the other hand, the language laws of 2019 are designed to protect and preserve the status of Ukrainian, not to suppress minority languages. We do not have to look far for the reasons for this concern about the future of the Ukrainian language. Both under the Imperial Russian and Soviet regimes, Ukrainian and other languages were systematically suppressed as part of various campaigns of "Russification." Consider, for example, what lay behind Tsar Alexander's Ems Ukase of 1876, which banned the Ukrainian language in *belles lettres* and education and otherwise restricted its use. The edict stated that Ukrainian language "has never existed, does not exist, and shall never exist in the future."

One might well think it strange that something that needs to be banned because it is politically dangerous nevertheless "does not exist." During most of the years under Soviet rule, the situation was the same or worse—and not just under the nightmare of the Stalin regime. A multi-dimensional campaign of Russification was in place throughout most of the Soviet period. The Kremlin's repression of Ukrainian language was a central part of that campaign. As just two of many illustrations, the Soviet language laws in the Brezhnev era made Russian the sole language of instruction in education, and there was next to no publication in the Ukrainian language.

The claim that Russians and Russian speakers are suffering under Ukrainian rule is surely fully discredited by now. By contrast, the last vestiges of a free press, freedom of assembly, and free expression have disappeared from Putin's Russia. Russian speakers in Ukraine have much more freedom of expression than Russians living in Russia. In Kharkiv, Mariupol, and other majority Russian-speaking parts of the country, resistance to the invasion has been as fierce as in predominantly Ukrainian-speaking areas. And let us not forget, of course, that in 2019 more than 73% of Ukrainian voters elected a Russian-speaking Eastern Ukrainian as their President. Ironically, Putin's brutal unprovoked war has united Ukrainians even further, so that now President Zelensky enjoys something close to universal approval in Ukraine. Meanwhile, the original 2014 "separatist" uprising in Eastern Ukraine was provoked by Putin and is supported, led, and actually partly manned by Russians from Russia. Given the appalling economic conditions in these territories, it is unlikely that language issues are at the forefront of popular worries.

Third false narrative

Russia's attack on Ukraine was motivated by Putin's determination to rid Ukraine of "fascists" who pose a threat to Russian speakers and to Russia. Ukraine must be "de-Nazified," and the Zelensky government and the Nazis around him must be removed and brought to justice.

Again, most people dismiss such suggestions as nonsense. Yet there are some disingenuous commenters from both Right and Left who for their own reasons are prepared to countenance this claim. Certainly there are extreme right wing forces at work in Ukraine, but their importance for Ukrainian political life has so far been minor and the extreme right attracts only a small part of the Ukrainian people — a much smaller proportion, in fact, than the far-right enjoys in many other European countries.

In 2019 more than 73% of Ukrainians voted for an Eastern Ukrainian, Russian-speaking Jew — whose grandfather, by the way, was a Holocaust survivor. Leaving aside the question of where to draw the line between radical nationalists and fascists, we note that the presidential candidate Ruslan Koshulynsky, who represented the Right Sektor, Svoboda, and several other right-wing groups, polled at only 1.6%. Subsequently, in the elections to Ukraine's parliament, the Verkhovna Rada, far-right parties gained less than 2% of the vote, reflecting a continuation of the decline of support for these parties from the results of the 2012 and 2014 elections. At the same time, Volodymyr Zelensky's "Servant of the People" party gained 254 of 450 seats and formed a majority government. The incumbent prime minister was Volodymyr Groysman, a Jew like Zelensky. To say the least, this would be a very strange formula for Nazism. On the other hand, the extremes of the authoritarian Putin regime fits a fascist model quite well — including its murderous treatment of any opposition, destruction of freedom of expression and freedom of assembly, imperialist foreign policy, and viciousness of its unprovoked aggression.

Fourth false narrative

Ukraine is not a real country. It belongs with Russia as part of a Great Russia and "Russkii Mir." There is no Ukrainian people, no language, no separate history. Ukraine is an entirely artificial creation of Soviet governments under Lenin and then Stalin.

The core element is getting the West to treat Russia as if it were the Soviet Union, a power to be respected and feared, with special rights in its neighbourhood and a voice in every serious international matter. The doctrine holds that only a few states should have this kind of authority, along with complete sovereignty, and that others must bow to their wishes. And the doctrine is tied together by Putin's overarching aim: reversing the consequences of the Soviet collapse, splitting the transatlantic alliance, and renegotiating the geographic settlement that ended the Cold War.

This is Putin's expressed position, and sadly there are those in the West who agree with him. However, objectively there is absolutely no question that Ukraine has its own language, which has been spoken for centuries and differs from Russian at least as much as Dutch differs from German. Ukraine's strong literary tradition was cemented in place in the 19th century by numerous Ukrainian writers and pre-eminently by the great poet and patriot Taras Shevchenko. After Shevchenko, no one can credibly claim that Ukraine does not have a language of its own.

There is no space here to review Ukraine's history at any length. But it is simply a fact that Ukraine has a state tradition which extends back more than a thousand years. In the modern era, a state emerged after the collapse of the Russian and Austrian empires at the end of the First World War. That state had a democratic constitution which aspired to consolidate Ukraine and separate it once and for all from Russia. However, with no sufficient and lasting support from the outside world, the new state finally succumbed to the superior power of Bolshevik Russia.

Conclusion

Ultimately, there is one sliver of truth in Putin's view of Ukraine. Ironically, with the Second World War it was Soviet power that drew together Ukrainian lands—pre-war Soviet Ukraine and Polish-occupied Eastern Galicia—into one geographic entity. Although the resulting consolidated Ukrainian SSR was to be completely subservient to Moscow, the groundwork was thereby unwittingly laid for the re-emergence of an independent Ukrainian state. It is not at all to credit Lenin and the early Bolsheviks with creating Ukrainian national consciousness. Rather, it is true that, unlike most other Russian rulers, Lenin acknowledged its reality. After the Bolshevik seizure of power and the conquest of the independent Ukrainian National Republic in 1921, Lenin set out to "domesticate" Communism in Ukraine He recognized that the new Communist regime had to adjust to the realities of Ukrainian national consciousness and national aspirations. So, in 1923 at the XII Party Congress a policy was launched that was designed to disarm nationalism as an enemy of Communism in Ukraine and in other non-Russian parts of the old empire.

As it applied to Ukraine, the officially approved "Ukrainization" program involved the promotion of Ukrainian language and recruitment of Ukrainians into the institutional life of Soviet Ukraine. The policy survived through the 1920s but was revoked by Stalin and replaced by the Bolshevik totalitarian terror state with its mass murder of Ukrainian intellectual, political, and religious leaders and its genocidal campaign of planned starvation against Ukrainian farmers. The Ukrainization policy had worked too well from Moscow's point of view and had in fact backfired, as Ukrainian national feeling and desire for autonomy came to be expressed even by the Communist Party of Ukraine.

The experience of the 1920s provides a clear reminder that in Ukraine, national consciousness, tolerance of diversity, and the demand for political, religious, and human rights are grassroots social values that can only be restrained by brute force. Stalin provided that brute force. Inevitably, with the end of Stalin and Stalinism civil society began to revive in Soviet Ukraine. It should have surprised no one that as the strength of Soviet state power continued to wane, the end result would be an independent and democratic society. That society has now had the experience of more than thirty years of independent national and democratic development. The Orange Revolution of 2004, the Revolution of Dignity of 2014 (Euromaidan), and the heroic resistance of Ukrainians to Putin's invasion in the eight years since provide the proof that now, even a new Stalin would not succeed in destroying that society and the unwavering aspirations which nourish it.

CHAPTER 3

Ukrainians have crossed the threshold of fear: They're fighting for victory

Mykola Bielieskov

Interview with Ostap Kushnir, published 11 April 2022

Mykola Bielieskov (MA in International Relations, Kyiv Shevchenko National University, 2016) is a Ukrainian military and security expert. In 2016-19, he served as an analyst at Institute of World Policy Ukrainian NGO. Since October 2019 he has been employed at the National Institute for Strategic Studies under President of Ukraine as an analyst in its Defence Policy Department. Alongside his service at the NISS, Bielieskov administers an open-access analytical channel on Telegram—Armchair General UA.

Kushnir: As an expert, you often emphasize the need to assess war dynamics at three levels: tactical, operational, and strategic. What is so specific about them and how effective are they overall? Is perfect knowledge of these levels all it takes to make someone a military expert, a full-fledged "armchair general"?

Bielieskov: These levels are used in standard assessments of warfare. Each of them is focused on a specific type of combat. At the tactical level the combat consists of an isolated skirmish, at the operational level it consists of an operation or sequence of clashes, and at the strategic level it is a complex of operations, which places the latter level on the margin between purely military and political activities. Therefore, for a proper assessment it is crucial to consider every situation at three levels—or at least at the first two, which are purely military.

Many people focus on the tactical level only, and this leads to distortions in their assessment of warfare. A major problem in late February 2022 was that the "armchair generals" observed the enemy's advancement towards Kyiv with panic and started lamenting that "Russia is winning." However, in due course the enemy retreated in a kind of "miraculous" way. This was not a miracle, though. Indeed, the Russians advanced rapidly at the very beginning, but they failed to achieve anything spectacular at the operational level of warfare.

They were winning individual fights but could not win all of them, stretching their forces for dozens of kilometres along the front line as well as deep inside Ukraine's territory.

At the tactical level, the effectiveness of isolated fights is assessed according to quantities of equipment destroyed, numbers of soldiers killed, and square kilometres of conquered land. On the other hand, effectiveness at the operational level is assessed according to the quantity of surrounded or incapacitated forces of the enemy. The Russians could not accomplish anything at this level. Notwithstanding their advancement and taking roads and population points under control, the Russians could not boast that they defeated Ukrainian forces, because the Ukrainians were being pushed back but were not incapacitated. They withdrew but simultaneously bided their time, limited the enemy to specific locations, and sabotaged its communications in the rearguard. Thus, when the Russians exhausted their offensive potential, the core of the Ukrainian forces still remained largely intact and was ready to move from manoeuvrable defence to offence. In this way Kyiv, Chernihiv, and Sumy oblasts were liberated.

Therefore, this war should not be perceived solely as isolated skirmishes, but as a sequence of clashes. If this is not done, then any enemy advancement will look disastrous. This was often the conclusion of many "armchair generals" during the first forty days of the Russian offence in the north of Ukraine.

Kushnir: Today, Western military analysts are making an interesting and seemingly contradictory statement. On the one hand, the war in Ukraine has shown that Russia is no longer a global power and that its capabilities are limited. On the other hand, Russia has learned from its mistakes and is about to start fighting "in full force," which leaves Ukrainian defenders no chance. Which aspect of this statement do you agree with?

Bielieskov: I would suggest that Russia's capabilities are limited. Russians have demonstrated their inadequacy in using the equipment and applying the training they acquired in recent years, during their army's supposed modernization. In February they had "perfect conditions" for the escalated invasion of Ukraine: an extensive front line of attack, thousands of troops gathered at the border, and sparse dispersal of units of Ukrainian defenders. Regardless, the Russians failed to inflict any considerable damage and stalled shortly after crossing the border. Their failure was related above all to their inability to coordinate different types and kinds of troops. They underperformed in what is called *combined arms warfare*.

I am sure that the Russo-Ukrainian war should be and will be compared to the Winter War of 1939/40 between the USSR and Finland. At that time, following rapid industrialization the Soviets possessed tons of equipment and developed some fresh warfare strategies, but it all proved to be futile in reality. The same scenario is taking place in Ukraine today. Waging a major war on numerous fronts, deploying different types and kinds of troops, requires experience that is impossible to gain in peacetime.

If you're wondering whether Russia will start fighting "in full force" soon, I doubt it. Already in the first wave of attack the Russian command deployed their best units: paratroopers, special forces, even elite armies such as the 1st Guards Tank Army or the 58th Army. Notwithstanding, they failed to achieve key objectives at both operational and strategic levels. All they accomplished were minor breakthroughs.

Certainly, the Russians may review their tactics and start attacking on the ground with powerful air support. However, this is easier said than done. As I have mentioned above, this requires combat experience and comes at a very high price. Without a doubt, the Russians have learned to fight better already, but they've suffered considerable losses along the way. According to estimates on the Ukrainian side, they have lost around 40 percent of their battalion tactical groups, entirely or partially. For that reason, they decided to move their remaining troops from northern Ukraine to its east and try to achieve success at least there.

As for me, any kind of training and drills that are conducted in peacetime will never replace combat experience—especially in today's Russian case. The paradox is that the Russians decided to execute a major offensive on numerous fronts while deploying a peacetime army. Similar offensives were executed by the USSR only in the fifth year of the Second World War, in 1944, with Soviet economics readjusted to the military purpose. Thus, it is not surprising that the Russians failed the initial strike and now need to downgrade their ambitions now.

Given the quality and quantity of remaining troops, even if their tactics are changed the Russians are limited in their options.

They cannot fight in full force as they lack both manpower and equipment. All the elite units have suffered damage and it will take at least six months to fully restore their battle capacity or create additional units.

In sum, so far Russia has demonstrated its inadequacy to wage modern warfare. This is not what a true great power should be capable of. The coming battles in eastern Ukraine will show what the Russians learned from their mistakes and how much of their "full force" was retained.

Kushnir: What is your opinion of the response of Ukrainian society to the war? The concept of "resilience" is commonly used in Western security studies today to explain the ability of a society to absorb shock and adapt to stress. How resilient do you think Ukrainian society is? To what extent is it ready to counteract aggression?

Bielieskov: Ukrainian society has demonstrated the best possible examples of how to enhance and uphold a defensive potential in short periods of time. Volunteer units significantly scaled up their activity and are providing consistent support to the Ministry of Defence and regional commands of the Armed Forces of Ukraine. Ukrainians' high level of social self-organization has allowed them to respond to many needs of the deployed units. Local activists supply them with surveillance drones, communication equipment, computers, individual first aid kits, food, and other goods.

Speaking of the wartime resilience, I would like to highlight the prompt response of Ukrainian society to the military mobilization. The grassroots motivation to defend their land is so impressive among ordinary Ukrainians, with the role of the state being secondary. This fantastic mobilization and self-organization effectively compensate shortcomings which the army experienced before the war, especially the lack of equipment.

I do not know much about other types of resilience, such as assistance to internally displaced people and mitigation of other outcomes of war. However, assessing readiness for war *per se*, Ukrainian society is doing phenomenally well. The amount of resources that ordinary Ukrainians have allocated and donated directly to combat efforts at the front, bypassing the state altogether, is unprecedented (and, it bears repeating, has been ongoing since 2013).

When future historians write about the Russo-Ukrainian war, they will doubtlessly dedicate much attention to the Ukrainian mobilization and self-organization. In the last 150 years it has been solely the state's task to prepare and support armies on the battlefield. However, since the first day of this war Ukrainians have willingly shifted much of this burden onto their shoulders. In Russia, on the other hand, the situation is quite the opposite. Their state-run war machine lacks a powerful grassroots support. Numerous problems observed in the invading army today, particularly its poor combat readiness and basic lack of food or fuel, stem from the state's incapacity to manage all needs fast. Therefore, a great number of Ukraine's victories belong to Ukraine's civil society.

Kushnir: What is the significance of the Western support to Ukraine in this war? Which aspects of Western engagement do you consider crucial for a successful defence: sanctions against Russia, arms supplies, diplomatic pressure? Is there anything missing in the Western engagement?

Bielieskov: Let me start from the optimistic statement that Russia underestimated the reaction of the West and Ukraine made a pivotal impact on framing that reaction. In the very first days, or even hours, of the war, many European officials claimed that Ukraine would not last long under the Russian assault. Very few officials in the US also believed in survival of the government in Kyiv. Nevertheless, the initial effort of the Ukrainian defence and security forces and their systematic resistance since then have made Western governments reconsider their opinion.

The Russians expected to complete a fast campaign and subjugate Ukraine before the West "awakens." They also expected that the Western reaction would be modest, even symbolic. However, the Ukrainian army crushed all these expectations by winning time and forcing the West to face the problem.

Speaking of aspects of the Western engagement — specifically, the sanctions against Russia — I have mixed feelings. On the one hand, the sanctions are in place and they look harsh. On the other hand, their effectiveness is dubious, as Russia continues benefitting from energy exports. Every day the government in Kremlin receives US$850 million from European states for its oil and gas exports. This money is of course redirected to feed the Russian war machine, support the existing regime, and continue fighting in Ukraine. The sanctions that are in place today are far below what is needed.

Western diplomatic support also needs to be more deliberate. For instance, on 2 March 2022 during the vote in the UN General Assembly to condemn the Russia's war in Ukraine, 141 states voted in favour and 35 abstained. I think the West could have done much more on the eve of the voting to further decrease the number of abstentions. The global support to Ukraine could be more articulate.

Western engagement in arms supplies is probably the most elaborate factor. Here, however, there is also much room for improvement. On the one hand, Ukraine has received large volumes of defensive weaponry from the West. On the other hand, it is light weaponry — mainly portable anti-aircraft and anti-tank missile systems. This weaponry neatly fit the initial objectives of Ukraine's defensive operation; however, it has never been enough. Heavy weaponry is what provides incomparable advantage and what is missing.

I share the feeling that many Western decision makers have a distorted image of how Ukraine fights. In modern warfare, defending with light weaponry only would lead to agony for the defenders. Only in combination with the old Soviet artillery complexes and new national systems, such as Stugna-P and Corsair, can the West's light weaponry lead to a positive result for Ukraine.

Heavy weaponry and artillery will allow Ukraine to destroy the columns of enemy vehicles much in advance, before they reach close combat range. This is incomparably more effective and live-saving when compared to destroying the individual vehicles with the help of Javelin or NLAW. Furthermore, the long-range heavy weaponry, supported with missile-carrying unmanned aerial vehicles like Bayraktar, allow to attack the enemy command posts and logistical infrastructure deep in the rear, 30-40 kilometres away from the combat zone. This is impossible with Western portable systems, which have been designed for close combat. In other words, abundance of Javelins and NLAW's by no means can compensate the scarcity of the classical long-range barrel artillery. Today, without the heavy systems and complexes, remaining from the Soviet times, the Ukrainian defenders would slowly agonize.

Kushnir: If I asked you to put it in a nutshell, what kind of Western weaponry would you say Ukraine needs now?

Bielieskov: Above all, the needs of Ukraine include long-range barrel artillery, heavy anti-aircraft and anti-missile weaponry, and thousands of manoeuvrable all-terrain vehicles, desirably with some armour on them.

Kushnir: What is your opinion of Russia's nuclear blackmail? To what extent do you find it probable that Putin will press the "red button"? Some of the Western states seem to take this blackmailing seriously and restrain their engagement in Ukrainian affairs. Is such restraint justified?

Bielieskov: Unfortunately, following the events of 24 February 2022, no threat should be disregarded. We live in a world where many "red lines" have been crossed already. I am afraid that if Russia continues underperforming in conventional warfare, its leadership may demonstratively resort to tactical nuclear weaponry. The territory of Ukraine is then, as now, a likely target.

However, nuclear blackmailing scares off Western states and makes them abandon Ukraine, the world will have get a precedent. The same blackmailing will be used then to return Poland, or the Baltic states to the Russian sphere of influence. Nuclear blackmailing will become a universal tool in the Kremlin's hands.

The West has already experienced similar pressure from the USSR during the Cold War. There was much lamenting among the European elites then: "Why should we die for the West Berlin"? Cold War history demonstrated that the readiness to die for West Berlin was necessary. It made the Soviets step back, moderate their rhetoric, and start negotiating.

The Russians should understand today—same as the Soviets understood decades ago—that nuclear blackmail fails to work as a tool of escalation. This understanding will push the Russians back to the path of negotiations. Otherwise, they will continue blackmailing the West on every occasion, whenever they decide to achieve any objective in future.

There is also a different side to the nuclear blackmail—the human side. I have observed that the Ukrainians are not afraid anymore and have prepared to endure all the calamities of war. They have crossed the threshold of fear. Paradoxically, the Western societies, having nuclear parity and unquestionable superiority over Russia, are afraid. This is a foolish situation. I understand all doubts and costs, but it is only the West that can truly counterweight Russia's rattling with nuclear sabres. The lessons of history should be learned. Unless the West wants to use nuclear blackmail as a comfortable reason to abstain from helping Ukraine in the war.

Kushnir: Do you agree that the Western states in talks with Russia downplay the importance of Ukraine's position? That is, are the discussions about Ukraine taking place behind Ukraine's back?

Bielieskov: Downplaying Ukraine's interests might have been the case earlier, but not today. In late December 2021 and early January 2022, the most active negotiations were held between US, NATO, and Russia. Today, Ukraine has a separate track of negotiations with Russia and speaks to the Kremlin directly.

The major problem, as I see it, is the obstinate desire of a part of the Western elites to strike a deal with Russia as soon as possible. They create pressure on Kyiv and advocate compromises at the expense of Ukraine. Luckily, Ukraine has also found support in the face of the UK government and some authoritative media. They put it straightforwardly: Ukraine has to win. I find this approach to ending the war more reasonable.

Western fans of the compromise continue overestimating the capabilities of Russia for fast mobilization and recovering of lost resources. The reality is that if the Russian command conducts one or two disastrous operations more, similar to the attacks on Kyiv and Mariupol, they will have no soldiers and equipment left to continue fighting. The aviation, missile, and artillery units will be useless without support of infantry on armoured vehicles. Under such a scenario, it is Russia who will seek for a peace deal on unfavourable conditions. What the West needs to do now is to provide Ukraine with heavy weaponry. This will also be right to prevent new atrocities which Russian soldiers have been observed committing in Ukraine.

To summarise, I do not think that the West and Russia speak about Ukraine behind Ukraine's back. Kyiv is actively engaged in all talks. The problem is that selected Western political circles and experts push for peace deals on unfavourable for Ukraine conditions. Instead, Ukraine is ready to fight, walk the thorny path till its end, and achieve a convincing victory. Only after such a victory, bolstered with the Western weaponry, a proper talk with Russia will take place.

Kushnir: You often say that predicting scenarios for the of the war is a tricky business because all scenarios anticipate political responses to changeable environment. However, from the purely military perspective, which status quo looks the most plausible to you?

Bielieskov: If Ukraine succeeds with its defensive operation in the east and Russia loses its offensive potential completely, the invaders would need to leave all the temporarily occupied territories. Afterwards, negotiations would start on numbers and armament of the Ukrainian Armed Forces, frameworks of Ukraine's cooperation with NATO, and other issues of military and technical cooperation with the West. The ongoing Russo-Ukrainian negotiations and initial peace drafts are tentative and non-binding. The provisions of the final peace treaty are yet to be written on the battlefield.

The recent Russian demands for the demilitarization of Ukraine and forfeit of NATO membership are totally unacceptable. Under such a scenario Ukraine would become defenceless against new Russian aggression. Therefore, Ukraine's major objective today is to obtain reliable security guarantees from external actors, including Russia. The architecture of these guarantees is a topic of heated debate and bargaining. Ultimately, this architecture will be decided by the successes of Ukrainian Armed Forces.

What Ukrainian diplomacy needs to do now is to clearly communicate to the Kremlin that its maximalist demands will never be put into practice, regardless of the outcomes of the war. The Ukrainian side also needs to avoid maximalist temptations; at least, not before Kyiv controls all the tools of pressure on Russia, including sanctions.

In case of a Ukrainian victory on the battlefield, the Kremlin will need to choose: either Ukraine joins NATO and has its armed forces reduced, or it remains a non-aligned state with a powerful army, much more powerful than it has ever had, built with the help of Western partners. Ukraine may also demand then the prohibition of stationing of Russian forces close to its borders.

The good news for today is that Ukrainian defenders have tasted victory. They've learned to wipe out invaders and have proved to the world that the Russian army can be stopped. In forty days of fighting, the presumably undefeatable Russian war machine could not accomplish anything on operational level.

Ukrainians are in it to win it. The West must decide if it is an engaged bystander or a trusted ally.

CHAPTER 4

"We are all on the front lines now": Baltic states' solidarity with Ukraine

Dovilė Budrytė

Essay published 13 May 2022

> Dovilė Budrytė (PhD, Old Dominion University) is a professor of political science at Georgia Gwinnett College, USA, and a member of the EUROPAST team at Vilnius University. She received research fellowships at Europa University Viadrina (Germany) and the Carnegie Council on Ethnic and International Affairs. In 2019, 2018, and 2015 she was a visiting professor at Vytautas Magnus University and Vilnius University in Lithuania. Her recent book is *Crisis and Change in Post-Cold War Global Politics: Ukraine in a Comparative Perspective*, co-edited with Erica Resende and Didem Buhari-Gulmez (2018). Her articles on minorities, women, and historical trauma in Lithuania have appeared in the *Journal of Baltic Studies*, *Gender and History*, and the *Journal of International Relations and Development*.

The experience of collective trauma leads to the creation of new identities. With Russia's war against Ukraine ongoing, we are seeing important changes in European identities, as Europe together with its allies seems to be galvanized to stand up for what have long been considered Western values and ideals, such as human rights and democracy. In the Baltic states, the genocidal war against Ukraine is perceived as an existential threat. The Baltic states have become the leading voices in Europe supporting Ukraine, arguing for its EU membership and for supplying Ukraine with what it needs most—weapons and other types of aid. There has also been strong support from the Baltic diasporas who have been engaged in pressuring governments in North America and other Western countries to aid Ukraine as well. As one of my colleagues in Lithuania remarked when the invasion started in February 2022, "we are all on the front lines now." Russia's aggressive war against Ukraine has become Lithuania's, Latvia's, and Estonia's war against Russia.

Baltic identification with Ukraine: Diplomacy, security, economy

Baltic countries' identification with Ukraine is not a new phenomenon. After the Russian occupation of Crimea in 2014 Lithuania became the first country to start delivering direct lethal military aid to Ukraine (Marzalik and Toler 2018), but the feelings of existential uncertainty and related anxieties go back to much earlier times. It matters that the Baltic states and Ukraine share similar collective memories about the Soviet past, especially the repressions under Stalin. They created similar memory regimes, both of which came to the fore in 2014, consolidating around the experience of previous traumas — including the Holodomor (in the case of Ukraine) and deportations under Stalin (in all cases). This explains the immediate identification of the Baltic states with the Ukrainians as well as their emotional adoption of Ukraine's self-defense.

When the invasion started in February 2022, Jaunius Kazlauskas, a 50-year-old Lithuanian teacher in Vilnius, said: "My grandparents were sent away to Siberia. My father was persecuted by the KGB. Now I live in a free democratic state, but it seems that nothing can be taken for granted" (Dapkus and Ritter 2022). Therefore, it does not come as a surprise that immediately after the invasion, many in Lithuania started demanding for more direct and hard-line NATO engagement in the war. Dalia Grybauskaitė, a former President of Lithuania, became one of the most vocal voices demanding a greater NATO role in Ukraine. During the early stages of the invasion, in early March, Grybauskaitė argued forcefully that economic sanctions imposed on Russia by the West were not enough, and that "only war that has already been launched can stop another war… The people of Ukraine are fighting the war for us" (LRT English 2022).

Grybauskaitė's opinion was shared by many in Lithuania and the other two Baltic states. In mid-March Estonia became the first NATO country to demand a no-fly zone over Ukraine. Several days later the Lithuanian parliament adopted a resolution arguing that this measure would help to ensure humanitarian corridors and the safety of Ukraine's nuclear power plants (BNS 2022a). Latvia followed, reiterating its full support for Ukraine's sovereignty and territorial integrity (LETA 2022). However, NATO refused to provide the no-fly-zone requested by Ukraine and the Baltic states, arguing that it would lead to escalation and potentially start a direct war with Russia. Nevertheless, the Baltic states continued to support Ukraine in every way possible—politically, economically, and militarily: sending massive amounts of humanitarian aid, taking in Ukrainian refugees into their homes, forming cyber-brigades to help Ukraine fight the disinformation war, and cutting off economic ties with Russia (Bankauskaitė 2022). In March 2022 Lithuania promised a significant amount of money to the International Criminal Court to launch investigations into war crimes and crimes against humanity perpetrated by Russia, aided and abetted by Belarus (BNS 2022b). This happened well before the term *genocide* was used by an increasing number of international actors, including President Biden, to describe Russia's crimes in Ukraine. Clearly, previous experience of mass deportations and political repression under Stalin made Lithuania especially sensitive to the similar crimes being committed in the 21st century.

Furthermore, the Baltic states started the challenging process of cutting off their energy ties with Russia and pressuring businesses engaged in Russia to also cut off their ties to this country. In April 2022 Lithuania became the first EU state to suspend all imports of Russian natural gas (Subramanian 2022). This escape from dependence on Russian gas was possible because Lithuania has been working on it since 2014—a significant achievement given that all of its gas imported that year was from Russia. To accomplish this it opened an LNG terminal in Klaipėda and began importing natural gas from other sources, mostly Norway. Latvia and Estonia followed Lithuania's lead in cutting off their dependence on Russian gas and calling on the entire EU to do the same (Dodman 2022). The three Baltic states became pioneers in Europe by eliminating their dependence on Russian gas and oil. Furthermore, Estonia proposed a model to the EU to use revenues from Russian oil and gas for the reconstruction of Ukraine (Sandford, Askew, and Carlo 2022).

Paradoxically, despite the Baltic countries' fears that they may be next, the eight-years-long war in Ukraine may have contributed to Baltic security, at least for the foreseeable future. Namely, since 2016 NATO's member states have forward-deployed four multinational battalion-size battle groups to the Baltic states and Poland on a rotational basis. Now the Baltic countries are calling on NATO to enlarge these battle groups to brigade size (MoND 2022). NATO is expected to make a decision regarding the requested enlargement of its battle groups at its upcoming summit in June. Moreover, in response to Russia's escalated aggression, Sweden and Finland have signalled that they are interested in abandoning their neutral status and joining NATO. This means that the NATO security blanket could potentially cover an even larger part of the Baltic region, adding over 800 miles to Russia's border with NATO countries.

Russia as the root of societal divisions in the Baltics

Collective traumas can also be a source of internal societal divisions, especially among individuals with different perceptions of the past. Latvia, Lithuania, and Estonia are home to Russian speakers and also, in the case of Lithuania, an ethnic Polish minority whose members in the past have been suspected of dual loyalties—harbouring some sympathies toward Russia and embracing a more positive view of the Soviet past.[1] In Latvia and Estonia there are still many individuals who identify themselves as Russians and do not have Latvian or Estonian citizenship.[2] In Lithuania, many

---

1. In 2021, 6.53% of Lithuania's population identify themselves as ethnic Poles, and 5% as ethnic Russians (Statistics Lithuania, "Population and Housing Census," https://osp.stat.gov.lt/en_GB/gyventoju-ir-bustu-surasymai1). Ethnic Polish minority has been traditionally more politically active than the ethnic Russian minority. In 2021, 24.5% of Latvia's residents identified themselves as Russians (CIA, "The World Factbook," https://www.cia.gov/the-world-factbook/countries/latvia/#people-and-society). In 2023, 28% of Estonia's population identified themselves as Russians (Global Estonian, "Survey: Less than a third of Russian residents in Estonia identify as such," 8 June 2023, https://globalestonian.com/en/news/survey-less-third-russian-residents-estonia-identify-such).
2. After the breakup of the Soviet Union, Lithuania, the most ethnically homogeneous Baltic state, chose the so-called "zero" option by awarding Lithuanian citizenship to everyone. Latvia and Estonia, which had a significant Russian speaking population, restored citizenship to those who had it before the Soviet occupation and their descendants. In Latvia and Estonia, many Russians (who migrated to Latvia and Estonia during the period of the Soviet occupation) ended up without Latvian and Estonian citizenship. However, under intense international pressure, hoping for EU and NATO membership, Latvia and Estonia revised their citizenship laws, making it much easier to obtain. Non-citizens can use the state as a "service station"; they have many rights except the right to vote (in Estonia non-citizen residents can vote in local elections). In 2021, 10.1% of Latvia's population consisted of non-citizens (Official Statistics of Latvia, "Press Release, 1 June 2022," "In Latvia similar number of emigrants and immigrants registered," https://stat.gov.lv/en/statistics-themes/population/population/press-releases/8686-number-population-latvia-2021). In 2020, in Estonia 71,361 individuals (or approximately 5% of the population) were classified as "stateless, unknown citizens and non-citizens" (European

members of the ethnic Polish community are attached to the Russian language and the Russian media, and thus some of them may have been susceptible to the Kremlin's propaganda—especially prior to February 2022, when Russian and Belarusan TV channels were banned in Lithuania over their "incitement of war and propaganda" (Janušauskienė 2021; see also BNS 2022c). After the 2014 occupation of Crimea by Russia, Valdemaras Tomaševskis [Waldemar Tomaszewski], a leading politician who claims to represent a large segment of Lithuania's Poles, publicly demonstrated support for Russia's position regarding Crimea (Černiauskas 2014). At that time as well, in Latvia a political party called "Harmony" that promotes the interests of Latvia's Russian-speakers, failed to condemn Russia's aggression (Bergmane 2022).

More recently, during the height of the Covid-19 pandemic, in all three states significant numbers of Russian speakers and (in the case of Lithuania) ethnic Poles expressed their preference for the Sputnik vaccine, thus demonstrating their trust in Russia and supporting Russia's "vaccine diplomacy" (Bakaitė 2021; Ostrovsky 2022). Nevertheless, despite these observations, research on ethnic minorities in the Baltic states suggests that their identities are complex and multi-layered (Janušauskienė 2021). There are divisions within these civic and ethnic communities, and they cannot be treated as unitary actors that automatically support Russia.

It appears that one clear line of division is generational. In Latvia the younger generation of Russian speakers is using social media to express its frustration with older family members who support Russia's war against Ukraine (Bergmane 2022). Some representatives of the older generation hold positive views of the Soviet past, which is associated with Russian hegemony (Stewart 2022). This often translates into support for Putin's Russia, which is seen as the inheritor of the USSR.

The other line of division seems to be related to religion. There are Orthodox churches in the Baltic states, and some of them operate under the jurisdiction of the Moscow Patriarchate (Bendžius 2022). Their relationship with the war has been complicated. The Orthodox Church of Latvia has condemned the war but did not condemn

---

Migration Network, "Estonia 2021: Main Developments in Migration and International Protection, Including Latest Statistics," August 2022, https://home-affairs.ec.europa.eu/system/files/2022-08/EMN_factsheet2021_EE.pdf).

Putin as the main culprit and perpetrator (Bergmane 2022). Similarly, the head of the Orthodox Church of Estonia has condemned the war (but not Putin) as well, joining the leaders of the Estonian Council of Churches in their condemnation of the bombing of humanitarian sites and causing the suffering of civilians (ERR News 2022). The archeparchy of the Russian Orthodox Church in Lithuania also condemned the war, and initially the metropolitan of the archeparchy, Inokentijus (Innocent), revealed publicly that he personally disagrees with Patriarch Kirill over the war in Ukraine (BNS 2022d). However, shortly afterward, in April Inokentijus's archeparchy was rocked by a scandal when three priests were removed after publicly criticizing Russia's war in Ukraine and Patriarch Kirill. Inokentijus accused the three priests of "conspiracy" by trying to switch to the jurisdiction of Constantinople (Bendžius 2022).

Russia becomes the common "Other"

Despite these divisions, there have been concerted efforts by politicians and civil society leaders in the Baltic countries to present a united front regarding the war in Ukraine and avoid internal tensions. Politicians such as Tomaševskis who openly supported the beginning of Russia's war in Ukraine in 2014 unambiguously condemned Russia's escalated invasion in March 2022 — although he had been critical of Lithuania's decision to shut down Russian TV channels after it started (Brunalas 2022). Zbignevas Jedinskis [Zbigniew Jedziński] — who served as advisor to a member of parliament representing the Electoral Action of Poles in Lithuania–Christian Families Alliance and who posted on Facebook arguing that Poland should leave NATO and establish friendly relations with Russia — drew widespread condemnation and lost his position due to this post (Vakarų ekspresas 2022). Meanwhile, civil society groups such as the Union of Lithuanian Poles organized public actions and humanitarian support for Ukraine, and the representative from the Department of National Minorities argued that attitude toward the Russo-Ukrainian war has nothing to do with ethnicity (Jakubauskas 2022).

In Latvia, leading pro-Russian politicians and "Harmony," supported by Russian-speakers, condemned the war and supported measures to help Ukraine (Bergmane 2022). In Estonia, according to Dmitri Teperik from the International Center for Defense and

Security in Tallinn, although there is a small number of pro-Putin Russians, "Russian-speakers who support Ukraine have gained visibility" (Narva 2022) as prominent government officials work to rally support for national unity. However, it appears that in Estonia a large group of Russian speakers has chosen to remain passive, referring to Russia's war in Ukraine as "not our war" instead of openly supporting or opposing it (Duxbury 2022). Although hundreds of Russian speakers in Latvia participated in anti-war demonstrations in April (RFE/RL 2022), it appears that passivity ("not supporting either side") is a common response among Latvia's minorities as well (Bergmane 2022).

This position may prove to be difficult to maintain in the future, as there are moves in the Baltic states to completely sever all links with the Soviet past and even with Russian culture. Discussions about removing all Soviet-era monuments have started. In Latvia there have been calls to dismantle the Monument to the Liberators in Riga—a memorial site associated with the glorification of the "Great Patriotic War" in Soviet Latvia (Bergmane 2022). Similar calls to remove monuments associated with the Soviet victory in the "Great Patriotic War" have been made in Lithuania as well. This idea has obtained support from some politicians and government agencies, but it has been resisted by leading memory politics experts (Bakaitė 2022). At the same time, in Lithuania (similarly to Ukraine) public discussions about how to relate to Russian culture, including its classics, have been taking place as well. Some have argued that there is a clear link between Russian expansionism and Russian culture; thus, the "correct" moral position given the war in Ukraine is to resist all expressions of Russian culture (Jakučiūnas 2022).

Considering the Baltic identification with Ukraine's collective trauma, such discourses of othering do not come as a surprise. These new identity discourses mark the borders of new communities of fighting and suffering that are likely to last a long time, even after this genocidal war is over.

Works cited

Bakaitė, Jurga. 2021. "'Niekas net nebando kovoti už tuos žmones': iš Vilniaus šnekėti, kad Visagine kas nors nevyksta, – tuščių puodų barbenimas" ['No one is even trying to fight for these people': To talk in Vilnius that nothing is happening in Visaginas amounts to talking nonsense"]. Lithuanian National Radio and Television, 29 March 2021. https://www.lrt.lt/naujienos/lietuvoje/2/1370786/niekas-net-nebando-kovoti-uz-tuos-zmones-is-vilniaus-sneketi-kad-visagine-kas-nors-nevyksta-tusciu-puodu-barbenimas.

— — —. 2022. "Entuziastingai sutikta sovietinės simbolikos iškėlimo idėja sulaukė kritikos: karas – blogiausias laikas paminklams griauti." Lithuanian National Radio and Television, 8 April 2022. https://www.lrt.lt/naujienos/lietuvoje/2/1667529/entuziastingai-sutikta-sovietines-simbolikos-iskelimo-ideja-sulauke-kritikos-karas-blogiausias-laikas-paminklams-griauti.

Bankauskaitė, Dalia. 2022. "The Baltic states' response to war against Ukraine."Centre for European Policy Analysis, 28 March 2022. https://cepa.org/the-baltic-states-response-to-war-against-ukraine.

Bendžius, Simon. 2022. "Rimtas signalas: trys lietuviai kunigai ortodoksai atleisti iš pareigų." Bernardinai.lt, 15 April 2022. https://www.bernardinai.lt/vienas-is-nusalintu-ortodoksu-kunigu-g-sungaila-tai-tik-pradzia-bus-ir-daugiau-atleistu-dvasininku.

Bergmane, Una. 2022. "Latvia's first response to Russia's war in Ukraine." Foreign Policy Research Institute, 11 March 2022. https://www.fpri.org/article/2022/03/latvias-first-response-to-russias-war-in-ukraine.

BNS. 2022a. "Lithuania bans Russian, Belarusian TV channels over war incitement." Lithuanian National Radio and Television, 25 February 2022. https://www.lrt.lt/en/news-in-english/19/1626345/lithuania-bans-russian-belarusian-tv-channels-over-war-incitement.

— — —. 2022b. "Lithuania intends to allocate EUR 100,000 to Hague Process over war in Ukraine." Delfi, 13 March 2022. https://www.delfi.lt/en/politics/lithuania-intends-to-allocate-eur-100-000-to-hague-process-over-war-in-ukraine-89663335.

— — —. 2022c. "Lithuanian parliament calls for no-fly zone over Ukraine." Lithuanian National Radio and Television, 17 March 2022. https://www.lrt.lt/en/news-in-english/19/1646939/lithuanian-parliament-calls-for-no-fly-zone-over-ukraine.

— — —. 2022d. "Lietuvos stačiatikių bažnyčia pasmerkė Rusijos karą prieš Ukrainą." Delfi, 18 March 2022. https://www.delfi.lt/news/daily/lithuania/lietuvos-staciatikiu-baznycia-pasmerke-rusijos-kara-pries-ukraina.d?id=89732439.

Brunalas, Ben. 2022. "Tomaševskis nenoriai komentuoja Rusijos sukeltą karą Ukrainoje: tai yra viena ilga nesąmonė." Delfi, 4 March 2022. https://www.delfi.lt/news/daily/lithuania/tomasevskis-nenoriai-komentuoja-rusijos-sukelta-kara-ukrainoje-tai-yra-viena-ilga-nesamone.d?id=89620765.

Černiauskas, Šarūnas. 2014. "V. Tomaševskis kartoja V. Putino argumentus." Delfi, 20 March 2014. https://www.delfi.lt/news/daily/lithuania/v-tomasevskis-kartoja-v-putino-argumentus.d?id=64326844.

Dapkus, Liudas, and Karl Ritter. 2022. "Ukraine attack leaves Baltics wondering: Are we next?" Associated Press, 24 February 2022. https://apnews.com/article/russia-ukraine-russia-estonia-race-and-ethnicity-soviet-union-187f098422b7a3170143de238865b526.

Dodman, Benjamin. 2022. "Baltic states end Russian gas imports, but can the rest of Europe follow suit?" France24, 5 March 2022. https://f24.my/8WX8.

Duxbury, Charlie. 2022. "Estonia fights back against pro-Russia messaging." Politico, 23 March 2022. https://www.politico.eu/article/estonia-fight-back-pro-russia-propaganda.

ERR News. 2022. "Head of Russian Orthodox Church in Estonia signs anti-war statement." ERR, 17 March 2022. https://news.err.ee/1608535288/head-of-russian-orthodox-church-in-estonia-signs-anti-war-statement.

Jakubauskas, Ramūnas. 2022. "Tautinių mažumų departamento vadovė: požiūris į karą Ukrainoje nėra susijęs su tautybe" [Leader of National Minorities Department: The attitudes toward the war in Ukraine have nothing to do with ethnicity]. 15 min, 18 May 2022. https://www.15min.lt/naujiena/aktualu/lietuva/tautiniu-mazumu-departamento-vadove-poziuris-i-kara-ukrainoje-nera-susijes-su-tautybe-56-1681518.

Jakučiūnas, Andrius. 2022. "'Didžiosios rusų kultūros' ypatumai. Ar Nabokovas atsakingas už tai, ką Ukrainoje iškrėtė Putinas?" [Peculiarities of the 'Great Russian culture': Is Nabokov responsible for what Putin is Doing in Ukraine?]. 15min, 26 April 2022. https://www.15min.lt/kultura/naujiena/literatura/andrius-jakuciunas-didziosios-rusu-kulturos-ypatumai-ar-nabokovas-atsakingas-uz-tai-ka-ukrainoje-iskrete-putinas-286-1671374.

Janušauskienė, Diana. 2021. "Identities of and policies toward the Polish national minority in Lithuania." *Ethnopolitics* 20 (1): 136–49.

LETA. 2022. "Latvian parliament supports imposing no-fly zone in Ukraine." Baltic News Network, 18 March 2022. https://bnn-news.com/latvian-parliament-supports-imposing-no-fly-zone-in-ukraine-233249.

LRT English. 2022. "Sanctions won't stop Russia, only war can stop war in Ukraine: Grybauskaitė." Lithuanian National Radio and Television, 2 March 2022. https://www.lrt.lt/en/news-in-english/19/1632601/sanctions-won-t-stop-russia-only-war-can-stop-war-in-ukraine-grybauskaite.

Marzalik, Peter J., and Aric Toler. 2018. "Lethal weapons to Ukraine: A primer." Atlantic Council, 26 January 2018. https://www.atlanticcouncil.org/blogs/ukrainealert/lethal-weapons-to-ukraine-a-primer.

MoND. 2022. "We aim for a reinforcement of NATO enhanced Forward Presence Battalions to Brigades, says Minister A. Anušauskas." Ministry of National Defence Republic of Lithuania, 11 April 2022. https://kam.lt/en/we-aim-for-a-reinforcement-of-nato-enhanced-forward-presence-battalions-to-brigades-says-minister-a-anusauskas.

Narva, Isabelle de Pommereau. 2022. "Will Estonia's Russians embrace the West?" Deutsche Welle, 11 March 2022. https://www.dw.com/en/amid-war-in-ukraine-are-estonias-russian-speakers-ready-to-embrace-the-west/a-61078050.

Ostrovsky, Simon. 2022. "Inside Estonia's approach in combating Russian disinformation." PBS, 15 January 2022. https://www.pbs.org/newshour/show/inside-estonias-approach-in-combating-russian-disinformation.

RFE/RL. 2022. "Latvian Russian-Speakers Protest Against Kremlin's War In Ukraine." Radio Free Europe/Radio Liberty, 23 April 2022. https://www.rferl.org/a/latvia-russians-protest-invasion/31817920.html.

Sandford, Alasdair, Joshua Askew, and Andrea Carlo, with AP, AFP. 2022. "Ukraine war: Where does each EU country stand on cutting off Russian oil and gas?" Euronews, 16 April 2022. https://www.euronews.com/my-europe/2022/04/16/ukraine-war-where-does-each-eu-country-stand-on-cutting-off-russian-oil-and-gas.

Stewart, Ashleigh. 2022. "Ethnic Russians in Latvia divided on war in Ukraine: 'There is a big division.'" Global News, 4 March 2022. https://globalnews.ca/news/8657202/ukraine-daugavpils-latvia-generational-divide.

Subramanian, Samanth. 2022. "How a Baltic nation ended its reliance on Russian gas." Quartz, 11 April 2022. https://qz.com/2152999/lithuania-became-the-first-eu-nation-to-stop-russian-gas-imports.

Vakarų ekspresas. 2022. "Jedinskis atleistas dėl įrašo apie Rusiją – Seimo pirmininkė." Vakaryų ekspresas, 13 April 2022. https://ve.lt/aktualijos/lietuva/jedinskis-atleistas-del-iraso-apie-rusija-seimo-pirmininke.

CHAPTER 5

The fallacy of "Russian culture" in Ukraine

Hiroaki Kuromiya
Essay published 16 May 2022

> Hiroaki Kuromiya taught Ukrainian, Russian, and Soviet history at Indiana University, USA, until his retirement in 2021. He is the author of *Freedom and Terror in the Donbas: A Ukrainian-Russian Borderland, 1870s–1990s* (1998), *Stalin: Profiles in Power* (2005), *Conscience on Trial: The Fate of Fourteen Pacifists in Stalin's Ukraine, 1952–1953* (2012), *Zrozumity Donbas* (Understanding the Donbas; 2015), and other books.

On 25 April the *New York Times*, a newspaper with more than nine million subscribers, published on its editorial page an essay [stating] "Russian artists aren't the problem," by Kevin M. F. Platt, a professor in the Department of Russian and East European Studies at the University of Pennsylvania and editor of the book *Global Russian Cultures* (Platt 2022). Although he is careful to blame Russia for "the depraved brutality of the unprovoked Russian invasion," he deplores what he sees as "retaliations against anyone and anything Russian" by other countries. He finds it "profoundly ironic that those who react to the war in Ukraine by aggressively or indiscriminately cancelling or restricting artists and artistic works simply for being Russian are reflecting the same kind of nationalist thinking driving the Russian invasion in the first place."

From such assertions one might be forgiven for assuming that Platt's intention is to defend Russian artists from unfairly being singled out and "cancelled." However, the substance of his essay is about something else. It is that "there is no one 'Russian culture' — there are many" — in Russia, Ukraine, Latvia, Uzbekistan, and other countries, namely, "global Russian cultures." Platt conflates "Russian culture" with "Russian-language literature" and "Russian diaspora cultures." These are not trivial but critical distinctions familiar to anyone who studies literature and culture in general. By muddying the water, Platt presents a fallacy that is tantamount to upholding the idea of the "Russian World" (*russkii mir*), a political brand or label heavily promoted by the Kremlin that appropriates as its own "anyone and anything Russian" beyond the borders of the Russian Federation.

Russian culture and the "Russian World"

Platt states disingenuously that "most Russians in Ukraine have no desire for Mr. Putin's 'salvation' — and a great many have taken up arms to resist it," adding that these "Russians" have a "different homeland. Now that is a demonstration of a distinct Russian culture." What Platt deliberately neglects to say is that these "Russians" are not Russians at all but rather Ukrainians (citizens of Ukraine). Even though they may be ethnic Russians, they are no more Russian than the many American or Canadian citizens who are ethnic Russians. Their culture may be Russophone, but it is not a "distinct Russian culture." Is the American culture a distinct English culture? American culture is largely Anglophone, but no one would accept the assertion that American culture is an English culture. Quebecois culture is not French culture but a Francophone Canadian culture. Platt contends that there are millions of people outside Russia who write in Russian, including Shamshad Abdullaev of Uzbekistan, creating "their own Russian culture." Although it is possible that Abdullaev is a Russophile, he would be surprised to learn that he has created a "Russian culture." Since, according to Platt, "his writing in Russian bears no relation to the Russian state or the territories it seeks to claim," it is not Russian culture, but Russian-language Uzbek literature. Platt also discusses Boris Khersonsky, "a Jewish poet from Odesa who writes mainly in Russian." He claims that Khersonsky "of course, might best be described as a Ukrainian poet. Yet his poetry forms part of a distinctive Russian culture. This is the crux of the matter." Actually, the crux of the matter is not this. Rather, it is that Khersonsky belongs (not "might best be described" as belonging) to Ukrainian culture, not to a "distinctive Russian culture." Here, too, Platt conflates Russian culture with Russian-language literature outside the Russian Federation.

To justify his claims, Platt repeats the platitude that languages and cultures transcend national borders:

> The idea of discrete national cultures, conducted in distinct languages and associated with states and their "proper territories" — French culture in France, German culture in Germany — is associated with the rising tide of ethnic nationalist ideology of the 19th century. Even then, this idea didn't correspond to reality. The forces of migration — as well as the more destructive means of war, conquest, and colonialism — have ensured the mingling of people, languages, and cultures throughout history. Borders between territories associated with one or another language or ethnic group have shifted over and over again, and so have the cultures they created.

All very well, but Platt omits the obvious fact that the world has evolved since the 19th century and that many countries (including the former European colonial powers) have learned not to press territorial and cultural appropriations beyond their respective political (or "national") borders, the kind of appropriations Platt purports for "Russian culture." To avoid this kind of cultural usurpation, we have learned to say, when it is ambiguous, "English-language literature," "Russophone diaspora culture," and the like. So as not to repeat our follies of the past, we do not appropriate history and culture beyond our national borders, and we acknowledge that the world was and is connected in a myriad of ways. Ukraine has Ukrainian culture, not a "distinctive Russian culture," even when it is written and expressed in the Russian language. What Platt is promoting is Russia's *cultural appropriation*, and he does so by conflating "Russian culture" with the various cultures and literatures created by the media of the Russian language beyond the borders of the Russian Federation.

Cases of Russia's cultural appropriation

True, ambiguous cases are legion. If Ukrainian citizens living in Ukraine write in Russian and publish their works in the Russian Federation, will they create a distinct "Russian literature" in Ukraine? If English citizens living in the United States publish in the United States, will they create a distinct "English literature"? One can perhaps speak of "English diaspora culture" in the United States, but it is not the same as "English culture."

Even more ambiguous are historical cases. Does Nikolai Gogol/Mykola Hohol (who mostly wrote in Russian) belong to Russian culture?[1] How about Ukraine's national poet, Taras Shevchenko (who mostly wrote in Ukrainian)? Both belong to the culture produced in the 19th-century Russian Empire, but in today's world, Russia is ambivalent about Shevchenko (a "proto-Ukrainian nationalist"), while it embraces Gogol as its own. But Ukraine, now independent, has also adopted Hohol as its own, because he was born and grew up in Poltava and his writing was heavily influenced by Ukrainian folk culture. Hohol's self-identification, which rested somewhere between Ukraine and Russia, confounds the question of belonging (Ilchuk 2021).

---

1. Much literature exists on Gogol/Hohol's position between Ukraine and Russia. The latest scholarly analysis emphasizes his "hybrid identity" (Ilchuk 2021).

It should be remembered, in any case, that the Russian Empire denied the very existence of Ukraine and Ukrainian culture and therefore did not even allow for an administrative unit called Ukraine to exist in the empire. It denied the very existence of the Ukrainian language (which was merely a "Little Russian dialect") but forbade its use all the same. Moscow takes advantage of these ambiguities to appropriate foreign lands and cultures. Platt fails to see through this Russian political scheme. Thirty years ago, shortly after Ukraine's independence, Michael Ignatieff, a prominent Canadian academic and politician whose Russian family was from Ukraine, frankly admitted that he had "difficulty in taking Ukraine seriously" and that he had "just a trace of old Russian disdain for these 'little Russians'" (Ignatieff 1993, 108).[2] While Ignatieff's view is nothing but a personal prejudice, Platt's is cloaked in a scholarly claim about what he calls "global Russian cultures."

This sort of ruse to obfuscate the inflated use of "Russian" is nothing new. Platt seems utterly oblivious to, or ignorant of, the long history of Ukraine's protestation of Russia's imperialist appropriations of things Ukrainian. To fully comprehend this, one must understand the origin of the terms Russia and Russian, which are derivatives of *Rus'*, referring to the medieval state that encompassed much of today's Ukraine and Belarus and parts of Russia, with the center in Kyiv, the capital of today's Ukraine. Russia may have some claim to the Rus' heritage, but it cannot disregard Ukraine's and Belarus's equally valid claims.[3]

Rus' and Russia are not the same

Yet Russia has been determined to appropriate the idea of Rus' for itself by denying the existence of Ukraine as an independent state. Both Ukrainian and Polish quite clearly distinguish between the names *Rus'* (Русь, руський/*Ruś, ruski*) and *Rosiia* (Росія, російський/ *Rosja, rosyjski*), whereas the Russian language obscures them (Русь,

---

2. Now, however, he seems to take Ukraine more seriously (CEU 2022).
3. In his chapter "The contest for the 'Kievan inheritance' in Russian-Ukrainian relations: Origins and early ramifications," Pelenski notes that Russia can claim some dynastic heritage of Rus', ignoring the fact that the Riurikide Rus' dynasty ended in the late 16th century, soon replaced by the Romanov dynasty. The Romanovs' rule, in any case, ended in Russia in 1917, more than one hundred years ago (Pelenski 1993).

Россия, русский, российский). In English, both *russkii* and *rossiiskii* are traditionally rendered as "Russian," complicating the already confusing terms. Putin calls the lands of Rus' "old Russian lands" (древнерусские земли, *drevnerusskie zemli*) and insists that Rus' people called themselves *russkie* 'Russians' (русские) (Putin 2022).

If the English and Russian languages were to adopt "Rusian" (or revert to the Latin equivalent "Ruthenian") and *ruskii*, respectively, to refer to the Rus', it would solve some of the confusion.[4] Although there has been much discussion on the difference between *russkii* and *rossiiskii*, effectively it has done little to challenge Russia's false albeit strenuous monopolization of the concept and culture-history of Rus'.

Sadly, many generations of North American Russia specialists were taught about "Kievan Russia." Here we must state emphatically that there was no such entity as "Kievan Russia," as Russia claims. Regrettably, however, even today if one puts this term in the keyword section of the OCLC library catalogue, it will return approximately 200 results, starting with George Vernadsky's classic work, *Kievan Russia* (published by Yale University Press in 1948, 1973, and 1976). As late as 2000, the hugely popular Russian history textbook (reissued numerous times) by Nicholas Riasanovsky and Oxford University Press, *A History of Russia*, called Rus' "Kievan Russia." In point of fact, the Muscovite Principality did not emerge as the state of Russia until the fifteenth or sixteenth century (i.e., two to three centuries after the collapse of Rus' in the thirteenth century), although the concept of Russia (*Rossiia*) may have appeared earlier. Muscovite tsars justified their territorial expansion as the "gathering of Russia," resolutely rejecting any concept of Ukraine and aggressively employing such terms as "New Russia" and "Little Russia" for Ukraine. Even now, most Western specialists of Russia use, without embarrassment, such terms as "Peter the Great" (instead of Peter I) and "Catherine the Great" (instead of Catherine II), as if intent on legitimizing Russia's imperialist self-aggrandizement.

Furthermore, in its war against Ukraine Russia has enlisted the Russian Orthodox Church. Ecclesiastically, the church claims to be the sole heir to "holy Rus'," asserting full control over the Ukrainian

---

4. On the use of "Rusian," see Horace G. Lunt (1975, 269–81; 1988, 276–313). Today, the English words "Ruthenia" and "Ruthenian," which derive from *Rus'* via Latin, nearly ubiquitously refer to Ukraine's westernmost region, south of the Carpathian Mountains.

Orthodox Churches and supporting the war against Ukraine. In this regard, Russia ranks with such aggressive theocratic regimes as the Islamic State. Indeed, cultural, linguistic, and religious appropriations can be as threatening and conducive to conflict as territorial ones. With the demise of the age of empire, the world has generally ceased to engage in such appropriations precisely because they are dangerous. Russia deliberately reverses this progress, and Platt appears to subscribe to these reactionary, imperialist Russian claims.

Concluding remarks

Platt is right that one should not cancel Russian culture indiscriminately and that Russian artists are not the problem. But the thrust of his essay is not about cancelling Russian culture. His real interest is to argue for the conflation of "Russian culture" with Ukrainian and other cultures. Putin has not turned a hair at just such statements, such as Platt's "depraved brutality of the unprovoked Russian invasion." On the contrary, Putin would be delighted with Platt's essay, which echoes his own "Russian World" slogan of cultural and territorial aggression. What is deeply regrettable is that this sort of Russian propaganda goes unnoticed in Western mass media and academia.

Works cited

CEU (Central European University). 2022. "Michael Ignatieff: The Historical Perspective of the War in Ukraine." YouTube, 17 March 2022. https://www.youtube.com/watch?v=FTsJe8-m6pw.

Ignatieff, Michael. 1993. *Blood and Belonging: Journeys into the New Nationalisms*. New York: Penguin.

Ilchuk, Yuliya. 2021. *Nikolai Gogol: Performing Hybrid Identity*. University of Toronto Press.

Lunt, Horace G. 1975. "On the language of Old Rus: Some questions and suggestions." *Russian Linguistics* 2 (3/4): 269–81.

— — —. 1988. "The Language of Rus' in the eleventh century: Some observations about facts and theories." *Harvard Ukrainian Studies* 12/13 (1988/1989): 276–313.

Pelenski, Jaroslaw. 1998. *Contest for the Legacy of Kievan Rus'*. Boulder, CO: Columbia University Press.

Putin, Vladimir. 2022. "Obrashchenie Vladimira Putina k rossianam v sviazi s situatsiei na Donbasse." Interfax, 21 February 2022. https://www.interfax.ru/russia/823522.

Platt, Kevin M.F. 2022. "The Profound Irony of Canceling Everything Russian." *The New York Times*, 22 April 2022. https://www.nytimes.com/2022/04/22/opinion/russian-artists-culture-boycotts.html.

CHAPTER 6

Contradicting Putin: Ukrainians and Russians are not "one people"

Nataliya Shpylova-Saeed
Essay published 18 May 2022

> Nataliya Shpylova-Saeed is a Preceptor in Ukrainian at the Department of Slavic Languages and Literatures, Harvard University. She has PhD degrees in Slavic studies (Indiana University, 2022) and American literature (Taras Shevchenko Institute of Literature, National Academy of Sciences of Ukraine, 2007). Her research interests include contested memory, with a focus on Ukraine and Russia. Shpylova-Saeed is an H-Ukraine review editor, Arrowsmith Press series editor, and a host on the New Books Network. Her book *Russia's Denial of Ukraine: Letters and Contested Memory* is forthcoming in 2024.

In 2014 the international community felt some responsibility to respond to Russia's military aggression against Ukraine. Ultimately, however, the hesitancy with which the international community acted when Russia annexed Crimea and occupied some regions of the Donbas sent a clear signal. Was it worthwhile to sacrifice old and profitable ties with Russia for a new post-Soviet state that was barely known? Was this sacrifice warranted for a country whose name was repeatedly pronounced with a misplaced definite article, "the" Ukraine? This was the attitude that justified the easy acceptance of Russian narratives about Ukraine. This attitude also justified and encouraged dismissive comments that easily aborted attempts to shift the emphasis from "the poked roaring bear" toward Ukraine. Ukraine received some compassionate comments about its citizens who lost their lives on the Maidan, but the political priority remained the same: do not aggravate "the bear."

The pretext for the Russo-Ukrainian war

Eight years after the initial aggression, on 24 February 2022 at 5 a.m. Eastern European Time the Russian Federation launched an armed invasion of Ukraine. Russian president Vladimir Putin disguised this assault as a "special military operation" in the Donbas. Instead, however, on 24 February the Russian military forces advanced not only in the eastern regions of Ukraine; towns and cities across the country awoke to the sounds of massive explosions. Within an hour it became clear that what Putin announced as a "special military operation" was Russia's escalated, full-scale war on Ukraine.

The pretext for the invasion was to "protect" Russian speakers living in the eastern parts of Ukraine who, according to Putin, were "oppressed" by the Ukrainian "neo-Nazi" government. Russia's accusations toward the Ukrainian government were not simply ungrounded but ambiguous. Following the Euromaidan events of 2014, Ukrainians stood up against their president's attempts to establish a dictatorship and fought for freedom and democracy. Nevertheless, in Putin's reality freedom and democracy can be presented as manifestations of Nazism and fascism, and since 2014 his rhetoric about Ukraine's "neo-Nazism" has been integrated into his vision of Ukraine.

Putin ignores the fact that the person who leads Ukraine today during its resistance against Russia's belligerence is of Jewish descent. Volodymyr Zelensky's relatives fell victim to Nazis during the Holocaust. Putin's rhetoric about the need to "de-nazify" the Ukrainian government reveals not only its duplicitousness but also its amorality.

In hindsight, we can look for facts that could have warned us about Putin's plan to launch a military assault against Ukraine. In his already well-known article on the "historical unity" of Russians and Ukrainians, Putin persisted in commenting on their "fraternal" relationship, underlining that they constitute "one people" (Putin 2021). Published in July 2021, just a month before Ukraine's celebration of 30 years of its independence — which had been overwhelmingly supported by Ukrainian citizens in 1991 — this screed was filled with historical inaccuracies and misconceptions. It was not the first attempt by Putin to construct a manipulative historical narrative for Russia, Ukraine, and the international community in general. During the 2014 invasion of Ukraine's Autonomous Republic of Crimea, the Russian president presented his view on the history of the peninsula, which, according to his statements, is part of the very essence of Russian history and Russian national identity (Putin 2014). Simultaneously, he mentioned the historic Novorossiia region in

Southern Ukraine during the occupation of the Donbas, attempting to resurrect another of Imperial Russia's territorial projects.

In his article, Putin lamented about the "wall" that emerged between the two countries over the last few years, declaring that it arose as the consequence "of our mistakes" which were made at different time periods. But "the wall" is also a result of the activities of those forces, which aimed to subvert "our unity"(ibid.). The consistent usage of the words "uniting," "we," and "our" was dominant in his essay: through this linguistic nuance, Putin again drew Russians and Ukrainians into one historical, political, cultural, and memorial space. To fulfill his goal to re-create an illusory "shared space" in which the Russians and the Ukrainians were "brethren" again, he conflated historical facts and created his version of the history of the two countries, which, when following his rhetoric, is/should be one—Russia. This vision was transmitted to a broad audience that extended beyond the borders of the Russian Federation.

Unquestionably, this article could have been taken as a warning in Ukraine, but many disregarded its threatening implications, commenting on it only briefly and then dropping the discussion. Some refused to even engage in any kind of analysis as they did not find it worthy of any attention. But it should have been taken more seriously, for only a few months later, on 22 February 2022 Putin would follow up with another "gesture of friendship"—recognition of the "independence" of the occupied parts of the Donetsk and Luhansk oblasts—and on 24 February 2022 would give orders to his militaries to "de-militarize" and "de-nazify" Ukraine, which did not welcome his historical visions in which Ukraine simply did not exist, does not, and should not exist.

The war as a tool to "Russify" regional political realities

As a result of the Russian aggression against Ukraine that started in 2014, more than thirteen thousand people lost their lives. Millions of people had to relocate from Crimea and the Donbas to different regions in Ukraine, European Union, as well as Russia (MSP 2021). Since the full-scale invasion in February, these numbers have increased to an unprecedented scale. Thousands of civilians have been murdered, hundreds of children killed, thousands of Ukrainians detained and tortured by Russians, and many deported to the Russian Federation. Russians place Ukrainians in "filtration" camps and force Ukrainian children to learn the Russian language. Airstrike sirens are activated across the entire country more and more frequently. The country's infrastructure has been severely damaged: many regions have been razed to the ground and will have to be completely rebuilt.

The current Russo-Ukrainian war revealed Putin's neo-imperialistic ambitions not only in Ukraine but in the rest of Europe as well (Kushnir 2022). In spite of the Kremlin's ceaseless rhetoric about friendship and cooperation that the Russian Federation prioritizes in its relations with *all* neighbouring countries, its policies of coercion constitute one of the major Russian international tactics. As the Russian officials, including Putin, made it clear in the fall of 2021, their priority is to stop the enlargement of NATO, which means barring countries such as Ukraine and Georgia from joining the alliance. This rhetoric intensified after 24 February. However, as the Russian war against Ukraine continues, Putin moves ever more threateningly toward NATO countries — not away.

Ukraine's divergence from Russian memorial programs

While the intricacies of international politics play a major role in the current Russo-Ukrainian war, we should not forget about another aspect that this war has already revealed. Ukrainians were consistently diverging from the imperial Russian memorial programs that attempt to strengthen the belief that Ukrainians and Russians are "one people." While these programs succeeded in Russia and to a certain degree in Ukraine, the cultural memory in Ukraine maintained a distinctiveness which was transmitted from generation to generation and which led to Ukraine's independence, fulfilling ambitions that had developed long before 1991.

Contested memory issues focusing on language, ethnicity, and memory were ultimately transmitted from generation to generation, becoming part of the very texture of cultural and national memory in Ukraine. This memory is rooted first and foremost in the uprooted (pun intended) sense of one's distinctiveness and otherness, national in particular. To be distinct from Russians, in many cases Ukrainians were meant to become invisible and, at times, to recognize their deficiency and inferiority. As a result of memory tactics exploited by the Russian Empire and later by the Soviet Union (and its official heir, the Russian Federation), Ukrainians had to remember themselves as inferior to their "great brother." *A priori*, Ukrainians' language and culture were positioned by Russian officials, critics, and, very often, intellectuals and intelligentsia as something beautiful but less sophisticated than all things Russian: not as "great" when compared to Russian culture and language. The official Russian rhetoric about the "great Russian language and culture" still has discriminative repercussions even today. The language bans that were implemented by the Russian Empire secured the stability of the prejudices against the Ukrainian language and led to the formation of an inferiority complex that was projected onto the Ukrainian speakers at a national level. The poetess Lesia Ukrainka was revolutionary in drawing attention to this national issue; not only did she encourage Ukrainians to embrace their language that some would regard as a "peasant" one but she also directly confronted Russians by advising them to deal with their own inferiority complexes. After all, the majority of the Russian aristocratic elite had long shunned the Russian vernacular until Alexander Pushkin subverted the non-Russian aristocratic linguistic elitism.

Ukrainians, after 2014 in particular, seem to have embraced the discovery of *their* memory, of memories that *they* choose of the past that *they* remember and transmit from generations to generations. Many will see this interest in memory as an attempt to nationalize memory, past, and history, which carries a number of risks potentially pernicious to the nation. But before making such accusations, it is worthwhile to entertain the idea that this interest in memory is part of a healing process.

The current war between Russia and Ukraine developed not only as a result of profoundly different political strategies and interests prioritized by each state, but also as a result of deeply rooted contested memory regarding the right to be distinct not only politically but mnemonically as well. In terms of the latter, Russia continues to deny Ukraine's right to its distinctiveness. For Putin, Ukrainians who do not agree with his maxim about Russians and Ukrainians being "one people" are "neo-Nazis" who should be eliminated. Thus, by waging the current war Putin is driven not only by his desire to re-establish Russia as a superpower. As Hiroaki Kuromiya aptly notes, he has already lost: "Clearly, from the beginning Russia was no match in spirit and morale for a country fighting for its very existence. Russia has already lost in the court of world opinion and will certainly lose in the court of world history" (Kuromiya 2022).

Russians and Ukrainians have never been "one people"

We can speculate about what Putin's ultimate geopolitical goal is, but at least one thing is quite evident: Putin endorsed the annihilation of an entire nation that he believes should not exist and cannot exist. His language echoes the language of imperial Russia's officials who declared bans against the Ukrainian language. Putin uses his mantra about Russians and Ukrainians being "one people." But how can one explain then the approval of killing the very people whom he regards as part of the Russian people?

The truth is that the political and cultural differences between Ukrainians and Russians are profound. Putin is probably not really sincere when he says that Russians and Ukrainians are "one people." Indeed they are not, and he most likely understands this quite well. In fact, it is precisely the profound differences between the two nations that threatens him. He also understands well that there is no grand Russia without Kyiv, without the culture-history of Kyivan Rus', and therefore the Russia he represents and promotes — an imperial Russia that cannot exist without Ukraine — is compelled to claim its right to Kyiv.

Ukrainians and Russians are not the same, they are different. They were made "almost the same" by imperial and Soviet Russians, and those who became fascinated and enchanted with the "great charm" of Russia and could not let go of this fascination, meanwhile turning a blind eye to Russia's imperialism and colonialism in politics and culture. As a result, Ukraine became almost invisible — until Russia's brutality made it visible. What a price Ukraine has to pay for the right to be distinct, to be taken as a sovereign state with its own history and culture, and not to be dismissed as a lesser-known region which does not deserve either political or academic attention since it is "very similar" to Russia. It is easier to focus on Russia, whose visibility has hardly ever been questioned. It has always been "prestigious" to do Russian studies since Russia is one of the regions that deserves much academic and political attention. Ironically, the events of 2022 puzzled the world. The war was waged by a Russia that the world still struggles to understand. Ukraine, its neighbour — the people of a country that cannot compete with

Russia in terms of geographical prevalence—have left the world in awe with their brave resistance against Russia's invasion. It was this significantly smaller country that for decades did not seem to deserve any "serious" attention from politicians and academics that has subverted the overpowering presence of Russia in the region.

After Russia's initial aggression in 2014, one could not find a unanimous opinion on the Russo-Ukrainian war in Ukraine; for some it was a war initiated by Russia, while for others it was the inability of the Ukrainian government to conduct an efficient domestic policy that led to the confrontation between the Ukrainians and the Russians. Russia's full-scale invasion of Ukraine in 2022 changed this significantly. More than 90% of Ukrainians across the country believe that Ukraine will defeat Russia, and the sentiment about Ukrainians and Russians being "brethren" has lost its supporters. Ukrainians have embraced and internalized their profound differences from Russians, not only political differences but cultural ones as well. Ukrainians are paying a very high price for their choice not to be Russians. On the other hand, today's decisive resistance against Russia's dictatorship would not have been possible without years and centuries of Ukraine's resilience against oppression perpetrated by Russia's manipulative narratives, targeting the distinctiveness of Ukrainians and attempting to turn Ukrainians into Russians.

Works cited

Kuromiya, Hiroaki. 2022. "Russia's war against Ukraine and the future of the Donbas." *Tyzhden,* 2 April 2022. https://tyzhden.ua/russia-s-war-against-ukraine-and-the-future-of-the-donbas.

Kushnir, Ostap. 2022. "Russia's neo-imperial powerplay in Ukraine: The factors of identity and interests." *Forum for Ukrainian Studies*, 31 January 2022. https://ukrainian-studies.ca/2022/01/31/russias-neo-imperial-powerplay-in-ukraine-the-factors-of-identity-and-interests.

MSP. 2021. "Oblikovano 1,473,650 vnutrishn'o peremishchenykh osib." Ministry of Social Policy of Ukraine, 6 July 2021. https://www.msp.gov.ua/news/20309.html.

Putin, Vladimir. 2021. "On the historical unity of Russian and Ukrainians." Presidential Executive Office, 12 July 2021. http://en.kremlin.ru/events/president/news/66181.

———. 2014. "Obrashchenie Prezidenta Rossiiskoi Federatsii." Presidential Executive Office, 18 March 2014. http://kremlin.ru/events/president/news/20603.

CHAPTER 7

"Never again" vs. "We can repeat it": Russians will pay any price to restore the glory of Soviet victory in WW II

Oleksii Polegkyi
Essay published 11 June 2022

> Oleksii Polegkyi is the academic director of the Center for Public Diplomacy in Kyiv and an Adjunkt at the Polish Academy of Science's Institute of Political Studies, also formerly a Bayduza Post-doctoral Fellow at the Canadian Institute of Ukrainian Studies and a member of the Political Communication Research Unit at the University of Antwerp. He was previously a research fellow with the Graduate Institute of Russian Studies at National Chengchi University, Taiwan, and a visiting fellow at the Institute of Advanced Studies Kőszeg (Hungary). Oleksii earned his PhD in Political Science from the University of Wrocław (Poland) and the University of Antwerp.

A key watershed between Ukraine and Russia is manifested in their respective relationships to World War II. In short, between the slogans "Never again" vs. "We can repeat it" there is an abyss. These two different and even contradictive approaches demonstrate the gap between orientations toward the past and the future. "Never again" is not just about the past, it is more about the future. Meanwhile, those who profess "We can repeat it" will try to wage war wherever possible.

One of the plausible reasons why Russia has lately become a de facto fascist state and is right now carrying out a genocide against Ukrainians is that the Soviet totalitarian regime and people responsible for enormous crimes during Soviet time were not really punished, and also that those terrible events were not reflected in Russian society. Germany after 1945 went through processes of purification and de-Nazification, but Russia did not have to undergo any real de-Communization or de-Stalinization.

Russia presents itself as a unique civilization, intent on challenging US domination in the world as well as the values that animate Western society. Vladimir Putin's regime tried to create an ideology of a "special path," having mixed Stalinism with conservative orthodoxy, neo-Eurasianism, and the idea of the "Russian World" (Polegkyi 2011, 1–25). But all those concepts are deeply based on trauma and resentment. Behind the search for Russia's true identity we find nothing except Russian collective traumas, myths of the country's origin and uniqueness, and a paranoid penchant for conspiracy theories.

Russia's status as a "great power" stands at the heart of its self-aggrandizing identity and feels entitled to a dominant role among the other major players in the world. President Putin, who proclaimed the collapse of the Soviet Union as "the greatest geopolitical catastrophe of the 20th century," introduced the paradigms of *unizhenie* 'humiliation' and *neuvazhenie* 'lack of respect' into Russian foreign policy thinking. Mikhail Yampolski argues that the entire Russian society, from Putin to the little man, are all bearers of profound resentment. "For Putin, it is the lack of recognition of Russia, and of him personally, as equal and respected players on the global scene; for the little man, it is the powerlessness in the face of the police, the bureaucracy, judges and bandits. The *ressentiment* of power coincided with the *ressentiment* of the common man" (Yampolski 2014).

Resentment in Russian public imaginary became powerful instrument of Russian political elites and was transformed into *ressentiment* in foreign policy. Russian *ressentiment* consists of two main elements. On the one hand, there is the theme of Russia's "humiliation" by the West. Putin's foreign policy thinking fully fits this paradigm of humiliation and lack of respect, as expressed in his Valdai speech on 24 October 2014: "You may remember the wonderful saying: 'Whatever Jupiter is allowed, the Ox is not.' We cannot agree with such an approach. The ox may not be allowed something, but the bear will not even bother to ask permission" (Kremlin 2014).

On the other hand, there is also massive rancour among large segments of the Russian population that have failed to adapt to the new and constantly changing reality (Medvedev 2020).

Transformation of the old cult of victory into a new cult of death

Putin is obsessed with history. Memories of World War II are exploited by the Kremlin in order to legitimize the political regime in Russia and its foreign policy. Putin's regime in Russia has actively exploited the legacy of the collective memory of former citizens of the Soviet Union. The myth of the "Great Patriotic War," as it was officially called in Soviet times, was one of the main cornerstones of Soviet identity and now possesses the same function in its sole, self-declared heir—the Russian Federation.

The aim of the politics of history is to introduce a dominant version of the past into the mass consciousness. The main feature of Soviet use of the politics of history was a monistic view that promotes only one "proper" interpretation of the past. In essence, it is the nationalization of the myth of the "Great Patriotic War"—highlighting imperial values but with very little room for acknowledging Stalinist crimes. Some years ago Russia even introduced a law prohibiting the "rehabilitation of Nazism," de facto muzzling any voice that contradicts the Kremlin's version of the past.

The cult of victory in the "Great Patriotic War" came into being during the era of Brezhnev's rule of the USSR; May 9, Victory Day, was not even a non-labour national holiday until 1965. Victory in the war was used as the main basis for legitimizing the Soviet Communist system, and commemorations of the holiday necessarily included references to the leading role of the Communist Party in the victory over Nazism.

Since the collapse of the USSR, Russia has utilized the concept of the "Great Patriotic War" to bind together the whole of the "post-Soviet space." On the one hand, it helps neighbouring countries to join in the shared ownership of victory in the war, while on the other it solidifies Russia's status as the main "defeater" of fascism:

> Today, we can say that the Great Patriotic War and our victory in it is the central event of not only Soviet but also Russian history. In 1941–45 the Russian people, using the Soviet regime and the Stalinist system as a sword and shield, defended their right not only to historical existence but also to greatness (Fursov 2015, 61–2).

Nowadays, Russian narratives concerning World War II are based on three main myths: power, liberation, and suffering-heroism.

The myth of power

The myth of power is the basis for representing Russia (and its leaders) as a powerful actor and to evoke feelings of "Great Country" glory. The concept of power is extremely important in the Russian public's imagination and helps its rulers to justify their actions. Power itself has a sacred significance in the perception of Russians.

From the very beginning of his rule, President Putin tried to create the image of Russia as a superpower. Putin began to build his version of Russian history, emphasizing the need to modernize the country, using a "strong hand" to lead the country back to the status of a superpower. For Putin and the majority of Russians, war itself has become not a symbol of tragedy but a cause for celebration.

Among the Russians who regret the collapse of the USSR, the main reason for this regret was that "people no longer feel they belong to a great power." In 1999 29% of respondents answered in this way, and by 2012 it was already 51%, according to the Levada Center (Zorkaya 2013, 196). This is why one of the main pillars for Putin's ideology is the *vstavanie s kolen* 'getting up off one's knees'.

The myth of liberation

Since the start of the new millennium, due to increased Russian ambitions to play a greater role in international politics, the symbolic capital of Soviet participation in the Allied victory over the Nazis in 1945 has been actively used by the Russian political elite to strengthen Russia's position in Europe—and to restore control over its "near-abroad." In 2014, the Russian historian Nikolay Koposov considered that the myth of the "soldier-liberator" was needed for Putin to carry out a kind of "rehabilitation" of the cult of the authoritarian state—a reanimation of the myth of the Soviet Union saving the world from fascism.

Recently, the Russian authorities even took steps toward "rehabilitating" the Molotov-Ribbentrop Pact of 1939. As a result of the secret annex to the Molotov-Ribbentrop Pact, Eastern Europe was divided into two spheres of influence. Thus, the Soviet regime under Stalin in 1939 was equally responsible together with Nazi Germany for dividing Europe, as well as providing support to Hitler policy. Soviet and, later, Russian historiography attempted to skip over or justify this fact of Soviet-German cooperation.

Perceptions of Stalin

In Russia, positive perceptions of the Bolshevik dictator Joseph Stalin have only been growing since Putin came to power. For a majority of Russians, when evaluating the role of Stalin in history the most important factor is that under his leadership Russia was victorious in World War II. Nearly 60% of respondents in 2012 (66% in 2008) agreed with the statement that regardless of any mistakes attributed to him, the most important factor was that the Soviet Union emerged victorious in the Great Patriotic War. In 2019, 70% of Russian respondents agreed that Stalin played a positive role for Russia—a record-high response since the question was first asked in 2003, according to the Levada Center (Levada 2019). Russians are united by Stalin, whom 56% consider to be a great leader and for whom respect is ever-growing, from 21% of respondents in 2012 to 45% in 2021. For them, Stalin is a symbol of a powerful state and a not unacceptable model of a society where the individual means nothing and state interests prevail over human life.

The myth of suffering transformed into a cult of heroism and cult of death

Suffering is another aspect of the Russian myth of power and is also a constituent element of the myth of the "Great Patriotic War." The price of victory is the suffering of a powerful country—and this myth also justifies the country's need for sacrifice. The main arguments used by defenders of Stalin are that he won the war and rebuilt a great country, all of which was impossible without sacrifice. During the last few years, there has been a significant increase in the number of people who believe that the Stalinist repressions may have been politically necessary and historically justified; correspondingly, the number has declined of those who thought that these repressions were a political crime and could not be justified.

It is hard to imagine another country that would be proud of the numbers of victims, as it appears in Russia. Essentially, the Kremlin realized that *the more blood and death, the more patriotism could be evoked*. The "Immortal Regiment" campaign, which began as a popular initiative to memorialize relatives who died in WW II, was intercepted by the state and soon acquired the character of some kind of wild pagan ritual. Portraits of dead people are carried around the streets every 9th of May. Sometimes these are portraits of strangers that schoolchildren and teenagers are ordered to carry.

The problem is that the "cult of death" formed by Putin's regime has become so deeply embedded in the psychology of millions of Russians that even many educated people in Russia do not understand how monstrous it is to arrange processions with images of the dead on sticks, turning one of the greatest tragedies in the history of mankind into a parade under the slogan "We can repeat it." While the whole world sorrows with the words "Never again" Putin's Russia, gripped by its cult of death, is celebrating with cries of "We can repeat it!"

Conclusions

The false and manipulative mythology, narratives, and symbols of the "Great Patriotic War" deliberately employed as Russian propaganda have served as a framework through which to justify the aggression against Ukraine. Moreover, they portray this "war with the West" at a mythological level because it contains powerful symbols that are still deeply rooted in Russian minds, whose deconstruction did not take place after the collapse of the Soviet Union.

The return of these myths and Soviet historical narratives has not been accidental. In our analysis, what is happening in Russia is primarily the manifestation of a cataclysmic national identity crisis, which has been exacerbated by Ukraine's inexorable movement toward open society and Europe. During the Soviet period, for the majority of Russians the dominant identity, assiduously cultivated by the Communist Party, was that of a "Soviet people." In the Soviet Union, the main foundational mythologizing event was the "Great October Revolution." Once Ukraine as a former imperial subject was out of the picture, victory in the "Great Patriotic War" has today become the same kind of foundational myth for contemporary Russia. Searching in the past for a mythological basis to unify the nation, especially in light of the trauma and disappointment associated with the collapse of the Soviet Union, was quite logical. Idealization of the Soviet past, identifying with the figures of Stalin and Brezhnev, became the answer to mass frustration of the Russian population, and victory in the "Great Patriotic War" became for the majority of Russians a singular and almost the only historical event that they could be proud of.

Works cited

Fursov, A.I. 2015. "Sovetskaia Pobeda, vsemirnaia istoriia i budushchee mira." *Strategicheskie prioritety* 6 (2): 49–69.

Koposov, Nikolay. 2014. "Pamiat' v zakone." Historians, 17 April 2014. https://www.historians.in.ua/index.php/en/istoriya-i-pamyat-vazhki-pitannya/1127-nykolai-koposov-pamiat-v-zakone.

Kremlin. 2014. "Meeting of the Valdai International Discussion Club." Kremlin.ru, 24 October 2014. http://eng.kremlin.ru/news/23137.

Levada. 2019. "Stalin's perception." Levada-Center, 19 April 2019. https://www.levada.ru/en/2019/04/19/dynamic-of-stalin-s-perception.

Medvedev, Sergei. 2020. *Return of the Russian Leviathan*. Cambridge: Polity Press.

Polegkyi, Oleksii. 2011. "Changes in Russian foreign policy discourse and concept of 'Russian World.'" PECOB's papers series no. 16 (2011).

Yampolski, Mikhail. 2014. "V strane pobedivshego ressentimenta." COLTA.RU, 6 October 2014. http://www.colta.ru/articles/specials/4887.

Zorkaya, N., ed. 2013. *Russian Public Opinion, 2012–2013*. Moscow: Levada-Center.

CHAPTER 8

Putin's dehumanizing discourses and the power of Ukrainian resistance and resilience

Cynthia Nielsen
Essay published 27 June 2022

> Cynthia R. Nielsen is a professor at the University of Dallas, where she teaches courses in the areas of hermeneutics, ethics, aesthetics, contemporary continental philosophy, and the history of philosophy. Her interest in hermeneutics applies to a broad range of topics, including aesthetics, animal studies, social and political (mis)uses of language (including disinformation and propaganda), war and trauma, and Ukrainian studies. Her most recent monograph is *Gadamer's Hermeneutical Aesthetics: On Art as a Performative, Dynamic, Communal Event* (2022), and she is currently working on a book entitled *Philosophical Reflections on War, Violence, and Responsibility: Listening to Ukrainian Voices*.

The violent war that Vladimir Putin has unleashed in Ukraine has now passed the four-month marker. Every day we hear new accounts of monstrous torture, rape, and killing of Ukrainian civilians, which includes children and the elderly. Putin's unjustified war of aggression is fuelled by a particular (pseudo)historical narrative, whose components, nonetheless, exhibit familiar colonial and imperialist tactics—tactics whose purposes are to dehumanize a purported enemy-other (i.e., the Ukrainians) and to destroy their culture, history, and identity. As a result of the indiscriminate bombing of civilian areas and objects, hundreds of breathtakingly beautiful cultural sites—churches, art museums, cultural monuments, architectural masterpieces, and many other cultural artefacts—have been and continue to be heavily damaged, and many have been destroyed.

Learning from Stalin: Putin's absolutization of falsehoods

In a recent article detailing the treasures of Ukraine's cultural heritage and the daily threat of their destruction, Olenka Z. Pevny describes the cultural significance of two world heritage sites in Kyiv—namely, the Monastery of the Caves and the Cathedral of St. Sophia, both of which date to the 11th century (Pevny 2022).

The Museum of Historical Treasures of Ukraine, located within the Caves Monastery compound, houses the Scythian gold pectoral, a priceless ancient work of art dating to the 4th century BC. As Pevny observes, "The shelling of this museum would efface the archaeological and visual record of numerous cultures unique to Ukraine. Works of Scythian art were already taken from Ukraine during the Soviet period and fill Russian museums."

Like so many aspects of the present war in Ukraine, Putin's brutality shares family resemblances with his predecessor Joseph Stalin, who under Putin's regime has been reconstructed as a great hero of the Fatherland. Of course, there are differences between the two leaders; Putin is not a mere repeat of Stalin.[1] However, their tyrannical repressive rule at home as well as their inhuman violence toward Ukrainians and refusal to acknowledge and respect Ukraine's autonomy and alterity show striking similarities. In a recent article comparing the two leaders, Simon Sebag Montefiore writes: "Putin's repression at home increasingly resembles Stalinist tyranny—in its cult of fear, rallying of patriotic displays, crushing of protests, brazen lies and total control of media" (Montefiore 2022). When it comes to their views of and actions toward Ukraine, Montefiore highlights the following common features: "Then there is Ukraine, a country that was brutally repressed by Stalin and is now attacked by Putin. The Russian president shares a part of Stalin's determination to liquidate the nationality and independence of Ukraine at any cost."

Putin's writings and propagandistic discourse about Ukraine and Ukrainians are replete with contradictions and historical inaccuracies. Such contradictions and calculated falsehoods are part and parcel of the disinformation component of Putin's hybrid warfare, which aims both to confuse and disorient his audience as well

---

1. Montefiore discusses many of the differences between Putin and Stalin in his article. Among these important differences are: "Stalin was a fanatical internationalist Marxist; Putin believes in the exceptionalist 'Russian world' starting with the Orthodox conversion of Vladimir [Volodymyr] the Great in 988. He despises Marxist ideology, believing that the Leninist revolution shattered the Russian imperium. Eschewing Communism, he promotes Kremlin-KGB-capitalism. Stalin, who had no interest in money and only possessed a couple of uniforms (though he enjoyed the use of comfortable mansions), would be disgusted by the vulgarity of the yachts and planes of Russia's ultra-rich" (Montefiore 2022).

as to control information and construct a rigid, authoritative discourse that cannot be publicly challenged or contested from within the Russian state. Putin's discourse depicts Ukrainians as "Nazis" and "fascists"—a dangerous enemy-other that must be destroyed. (The fact that Ukraine's President Volodymyr Zelensky is Jewish underscores the absurdity of Putin's Nazi discourse.[2]) In a recent article by the pro-Kremlin political pundit—or, better, "political technologist"—Timofey Sergeytsev titled "*Chto Rossiia dolzhna sdelat' s Ukrainoi?*" (What should Russia do with Ukraine; Sergeytsev 2022), a narrative is created that ultimately equates *all* Ukrainians with Nazis and the process of "denazification" with an "inevitable" process of "de-Ukrainization" [Денацификация неизбежно будет являться и деукраинизацией]. That is, Sergeytsev not only asserts that the Armed Forces of Ukraine, Security Service of Ukraine, and organized territorial defense forces are war criminals and Nazis, all of which must be "punished in such a way that an example is made" [примерно и показательно наказаны] through a process of "total lustration" [тотальная люстрация] or purging. According to Sergeytsev, not only are the military and top Ukrainian leaders deemed Nazis but likewise he asserts that "a significant portion of the masses are also guilty of being passive Nazis and collaborators of Nazism" [виновна и значительная часть народной массы, которая является пассивными нацистами, пособниками нацизма]. The masses—that is, those who survive—must be denazified, which, among other things, will require "re-education" [перевоспитания] and "severe censorship" [жесткая цензура]. (We have already seen these tactics enacted in Mariupol.) Sergeytsev's essay was published on RIA-Novosti, a Russian state news agency with significant audience impact.

Russian neo-colonial discourse regarding Ukraine

Whereas many European colonial discourses construct the "other" as exotic, Putin's (pseudo) historical-narrative, which nonetheless exhibits its own colonial inflections, completely denies any

---

2. See also Timothy Snyder's discussion of Russia's new version of fascism as schizofascism—that is, "actual fascists calling their opponents 'fascists'" (Snyder 2018, 145). Snyder also highlights how antisemitic and racist rhetoric is often employed in contemporary Russia's "schizofascist" discourses (see especially Montefiore 2022, 145–58).

Ukrainian otherness or alterity.[3] For example, he proclaims that Russians and Ukrainians are "one people—a single whole" who share "essentially the same historical and spiritual space." That is, according to Putin's narrative Ukrainians are not Ukrainians but Russians who have failed to recognize their "true" (fixed, essentialist) identity, having been seduced by Western forces, and whose political paradigms and alleged decadent values have enticed them to abandon their destiny as descendants of "Ancient Rus" (Putin 2021). Seen in this distorted light, Ukrainian identity and self-understanding are false constructions that must be dismantled so that Ukraine's supposed true essence can be liberated and its fragmentary, fallen existence can be made whole again through its reunification with Holy Rus. To achieve this goal, the most horrific violence imaginable is not only acceptable but celebrated and bestowed with the highest military honours (Ritchie, Angelova, and Picheta 2022). Such brutality and violence, according to Putin's logic, is apparently necessary in order to reunify the fragmented "mystical body" of Holy Rus. Although in his essay and in other recent writings and public statements Putin claims to be concerned about the safety and well-being of Russian-speakers in the Donbas, his actions cut through the propagandistic double-speak. In the context of his discussion of the ongoing fighting in the Donbas region prior to the current full-scale war, he claims that "Russia has done everything to stop fratricide" (Putin 2021). And yet the reality is that today some of the heaviest, most brutal Russian bombing and missile strikes have taken place in Mariupol and now the Donbas region—precisely where so many Russian-speaking Ukrainians live. Consequently, thousands of Ukrainians in these regions have died, many of whom are unquestionably Russian speakers. Similarly to the falseness of

---

3. For a detailed discussion of the complexities and peculiarities of Russia's colonizing practices, see Von Hagen (2014). Regarding Soviet colonizing violence, see Snyder (2015). Unlike maritime empires such as Great Britain, France, and the United States, which travelled to distant lands to conquer territory and subjugate and murder indigenous people, the Soviet Union and today's Russia colonize and terrorize their neighbours, denying their sovereignty, territorial integrity, and right to self-determination. As Snyder explains, Stalin used the term "internal colonization," which describes the Soviet regime's treatment of Soviet territories—with Ukraine a central target of its cruelty—as analogous to the way in which "maritime empires treated their distant possessions" (Snyder 2018, 697). See also Etkind (2011) for a detailed study of Russian history and its inflection of colonizing violence.

Putin's claims that he would not invade Ukraine, his empty talk of preventing fratricide rings not only hollow but cynical, cruel, and perverse.

Repeatedly throughout his essay, Putin emphasizes the shared language and Orthodox faith of Russians and Ukrainians as indelible signs signifying Ukrainians' "true" identity as Russians (Putin 2021). However, Putin's narrative floats above the actual diverse, concrete reality of Ukrainian life and society's embrace of a plurality of languages and religions. Many Ukrainians speak both Ukrainian and Russian, and code-switching is a common phenomenon in everyday Ukrainian life. Moreover, many Ukrainians whose first language is Russian strongly identify as Ukrainians and see Ukraine's bilingualism in a positive rather than a negative light. (Of course, there are tensions and controversies within Ukraine about how each language should be viewed, and this will likely intensify after the war.) The point, however, contra Putin, is that language, although an important part of culture, does not rigidly determine or fix one's cultural, social, or national identity. The same applies to religious faith. There are Ukrainian Jews, Ukrainian Orthodox Christians, and Ukrainian Muslims, and within these categories one encounters diverse expressions of Christianity, Judaism, and Islam.[4] Multiple expressions of religious faith not only coexist in Ukraine but even work together — and Putin's war has only strengthened this collaborative work. Within Orthodoxy itself, and especially in light of the Russian patriarch Kirill's blessing of Putin's war, there are divisions and differences of opinion regarding faith, doctrine, and what the proper relationship should be between Church and state. Ukrainian Orthodox priests as well as Christian priests and leaders worldwide have strongly condemned Kirill's teaching and actions, calling him an ideologue who preaches the doctrine of the "Russian World" rather than the "Gospel of Christ." Here again, Putin's imaginings of Ukraine and Ukrainian identity widely miss the mark. Whereas Putin's discourses and tactics seek to eradicate difference and plurality by violently imposing its conjured unity on Ukraine through indiscriminate bombardment of civilian areas and cultural sites, Ukraine's actions and self-understanding promotes unity in difference. That is, a recognition and embrace of plurality, diversity, freedom, and democratic

---

4. For example, within the Christian realm one finds Ukrainian Roman Catholics, Ukrainian Protestants, and Ukrainian Greek Catholics.

principles, forged through solidaristic actions and lived experience, constitutes Ukraine's values and way of life—values that Ukrainians have chosen and which they share with the West. As the Ukrainian philosopher Volodymyr Yermolenko stated in his recent essay in the *Economist*, "Freedom is the key trait of Ukraine's identity as a political nation. Ukrainian political culture is based upon anti-tyrannical, democratic, and republican values" (2022). In stark contrast, Putin and his cronies detest democratic principles, values, and institutions. Early in the present war, the Kremlin cracked down on any independent news coverage of the war, threatening journalists with up to 15 years of imprisonment for reporting that deviates from the official state narrative. Consequently, any vestige of journalistic freedom, independent reporting, and genuine media diversity no longer exists in Russia.

Ukrainian resilience and its price

As this hellish war rages on, Ukrainians continue to inspire us with their courage, resilience, compassion, and creativity. For example, the Ukrainian cellist Denys Karachevtsev finds the strength to perform a Bach cello suite amidst the decimated buildings in Kharkiv, showing that beauty cannot be destroyed by Putin's bombs (Hall 2022). Others plant flowers in the colours of the Ukrainian flag to beautify areas recently hit by Russian missile attacks. The band Kalush showcases its talent with a stellar performance of "Stefania" and wins the 2022 Eurovision song contest, helping to raise awareness of the war and the need to continue to support Ukraine. Communities work together to rebuild their lives and homes and reopen their businesses, despite the tremendous challenges, not to mention existential dangers, posed by the ongoing active war. Through their individual and solidaristic actions Ukrainians demonstrate to the world who they are and what they believe. Their willingness to give their lives for their own self-determination and freedom has not only been a source of inspiration but has also reanimated key democratic institutions (including NATO). Their individual and collective actions to forge their own multivalent Ukrainian identity and to secure their future as a sovereign democratic country serve as reminders that our own democracies and the democratic principles which we cherish are not givens but rather require constant nurture, building, and rebuilding.

It is worth remembering that Ukraine's 2013-14 Maidan Revolution is also called the "Revolution of Dignity." During some of the coldest months of winter, thousands of Ukrainians both young and old took to the streets, risking their lives for their belief in fundamental human rights, the freedom to determine their own political future, and human dignity. To quote Yermolenko again, "Ukraine's recent history is a story about the values of dignity moving east. [...]"[5] Today's Ukraine is a country in which the values of dignity for all are taking root. This provokes horror in today's Russia, which wants to re-establish authoritarian values, and where the only person with dignity is the tsar or dictator." As Ukraine enters its most difficult phase of the war thus far, our support for Ukraine cannot waver; the thousands of Ukrainian lives that have been lost cannot be lost in vain. Nor can we allow brutal autocratic leaders like Putin to inspire others of his kind to enact their own wars of aggression. A defeat in Ukraine would be a defeat to democracies worldwide.

Works Cited

Etkind, Alexander. 2011. *Internal Colonization: Russia's Imperial Experience.* Cambridge: Polity.

Hall, Sophia Alexandra. 2022. "Ukrainian cellist plays solitary Bach suite in abandoned bombed-out streets of Kharkiv." Classic FM, 24 March 2022. https://www.classicfm.com/music-news/videos/ukrainian-cellist-bach-suite-kharkiv.

Montefiore, Simon Sebag. 2022. "Why Putin is beholden to Stalin's legacy: The Russian president has embraced the Soviet cult of fear and control; his invasion of Ukraine is a colossal gamble to secure his place in history." The New Statesman, 9 March 2022. https://www.newstatesman.com/culture/2022/03/a-tale-of-two-dictators-why-putin-is-beholden-to-stalins-legacy.

Pevny, Olenka Z. 2022. "Ukraine's cultural heritage faces destruction as Russia's bombing continues." The Conversation, 9 March 2022. https://theconversation.com/ukraines-cultural-heritage-faces-destruction-as-russian-bombing-continues-178563.

Putin, Vladimir. 2021. "On the historical unity of Russian and Ukrainians." Presidential Executive Office, 12 July 2021. http://en.kremlin.ru/events/president/news/66181.

---

5. Yermolenko, "national identity."

———. 2022. "Transcript: Vladimir Putin's televised address on Ukraine." Bloomberg, 24 February 2022. https://www.bloomberg.com/news/articles/2022-02-24/full-transcript-vladimir-putin-s-televised-address-to-russia-on-ukraine-feb-24.

Ritchie, Hannah, Masha Angelova, and Rob Picheta. 2022. "Putin gives honorary title to Russian brigade accused of war crimes in Bucha." CNN, 19 April 2022. https://www.cnn.com/2022/04/19/europe/russia-bucha-brigade-honorary-title-putin-intl/index.html.

Sergeytsev, Timofey. 2022. "Chto Rossiia dolzhna sdelat' s Ukrainoi." RIA-Novosti, 3 April 2022 (updated 5 April 2022). https://ria.ru/20220403/ukraina-1781469605.html.

Snyder, Timothy. 2018. *The Road to Unfreedom: Russia, Europe, America.* New York: Tim Dugan Books.

———. 2015. "Integration and disintegration: Europe, Ukraine, and the world." *Slavic Review* 74 (4): 695–707.

Von Hagen, Mark. 2014. "From imperial Russia to colonial Ukraine." In *The Shadow of Colonialism on Europe's Modern Past*, edited by Róisín Healy and Enrico Dal Lago, 173–93. New York: Springer.

Yermolenko, Volodymyr. 2022. "Volodymyr Yermolenko, a Ukrainian philosopher, considers his national identity." *The Economist.* 5 March 2022 (updated 11 March 2022). https://www.economist.com/by-invitation/2022/03/05/volodymyr-yermolenko-a-ukrainian-philosopher-considers-his-national-identity.

CHAPTER 9

Explaining the "Westsplainers": Can a Western scholar be an authority on Central and Eastern Europe?

Aliaksei Kazharski

Essay published 19 July 2022

> Aliaksei Kazharski received his PhD from Comenius University in Bratislava (Slovakia) in 2015. He has also been a visiting researcher at the University of Vienna (2016) and the Polish Academy of Sciences (2021) and has worked as a researcher and lecturer at Charles University in Prague (Czechia) and Comenius University. Kazharski's doctoral dissertation was published as a monograph, *Eurasian Integration and the Russian World: Regionalism as an Identitiary Enterprise*, in 2019. His second book, *Central Europe Thirty Years after the Fall of Communism: A Return to the Margin?* (2022) won the International Studies Association's Global International Relations 2022-23 Book Award.

Following the 2022 escalated invasion of Ukraine, the terms "Westsplaining" and "Westsplainer" seem to be gaining momentum. They are used in reaction to commentary that is delivered by established Western intellectuals—be they American realists, German idealists, or sometimes even critical scholars from Ireland. Many people from what is typically known as Central and Eastern Europe, as well as some of their Western colleagues, tend to find such commentary not only useless but, in fact, harmful. Far from being purely theoretical academic contemplation, it uses influential Western media forums to provide policy advice that is often based on false assumptions and projections.

At the same time, some Westerners may feel wronged here, as the term "Westsplaining" could sound too much like an attempt to deny them the right to participate in expert debate based solely on their personal background. Without pretending to have a monopoly on the definition, I will try to explain why, in my opinion, the term makes sense and how it can be used critically without being reduced to a vulgar *ad hominem*.

From "mansplaining" to "Westsplaining": Birth of the portmanteau

The term "Westsplaining" is obviously modelled on "mansplaining." Coined some years ago, "mansplaining" was defined as the intersection between (male) "overconfidence and cluelessness" with respect to women (Solnit 2022). It was meant to refer to situations when a man tries, in an authoritative manner, to explain to a woman something that she knows better than him anyway (Rothman 2012).

As such, the term should also be seen as part of a much broader trend of critical thought that urges us to reflect on the backgrounds of speakers — including, above all, ourselves — and think of how they may influence ways in which individuals see the world. Thus, much of contemporary social science seems quite preoccupied with various "positionalities" of researchers. The impact of critical theory on social scientific research has been mixed, as postmodernist relativization of epistemologies has also contributed to mounting ideological pressures in academia. This did not always improve the quality of the scientific debate or of scholarly output (to put it mildly).

Outside the ivory tower, terms like "mansplaining" and "Westsplaining" could also easily be weaponized, as they provided an easy way of attacking the person's background instead of their arguments. Sadly, for too many people the temptation to go *ad hominem* is simply too strong to resist.

Having said this, we should probably also remember that the Delphic maxim "know thyself" is much older than any postmodernist critical theory. Therefore, reflecting on oneself — which should be accompanied by acknowledging your own limits — is likely to be a useful exercise.

Is "Westsplaining" about backgrounds? Spoiler: no, it is not

The original portmanteau ("mansplaining") could ultimately be justified by the fact that apart from sometimes very different social roles, gender differences are also rooted in experiences that are, so to speak, existential and non-transferable (e.g., childbirth pain). Fortunately, cultural differences are not in any way biological. Despite what Samuel Huntington and his followers may preach, these differences can certainly be overcome — although it does not take place automatically and often requires investing significant amounts of time and intellectual effort.

So, the question of whether a Westerner can become an authority on Central and Eastern Europe — or any other region — is obviously rhetorical. Personally, my favourite example has always been the Norwegian international relations scholar Iver B. Neumann. His analysis of the nexus between Russian identity and foreign policy, to my taste at least, provides a keener understanding of the subject than that which is available to many Russians (Neumann 2017). Taking a quick look around, I also see people like Andreas Umland and Timothy Snyder, whose admonitions about fascism in Russia we may have taken too lightly; as well as the amazing, multi-lingual Marci Shore, the brilliant erudite Marlène Laruelle, and this is just to quickly throw in a few very "big" names off the top of my head.

Along with many other Western scholars, these people demonstrate to us on a regular basis that differences in cultural background can actually be an asset. They can help us overcome what is known as home blindness, i.e., failing to see certain things because we are used to them.

So, what is Westsplaining about if not backgrounds?

It is very simple. "Westsplaining" is speaking without sufficient expertise but from a position of authority, often making false projections and assumptions that are based on the Western experience but are not necessarily relevant to the region in question. The point is not where you are from. Rather, it is whether you possess the necessary expertise and whether, before you decided to comment, you spent enough time following the region, learning the languages, and gaining some intimate understanding of the countries involved.

Thus, for example, the problem with prominent American international relations realists who are keen to comment on Russia and Ukraine is that they have a very vague notion as to what actually drives Russian foreign policy. To some extent this is rooted in the original sin of their "structural" theory, which famously takes pride in ignoring ("black-boxing") domestic politics.

This "structural" approach is rather convenient, because it allows one to comment on various regions and countries without specific expertise. It also seems congruent with a (naïve) image of the liberal, globalized world, where different cultural and political contexts are supposed to be progressively converging. This image creates a false sense of universal transparency and relegates country and region-specific expertise and "area studies" as something secondary or residual.

However, following a closer examination, pseudo-universal explanations delivered by some established Western scholars turn out to be merely a form of intellectual parochialism, which takes it for granted that its own Western assumptions are universally applicable. Thus, the aforementioned American international relations realists apparently feel sufficiently emboldened by the wisdom of their universalist theory to provide policy advice on Ukraine. In the process, they make some very naïve assumptions, ascribing to Russia the realist virtues of prudence and cold strategic calculus, i.e., that model of rationality which is often found in their own theories but unfortunately not in the Kremlin. Here, the post-February 24th developments clearly speak for themselves—as even Kremlin-associated policy experts have pointed out.

Russo-centrism is also a part of Westsplaining

Furthermore, Western discourse on Central and Eastern Europe more often than not suffers from distortions caused by its deep Russo-centrism. Too frequently this becomes a discussion about what these countries mean to Russia and how Moscow's "legitimate" interests could be accommodated without "humiliating" Russia. This is a structural problem of "knowledge production." Apparently, some Western media outlets have seen no problem when their correspondents report on countries like Belarus from Moscow but not from Minsk. Some Western academics also seem to believe it is enough to know Russian to write about the post-Soviet countries.

This Russo-centrism also borders on what international relations scholars call "great power management," i.e., the assumption that powerful players can and should talk to Moscow over the heads of Central and Eastern European countries and strike great power deals in the manner of the 19th–early 20th century. Thus, in the new round of debates following the outbreak of the Russo-Ukrainian War, the agency of the people of Ukraine (and of other Central and Eastern European nations) has once too often been overshadowed by "geopolitical" considerations and seemingly smart "realpolitik" approaches. This is where "Westsplaining" probably comes closest to the original "mansplaining," because its "authoritative" tone also implies a system of hierarchical, unequal relations. This time, not between genders but between nations.

Is "Westsplaining" endemic to the West?

Not at all. Wanting to comment without proper knowledge and understanding seems to be very much "part of the human condition." It is also a phenomenon to be found among "Eastern European" countries themselves. Thus, I was personally "fortunate" to witness this in 2020 when, in the runup to the presidential "election" in Belarus, the independent Russian *commentariat* suddenly developed a keen but superficial interest in Belarus. The majority of these people had not followed Belarus systematically before 2020, which ultimately resulted in producing much naïve "Russosplaining" of Belarus and its regime. Linguistic proximity must have played a trick on many Russian commentators, contributing to the sense of false transparency. Later on, Russian spin doctors, who were apparently deployed by the Kremlin to save Lukashenka's regime following the outbreak of the protests in August 2020, famously fell into a very similar trap.

Incidentally, "Russosplaining" not only stems from the legacy of Russian language domination in the so-called "post-Soviet space" but also from an implicit sense of political, social, and cultural entitlement shared by many Russians. The ambiguous, fuzzy notion of the "near abroad" has long informed their mental maps. The "near abroad" operates as a liminal space that is imagined as being not exactly inside but also not quite outside Russia. Consequently, it was taken for granted that, in this post-imperial space, Russians simply would not run into something they would genuinely not know or understand (Kazharski and Kubová 2021).

The "Russosplaining" trap and the *Postsovieticum*

This grand illusion has entailed a general disregard for knowledge of the local "reality on the ground." Just think of how little the decision-makers in Moscow have cared to know about what was actually happening in Ukraine in terms of its politics, culture, and nation-building. The initial goals of Putin's "special operation" were meant to prompt a quick regime change in Kyiv, happening against the background of the Ukrainian state collapsing like a house of cards. Moscow's spectacular failure in Ukraine — where, contrary to its expectations, Russian forces encountered fierce resistance put up by a consolidated Ukrainian nation — should ultimately be attributed to this disregard for knowledge. The arrogant, patronizing imperialist attitude, which treats smaller neighbours as inferior, subordinate, and unimportant, is an integral part of "Russosplaining."

Unfortunately, at this point, I must add that Ukrainians have also not been immune to the universal illness. Since the start of the popular uprising in Belarus 2020, many Ukrainian commentators adopted a patronizing and sometimes denigrating attitude toward Belarusan protesters. This attitude showed a complete disregard for the obvious differences between the Ukrainian experience, which essentially amounted to organizing popular revolts in an oligarchic democracy, and the Belarusan experience of 2020, which was about facing a consolidated authoritarian regime directly backed by the Kremlin in its critical moments.

This "Ukrosplaining" of Belarus stemmed from a widespread lack of knowledge about the northern neighbour and naïve assumptions that the domestic situation in Belarus generally resembled the one in Ukraine. It also gained new momentum after the regime provided Belarusan territory for the Russian attack on Ukraine in 2022. As the Ukrainian public intellectual Pavlo Zubiuk aptly pointed out, Ukrainian commentary on Belarus also stems from a basic lack of understanding combined with a "chauvinist" attitude (Zubiuk 2022).

The habit is universal, but "Westsplainers" do more damage

At the end of the day, the sin of "-splaining" seems to be quite universal. Returning to my original point, I think the notion of "Westsplaining" certainly has its merits. But it does only insofar as it does not target the immediate background of the interlocutor but rather the limits of their expertise and insight and their proneness to serve as self-appointed authorities on subjects which they did not spend enough time with.

Unfortunately, all of us are sometimes prone to comment on things we think we understand all too well. However, the problem with Western commentary on the Russo-Ukrainian war in particular is that, compared to voices from Central and Eastern Europe, it enjoys a much higher degree of international influence. In spreading their messages, "Westsplainers" tend to benefit from access to the best-known European and American media outlets that have a global outreach. This is where we should probably return to the original parallels between "mansplaining" and the structural inequalities embedded in the present international system.

Works cited

Kazharski, Aliaksei, and Monika Kubová. 2021. "Belarus as a liminal space for Russia's ontological security before and after the 2020 protests." *New Perspectives: Interdisciplinary Journal of Central & East European Politics and International Relations* 29 (3): 249–71. https://doi.org/10.1177/2336825X211032900.

Neumann, Iver B. 2017. *Russia and the Idea of Europe: A Study in Identity and International Relations*, 2nd ed. Milton Park: Routledge.

Rothman, Lily. 2012. "A cultural history of mansplaining." *The Atlantic*, 1 November 2012. https://www.theatlantic.com/sexes/archive/2012/11/a-cultural-history-of-mansplaining/264380.

Solnit, Rebecca. 2022. "Men still explain things to me." *The Nation*, 20 August 2022. https://www.thenation.com/article/archive/men-still-explain-things-me.

Zubiuk, Pavlo. 2022. "Persha ukraïns'ko-bilorus'ka viina." Zaxid.net, 2 July 2022. https://zaxid.net/persha_ukrayinsko_biloruska_viyna_n1545743.

CHAPTER 10

The fall of Lysychansk and the fate of the Donbas

Hiroaki Kuromiya
Essay 28 July 2022

> Hiroaki Kuromiya taught Ukrainian, Russian, and Soviet history at Indiana University, USA, until his retirement in 2021. He is the author of Freedom and Terror in the Donbas: A Ukrainian-Russian Borderland, 1870s–1990s (1998), Stalin: Profiles in Power (2005), Conscience on Trial: The Fate of Fourteen Pacifists in Stalin's Ukraine, 1952–1953 (2012), Zrozumity Donbas (Understanding the Donbas; 2015), and other books.

Lysychansk, a city in Luhansk oblast, fell on 2 July, a week after the Russian capture of Siverskodonetsk, its sister city across the Siverskyi Dinets River. It effectively signified the Russian occupation of all of Luhansk oblast. It was not a "liberation," as Vladimir Putin is fond of saying, but an occupation, ruin, and enslavement. The extent of the destruction of the cities, towns, and villages in the wake of the Russian advance is beyond our imagination. What does all this mean for the fate of Ukraine in general and of the Donbas in particular?

The reality of war

As expected, Russia conquered Siverskodonetsk and Lysychansk using a tried-and-true method — that is, by levelling everything to the ground, as it had done in Chechnya and Syria earlier. Destruction of non-military civilian objects and people is of no concern to Russian politicians and military commanders. When Ukraine's armed defences fail, Russia moves in to de-Ukrainianize areas by killing and deporting Ukrainian citizens. As Russia advances farther into Ukraine, particularly in Donetsk Oblast, it will certainly employ the same method in trying to capture additional Ukrainian territory. This strategy reflects Moscow's complete indifference to human life and suffering, including of its own soldiers.

Russian President Vladimir Putin has positioned himself as the successor to Iosif Stalin, the Soviet dictator. During World War II, on average more than 5,000 Soviet soldiers were killed every day, totalling some 7.5 million deaths in the war against Germany. The vanquished Third Reich, which fought on two fronts and on land and sea (whereas the Soviet Union fought on just one front and almost exclusively on land), lost far fewer soldiers—four to five million dead. The Soviet fatality numbers likely also include more than 150,000 of its own soldiers who were executed by the Red Army for cowardice, insubordination, desertion, and other offenses, whereas the Germans executed approximately 15,000 of their own soldiers, only some ten percent of the Soviet figures. The Russian war hero Marshall Georgii Zhukov was responsible for many of the Soviet executions. During WW II Zhukov got along very well with Stalin, who famously trusted no one. They held a shared belief in political and military priorities over all else (including human lives). To best the Allied forces in the capture of Berlin in 1945, Stalin and Zhukov marched on without regard for the losses of Soviet soldiers, needlessly multiplying their casualties. Zhukov had already displayed an affinity with Stalin in 1939, in the battle of Khalkhin Gol against Japan. Although the Soviets won a resounding victory, their casualties were almost certainly higher than those of Japan. Zhukov's own subordinates later expressed doubts about his command: "Zhukov did not care about any losses [of human lives] we suffered."[1]

Similarly, in the present Russo-Ukrainian War one should not expect Putin to cringe from further assaults on Ukraine's lands regardless of the cost to Russia in human and material resources. Unless he or his commanders are overthrown by the Russians themselves (or defeated on the battlefield by Ukrainian forces), it seems certain that Putin will continue to fight with fury and dirty tactics until he achieves his goal of usurping the Kyiv government and Russifying Ukraine. This is a truly gloomy prognosis, but it behooves us to prepare for a war of total destruction. One of Putin's aims is to demonstrate to the world that Russia is invincible. This was made clear when on 7 July Putin claimed that the West was supporting Ukraine for the sole purpose of defeating Russia on the battlefield. Dismissing the huge loss of Russian lives (estimates range from 20,000 to within a whisker of 40,000) in the war so far, Putin has declared that Russia has barely begun to fight "in the larger scheme of things" (Kremlin 2022). Unless Putin is bluffing, it

---

1. On Zhukov and Stalin, see my review of Zhukov's memoir in H-Diplo (Kuromiya 2014).

appears that Russia's aggression can only be stopped by superior military force. This is the reality of the war in Ukraine.

Moscow and the Donbas

Moscow now claims that Russia's aim in its "special military operation" against Ukraine is to "liberate" the Donbas. Initially, as in 2014, Moscow exhibited no special interest in prioritizing the capture of the Donbas. In 2014 Moscow had no illusions regarding the political loyalties of the people of the Donbas. In Moscow's scheme for resurrecting "New Russia" — which ultimately failed — the Donbas did not occupy center stage. Moscow's capture of parts of the Donbas in 2014, which led to creation of the Luhansk and Donetsk "people's republics," was more accidental than carefully planned, due in large part to Moscow's failure to capture the eastern-southern Ukrainian lands extending from Kharkiv to Odesa. It is indisputably not the case that the Russophones in the Donbas were being terrorized, as Moscow claimed at the time as an excuse for invading. Nor was there any strong popular desire in the Donbas for Russia's to meddle in its political life — in 2014 or 2022 — notwithstanding Moscow's contrary claims. In February of this year Putin falsely *or* duplicitously *or* mendaciously claimed that it was necessary for him to end the "genocide of millions of people living there [in the Donbas] who trust only us [Russia]" (Kremlin 2022). Nothing could be farther from the truth.

The Donbas has historically been a baffling region, characterized by distrust of all outside political forces, particularly Moscow. In a poll taken in April 2014 after Russia's covert military takeover of Crimea and just as armed conflict was beginning in the Donbas, 67 percent of the four eastern Ukrainian oblasts (including Donetsk and Luhansk) answered "No" to the question "Do you support the decision of the Russian Federation to send its army into Ukraine under the pretext of protecting Russian-speaking citizens?" Only 19 percent answered "Yes." Another poll taken in the same month showed that the majority of people in the Donbas regarded themselves as citizens of Ukraine: 79.7 percent and 72.7 percent in Donetsk and Luhansk oblasts, respectively, supported the idea that "Ukraine and Russia must be independent but friendly states, with open borders, without visas, and customs houses" (KIIS 2014). Although difficult to quantify, there was certainly no evidence in 2014 that anti-Ukrainian, pro-Russian forces in the Donbas were strong enough to take over the Donbas politically or militarily, even had they been so inclined. The Donbas people themselves were surprised by the unexpected turn of events in 2014, which resulted in the formation of two "people's republics." True, there had been discontent with and distrust of successive governments in Kyiv, in the Donbas, as well as much of Ukraine, yet this did not mean that the Donbas population wanted a takeover by Moscow. What happened in the Donbas was not a "civil war" but an elaborately camouflaged military and political intervention by Russia. By all accounts, what happened was seen as Russia's meddling in the Donbas. The idea of the Donbas as a bastion of pro-Russian forces is simply a myth. One needs to understand this myth in order to see clearly the future confronting the Donbas and Ukraine.

Were Kyiv and the West to accept as fact the myth that the Donbas has always been a pro-Russian bastion, relinquishing the Donbas to Moscow (e.g., to negotiate a cease-fire) would be easy. This is almost certainly what Moscow is counting on by occupying the Donbas after its failure to capture Kyiv, Kharkiv, and other major cities. The capture of the Donbas may seem a negligible consolation prize for Moscow, but it is one that Putin can live with until resuming his inevitable aggression farther into Ukraine. Fortunately, neither Kyiv nor the Ukrainian military buy into this myth about the Donbas and since 2014 have been fighting for the Donbas lands.

The danger of losing the Donbas is still real, however. The Western press, politicians, academics, and observers continue to speak as if they accept at face value the Russian propaganda that the Donbas is historically Russian. What they fail to understand, or wilfully ignore, is that the Donbas was historically Ukrainian Cossack territory and was never Russian. However Russified linguistically it became, the Donbas has always been Ukrainian, and at no point in modern history did its ethnic Russian population surpass that of ethnic Ukrainians.

Unfortunately, there is also a danger to the Donbas from within Ukraine itself. Some Ukrainians who are unfamiliar with the Donbas are dismissive of it. Quite dishearteningly, a number of leading Ukrainian intellectuals are among them. One prominent Ukrainian writer wrote in the wake of the Orange Revolution that the Donbas was a region that "easily succumbs to political manipulation in connection with a black-and-white view of the world," and that its people were "medieval-feudal" or "Cro-Magnon-Neanderthal" (*кроманьйонської та неандертальської*); the "ballast of the Donbas," which the writer called a "big proto-cultural wasteland" (*велику протокультурну пустку*), could become an impediment to Ukraine's integration into Europe (Andrukhovych 2005, 2006). Russia exploits this sort of errant prejudice with the aim of dividing and conquering Ukraine. Such discourse is the subject of Russian political life but not Europe's.

True, the Donbas is not free of its own kind of prejudice. Some people in the Donbas may regard their compatriots from Ukraine's western regions as "Banderites" — supporters of Stepan Bandera (1909–59), a mid-twentieth-century Ukrainian nationalist leader. Yet the Donbas is also known among Ukrainian nationalists from the western regions as a force that helped to democratize their nationalist platform. During World War II, for example, Ievhen Stakhiv (1918–2014) worked in the Donbas as a secret organizer of the Organization of Ukrainian Nationalists and found that people in the Donbas treated the ideologue of Ukrainian nationalism, Dmytro Dontsov (1883–1973), as a "fascist." Influenced by the people in the Donbas, Stakhiv, who had once idealized Spain's Franco regime, "abandoned a narrowly defined Ukrainian nationalism and embraced the ideal of a democratic Ukraine without discrimination against its national minorities." Stakhiv attributed his democratic conversion to the Donbas people and was grateful to them for it (Stakhiv 1995, 133–4, 308).

In any case, Russia's military invasion of the Donbas has ironically served to blunt the prejudice toward the Donbas, although it has not died easily. In contrast, one cannot but be struck by the passion and tenacity of the Ukrainian soldiers who have been fighting for the Donbas since 2014. For them, the Donbas and its people are unqualifiedly Ukrainian.

Moscow and the "people's republics" in the Donbas

It is also noteworthy that Moscow, while it occupied and swiftly annexed Crimea in 2014, has been in no such hurry to annex the Donbas. On the eve of invading Ukraine in late February this year, Moscow made a point of recognizing the two "people's republics" in the Donbas as sovereign states. It could have declared their annexation but did not. It is possible that Moscow is waiting for the capture of all of the Luhansk and Donetsk oblasts before annexing them. As has been argued by many, interest in incorporation does have a voice among the leaders of the "people's republics" and among the population of the occupied parts of the Donbas. As if to encourage this, Russia has been distributing Russian passports among the Donbas population, although exactly how many people have willingly received them or received them as insurance against an uncertain future is difficult to determine. As of the end of January this year, it is estimated that 635,000 residents, or 22 to 35 percent of the population in the two "people's republics," had obtained Russian passports (Burkhardt et al. 2022).

It should be pointed out, however, that just before the full-barrel war began in February, popular sentiment even in the Russian-occupied Donbas territory was ambivalent. An opinion poll conducted by a joint team of Ukrainian, Russian, and Western researchers just before Russia invaded Ukraine shows that more than half of the respondents had no interest in which government, Kyiv or Moscow, controlled the Donbas. There was little difference between those living in the Kyiv-controlled areas and the Russian occupied ones in the Donbas.[2] This was the view after almost eight years of occupation, one hardly encouraging to Moscow (or to Kyiv, for that matter, as far as the Kyiv-controlled parts of the Donbas are concerned). This kind of outlook faithfully reflects the historical and political nature of the Donbas: its population have distrusted and spurned all outside political authority, even though, like the Cossacks in the old days, they are happy to strike up an alliance with whoever might help them. This is a survival strategy for those straining to sustain life in the precarious border regions.

It seems probable that Moscow and the leaders of the "people's republics" installed in parts of Donetsk and Luhansk oblasts have not been operating on the same wavelength. Putin's blatant embrace of Russian imperialism must be alarming for some of the Donbas republics' leaders. On the one hand, they need the Kremlin's full support to secure and maintain their power and territory. On the other hand, if the Donbas should become part of Russia, it would become just one tiny region of the federation. With its antiquated industrial infrastructure, the uncertain future of the coal industry, and total

---

2. See O'Loughlin, Sasse, and Toal (2022).

devastation of the regions subjected to Russian conquest, the Donbas would be an enormous burden by any estimate. Impoverished by Western sanctions and isolated from the world economy, Russia would not and could not restore the Donbas to any meaningful degree. The onus of reconstruction would fall squarely on the shoulders of the Donbas people themselves. Under Ukrainian control, however, the Donbas would benefit from post-war reconstruction aid from abroad. Kyiv should make the most of these contrasting perspectives.

In the occupied lands of the Donbas and in the south of Ukraine, flags are hoisted of the defunct Soviet Union or with hammer-and-sickle symbols, along with the Russian national flags. Is this a sign of nostalgia for the "good, old, and stable" days under Soviet rule? Or might it be a sign of political disorientation in a population that trusts neither Moscow nor Kyiv? If it is a nostalgia, one aspect in particular of Soviet history could be inconvenient for Moscow, bent as it is on exporting the "Russian World" to Ukraine. Namely, in declaring Russian Federation's recognition of the "people's republics" on the eve of the war, Putin criticized Vladimir I. Lenin and the Bolshevik government for creating an "artificial" Ukrainian (Soviet) Republic in lands that belonged to Russia's "historical territory." (In 1918 Lenin disapproved of the separatist "Donets–Kryvyi Rih Soviet Republic" as harmful to the interests of Ukraine, disbanded it, and incorporated it into the Ukrainian SSR.) Instead of being grateful to Lenin, Putin notes, the Ukrainians have for some time been at work on "de-Communization," demolishing memorials to Lenin. If Ukraine wants de-Communization, Putin has declared, it can have a real "de-Communization" — entailing in the establishment, or more appropriately, the restoration of the "Russian World" or Russian imperialist rule in Ukraine that would supposedly do away with the Soviet Communist legacy in Ukraine (Putin 2022).

Will this overt revival of Russia's imperial ambitions be accepted by leaders of the Donetsk and Luhansk "people's republics"? One possible development might be the "Chechenization" of the Donbas, achieved politically by co-opting local bigwigs in exchange for a degree of "autonomy" (i.e., local dictatorship) in the Russian-controlled Donbas. Ramzan Kadyrov, the Putin-appointed dictator in Chechnya — a region in the Russian Federation known for its fractious history — has been sending soldiers to the Donbas for the Russian side in the current war. In a sense, since 2014 the two "people's republics" of the Donbas have been functioning as Russian client regimes akin to Chechnya. "Chechenization" of the Donbas might enforce a degree of peace, but for how long? Time will tell whether Moscow can keep the Donbas (or Chechnya) under control.

Conclusion

If any in the anti-imperialist, anti-colonialist camp in Europe, the Americas, Asia, Africa, or elsewhere in the world have had lingering illusions about Russia and Putin, the war against Ukraine should have dispelled them. Yet it has not. Meanwhile, those on the anti-democratic right continue to appear to be enchanted by the Russian dictator. Putin thus enjoys noticeable support at both ends of the political spectrum. In his speeches Putin has essentially declared an end to the liberal-democratic world order. The global order he seeks to build in its place is a Russian-controlled, anti-democratic one. The brunt of the struggle against Putin's crusade has fallen upon Ukraine and upon the Donbas in particular. In Russia, as in many parts of the world, it is difficult to distinguish today between Communists and radical right-wing nationalists. Anyone familiar with world history should not be surprised by this political configuration. As just one example, in 1939 Hitler and Stalin conspired and jointly destroyed Poland.

Political developments in the Donbas are the key to understanding the future for Ukraine. The Donbas often appears an eternal puzzle to outside observers. Historically, almost every political force has gotten its hands burned in the Donbas. A century ago Trotsky observed, "one can't go to the Donbas without a [political] gas mask," alluding to the difficulties he encountered there. Ivan Maistrenko went to the Donbas after Trotsky. Initially he was pleased that his party, the *Ukapisty* (the Communist wing of the Ukrainian Social Democrats, who later, in 1925, would join the Bolsheviks), appeared to have more support among the Donbas workers than did the Bolsheviks. Yet those workers who supported the Ukrainian Communist Party, according to Maistrenko, had no sense of nationality issues. They just wanted to see how the Ukrainian Communists would improve their lives, their thought being, "Well, if nothing comes of the All-Russian party (Bolsheviks), let's try the Ukrainians." In despair, subsequently, Maistrenko refused to work in the

Donbas (a "culturally joyless province").[3] Although the Donbas has changed a great deal since the 1920s, it is still enigmatic and frustrations like Maistrenko's have not died easily. Be that as it may, we can ill afford to ignore Russian encroachment in the Donbas, as it holds the key to understanding Putin's strategy for furthering his imperialist goals in Ukraine—and beyond.

Works cited

Andrukhovych, Iurii. 2005. "Shukaiuchy Dreamland." *Krytyka* 9 (1–2): 3.

— — —. 2006. "Atlas: Medytatsiï." *Krytyka* 10 (1–2): 10–11.

Burkhardt, Fabian, Cindy Wittke, Elia Bescotti, and Maryna Rabinovych. 2022. "Russlands Passportisierung des Donbas: Von einer eingeschränkten zu einer vollwertigen Staatsbürgerschaft?" *Ukraine-Analysen*, no. 262 (22 February 2022): 11.

International Republican Institute. 2014. *Public Opinion Survey: Residents of Ukraine (3–12 April 2014)*. Kyiv: USAID. https://www.iri.org/wp-content/uploads/2014/04/201420April202420Survey20of20Residents20of20Ukraine2C20April203-122C202014.pdf.

KIIS. 2014. "Opinions and views of the citizens of Southern and Eastern regions of Ukraine: April 2014." Kyiv International Institute of Sociology, 20 April 2014. https://www.kiis.com.ua/?lang=eng&cat=news&id=258.

Kremlin. 2022. "Vstrecha s rukovodstvom Gosdumy i glavnymi fraktsii." Kremlin.ru, 7 July 2022. http://kremlin.ru/events/president/news/68836.

Kuromiya, Hiroaki. 1998. *Freedom and Terror in the Donbas: A Ukrainian-Russian Borderland, 1870s–1990s*. New York: Cambridge University Press.

— — —. 2014. "H-Diplo Review Essay on Georgy Zhukov. *Marshal of Victory: The Autobiography of General Georgy Zhukov*. Ed. Geoffrey Roberts. Barnsley: Pen & Sword Military. 2013" (no. 111). H-Diplo, 6 June 2014. http://h-diplo.org/essays/PDF/E111.pdf.

O'Loughlin, John, Gwendolyn Sasse, and Gerard Toal. 2022. "Will Russia recognize the independence of two eastern Ukraine republics? Here's what people there think." *The Washington Post*, 17 February 2022.

Putin, Vladimir. 2022. "Obrashchenie Prezidenta Rossiiskoi Federatsii." Kremlin.ru, 21 February 2022. http://kremlin.ru/events/president/news/67828.

Stakhiv, Ievhen. 1995. *Kriz' tiurmy, pidpillia i kordony: Povist' moho zhyttia*. Kyiv: Rada.

---

3. On Trotsky, Maistrenko, and others on the Donbas, see Kuromiya (1998, 4, 124).

CHAPTER 11

Russian foreign policy and the origins of the "Russian World"

Oleksii Polegkyi and Dmytro Bushuyev
Essay published 6 September 2022

Oleksii Polegkyi is the academic director of the Center for Public Diplomacy in Kyiv and an Adjunkt at the Polish Academy of Science's Institute of Political Studies, also formerly a Bayduza Post-doctoral Fellow at the Canadian Institute of Ukrainian Studies and a member of the Political Communication Research Unit at the University of Antwerp. He was previously a research fellow with the Graduate Institute of Russian Studies at National Chengchi University, Taiwan, and a visiting fellow at the Institute of Advanced Studies Kőszeg (Hungary). Oleksii earned his PhD in Political Science from the University of Wrocław (Poland) and the University of Antwerp.

Dmytro Bushuyev is a political analyst and writer. He worked as a speech-writer for the Government of Ukraine in 2019–22. He authored the book *The History of Undefeated: Ukraine on Defending the European Civilization* about the origins of the Russo-Ukrainian war.

Just a few months ago, Irpin and Bucha were cozy towns on the outskirts of Kyiv, Ukraine's capital, popular among young families and retirees thanks to their parks, peaceful atmosphere, and reasonable housing rates.

Things changed drastically after 24 February, when Russia launched its escalated invasion of Ukraine. In its attempt to capture Kyiv, the Russian Army besieged Irpin and Bucha and took hostage their inhabitants. A month later, after the Russians were forced to retreat, Ukrainians revealed mass graves of civilians killed during the occupation. As witnesses reported, torture and rape were common, as well as looting. The senseless cruelty of Russian soldiers went far beyond the usual violence of war. The war crimes in Irpin and Bucha became only the first in a long and growing list of wanton atrocities committed by the invading Russians.

On the same day that the bodies were discovered in Bucha, an article by Timofey Sergeytsev, one of the Kremlin's ideologists, was published by RIA Novosti, a Russian state-owned news agency.

The title (here translated) was rather pithy: "What should Russia do with Ukraine?" (Sergeytsev 2022). The author praised the supremacy of Russian civilization and insisted that Ukraine and Ukrainian identity should be eradicated.

Thus, everything that had happened in Bucha, Irpin, and other Ukrainian cities and towns — and is continuing to happen — was not just a tragic accident. It is a deliberate genocidal policy of Russia against Ukraine, inspired by the concept of the *Russkii mir* or "Russian World."

Origins of the "Russian World"

At the beginning of the 2000s, Russian government policy started pivoting away from previous attempts to effect democratic change, which were hindered by the corruption of Russian elites, and towards a neo-autocracy led by the federation's second president, Vladimir Putin, a former KGB officer. The Russian state treasury had swelled with money from oil and gas exports, which brought not only higher standards of life for Russians but also an assiduously cultivated feeling of nostalgia for the Soviet Union, the political successor of the Russian Empire.

The West, which had been viewed as a partner to Russia in the 1990s, was re-assessed in the 2000s as an adversary whose covert actions had destroyed the USSR and broken the unity of its "brotherly nations" and satellite countries of the "near abroad." The external threat that was at the core of the Russian mindset for ages emerged again.

This resentment was quite promptly reflected in the federation's state military budget, which increased from 9 billion dollars in 2000 to almost 35 billion in 2006 (Macrotrends, n.d.). But the call for a revanchist empire demanded a new ideology — neither a pure Soviet nor a czarist ideology, but one that matched the realities of the 21st century.

Changes in Russia's foreign policy became evident in 2005 after Ukraine's "Orange Revolution," a months-long civilian protest against the falsification of the presidential election, where Russia had backed a pro-Russian candidate, Viktor Yanukovych, and appeared to influence the results.

In Russia's perception, the Orange Revolution was an organized operation to provoke an anti-Russian and pro-American uprising in Ukraine using soft-power means. It was regarded by Russian elites as the result of a Western coup and awakened fears in the Kremlin that the Ukrainian experience might serve as a model for political change in Russia itself. The Kremlin then resorted to its centuries-old playbook, using the power of ideas to exert soft-power influence on other countries to its own nefarious ends.

In particular, Russia started re-shaping its public policy, language issues, and historical narratives as a way of exerting its power on neighbouring countries and as a way of imposing its own geopolitical interests in the post-Soviet space. The idea of the "Russian World," which was initially conceptualized by a quasi-philosophical circle of Russian methodologists in the early 2000s, was taken up as a starting point and name for a new doctrine.

The declared bases of the "Russian World" are Russian language and culture, Orthodox faith, historical memory, and a common past, especially a reverent attitude toward the Great Fatherland War (Russia's term for World War II, aka "Great Patriotic War"), which is considered the greatest military victory of the Soviet Union. After applying the concept of the "Russian compatriot abroad" to citizens of neighbouring countries who have connections to the Russian culture, language, and traditions, Russia announced its wish to "protect" these compatriots' rights and interests and declared it will battle for the hearts and minds of the citizens of these independent countries.

The world has since discovered that they meant "battle" literally, and the first to feel it was Georgia, which faced a Russian invasion in 2008.

Two more factors subsequently galvanized President Putin's policy and pushed him to strengthen the "Russian World" doctrine, making it tougher and more severe. The first factor was a series of Russian opposition protests in 2012 — a civic reaction to presidential elections which, according to opposition leaders, were rigged in Putin's favour. His nightmare of an Orange Revolution in Moscow seemed to be coming true, despite the protests failing. The second factor was yet another revolution in Ukraine — this time in 2014, resulting in the abdication and escape to Russia of the pro-Russian Viktor Yanukovych, who had been the President of Ukraine since 2010. Spurred by student activism, the Euromaidan Revolution (aka Revolution of Dignity) was a successful Ukrainian response to his policy of autocracy and attempts to curtail the European choice of

Ukraine. In fact, the protesters descended on Kyiv's Independence Square (*maidan*) after Yanukovych's government suddenly reversed its position and refused to sign the Association Agreement between Ukraine and the EU, which a lot of Ukrainians considered crucial for the country's future.

Putin could not believe that a head of state could be fired as a result of civilian protests. His KGB past and Russia's history told him that it could only be done through government backroom dealings. The fact that the world's democracies supported the Euromaidan Revolution enhanced Putin's conviction that the West, and the US in particular, were acting against him directly.

The Kremlin developed a rival "counter-revolutionary" propaganda to justify Russia's "special path," consisting of a mélange of ideologies where Stalinism is combined with conservative Orthodoxy and selected modern philosophical approaches of methodologists, formulated in the latter 20th century (Popescu and Wilson 2009).

Putin seized upon the idea of civilizational differences between Russia and the West, citing the philosopher Ivan Ilin, a direct disciple of the intellectual tradition of fascist ideology. The looming threat of a new "colour revolution" within the borders of the Russian Federation was one of the Kremlin's biggest fears. The 2013–14 Euromaidan protests in Ukraine were labelled by the Kremlin as another "special operation" of the West directed against Russia (Tsygankov 2015; van Herpen 2015).

To a large extent, Russian foreign policy has always been part of its domestic policy, and the role of foreign policy issues increased significantly during certain periods of its history as an instrument of mass mobilization. Putin's regime depends on militarism to retain power. In 2014, 86% of Russians supported the annexation of Crimea immediately after it took place. Popular feelings of victimhood and imperial longing help to justify Russia's military aggression abroad.

When Russia annexed Crimea in 2014 and initiated a proxy war in the Donbas region of Ukraine, right through to the escalated war against Ukraine eight years later, President Putin and Patriarch Kirill, leader of the Russian Orthodox Church, have used "Russian World" ideology as their principal justification for the invasion.

In his so-called 2014 "Crimea speech," Putin claimed that Russia was a divided nation: "Millions of Russians went to sleep in one country and woke up in a foreign land. Overnight they became national minorities in the former union republics. The Russian people became one of the largest, if not the largest divided people in the world" (Putin 2014).[1]

Essence of the "Russian World"

The concept of the "Russian World" is a geopolitical imagining, argues Marlene Laruelle, "a fuzzy mental atlas [...] on which different regions of the world and their different links to Russia can be articulated in a fluid way. This blurriness is structural to the concept and allows it to be reinterpreted within multiple contexts" (2015).

According to this approach, Russia should be represented as a unique civilization whose great power status is based on strong moral values, economy, and military capacity. It supports the belief that Russia should pursue independent, assertive, and opportunistic foreign policy in order to defend Russian interests and establish Russia as a great power that presents an alternative to Western democracy.

Several key characteristics of *Russia-specific nationalism* comprise the foundation for the "Russian World": *essentialism* — the idea that there are special, eternal cultural qualities of the Russian people that distinguish them fundamentally from other peoples; *aggrandizing imperial drive* — from the start, Russian nationalists saw autocracy and preservation of empire as vitally important goals of their political activity; and *imperial consciousness*. This includes an intricate complex of traditional stereotypes that preserve stable statist values, hopes for "a wise tsar" and "a firm hand," and imperial ambitions. The elitist variety of the "imperial consciousness" is above all connected with a geopolitical essentialism that arises in two interrelated notions: first, that the special Russian civilization exists eternally in the "Russian soul"; and second, that Western civilization continually threatens Russian civilization (Pain 2016, 60).

The conception of the "Russian World" as a transnational space of those who understand Russian language and have been touched by Russian culture was formulated in the 1990s by intellectuals and methodologists such as Petr Shchedrovitsky, Efim Ostrovsky, Gleb Pavlovsky, Valery Tishkov, and others. From a

---

1. Here and below, translations and emphases are by the authors.

civilization perspective, the Russian language has been seen as a way of holding the "Russian World" together as a sort of a transnational tie that crosses state borders. Because belonging to a cultural-linguistic group is considered to be the main determinant of one's membership to the "Russian World," its boundaries are not strictly delimited. Therefore, while the Russian Federation as a state has its limits, the "Russian World" does not.

In the mid-2000s, these ideas were accepted as a part of the Russian Federation's re-formulated foreign policy. The term "Russian World" was generally understood to comprise not only the Russian diaspora itself but also an ideological concept of Russian culture and its mission in the world.

Furthermore, methodologists brought an additional dimension to the "Russian World" doctrine. From the point of view of methodology, activity is a fundamental reality of the world, and everything else, even humans, are just tools for activity. It gives special credit to technocracy as a way to turn whatever you need into a "tool"; the more effective you want to be, the more precise tool you need (or have to be), ideally a tool which follows its mandate without moral hesitation. To disseminate this thinking, the philosophy requires the total dehumanization of its followers, because effectiveness, as a main merit of technocracy, does not care about specific human "weaknesses" such as kindness, compassion, or empathy.

This approach has become extremely popular among the Russian political elite, and many officials have taken specific training, including Sergey Kirienko, first deputy chief of the Presidential Administration of the Russian Federation.

It is more than likely that this technocratic approach on the part of the Russian elite has made its way through the entire Russian state system—resulting, among other things, in the cruelty of Russian soldiers who are "just trying to do their job" in the most efficient way. But being only a "heartless technocrat" is not enough, one has to attain certainty of his moral righteousness to turn into a perfect war machine.

Russians get this feeling of self-righteousness from their Orthodox Church, which has become the second pillar of the "Russian World" doctrine.

The Russian Orthodox Church has become a major player in the discourse on Russian identity and on Russia's relations with neighbouring states. Orthodoxy is now one of the most important institutions for preserving supranational principles in the Russian consciousness and maintaining the unity of the "Russian World" civilization. Patriarch of Moscow and All Russia Kirill has begun to pose not just as the head of the Russian Orthodox Church but as a supranational spiritual leader of "Holy Russia," which purports to include Russia, Ukraine, Belarus, Moldova, and—on a broader scale—all Orthodox Christians. From this perspective, Moscow views itself as the "Third Rome" and the only legal inheritor of the Byzantine Empire—in contrast to the "false Rome" of Washington. Today, the Russian Orthodox Church has become the "moral foundation" for the Russo-Ukrainian war (Kelaidis 2022).

The third basis for the "Russian World" is a common historical memory. History and the past as a symbolic resource have become instruments for achieving political goals and strongly influence Russian politics. As mentioned above, the Great Fatherland War is certainly one of the most (if not the most) evocative historical events in the Russian imagination. The Soviet Union's victory in WW II— the "Great Victory in the Great War" [sic], according to Russian mythology—became a cornerstone of the neo-imperialist Russian identity, especially under President Putin, and has been actively exploited in order to mobilize support for current political regimes in the Kremlin. The heritage of victory in 1945 provides the foundation to represent Russia as a great power and claim a special position in Europe. Any challenge to the myth of victory in WW II amounts to a threat to Russian hegemony in the post-Soviet space—and even a direct threat to the existence of Russia as a state.

The article by Sergeytsev, who belongs to the Methodologist circle mentioned above, is a perfect reflection of the "Russian World" idea. Ukraine is a "Nazi" state just because it dares to question the exceptional role of Russia in World War II, viewing it as a joint victory of allies in which not only Russian but also Ukrainian lives were sacrificed, along with the Americans, British, Poles, French, and others all over the world.

German Nazism of 1930–40 is interpreted by Russians as a consequence of the Western mindset crisis from which Russia "redeemed" the world; and today the West, soaked with moral decay, has rejected Russia's sacrifice and decided to punish it for selfless help.

Ukraine is viewed not as an independent state and self-sufficient nation but as a tool of the hostile West, artificially created to hurt Russia. Ukraine, which consciously made European and democratic choices, undermines the Russian imperialist doctrine of the "divided nation." Therefore, Ukraine is guilty because it does not want to share the common fate of the "Russian World" that had been imagined by intellectuals and clergymen. Ukraine should be tied to Russia, otherwise it must be de-Ukrainianized and de-Europized. The historical self-righteousness of Russia and the blessing of the Russian Orthodox Church justify all the crimes of the Russian Army for the sake of the Russian World.

The "Russian World," a concept and propaganda tool deliberately created and cherished in Russia during the last few decades, has a profoundly weak basis. It has no answer for the question of how to coexist with those who do not consider themselves to be a part of it.

Works cited

Kelaidis, Katherine. 2022. "The Russian Patriarch just gave his most dangerous speech yet—and almost no one in the West has noticed." *Religion Dispatches*, 4 April 2022. https://religiondispatches.org/the-russian-patriarch-just-gave-his-most-dangerous-speech-yet-and-almost-no-one-in-the-west-has-noticed.

Laruelle, Marlene. 2015. "The 'Russian World': Russia's Soft Power and Geopolitical Imagination." Center for Global Interests Papers, May 2015. https://www.researchgate.net/publication/344222398_The_'Russian_World'_Russia's_Soft_Power_and_Geopolitical_Imagination_Center_for_Global_Interests_Papers_May

Macrotrends. n.d. "Russia military spending/defense budget 1992–2023." Macrotrends LLC. https://www.macrotrends.net/countries/RUS/russia/military-spending-defense-budget.

Pain, Emil. 2016. "The imperial syndrome and its influence on Russian nationalism." In *The New Russian Nationalism: Imperialism, Ethnicity and Authoritarianism 2000–2015*, edited by Pål Kolstø and Helge Blakkisrud, 46–74. Edinburgh University Press.

Popescu, Nicu, and Andrew Wilson. 2009. *The Limits of Enlargement-lite: European and Russian Power in the Troubled Neighbourhood*. London: European Council on Foreign Relations.

Putin, Vladimir. 2014. "Obrashchenie Prezidenta Rossiiskoi Federatsii." Kremlin.ru, 18 March 2014. http://kremlin.ru/events/president/news/20603.

Sergeytsev, Timofey. 2022. "Chto Rossiia dolzhna sdelat' s Ukrainoi?" RIA, updated 4 June 2022. https://ria.ru/20220403/ukraina-1781469605.html.

Tsygankov, Andrei. 2015. "Vladimir Putin's Last Stand: The Sources of Russia's Ukraine Policy." *Post-Soviet Affairs* 31 (4): 279–303.

van Herpen, Marcel H. 2015. *Putin's Propaganda Machine: Soft Power and Russian Foreign Policy*. London: Rowman & Littlefield.

CHAPTER 12

To be or not to be: Attitudes of Ukrainian society about gender equality and diversity after Russia's invasion of Ukraine

Tamara Martsenyuk
Essay published 6 September 2022

> Tamara Martsenyuk is an associate professor in the Department of Sociology at the University of Kyiv-Mohyla Academy. Since 2022 she has been a visiting scholar at Leuphana Universität Lüneburg. Her research interests relate to gender and social structure, including women's participation in protests and women's access to the military. She authored chapters in *Feminist Perspective on Russia's War in Ukraine* (2024), *Dispossession: Anthropological Perspectives on Russia's War Against Ukraine* (2023), *Ukraine's Many Faces: Land, People, and Culture Revisited* (2023), and other books. In 2023 she received the Emma Goldman Award for outstanding research on feminist and inequality issues.

Since acquiring independence after the collapse of the USSR in 1991, Ukraine has achieved visible progress in establishing gender equality in the different spheres of society. At the national level, gender equality is guaranteed first of all by the Constitution of Ukraine (1996) and the Law of Ukraine "On ensuring equal rights and opportunities for women and men" (2005). At the international level Ukraine has ratified major international documents on providing equal rights and opportunities for men and women, including the UN Convention on the Elimination of all Forms of Discrimination Against Women and the UN Sustainable Development Goals. A very big success for Ukraine was its ratification in July 2022 of the Council of Europe's Convention on Preventing and Combating Violence Against Women and Domestic Violence (aka Istanbul Convention).

On 23 June 2022 the Council of Europe granted Ukraine candidate status for accession to the European Union. Gender equality and respect for diversity are among the EU's founding values. Therefore, it is important for Ukrainian society to continue promoting them through legislation, monitoring, policy guidance, raising awareness, and support to grassroots projects and NGOs.

105

Even though political will is crucial to implement gender equality at an institutional level, societal attitudes toward diversity and dignity are also an important factor. Public opinion on gender equality (especially in such traditionally "male" spheres as the armed forces and military) and rights for LGBT people could be a litmus test of democratic values.

Public opinion on gender equality in the Armed Forces of Ukraine

The topic of women's access to the armed forces has become a visible part of Ukraine's political agenda since the 2014 Russo-Ukrainian war in the Donbas. A sociological study titled "The 'Invisible Battalion': Women's participation in the ATO military operations" was conducted in summer–autumn 2015 (Martsenyuk, Grytsenko, and Kvit 2016). The study found that just like the Ukrainian job market in general, the Armed Forces of Ukraine (ZSU) manifests vertical and horizontal gender segregation. Two subsequent studies focused on the status of female veterans (2018–19) and the problem of sexual harassment in the military (2021). Thus, "Invisible Battalion" became a large advocacy campaign for researching and documenting women's participation in the war.

Let us review Ukrainian public opinion on gender equality in the Armed Forces, especially after the Russian invasion. I propose to compare the results of two public opinion surveys that are representative of Ukraine, which covered only the territories under Ukrainian control.

The first poll was conducted by the Kyiv International Institute of Sociology (KIIS) on 8–23 September 2018 for our study "'Invisible battalion 2.0': Women veterans returning to peaceful life" (Martsenyuk et al. 2019). The survey was held in 109 localities in all oblasts of Ukraine, except for occupied Crimea and selected districts of Donetsk and Luhansk oblasts. In the field stage, 2,026 questionnaires were collected, of them 915 from men and 1,111 from women.

The second poll was conducted by the research agency "InfoSapiens" on 10–14 April 2022. The method of data collection was telephone interviews (CATI). The sample size was 1,000 respondents (454 men and 546 women).

Overall, as shown by the representative public opinion surveys conducted in 2018 and 2022, Ukrainian society supports the idea of equal rights and opportunities in the ZSU. After Russia's invasion, Ukrainians supported gender equality in the military sphere even more than just a few years previously.

As we can see in Table 1, in 2018 more than half agreed that women in Ukraine should be granted equal opportunities with men to work in the ZSU and other military formations. In 2022 the percentage of these supporters increased from 53% (in 2018) to 80%. Moreover, the respondents became more certain about this question, as the percentage of undecided in 2022 was only around 1%, compared to 14% in 2018.

Table 1. Answers to a question twice surveyed: "Women should be granted equal opportunities with men to work in the Armed Forces of Ukraine and other military formations."

Answers	KIIS September 2018, N=2,026, %	InfoSapiens April 2022, N=1,000, %
Agree completely	24.0	44.0
Sooner agree than disagree	29.3	35.7
Sooner disagree than agree	18.9	12.9
Completely disagree	12.2	5.9
Difficult to say	14.3	1.3
Decline to answer	1.4	0.2
Total	100	100

In 2022, the breakdown of those who "agree completely" with this statement of gender equality in the ZSU is: 54.4% of young people (16–19 y.o.), 50.4% of the Ukrainian-speaking population, 51.7% of the population in Western Ukraine, 53.6% of the population in Central Ukraine, and 57% of students.

There are different factors to explain why Ukrainian society (especially after Russia's invasion) supports equal opportunities for women and men to work in the ZSU and other military formations. The Euromaidan protests in 2013–14 and the invasion of the Donbas in 2014 inspired women in Ukraine to fight more actively for their rights, especially in the military sphere. Women became more visible in the ZSU and in the front lines of Russia's war against Ukraine. The percentage of women in the ZSU increased to 22% in 2022. Some women are now even found in the rank of general. Thus Ukrainian society has become used to the presence and the positive image of military women.

Moreover, Russia's full-scale invasion of Ukraine and the necessity to mobilize more people to be ready for armed resistance have encouraged Ukrainian society to see women as (potential) soldiers. Finally, Ukrainian women have always been an active part of the fight of Ukrainians for their independence and recognition. That tradition of resistance also continues in these hard times. For example, according to an all-Ukrainian nationally representative poll conducted by InfoSapiens for the British Research Agency ORB on 3–4 March 2022, 59% of women are ready to personally participate in the armed resistance to end the Russian occupation of Ukraine.[1]

The second question is about the type of army that Ukraine should introduce. As we can see from Table 2, the situation did not change radically between 2018 and 2022. "Professional army with enlistment of both men and women only on a voluntary (contract) basis" is the most popular answer, chosen by 62% of respondents in 2018 and 64% in 2022. The current Ukrainian situation—conscription of all the men and only some women—in 2022 is supported by 14.5% of respondents, while conscription of men only is supported by 14%. In 2018, less than 2% supported the idea of conscription of all men and all women. In 2022 the percentage increased to 4.2%, which also may be explained by the factors of full-scale invasion and necessity of strong resistance.

Table 2. Answers to a question twice surveyed: "In your opinion, what kind of army should Ukraine introduce?"

Answers	KIIS, September 2018, N=2,026, %	InfoSapiens, April 2022, N=1,000, %
Only voluntary enlistment of both men and women (enlistment by contract)	62.0	63.6
Conscription of all men and only of some women	10.6	14.5
Conscription only of men	17.0	14.2
Conscription of all men and all women	1.6	4.2
Other	0.4	1.4
Difficult to say	7.3	1.8
Decline to answer	1.1	0.2
Total	100	100

---

1. See Berger (2022).

Currently, according to Article 6 of the Law of Ukraine "On ensuring equal rights and opportunities for women and men," compulsory military service for men is not considered sex-based discrimination. Meanwhile, in 2018 a law was signed on equal rights for women and men while serving in the ZSU and other military formations. It provides equal opportunities for women and men to serve under contract, with equal access to positions and military ranks and equal responsibilities in the performance of military service.[2]

In sum, according to representative all-Ukrainian surveys of public opinion conducted in 2018 and in 2022 after Russia's invasion, Ukrainian society generally supports egalitarian ideas as to engaging women in the armed forces on a par with men, as well as having a professional army of those enlisted voluntarily (based on contracts). Therefore, further reforms should be implemented in the armed forces in order to better integrate women in the military sphere, and to prevent gender discrimination and gender-based violence.

Public opinion on human rights for LGBT people in Ukraine

Respect for diversity, especially on the basis of sexual orientation or gender identity (SOGI), is another value of the European community. Even though Ukraine was the first post-Soviet country that decriminalized homosexuality in December 1991, homophobia has remained a challenge for Ukrainian society (Martsenyuk 2016). LGBT people actively participated in the Euromaidan protests of 2013-14 and in the Donbas war since 2014. A union of LGBT military, veterans, and volunteers was established in 2018 by Viktor Pylypenko, an openly gay veteran of the Donbas Volunteer Battalion. The organization states, "We are currently gaining strength, taking an active part not only in defending Ukraine from the Russian invasion on the front line but also defending democracy and equality for all citizens of Ukraine." Since the 1990s LGBT organizations of Ukraine have been fighting for their rights and visibility. Thus, let us check the public opinion of Ukrainian society on this very topic.

---

2. Law of Ukraine No. 2866-IV "On ensuring equal rights and opportunities for women and men" dated 8 September 2005. http://zakon.rada.gov.ua/laws/show/2866-15.

For many years the "Nash Svit" [our world] Center, with cooperation of sociological agencies, has been monitoring the public opinion of Ukrainian society toward LGBT people. After Russia's invasion of Ukraine, they repeated some questions to reveal possible changes in attitudes. Table 3 and Table 4 compare the results of the representative surveys conducted by KIIS in 2016 and 2022. Nash Svit summarizes: "As expected, Ukrainians have demonstrated an overall increasing trend of accepting their LGBT fellow citizens" (2022).

As we can see from Table 3, in 2016 almost half of Ukrainians (45%) believed that there should be certain restrictions on the rights of persons of homosexual orientation; and 33% of Ukrainians were in favour of equal rights. And more than one-fifth of respondents could not answer this question. As we can see from more detailed KIIS data (2016), women, younger people, and more educated respondents tend to be more gay-friendly (Nash Svit 2016).

Table 3. Answers to a question twice surveyed: "In your opinion, should residents of Ukraine of homosexual orientation have the same rights as other citizens of our country?"

Answers	KIIS, September 2018, N=2,026, %	InfoSapiens, April 2022, N=1,000, %
Yes, everybody should have equal rights	33.4	63.7
No, there should be some restrictions	45.2	25.9
Difficult to say / Decline to answer	21.3	10.4
Total	100	100

In May 2022 the results of a public opinion survey demonstrated a visible tendency to an increasingly gay-friendly attitude. Twice as many respondents as 6 years ago (64%) support the idea that residents of Ukraine who have a homosexual orientation should have the same rights as other citizens of our country. The percentage of undecided respondents halved, down to 10%. Younger respondents, residents of larger cities, more educated, and wealthier people are the most supportive of equality for LGBT in Ukraine. Regarding participation of LGBT people in protecting Ukraine from Russian aggression, then 66% of respondents approve; only 11% are negative about LGBT people coming to the defense of Ukraine, and 15% are indifferent (Nash Svit 2022).

Very important for the LGBT community in Ukraine is the question of support for the introduction of registered partnership for same-sex couples. As shown in Table 4, in 2016 only 5% of Ukrainians were in favour and 19% were indifferent, but 69% were against it. Even among those who were in favour of equal rights for LGBT in Ukraine, 56% opposed registered partnerships and only 10% supported them (Nash Svit 2016).

By May 2022 public opinion improved on this issue. The percentage of supporters of registered partnerships for same-sex couples quintupled, up to around 24%. At the same time, 42% did not support this right, but that number had decreased in last six years. Comparing answers from Table 3 and Table 4, we see that respondents are inconsistent in their perception of basic rights for LGBT people, in this case the right to official relationships. Either way, the total of those who answered "yes" or "I don't care" is 51%, which is a majority of opponents. In this situation, the LGBT Nash Svit Center notes that "Ukrainian churches and conservative politicians need to learn that the majority of Ukrainian citizens do not object to the legalization of same-sex civil unions" (Nash Svit 2022).

Table 4. Answers to a question twice surveyed: "Do you support registered partnerships for same-sex couples, similar to ordinary marriage but without the right to adopt children?"

Answers	KIIS, September 2018, N=2,026, %	InfoSapiens, April 2022, N=1,000, %
Yes	4.8	23.6
No	69.0	41.9
I don't care	18.5	27.1
Difficult to say / Decline to answer	7.7	7.4
Total	100	100

Anyway, the May 2022 survey results about support for registered partnerships for same-sex couples could explain the success of a recent petition for the legalization of same-sex marriages, supported by over 28,000 people.[3] President Zelensky reacted to the petition as follows:[4]

---

3. Sovenko, Anastasiia. "Tekst petytsiï." 3 June 2022. https://petition.president.gov.ua/petition/144562.
4. Zelensky, Volodymyr. "Vidpovid' na petytsiiu." 2 August 2022. https://petition.president.gov.ua/petition/144562.

The government has developed options for legalization in Ukraine of registered civil partnerships under the parameters of our work on the affirmation and provision of human rights and freedoms. In accordance with Article 116 of the Constitution of Ukraine, the Cabinet of Ministers of Ukraine is taking measures to ensure the rights and freedoms of persons and citizens. Considering the above, I have requested that the Prime Minister of Ukraine consider the issue raised in the electronic petition and inform me about relevant results.

Thus, Ukraine is likely to follow the European way in ensuring equal rights and opportunities for LGBT people.

In our "civilizational battle" between the *Russkii mir* (Russian world, which promotes ideas of criminalizing "gay propaganda" and patriarchal gender norms) and European values of support for diversity and equal rights, the latter is winning. Let us hope that recent successes in the implementation of equal rights and opportunities policy in Ukraine will continue and that it will be helpful in the further Euro-integration process.

Works cited

Berger, Miriam. 2022. "A majority of Ukrainians support armed resistance and oppose concessions to Russia, new poll finds." *The Washington Post*, 10 March 2022. https://www.washingtonpost.com/world/2022/03/10/ukraine-poll-majority-ukrainians-support-armed-resistance-oppose-concessions-russia-new-poll-finds.

Martsenyuk, Tamara. 2016. "Sexuality and revolution in post-Soviet Ukraine: LGBT rights and the Euromaidan protests of 2013–2014." *Journal of Soviet and Post-Soviet Politics and Society* 2 (1): 49–74.

Martsenyuk, Tamara, Ganna Grytsenko, and Anna Kvit. 2016. *"Invisible Battalion": Women's Participation in ATO Military Operations*. Kyiv: Ukrainian Women's Fund. https://ekmair.ukma.edu.ua/items/7ae6ded8-6e5c-48f1-8a6b-ddf031f54071.

Martsenyuk, Tamara, Ganna Grytsenko, Anna Kvit, Lesia Vasylenko, and Maria Zviahintseva. 2019. *"Invisible Battalion 2.0": Women Veterans Returning to Peaceful Life*. Kyiv: UN Women Ukraine.

Nash Svit. 2022. "Ukrainians have dramatically improved their attitude towards LGBT people." Nash Svit Center, 1 June 2022. https://gay.org.ua/en/blog/2022/06/01/ukrainians-have-dramatically-improved-their-attitude-towards-lgbt-people.

— — —. 2016. "Stavlennia do liudei homoseksual'noï oriientatsiï: liutyj 2016 roku." Nash Svit Center, February 2016. https://gay.org.ua/publications/soc-poll2016.pdf.

CHAPTER 13

Russia's war against Ukraine: Empires don't die overnight

Serhii Plokhy

Interview with Kevin Theriault, published 26 September 2022

Serhii Plokhy is the Mykhailo Hrushevsky Professor of Ukrainian History and director of the Ukrainian Research Institute at Harvard University. His interests include the intellectual, cultural, and international history of Eastern Europe, with an emphasis on Ukraine. He is the author of *Atoms and Ashes: A Global History of Nuclear Disasters* (2022), *The Frontline: Essays on Ukraine's Past and Present* (2021), *Nuclear Folly: A History of the Cuban Missile Crisis* (2021), *Forgotten Bastards of the Eastern Front: American Airmen behind the Soviet Lines and the Collapse of the Grand Alliance* (2019), *Chernobyl: The History of a Nuclear Catastrophe* (2018), and *The Gates of Europe: A History of Ukraine* (2015).

Theriault: Putin has been distorting history to justify Russia's invasion of Ukraine. What is the real role of history in this war? Can you think of other reasons for his actions?

Plokhy: Well, history is important here on two levels. First of all, history was used as a justification for Moscow's aggression—a particular way of reading history and misreading history. Before the all-out invasion of Ukraine started, in July of last year Putin published an article on the historical unity of Russians and Ukrainians. According to the majority of Kremlin watchers, it was actually at least drafted by him, so it wasn't just Putin putting his name there: he was purposefully developing and supporting his old argument that Russians and Ukrainians are one and the same people, which means that Ukrainians did not exist and are not supposed to exist as a separate nation.[1]

Putin's argument goes back to the imperial Russian historiography of pre-1917 and belief in one big Russian nation. But it has

---

1. For more background on the genesis of nations and why the Ukrainian nation should be regarded as no less legitimate than any other in present-day Europe, we recommend Prof. Timothy Snyder's lectures for his undergraduate course "The Making of Modern Ukraine" at Yale University, posted and freely available on YouTube.

been "retranslated" by Putin and become part of the Kremlin's broader propaganda — slogans and posters in the occupied territories that "we and Russia are the same people." Maybe even more importantly, the planning of the war was made on the same premises and same misreading of history. So the expectation was that Ukrainians would welcome the Russian troops as liberators and so on and so forth. And that is one level in which history is important.

Another one is, at least in my interpretation, that this war is basically a war about the Soviet succession. And more than that, a war about the imperial Russian succession. This is a continuation of the disintegration of the Russian Empire that had started during World War I, was arrested by the Bolsheviks, and then continued in 1991 with the fall of the Soviet Union. And history is particularly important — as in the history of the disintegration of empires *and* the history of the formation of modern nations — both when it comes to Ukraine and also when it comes to Russia as well. So really, history is a very important discipline when it comes to understanding the causes of this war, the course of the war, and also the rhetoric and ideology that are associated with it.

Theriault: Does Putin view Ukrainian democracy as a threat to his power?

Plokhy: Yes, we see that democracy is something that clearly bothers Russia. You can go back to the same article that I just mentioned by Vladimir Putin, "On the Historical Unity of Russians and Ukrainians," and there is a very important paragraph where he attacks the Ukrainian president, Volodymyr Zelensky, without mentioning his name. And the argument there is that the West installed in Ukraine a system of government in which people change, personalities change, promises are allegedly made, but the policy toward independence doesn't change. This is a direct attack on democracy in the sense that Putin is much more comfortable dealing with the Lukashenko type of regime in Belarus, and he was trying to do the same with the Yanukovych regime in Ukraine.

The resistance of the people to pressure to accept deals is something that Putin [apparently — *Ed.*] considers to be a Western ploy against Russia. So really, he is not realizing or is not willing to realize that what is at stake, what bothers him so much is the democratic development of another country and that indeed in democracies elections do take place. Politicians are there not to follow the conservative utopia (like it is happening with Putin himself) but to be responsible to the electors and to the people. So that's just one indication of how important the story is from the Russian side.

On the Ukrainian side there was a very interesting article by Nataliya Gumenyuk, a leading Ukrainian journalist who travelled all over Ukraine this past spring and heard the same phrase that we did from the people in the armed forces and people in the rear when they were speaking about the war and their determination to fight back. They were talking not about language, not about a culturally understood nation but about democratic freedoms. And that's what they were defending. Again, that's not the only reason why the Ukrainians are fighting, but it is certainly one of the key ones.

Theriault: Ukraine is now an EU candidate. Do you see this as a significant marker of Western support behind Ukraine? What does this mean to you in terms of Ukrainian identity?

Plokhy: The Ukrainian modern national project emerged in the 19th century as having basically two poles. The first pole was Russia and the Russian Empire—and that's what the Ukrainian national project is trying to distance itself from. Then there is another pole—the pole of attraction, which is basically Europe. This emerged in the mid-19th century and has continued all the way through the 20th century, irrespective of who the people are who are formulating the Ukrainian national project—be they the numerous national awakeners of the 19th century, later liberals like Mykhailo Drahomanov, national communists like Mykola Khvyliovyi, or members of the Ukrainian Helsinki Group, who all put Europe at the centre of the Ukrainian political agenda.

Thus Europe was for Ukraine quite a very important place long before the creation of the European Union and before the creation of any alternative structures as [Ukraine attempted to extricate itself from] Russia. And from that point of view, again, candidate membership is an important factor in getting closer to the EU, getting closer also to this idea of an orientation toward Europe. The war, it's sometimes forgotten, didn't start in February of 2022. It started in February of 2014 with the Russian takeover of Crimea. And it started as a result of Moscow's inability to stop the signing of the Association Agreement between Ukraine and the EU.

So the trigger for the start of this war was the European orientation of Ukraine. And from that point of view, now is the beginning of the new stage: all-out war. That European component is an important part of the story, and acceptance of Ukraine as a candidate member shouldn't come as a surprise.

Theriault: You wrote about the demise of the Soviet Union and that empires don't die overnight. Is Russia's war in Ukraine an indication that the empire is approaching its end, or is it an indication of something else?

Plokhy: Well, the history of the fall of empires, it can be a really long history. Looking at the Ottoman Empire, the process of its fall and disintegration really started in the late 17th and 18th centuries. And if you look today at the Middle East—at the situation in Palestine, Israel, at the emergence of the Islamic State—this is still a continuation of the story of the reshaping and rearranging of the former Ottoman Empire's realms. So I *want* to say that things can happen fast and that we are approaching the end, but I really don't know.

One thing that I do know is that this war is really part of a longer continuum that is related to not just the fall of the Soviet Union but the fall of [its direct predecessor—*Ed.*] the Russian Empire. The fact that Putin is back on the international scene with ideas that come from the Russian Empire, from imperial Russian thinkers, is just one more indication that long-range history is at play here.

What I think will be a long-term outcome, which brings the end of the Empire closer, is that as a result of this war there is less and less incentive for anyone in Russia, but also in Ukraine, to subscribe to Putin's imperial ideology of Russia and Ukraine being one of the same people and of the same nation. So this war really puts an end to that sort of rhetoric, and in that sense it will be a major contributing factor for hopefully the formation of post-imperial nations.

So it is another bloody step on the long road of disintegration of the Russian Empire. And it certainly points in toward the eventual end of that process. We know historically that empires collapse. We know historically that imperial nations reinvent themselves as nation-states. We also know from history that it takes time, unfortunately, and very often is accompanied by bloody wars.

Theriault: There are in the media lots of discussions about how the post–Cold War period has ended and indications that a new multi-polar world is emerging. What are your thoughts about significant structural shifts happening in the world? Are you seeing something else?

Plokhy: Yes, I think that shifts and changes do happen. And we are seeing that the Russian version of the multi-polar world is basically suffering a defeat in this war. I already mentioned that the trigger was the Association Agreement between Ukraine and the European Union. The agreement was extremely important, but it wasn't even about candidate-member status nor membership status in the EU. The agreement was important because if Ukraine signed that agreement, then it couldn't join the "Eurasian Union" that Russia was meaning to build. And establishing it was the vision of Russia and the Kremlin of becoming one of the poles of the multi-polar world—really by reintegrating at a certain level the former post-Soviet space—and being able to play the game on par with China and the EU. And that certainly did not happen in 2014.

And now, with Russia's military defeats and economic isolation, sanctions, what you see is certainly the end of this "Eurasian Union" dream, the implosion of Russia as an economic and military power as it drifts away from Europe and toward China. It is a push in the direction of recreating the bi-polar world, with Beijing emerging already, economically, as the other pole on a par with Washington, and certainly with Russia at this point having nowhere to go but to China.

This is the end of the Russian multi-polar dream. So yes, this war is cataclysmic for major geopolitical shifts and changes, but not of the sort that were envisioned by Russia.

Theriault: You have written extensively about Chornobyl and its political consequences. Are the lessons learned from Chornobyl being forgotten at the Zaporizhia Nuclear Power Plant?

Plokhy: Some of the lessons *were* learned, in the sense that the international community is trying to play a more active role through the International Atomic Energy Agency. So we see the international community being present before an accident, actually trying to prevent an accident, not just acting afterward, which is a plus. What is a minus is that the IAEA has no real power—the same way it had no real power back in 1986; it is open for manipulation.

It was manipulated by the Soviet Union back in 1986, and it has been very reluctant to take any clear stand now in the first months of the war. During the first weeks it was calling on both sides to exercise restraint, and so on and so forth, because it is part of the United Nations organization, whose highest body is the Security Council with Russia being a member. Therefore, some lessons were learned, but the big lesson is that we have to have an international regime and an international organization that would be able to deal with emergencies like that and override either the sovereignty of countries or interfere in conflicts like this one. It is something that we are clearly not prepared to deal with today.

If you want to think about the future of nuclear energy and want to consider it as part of a mix that would help us to deal with the climate change crisis, the security of the 440 reactors that are today in the world is an issue that has to be resolved at the level of international law, at the level of international organizations. We are not even close to doing so.

CHAPTER 14

Ukraine must restore control over its sovereign territory

Mariia Zolkina

Interview with Ostap Kushnir, published 17 October 2022

> Mariia Zolkina, is the Head of Regional Security and Conflict Studies at the Ilko Kucheriv Democratic Initiatives Foundation and a co-founder of the Kalmius Group. Working as a researcher and public opinion analyst—particularly in the areas of public perception of foreign policy issues, Ukraine's European and Euro-Atlantic prospects, security, and reintegration of temporarily occupied territories—since 2014 she has been providing expert commentary on the political component of the Russia-Ukraine conflict, especially regarding the Donbas, and the socio-political implications of the conflict at both national and international levels. Author of policy papers as well as publications in prominent Ukrainian and international mass media.

Kushnir: Looking at the Russo-Ukrainian war from a wider international perspective, what are, in your opinion, the prevalent narratives about the war that are circulating in the public and professed by experts in countries of the Middle East and North Africa?

Zolkina: There are a few dominant narratives of how the war is portrayed and assessed in the Middle East and North Africa region (MENA). Above all, the war falls in line with the spirit of anti-Americanism that is strongly articulated in the informational space of the region. This spirit draws from the misfortunes that followed the US military operations in the Middle East, especially in Iraq. Russia has tried to make use of anti-American sentiments and reinforce the message all across the MENA that the US is the biggest global evil of the contemporary world and that if the US supports Ukraine, the latter could not be independent. Moreover, Moscow puts special emphasis on the idea that Ukraine is a "puppet government" ruled from Washington. However, the latter narrative is not as successful as Moscow would like. Thus, Ukraine is perceived mainly as a victim of aggression and as a nation that is fighting to defend itself. At the same time, in the MENA the position that Western partners of Ukraine should not be trusted unconditionally by Kyiv is very strong.

The second narrative is that Ukraine and Russia have many similarities. This narrative draws on the lack of understanding of pre-2022 relations between the two states, as well as between Russia and the West. MENA residents have a very poor awareness of Ukraine's having been an independent, truly democratic non-bloc state when Russia invaded in 2014, or that the war had in fact started in 2014, not 2022, that there was no overwhelming majority of separatists (if any at all) in the east of Ukraine, and that the Donbas region and Crimea were annexed illegally. Also, they do not understand clearly the global magnitude of the conflict or the depth of the political split between Ukrainians and Russians. Finally, if anti-Americanism is added to this melange, the confusion in perceptions of ongoing war by the public in the region becomes more understandable.

The third narrative, which is present not only in the MENA but across many Western states, is that Russia cannot be defeated—namely, it is simply impossible to defeat a nuclear state with a large army and unlimited mobilization resources. Therefore, public opinion holds that Russia's retreat, demilitarization, and denuclearization are inconceivable. Oppositely, there is the idea that some concessions on the side of Ukraine are unavoidable. This narrative was quite prevalent among Ukraine's Western partners during the first months of the invasion but started waning with time. In the MENA, it is still popular but is also gradually weakening in light of Russia's many military debacles in Ukraine.

The fourth narrative is more specific to the states of Africa than to the MENA overall—that is, that Russia is a "good" global power that stands against "bad" powers. This narrative draws from the history of support being provided to African governments and nations by the Soviet Union, to which Moscow decided unilaterally that Russia would be the successor. It also draws from Russia's mutually beneficial weapons trade with African countries during recent decades. And of course, Russia has also been investing a lot of money in building its propaganda networks on the continent. As a result, Ukrainian positions and appeals are downplayed, if not ignored. One of the most recent difficulties for Ukraine has been to convince its partners in Africa that the food crisis they are suffering from was artificially created by Moscow by imposing a blockade of Ukraine's seaports. These rational pro-Ukrainian arguments have little credibility in the African information space. Instead, an *a priori* irrational perception of Russia as a counterweight to Africa's former colonizers from the West remains undisputed and, consequentially, works against Ukraine.

Kushnir: What is your opinion of the current Western perception of the Russia-Ukrainian war? What narratives were present in discussions at the Warsaw Security Forum that you attended in early October?

Zolkina: In general, the perception of the Russo-Ukrainian war by Western politicians and experts is aligned with the one in Kyiv: Ukraine has to restore its control over its sovereign territory. However, there are a few differences in perceptions between the eastern and western flanks of the European Union.

Poland, Slovakia, Romania, Czechia, and the Baltic states consider Russia's ongoing war to be a security threat not only for Ukraine but also for themselves. This perception was articulated numerous times during the Security Forum discussions. Also, I encountered neither any willingness of the mentioned states to accept territorial concessions from the Ukrainian side nor any belief that such concessions or other compromises restricting the sovereignty of Ukraine would lead to positive outcomes.

The states from the EU's eastern flank, especially the Baltic countries and Poland, have a very clear vision of how the settlement with Russia should be organized. They advocate for the collapse of the current political regime in Russia. Their representatives declare openly that Russia must be defeated militarily. It must be weakened to the point that any further aggression becomes technically, politically, and economically impossible. Such a straightforward perception of reality, in my opinion, is the one most justified.

Putin's dictatorship would not survive Russia's military defeat. If Ukraine is victorious on the battlefield, this will provide the impetus not only for the removal of Putin from office but most probably for the destabilization and disintegration of Russia. Political elites would reshuffle their spheres of influence, and national republics would probably try to secede from under Moscow's rule and carve up states within their current borders. Ukraine's partners from the EU's eastern flank are in favour of dismantling the Russian Federation. They consider this scenario seriously and weigh the various consequences.

And at the same time, the position of the European Union's western states looks more ambiguous. On the one hand, they provide military, financial, economic, and humanitarian support to Ukraine. They say that Ukraine does not need to seek compromise with Russia. I believe that for the next five to six months Western Europe will not place much pressure on Ukraine, and Kyiv will have a green light to liberate as much of its land as possible. In winter, there will be new variables to consider, but as of now Kyiv is fully supported in its counteroffensive operations.

On the other hand, when it comes to the defeat of Russia and its post-war fate, or the personal downfall of Putin, there is no clarity. They do not want to discuss it. And I would say there is fear and uncertainty on the side of Western Europe that the scenario of Russia's disintegration will eventually take place. I do not see any readiness, neither in political nor in expert communities of these Western states, to seriously consider such a scenario and prepare themselves for it. For me this looks strange, because the EU's western flank purposively avoids alternatives that anticipate radical changes in the Russian regime and territorial composition.

Kushnir: Why should Kyiv care more about Ukraine's informational presence of in the Global South? How can it be boosted?

Zolkina: In the first place, Ukraine needs to develop and strengthen its cultural and political relations with the Global South because these relations are rather poor. Also, the Global South states are members of the United Nations and have a right to vote in the General Assembly. Many procedures in the UN can be completed through the General Assembly instead of the Security Council, where Russia has veto power. Therefore, support within the General Assembly is critical for Ukraine, especially if there is a probability that the resolution condemning Russian misconduct will be vetoed at the highest level.

Thus, Ukraine needs the support of the Global South states when establishing international tribunals or applying other international judicial mechanisms to prosecute Russian war criminals. Such prosecutions and trials, no matter what legal form they take, should be conducted under a legitimate umbrella. And most probably this umbrella will be the UN. Therefore, the more voices Ukraine gains here, the better for the restoration of justice.

Apart from this, Ukraine should countermand the continued and blatant exploitation by Russia of the Global South states as its proxies in international organizations. The food crisis, for instance, was a scheme applied by Russia. The Kremlin intensified its relations with the African Union, played on its fears of food shortages, and made it create pressure on UN structures. In other words, these fifty countries of the African Union knocked on the UN door and declared that they had been starving and dying because of Ukraine.

Ukraine should also start being present in the African informational space, as otherwise Russia will continue dominating it. The task for Ukraine is to make its perspectives known to the local audience and simultaneously counter Russian arguments and propaganda. The tides will not turn for Ukraine automatically, but it should make an appearance in the African informational space and respond to Russian provocations in order to have any hope of counting on anything in the future.

One of the arguments that African politicians and experts use to explain why they do not support Ukraine, or simply abstain from crucial voting in the UN, is that the ongoing war is not of their direct concern. They raise the question of why their countries should care about a European conflict when Europe does not want to hear about their numerous conflicts. If international law was not working in their cases in Africa, then why should they pay attention to Ukraine today? One of the counter-arguments here is that Ukraine is fighting in order to make international law finally work.

Another important instance is the Middle East. Ukraine has yet to discover and benefit from its potential. The Middle Eastern countries claim to be keeping up a political neutrality in the Russo-Ukrainian war. However, that neutrality has an "Arab spirit" to it. For instance, Qatar is considered to be a partner of the US while at the same time the public may still harbour some caution and anti-American moods. Notably, Qatar participates in the Ukraine Defense Contact Group, a voluntary coordination ("Ramstein format") for defensive support of Ukraine. Thus, as a neutral state Qatar sends no military support to Ukraine but its representatives attend Ramstein meetings regularly because they have pretty close relations with the West.

The Middle Eastern states, especially the Gulf area, have money and willingness to invest. Some of them, like Qatar, decided to freeze their investments in Russia. Today, these countries are waiting to see how the war ends and to offer cooperation to whomever becomes the winner. These states share rational economic thinking and pragmatic interests that dictate their foreign policy. When it comes to cooperation with far-away partners, they are looking for benefits.

In three or five years, when Ukraine will be in the process of restoration, it will need investments. And who said that such investments should come only from Western countries?

Kushnir: How do you envision the post-war reconstruction of Ukraine? How hard will it be to deal with Russia's legacy on the occupied territories: atrocities, indoctrination, Russification? What long- and short-lasting effects will this legacy bring and how will it influence reconstruction?

Zolkina: Above all, I want to highlight two aspects of Ukraine's reconstruction. The first is purely economic. It is focused on the creation of domestic and international platforms for investments, on reaching a consensus on reconstruction priorities, as well as on the negotiation of deals between investment partners. This aspect is about answering questions about who is responsible for what, how much money is needed for which specific task, and how to manage tasks and distribute responsibilities between the regional, local, and central authorities in Ukraine. It is a technical process to a large extent.

Moreover, some reconstruction projects are already being implemented. Certainly, local infrastructure and public utilities need to be repaired immediately after they become damaged or worn out. Some infrastructure requires constant maintenance. Therefore, economic reconstruction is also about *ad hoc* ideas and *ad hoc* means, which are parts of bigger projects that will be fully launched after the war, when an agreement on the fate of Russia is achieved.

The second aspect of reconstruction is more about society and its return to normalcy. I am speaking here of people who experienced the occupation, stress from the myriad ways Russia is present in Ukraine, and other violations of their human rights and civil liberties. For these people and their return to normalcy, the duration of the occupation *matters*. Apart from this, much depends on how smoothly Ukraine's army expels Russians from the occupied territories. The less destruction the liberated villages and towns encounter, the faster their residents will be able to restore their pre-war lifestyles. The task for Ukraine's army here is to inflict as little damage as possible. Ukrainians should avoid using artillery or assaulting the property of locals, which is what the Russians did in the western parts of Donetsk and Luhansk oblasts when they first levelled all the population points and then captured the scorched earth.

Of course, Ukraine's cautiousness in liberating occupied territories will take more time. Local residents will have to endure more stress, which will take its psychological toll. However, it is one story when Russians abandon the occupied settlements and the properties and land remain untouched; the price then is not too high for the local residents. Another story is when the liberation follows a fierce battle and is accompanied by massive destruction and numerous deaths among the civilians. Social recovery from such experiences will take much longer. As I see things now, unless a professional and well-trained Russian army miraculously appears to block its way, Ukraine will not stop until all of its territories are liberated.

I do not believe it will take decades for the liberated societies to reconstruct themselves under Ukrainian rule. The implications of occupation will be mainly psychological, they will concern the feelings of the people. Instead, all these artificial attempts to de-Ukrainize, forcibly Russify, or impose the "Russian World" (*russkii mir*) of its own cultural and political understanding will not take root. I do not believe that the legacy of the Russian occupation is something that Ukraine needs to be afraid of—for example, in terms of how to tackle it. Therefore, as just Russia withdraws, many of the problems will disappear on their own. In fact, in the currently occupied territories there has never been high support for Russia or demand for some kind of *russkii mir*.

Kushnir: Do you think that ordinary Russians will ever understand and acknowledge their contribution to the war? Will they ever feel remorse?

Zolkina: Maybe I will sound hawkish in this interview (indeed, perhaps I really am!), but I think that the military defeat of Russia is the only possibility for Russian society to conceivably change their perception of the world. It is very important that they accept some kind of common political responsibility for the war. Because what we see today is an attempt to distance themselves from their political elites and the overall Russian system. Ordinary Russians comfortably claim that they have nothing in common with their elites, or that they cannot influence their elites, or that they are fine with the invasion as long as it does not touch them personally.

Even now, when many of them are being mobilized, forcibly deployed on the battlefield and risking getting killed, Russians are not appealing to their government. It seems that they are failing to establish, or do not want to establish, the cause-and-effect links and understand the situation in which they are. Instead, they often appeal to the Western governments and blame them, for instance, for not issuing humanitarian visas for people escaping from the system. Ordinary Russians perceive themselves as victims. Even the threat of mobilization and heavy losses that their army is suffering are not enough for Russians to understand that they cannot just keep their eyes blind.

And this is why I think that only in the case of Russia's defeat there is a chance for the revision of public opinion. Make no mistake, public opinion has always backed the Kremlin's aggressive foreign policies, be they the policies of Russian emperors, Bolsheviks, or Putin. People are fine with the expansion of their state at the expense of others.

And this is why if public opinion is not shaken by the military defeat on the ground, Russians will not draw any useful conclusions and we will have an even worse situation in future. When I think of a partial defeat of Russia, of some kind of compromise "to save face," I see no room for collective reassessment. Russians will likely feel that they did not win and had to withdraw under pressure. They will feel humiliated and instead of concentrating on their losses they will think of *revanche*. Their logic will be similar to the times between the First and Second Chechen wars, when they fought and failed but felt that the matter had not been finished and that they needed to return. This is why Russians should experience a complete defeat today which will—maybe—destroy nation-wide passive support for their system.

As a public opinion researcher, I have always stressed that if people are not in favour of the aggressive policy of their state but they remain passively loyal, meaning "let it be, as long as it doesn't affect me," then this still counts as support. Because what really matters is when people speak *against*.

CHAPTER 15

Ukrainians forced into fighting an asymmetrical war, getting good at it

Mykola Bielieskov

Interview with Ostap Kushnir, published 25 October 2022

Mykola Bielieskov (MA, international relations, Kyiv Shevchenko National University, 2016) is a Ukrainian military and security expert and senior analyst with the Come Back Alive Foundation [Povernys zhyvym, savelife.in.ua]. In 2016–19 he served as an analyst at the Institute of World Policy Ukrainian NGO. Since October 2019 Bielieskov has been employed at the National Institute for Strategic Studies under the President of Ukraine as an analyst in the Defence Policy Department. He also administers the open-access analytical channel "Armchair General UA" on Telegram.

Kushnir: Since April 2022, when we last spoke, what have been the major changes in Ukraine's warfare tactics? What achievements or failures have they brought?

Bielieskov: Since war is a process of continuous mutual adjustment, Ukraine's defensive tactics have evolved in response to the evolution of Russia's offensive tactics. From mid-April 2022, Russians began to rely disproportionately on heavy artillery bombardment. Thus, the main Ukrainian task became to withstand those continuous attacks and prevent Russians from using them to penetrate the defensive lines or carry out large envelopment of Ukrainian forces in the Donbas. Up to the end of the summer, Ukraine had to prioritize negating Russia's disproportionate reliance on artillery and depleting Russian forces to the fullest possible extent.

Before the West started delivering tube artillery and then multiple-launch rocket systems, Ukrainians relied on their infantry, defensive depth, and numerical superiority, which were combined with an abundance of anti-armour [e.g., Javelin missiles] supplied by the West. The logic was as follows: Ukrainians engineered effective defensive positions beforehand and used them to withstand all incoming barrages of artillery. While the Russians had problems moving with armour and infantry after heavy shelling, the

Ukrainians appeared relatively unscathed and could inflict further damage. It was a continuous game of Russians moving back and forth from Ukrainian positions.

In the Donbas, the situation was threatening north of Izium in the summer. However, the Ukrainian positions did not crumble and all that the Russians could accomplish was frontal assaults and slowly pushing the Ukrainians out from Siverskodonetsk, Lysychansk, and Popasna districts. The frontal assaults came at a high cost. In turn, the Ukrainians won time, saved troops' lives, and prevented the Russians from quickly penetrating their defensive lines, especially on the flanks. Winning time was crucial for Ukraine, as it waited for the US delivery of long-range precision weapons, above all M142 [HIMARS] and guided multiple-launch rocket systems [MRLS or M270].

Having received that delivery, the Ukrainians were able to apply another tactic—an asymmetrical one. In fact, the latter tactic was to a significant degree dictated by Western decisions. Instead of providing Ukraine with considerable numbers of tube artillery so that it could symmetrically match Russia's firepower, the US and other partners opted for multiple-launch systems of longer range and more sophisticated performance. This allowed the Ukrainians to target Russian warehouses and command-and-control nodes in the rear instead of attacking troops on the front line. As we see today, this worked well.

Basically, Ukraine proved right the whole concept under which the M142 and M270 were created: if it is possible to target priority enemy sites in the rear and destroy them, then ultimately the enemy will slow down its advance. We see today that the Russians dispersed too much of their offensive potential. They gained almost no ground when they pushed toward Bakhmut after the capture of Siverskodonetsk and Lysychansk. Bakhmut remains under Ukrainian control despite three months of active fighting on its outskirts. In the other theatres, Russians also ceased any advances. They predominantly switched to defence in the Kharkiv region, Zaporizhia, and Kherson. In a word, Ukraine proved that you do not always need to match the enemy symmetrically in firepower to be effective.

Some time in mid-summer, Russia started to lose initiative. The nature of the war became different compared with its first stage, which was discussed in the previous interview. From midspring until the end of June, it was the enemy who possessed the initiative and Ukraine had to adjust: for instance, if Russia concentrated its forces in the eastern theatres, then Ukraine had to do the same. However, at the beginning of August, when Kyiv publicly promised the counter-offensive in the south, the first signs of Russia's major realignments became apparent. That provided the best evidence that the enemy was losing initiative, and subsequent operations only proved it true.

A very good example of Ukraine using its initiative was the liberation of the Kharkiv region. It was mainly about misleading the enemy: Ukrainians "convinced" the Russian command that they would go on a major offensive in the south, in the Kherson region, yet they performed a classic offensive operation in the northeast. The latter was something that the Russians had not managed to do for months and were forced to rely on slow frontal assaults. Instead the Ukrainians—even while lacking air superiority, means of mobility, armour of different kinds, or artillery—managed to quickly penetrate the enemy's depths of defence and made it flee. Russians were running away so fast that they had no time to destroy warehouses with equipment and ammunition, leaving them to Ukraine. This is how successful the operation in the Kharkiv region was.

In sum, first, in spring Ukraine needed to, and eventually managed to, adjust to the new Russian tactics, which were heavily dependent on artillery, despite the fact that Ukraine lacked effective countering means. Afterwards, in mid-summer, when Ukraine received means of asymmetrical response from the West, it employed them on the battlefield effectively and, little by little, made the Russians switch to defence. Finally, in late summer Ukraine gained the initiative, epitomized in the successful Balakliia-Kupiansk military operation. It took Ukraine only one week to liberate a major swath of its territory.

Kushnir: What do you think about the ambition to liberate the whole of Ukraine in a powerful counter-offensive, as declared by President Zelensky in September? How realistic is it to "come back to where it all started" and de-occupy Crimea? How is the counter-offensive in the south going?

Bielieskov: Firstly, everything President Zelensky said was not on his own whim but a direct reflection of the Ukrainian public mood. This is the crucial thing that the Western audience needs to understand. If one looks at surveys conducted by different sociological agencies, it becomes clear that Ukrainians are not ready for compromises, given their great sacrifices and the destruction they are suffering.

Considering such a public mood, it is natural and logical that since it all started in Crimea, everything needs to end in Crimea. Moreover, Ukrainians learned their lesson from 2014 and 2016, when the negotiated ceasefires and truces did not hold for long, as they could not solve the major source of the problem—which was Russian imperialism. Today, as a legitimate democratic leader Zelensky has no other option but to reflect the general mood of Ukrainian society.

Definitely, Ukraine could liberate Crimea in a sequence of operations; the experience of the Second World War proves that it is possible. However, Ukraine cannot do everything fast, especially given the lack of heavy weaponry. In his address, Zelensky communicated a broad strategic objective: some time in the future, Ukraine will attrit the Russian forces both in offence and defence and will reclaim Crimea in a natural way. Zelensky never provided a strict timeline of de-occupation, he is quite wise and prudent not to do so. He just spoke about what will happen because society wants this to happen.

As for the offensive in the south, it could have developed more swiftly. However, its slow pace is an indirect result of Ukraine's success in the Kharkiv region. Being misled by Ukraine's promises to attack Kherson, Russia concentrated a great amount of forces there, disproportionately to the territory. Today, it is taking more time to break through those forces.

Ukraine announced the start of its counter-offensive in the south at the end of August, but the first major successes came only towards the end of September. Ukraine's gains in the northern part of a Russian salient on the right bank of the Dnipro in Kherson region were the result of a very slow attrition fight. The Ukrainians performed continuous harassing actions on the front by intercepting Russian resupply and damaging reserves. In my opinion, the forthcoming battle in the south will continue being slow, especially after Putin has made it clear that Russia has to retain Kherson at any cost.

As with Crimea, the south of Ukraine will not be liberated in one decisive strike but in a sequence of operations, given the deficit of heavy weaponry and the specificity of the terrain. Ukraine will keep on using long-range attacks to target warehouses, command headquarters, and control hubs, and to disrupt logistics. This tactic of harassing actions should be especially effective in winter, when the logistics will revolve around not only fuel and ammunition but also warm clothes and food. It may happen that by early spring Russia's army will cross the point of no return. The Russian soldiers may become so demoralized that they will just refuse to fight and the front line will disintegrate on its own—as it happened to their army during the First World War.

Kushnir: In September President Putin announced a partial mobilization in Russia, to which President Zelensky responded with Ukraine's application to NATO. Then there was an explosion on the Kerch Strait Bridge in Crimea, followed by mass bombardments of Ukrainian cities and infrastructure. What changes in the nature and dynamics of war do you anticipate following the logic of these events?

Bielieskov: I am not convinced that Russians will be able to sustain the same intensity of strikes that they demonstrated on 10–11 October, especially using cruise missiles. Definitely they will continue using kamikaze UAVs [drones] procured in Iran, but relying on them only has its limits. These drones cannot be used against moving targets, like HIMARS, as they do not feed video to their operators. As for attacks on infrastructure such as electricity generators and distribution facilities, these vehicles will be effectively shot down by Ukraine's air defence systems. Even today, the rate of interception of Russia's drones is comparatively high, 40 to 60 per cent, depending on the situation.

To create a proper level of damage, Russia would need to resort to piloted aviation, which is easier said than done. Ukraine's sky remains contested, and Russians are not likely to gain air superiority, especially when the West made a commitment in early October to strengthen Ukraine's mid-range air defences. Therefore, without piloted aviation Russia will not be able to demolish cities on a wide scale, inflict damage on critical infrastructure, destroy M142 and M270, or significantly reduce the effectiveness of Ukraine's manoeuvring.

Speaking of the other developments, they will largely depend on the Ukrainians' boldness. To date (mid-October), notwithstanding

Putin's nuclear threats, Ukrainians are continuing to wage the war as they deem appropriate. A month ago they masterfully liberated the Kharkiv region. When Putin declared that some parts of Ukraine were being incorporated into Russia and any assaults on them would lead to escalation, Ukrainians brushed these threats aside, regaining Lyman and approaching Svatove.

One of the most important factors influencing the dynamics of the war is the consistency of Western support. Luckily, as of today, Ukraine's partners are no longer buying into Putin's nuclear blackmail. Ukraine was granted two new packages of immediate assistance from the US, which include multiple-launch rocket systems and other priority weapons. The Western message to Ukraine is clear: continue doing your job as you have been doing it before.

Also, it would be very difficult for Russia to employ nuclear weaponry. And here I do not mean technically difficult but psychologically. The majority of the world's governments have placed the responsibility for the 24 February escalation on the Russian side. These governments will not accept its launches of tactical nuclear missiles as legitimate. In turn, Putin seems to be concerned about legitimacy in this context.

To sum up, I think that the nature and dynamics of the war will not change much in the foreseeable future. We will continue experiencing what we have already experienced in the previous month and a half. The Ukrainians will exploit their initiative and do everything they can to inflict damage and attrit the Russian forces. In turn, the Russians will do everything they can to hold their front lines and terrorize civilians. The winter will be a period of relatively moderate fighting, as additional strain on soldiers and equipment will be unavoidable. Therefore, I expect that the major accomplishment for Ukrainians in winter will be to endure it unscathed, regroup, recuperate, and retain as much morale as possible. I do not anticipate that Ukrainians will launch a major offensive operation in low temperatures, but such a development should not be considered totally impossible.

Kushnir: You mentioned in your previous interview that no red lines existed for Putin and that he could resort to nuclear weapons at any time. A few minutes ago, you mentioned that it is psychologically hard to do so. How do you assess the real probability for

Russians to use nuclear weapons against Ukraine in the situation they face now? Is this probability higher or lower than in spring?

Bielieskov: Definitely things are not developing in Putin's or Russia's favour. The probability of Russia employing nuclear weapons increased because the stakes have increased. The war has become a matter of political survival for Putin and his regime.

However, the fact that nothing can be excluded today does not mean that nuclear escalation is inevitable. During one week in September, after Russia lost its battlefield initiative, Putin twice threatened to use nuclear weapons. It would be a grave mistake not to take such threats seriously. At the same time, Ukrainians continued their counter-offensive and no "ultimate response" followed.

I am 100 per cent sure that the governments in Washington and Kyiv have already designed a number of retaliatory measures, depending on what Russia will do. This is a natural thing: to be prepared for any development in times of war, especially for the worst-case scenario. However, we also need to look at the accompanying risks. If Russia employs tactical nukes against a military or civilian target in Ukraine, it is difficult to predict what it might gain.

The whole idea behind possessing nuclear weaponry is to scare opponents off, make them retreat, and agree with the proponent, because the stakes are so high. However, in the case of Ukraine the stakes have been the highest since February, while its choices have been very limited. Ukrainians are already in an existential fight, and I am not sure that the Russian nuclear threats would work, especially considering the damage it suffered from conventional weaponry.

I am inclined to think that the nuclear strike option is actually very risky for Putin and his regime. If it happens, then all the states which adopted favourable or neutral positions toward Russia will revise them. The strike will also be the point of no return for the West. Up to now, the Biden Administration has regularly emphasized that the US policy endgame is not regime change in Russia but a change of Russian foreign policy. However, if the nuclear taboo gets violated, then I think regime change will become a primary goal of US policy. Global security should not be dependent on one person who is, I would say, out of touch with reality.

I think Putin understands these circumstances quite well. Thus, the likely key objectives behind his nuclear threat are: win time to finish additional preparations in Russia and wait for the mobilization to take effect. For their part, Ukrainians have already crossed the threshold of fear. The damage they have suffered in terms of human lives and demolished infrastructure is unprecedented. At this point, it would take a couple of tactical nukes to replicate a similar level of damage.

In conclusion, we should not underestimate the probability of the worst-case scenario. However, personally I am not inclined to take the nuclear rhetoric seriously.

Kushnir: In your opinion, what equipment is of crucial importance for Ukraine today? What does Ukraine expect the West to provide it as soon as possible?

Bielieskov: The list of crucial equipment has not changed much since the outbreak of the invasion. In July, [the Commander-in-Chief of the Armed Forces of Ukraine] Gen Valerii Zaluzhnyi spoke to [the Chairman of the US Joint Chiefs of Staff] Gen Mark Milley, saying that more tube and multiple rocket artillery was needed to fully negate the Russian advantage in firepower. I would say that this remains Ukraine's number one priority up to now. But it is by no means the only one.

Ukraine needs air defence systems. This was made clear in the aftermath of the bombardments on 10–11 October. Yet again, such a need had been clearly communicated by President Zelensky already in February. At that time, Ukraine requested surface-to-air missiles of medium range and fighter jets to defend its skies. Also, as the offensive in the Kharkiv region demonstrated, Ukraine needs specialized transport vehicles. To perform effective offensive operations, any army has to rely on speed, manoeuvrability, protection, and firepower. These all are secured by the main battle tanks, armoured personnel carriers, and infantry fighting vehicles.

Apart from this, Ukraine needs reconnaissance UAVs to arm with artillery and make it more precise, as well as communication equipment to coordinate the whole grouping of forces. Short-range ballistic missiles, the delivery of which remains the major point of disagreement between Kyiv and Washington, are also of pivotal importance.

In a nutshell, to succeed at combined arms warfare, Ukraine has to obtain a specific set of equipment: artillery, means of mobility, communication devices, reconnaissance devices, surface-to-air missiles, jet fighters, anti-ship missiles, ballistic missiles, and others. It is pointless to determine exclusive priorities or cherry-pick one weapon over the other, as all are mutually reinforcing.

Kushnir: What do you think are the lessons that the West has learned from this war?

Bielieskov: The crucial lesson for the West, and I would say the scary one, is the discovery that the rate of consumption of ammunition exceeds the rate of production. In the case of the US, despite them having one of the world's biggest manufacturing capacities, the speed of supply of the missiles to HIMARS is falling short of Ukraine's demand. Besides, Javelins are not in active production, and no new Stingers have been made since 2005. Therefore, the Western states have learned that to wage contemporary wars effectively, they should store tens of thousands of high-precision ammunition items in their stockpiles.

Of course, we may discuss some specific tactical lessons from the Russo-Ukrainian conflict, yet I am not sure that it has really revolutionized warfare. I would say that the Ukrainians have proven true some concepts that had been invented earlier but never properly tested. Such, for instance, was the concept of using precision ammunition with a range of 70-80 kilometres to destroy priority targets in the enemy's rear and slow down its advances. Or the concept of command delegation which made the Ukrainian army more decentralized and therefore more flexible, improvisational, and adaptive compared to the Russian one. However, the Russo-Ukrainian conflict as such has not changed the understanding of modern warfare. Military establishments are not about to reflect on its dynamics and write new books from scratch.

In the end, I can say that the Russo-Ukrainian war will definitely redesign international relations, but not in the aspect of national militaries preparing for combat. Let us be honest: the Russo-Ukrainian war is one of high intensity where two armies with many deficiencies and shortages clash in a rather old-school fashion.

CHAPTER 16

What we are seeing now in Ukrainian society is grassroots Ukrainization

Olexiy Haran

Interview with Ostap Kushnir, published 15 November 2022

Olexiy Haran is a professor of comparative politics at the National University of Kyiv-Mohyla Academy (UKMA). In 1991–93 he was the founding dean of its Faculty of Social Sciences, and since 2002 he has been the founding director of the UKMA School of Policy Analysis. In 2015 he became the research director at the Democratic Initiatives Foundation, a leading Ukrainian think tank. He is a co-editor of *Constructing a Political Nation: Changes in the Attitudes of Ukrainians during the War in the Donbas* (2017), and his latest book (title here transl. from Ukrainian) is *From Brezhnev to Zelensky: Dilemmas of a Ukrainian Political Scientist* (2021).

Kushnir: Having observed Ukrainian and Russian political life for years, did you foresee the Russian invasion of Ukraine on 24 February 2022?

Haran: Before answering this question, I need to address a different one, namely, the Russian invasion in what form? My colleagues and I were aware that Russia had been gathering troops at Ukraine's border, but we did not know if it would launch a full-scale invasion or a series of targeted strikes. The events of 2014 demonstrate that many of Vladimir Putin's moves are hard to anticipate.

From a rational point of view, Putin should have never annexed Crimea or invaded the Donbas. Russia's international and domestic positions were strong before 2014. The state was even accepted as a legitimate member of the G8 and could promote its vision of a multi-polar world. Then, however, Putin decided to annex Crimea and thereby started the isolation of Russia. In my opinion, the annexation of Crimea was counterproductive to Russia's national interests. The West seems to have shared the same belief, as they also got caught by surprise. Actually, very few experts in Ukraine and abroad, including myself, anticipated the annexation of Crimea because it was so irrational.

When the annexation was completed, I guessed that Putin would announce the creation of an "independent" Crimean republic, similar to Transnistria. However, he decided to incorporate Crimea into Russia. By doing so, Putin managed to increase his support among ordinary Russians but lost a lot of respect internationally.

Another irrational move was sending regular troops to the Donbas. Regardless of Russia's official declarations, all careful observers did not doubt that the "little green man" (mercenaries with no military insignia) are Russian soldiers. Ukraine's decision makers and the majority of Western ones did not buy into the Russian game *"nas tam net"* [we are not there] and identified skirmishes in Donbas as an illegal invasion.

My colleagues and I tried to analyze a whole spectrum of scenarios related to the Russian invasion. However, before 24 February 2022, when bombarded with questions about "what will happen" and "how to behave," I used to answer that Putin would likely escalate the situation in the Donbas and try reaching the North Crimean Canal and strategic ports on the Black Sea. I believed that the Kremlin would employ targeted strikes against command posts of the Ukrainian military, nothing more. It seemed irrational for Putin to start a full-scale invasion and try to conquer Kyiv and other major cities in the north. Therefore, I cannot say that I anticipated the invasion in the form that it took.

Kushnir: Was the response of Ukrainian society to the invasion a surprise for you, or did you expect something similar?

Haran: The response of Ukrainian society was predictable. The Democratic Initiatives Foundation conducted polls on the eve of the invasion on what would be the reaction to Russian military aggression if it occurred. The polls demonstrated that almost half of Ukrainians would resist, either directly by joining the army or indirectly by helping the army in any possible way. This is a very high figure. That being said, 1/5 of Ukrainians did not expect the invasion to happen. Additionally, 1/5 responded that they would simply try to survive.

In the first days of the invasion, when the fights for Hostomel airport broke out and diversionary groups appeared north of Kyiv, people got nervous. The worst-case scenarios, such as grinding urban skirmishes and total evacuation of civilians, suddenly became possible. My colleagues encouraged me to leave Kyiv because they thought I was on the Russian detention list. However, I decided to stay. I was publicly advocating the necessity to resist and support the Ukrainian army. In this situation, from a moral point of view I could not leave.

At a certain moment I went to the military registration point to get issued a weapon. However, there stood such a huge line of other volunteers that it was impossible to obtain anything. I tried my luck two times, unsuccessfully. That line — where one heard different languages and saw different ages and social strata — became the best evidence that Ukraine would win. I saw the desire to resist in the flesh, not numbers on paper. Unlike actions taken by people, numbers can be misleading.

In this respect, the reaction of the Western states was exemplary. They recognized the braveness of Ukrainians and praised President Volodymyr Zelensky for not leaving the country, unlike what President Ashraf Ghani of Afghanistan did in August 2021. I remember hearing from my Western colleagues about how bold our President was and how lucky we were to have such a leader. I responded that it was President Zelensky who was lucky, as he could rely on Ukrainian society. In other words, Zelensky was able to behave so boldly exactly because he was backed by a brave society.

It is also important to highlight that President Zelensky is a Russian-speaking Ukrainian of Jewish heritage. In this sense, yes, Ukrainian society is lucky: this sole fact undermined Russian propaganda claims that Ukraine had been "governed by Nazis." In the figure of Zelensky, Western journalists and public opinion acquired a powerful counter-argument to shatter the Russian war narratives.

Since the escalation of this war Zelensky has undergone a major transformation. He fully switched to Ukrainian language for communication and started promoting valiant political objectives that had earlier been voiced only by nationalists. In his example, Zelensky demonstrated how a Ukrainian political nation could be built.

Speaking of political nation and the overall resilience of Ukrainian society, they did not miraculously appear overnight in February 2022. I have observed distinctive nation-building trends in Ukraine since 2014 — not to mention that many of these trends revealed themselves much earlier, in 1991, right after Ukraine declared independence. Both Maidan revolutions as well as the powerful response to the Russian invasion since 2014 simply made these trends more visible to everyone.

Kushnir: In his interview for *Forum*, Mykola Bielieskov highlighted that Ukrainian civil society has often shouldered the burden of functions normally assigned to the state, resorting to informal institutions and practices in order to achieve desired objectives. This could be observed, in particular, in the volunteer movement to support the army, as well as self-mobilization, delivering logistics and communications, assistance to displaced persons, and other activities. To what extent do you agree with the statement that Ukrainian civil society is acting in parallel with state institutions, sometimes demonstrating even greater effectiveness?

Haran: I find this statement rather convincing. If we look into the history of Ukraine, we may encounter abundant evidence that Ukrainians habitually distrusted the state and its authorities, which in most cases were foreign to them. At the same time, Ukrainians eagerly formed networks of cooperation and resistance. The latter networks, be they active or passive, usually targeted and sabotaged political figures who wanted to monopolize power.

In the 1980s the Ukrainian Rukh movement was born in an unwelcome Soviet environment with no Western support. In a way, Rukh became a genuine grassroots movement that addressed the domestic social demand. Afterwards, since 1991, the maturation of Ukrainian civil society has often surpassed corresponding state institutions. In this context, I would like to express my gratitude to Western partners, whose role was also important. Afterwards, the strength of Ukrainian civil society was successfully tested during both Maidan revolutions, in 2005 and 2014.

Post-2014 polls conducted by the Democratic Initiatives Foundation proved that Ukrainians have continued to distrust the authorities. Instead, their highest trust was put in institutions where the social component was the most articulate: the armed forces, church, volunteers (*volontery*, who provide direct army support), and civil society organizations.

The most recent poll conducted by the Democratic Initiatives Foundation together with the Razumkov Centre (August 2022) also proved the validity of the earlier trends. The institutions with the highest balance of trust and distrust were the armed forces (91 per cent), national guard (81 per cent), volunteer organizations (77 per cent), volunteer detachments (73 per cent), and finally the President of Ukraine (71 per cent). Instead, the balance of trust was negative for the strictly governing institutions: the government (–7 per cent), the parliament (–11 per cent), the courts (–46 per cent), and finally the political parties (–55 per cent).

Kushnir: In light of the war needs, the current government restricted the rights and freedoms of citizens and introduced many monopolies, in particular on the dissemination of information in the media. Will the government be tempted to keep these restrictions and monopolies after the war?

Haran: Indeed, there are restrictions in war-time Ukraine. We live in a time of martial law. However, I would like to stress that the level of freedom of speech remains extremely high. This is a very uncommon practice under martial law.

The opposition's television channels continue to function. There are some challenges in reaching them, but if citizens of Ukraine want to hear their messages, they can. Apart from this, the Internet media and newspapers exist for all people who want to be active in politics or simply ascertain different perspectives. These media and newspapers offer a plurality of views, openly criticizing authorities and discussing the effectiveness of government actions.

I also consider it a positive development that the opposition supported the government and voted for martial law in February 2022. A tacit agreement is in place between the government and the opposition that the latter will not excessively criticize the former in wartime. Considering the situation, this looks like a reasonable and healthy compromise.

When speaking to Ukrainian media, I follow a simple rule: never criticize military operations, actions, Ukrainian command, or military leadership. Today is not the best time and circumstances for this. However, I do not feel restrained, and I also deem it justifiable to criticize certain political occurrences. I think it is important to talk about non-war-related misconduct even during a war. Ukrainians are fighting not only for the freedom and restoration of their territorial integrity today but for a new and prosperous country.

Moreover, I want to praise the decision of the EU to grant candidate status to Ukraine. While this status may not turn into full-fledged membership for a long time, the very fact of its granting serves as a powerful tool for domestic transformation. To illustrate, let us look at the dynamics of the appointment of Director of the National Anti-Corruption Bureau. For several months, the appointing commission could not meet because some of its members were allegedly ill. However, after the government started preparations to fulfill the EU's candidacy criteria, suddenly all the members of the commission recovered, the meeting took place, and the Anti-Corruption Prosecutor got appointed—the same one who earlier had won in transparent elections. I can only imagine how much the Office of the President was against such an appointment, but it finally had to agree to the demands put forward by the Ukrainian civil society and the EU.

Therefore, I believe that the doubled domestic and international pressure on Ukraine's government will continue. Monopolization of power is hardly possible. I am sure that Ukraine will remain democratic after the victory.

Kushnir: Religion, language, identity, regional self-identification—to what extent did these factors fade, or on the contrary, became more pronounced in Ukrainian society during the war?

Haran: We are experiencing a consolidation of Ukrainians today to an extent that has never existed before. Having said that, I would like to return to my thesis that the consolidating trend first appeared in 1991. Afterwards, it was proven true and strengthened in the events of 2004, 2014, and 2022.

What we are seeing now in Ukrainian society is grassroots Ukrainization—at least, this is how I define it. National values are not imposed by the government or political elites, but rather they are spread within and between people. To illustrate, let us take decommunization. There were attempts to get rid of the Soviet legacy under President Viktor Yushchenko, in the late 2000s. However, these attempts were not successful. On the contrary, the decommunization and Leninopad after 2014 were incomparably more effective as the demand came from below. Therefore, it was easier for the government to conduct an official campaign against the Soviet legacy because the people supported it.

The consolidation of Ukrainians that we see today has deep roots. It reflects the existential necessities of society. Even before February 2022, the majority of Ukrainians agreed that there should be one official language. Every public figure was supposed to know and actively use Ukrainian in communication. Basically, a language consensus in Ukrainian society was successfully developed by the end of the third decade of the state's existence.

I used to visit the front lines as a volunteer and have been doing it regularly since 2014. Around half of the Ukrainian army, both soldiers and their command, spoke Russian in my presence. At the same time, they did their best to master the Ukrainian language and switch to it on every occasion. The trend was apparent.

Also, I do not see a problem with the people who continue speaking Russian in Ukraine's south or east, even in Kyiv. It often happens that they use the Russian language and practice Russian culture in their private circles. As for the public sphere, they reveal a deep understanding of the importance and role of the Ukrainian language and culture. This trend will only be strengthening in the future.

Our poll from August 2022 demonstrates that Ukrainians, regardless of their backgrounds, are proud of their citizenship, which is a healthy indicator of the formation of a political nation. They also believe in Ukraine's victory. An interesting observation is that Ukrainians do not support concessions to Russia to end the war. For its part, the Western public still perceives concessions as something inevitable. I was asked many times by foreign experts when Ukrainians would finally get tired of the resistance and agree to trade a part of their land for peace. However, they did not want to. For me, it looks even strange that the polls did not indicate fatigue. But indeed Ukrainians looked angry, not tired.

Having said that, the mentioned consolidation does not come without challenges. In most regions, when we asked respondents for their attitudes toward the renaming of toponyms that reflect Russian or Soviet legacy [e.g. streets, settlements — Ed.], the reaction was positive. However, only 27 per cent of respondents in the south supported the renaming while 42 per cent spoke against it. This observation is disturbing and shows that much remains to be done in order to overcome the remnants of colonial influence in the south. I am very curious to see what happens to the monument of Empress Catherine II in Odesa. My guess is that sooner or later it will be demolished.

Finally, there is the attitude to the Russian Orthodox Church of the Moscow Patriarchate. Our August 2022 poll enquired respondents to choose one of two options: "Actions of Moscow Patriarchate rather encourage Russian aggression" or "Actions of Moscow Patriarchate rather help to defend Ukraine." 52 per cent chose the former option while only 11 per cent chose the latter. 37 per cent of respondents answered "hard to say" or disagreed with both options. However, only 26 per cent in the south and 33 per cent in the east blamed the Moscow Patriarchate for encouraging Russian aggression. These percentages are still higher than those who believe in the help of the Moscow Patriarchate to defend Ukraine, but the largest category of respondents remained in-between or undecided.

When we deal with the functioning of the Moscow Patriarchate in the context of national unity, I believe that it is crucial to have a "wave from below," a grassroots demand for change. Religious convictions are very hard to influence, as they often rely on well-established conservative structures on the ground. Therefore, it will be very difficult to have a swift decision on the fate of the Moscow Patriarchate. And here I think that the state should abandon so called neutrality, become proactive, and lead reforms especially when there it is known that many hierarchs of this church supported the aggressor.

Kushnir: Do you agree with the statement that Russia invaded Ukraine because the latter became an existentially dangerous "Anti-Russia"? To what extent is the current war a war of values?

Haran: I believe that Ukraine has never been "Anti-Russia." Even today, in the conditions of a full-scale invasion, the attitude toward the Russian culture is sceptical or even negative, but not vicious or utterly intolerant. Ukraine is a democratic country. That being said, it may become "Anti-Russia" after the gravity of crimes and atrocities that Russians committed on its lands is fully acknowledged.

As I mentioned, more and more people in Ukraine will switch from Russian to the Ukrainian language and culture. However, there will never be 100 per cent of switches. Many people will continue practising Russian culture, speak Russian, and even attend churches of the Moscow Patriarchate, especially if the latter re-brands itself.

When we speak about ethnic Russians in Ukraine, I believe, there are no major problems with their safety and liberties. They are not existentially threatened. Ethnic Russians are also legitimate parts of the Ukrainian political nation. In this sense, again, Ukraine has never been "Anti-Russia."

However, the overall public mood changed significantly after February 2022. Ukrainians became suspicious of everything which originates within the Russian domain. I believe this feeling of suspicion is justified. It can be observed not only in Ukraine but in many Western societies too.

I also agree that Russia and Ukraine are fighting a war of values today. We have a clash between democracy and authoritarianism or even totalitarianism.

Kushnir: How do you see Ukrainian-Russian relations after the war?

Haran: Unless Russia changes its imperial approach to Ukraine, there will be no normal relations. When we ask Ukrainians in polls about what they understand as "victory," 20 per cent say that it is the defeat of the Russian army accompanied by the disintegration of the Russian Federation. The narratives about the necessity for Russia to split into smaller parts are being promoted even by some of Ukraine's political elites.

I strongly believe that only the ethnic minorities in Russia should decide on their belonging to the Russian Federation. In turn, all Russian citizens should decide together on the nature of the federation moving forward. Therefore, Ukrainian officials should not be expressing their opinions on the disintegration of Russia. It is not their business to bring such opinions to the public. Excessive expostulation on this topic may be counterproductive.

The business of Ukraine today is to make Russia stop being an imperialist state. Only this scenario will allow for the gradual restoration of good-neighbourly relations.

Kushnir: Do you think that Western countries and Western societies have understood Ukraine better since 24 February 2022?

Haran: I think they have. Ursula von der Leyen, the President of the European Commission, for instance, stated that "Ukraine is one of us." The change of position of Frank-Walter Steinmeier, the president of Germany, to a more pro-Ukrainian one was also eloquent. He openly recognized his mistakes in mistreating Ukraine and appeasing Russia in a brave and self-critical move.

I want to emphasize again that Moscow's actions and policies in the West were totally counterproductive for Russia. The image of the state suffered a lot. However, there still remain many Putin-understanders, or *Putin-Verstehers*, in the West. They have eventually agreed today that Ukraine is waging a just war, they even subtly support Ukraine, but nevertheless advocate for a compromise with Russia which may, for instance, reside in recognizing the annexation of Crimea. For me, this looks like an appeasement policy again. This looks like flirting with Adolf Hitler.

There are also many experts who criticize Ukraine for not being willing to negotiate peace, Minsk agreements, or carry a part of the responsibility for escalation. There also are those who portray Ukraine as a corrupted and failed state that will eventually fall to Russia. I am not sure that we should treat comments from such Western experts seriously. Some of them indeed change their positions with time, but very few recognize their mistakes.

Volodymyr Kulyk actually raised the issue of the absence of repentance coming from Western experts and decision-makers for their mistaken approach. Since 2014 they have been blaming Ukraine, not Russia, for the bloodshed. In the best case, they put equal responsibility on both belligerents. Do they recognize their own responsibility?

To sum up: Unfortunately, Western media and experts continue to support Russian narratives in many cases. Fortunately, the truth is on our side. Zelensky's speeches and media addresses sound so powerful exactly because he speaks the truth.

Kushnir: In her interview last month, Mariia Zolkina stated that Western decision-makers and experts avoided discussing the possible disintegration of Russia if Putin loses the war. They regard the scenario of disintegration with fear. In your opinion, has something changed in a month?

Haran: As I have mentioned above, Ukraine should recognize and support movements in Russia that speak against political oppression, but it is not Ukraine's business to decide on the future structure of Russia.

Regarding the perceptions of the West, I believe that we can draw parallels to what happened in the 1990s. The West was afraid of the collapse of the Soviet Union, yet it happened. Similarly, the West is afraid of the disintegration of Russia and, if it happens, that the situation in the whole world may become unstable.

However, I think that all sides should seriously analyze the potential scenario of Russia's disintegration today. Whether they like it or not, such a prospect should not be rejected by responsible decision-makers and experts. The case of the Soviet Union provides the best evidence for the necessity of getting ready for unpredictable events, even if the probability of these events seems to be low.

CHAPTER 17

I hope that Ukrainians will encourage new voices in Poland

Elżbieta Kwiecińska

Interview with Ostap Kushnir, published 23 November 2022

Elżbieta Kwiecińska (PhD, European University Institute, Florence, Italy, 2021) is a historian and social scientist. Right after the beginning of Russian full-scale invasion against Ukraine, she turned her flat in Warsaw into a humanitarian aid hub. Since 2022 she has been a mentor to Ukrainian students and an instructor at the Invisible University for Ukraine (Central European University, Budapest/Vienna). From June 2022 to September 2023 she recorded oral testimonies with Ukrainian refugees for the project "24.02.2024, 5 am: Testimonies from the War" at the Institute of Philosophy and Sociology of the Academy of Sciences of Poland.

Kushnir: How has pro-Ukrainian volunteer activity evolved in Poland since February 2022? What have been your personal observations and experiences?

Kwiecińska: I would need to share my observations from two perspectives: as an actor and as an expert.

As an actor, my pro-Ukrainian volunteering effort evolved from multi-tasking 24 hours a day into a more focused and structured activity. From the first days of the Russian invasion, I was engaged in fundraising, purchasing protective equipment for Ukrainian soldiers (often in weird places across Poland), escorting shipments from Western Europe and the US to Ukraine, storing army equipment in my flat or my mom's basement, hosting displaced people in my flat, and serving as a translator from Polish or English into Ukrainian or Russian. As you can imagine, at a certain point I became very exhausted.

An interesting experience for me as well as for many other Poles was using and expanding our personal networks to help Ukrainians. For instance, I do not drive, so I had to ask my friends or my mom to transport migrants and refugees from one point to another. If there was no room in my flat to shelter people, I had to ask someone else. Some Poles made tea and sandwiches, some purchased clothes and food, some met Ukrainians arriving in groups by train, and some helped them to adapt to a new location. Impressive numbers of Poles united their efforts and volunteered from February till May or June.

In May my activities began to narrow down. I stopped doing everything. Many of my friends also decided to specialize in specific tasks. For instance, Oleksii Rudenko, who once stayed under my roof, created his NGO Stand with Ukraine and started supplying the Ukrainian army with protective equipment — hundreds of items.

For three months I worked at an NGO and translated guidelines for Ukrainians about how to arrange their lives in Poland. I tried to help different kinds of people in need: migrants with Roma heritage, representatives of the LGBTQ+ communities, moms with kids, and others. They urgently required information on how to get enrolled in schools or universities, apply for medical assistance, and obtain state registration or financial support from the government.

As an expert, I see the growing interest in studying the phenomenon of the Russo-Ukrainian war, and specifically its human component, in academia. Here, it is worth mentioning the project "Testimonies from the War" to which I contribute. The project unites researchers from the Polish Academy of Sciences, Lviv Center for Urban History, Luxembourg Centre for Contemporary and Digital History, the University of St. Andrew in Scotland, and other institutions. We use our language and scholarly skills to create an oral history archive about Ukrainians who have fled the war to Poland.

We started doing interviews in Warsaw but are gradually moving to smaller cities and working-class neighbourhoods in order to reach a wider audience. We hope our interviews will help future researchers to get a better insight into the impact of war on human lives.

In turn, Poland's universities and the government also started providing more targeted and organized support to the people from Ukraine. A few months ago, I became a lecturer in the Faculty of History at the University of Warsaw. I teach the history of Ukraine for Poles in Polish and Ukrainian-Polish history for Ukrainian refugee students in Ukrainian. My students fleeing the war are of different ages and backgrounds: from 16-year-old teenagers to experienced individuals, predominantly women, in their 50s. Tuition fees for academic degrees at Polish public universities have been waived for Ukrainians. In a way, everyone who wants to start a new life in Poland is offered an attractive opportunity to get a new education. Moreover, Ukrainians receive free classes in the Polish language for foreigners, and they can apply for scholarships. They enjoy equal rights with Polish students.

Offering classes in Ukrainian by my department became a significant milestone, if not a pivotal turn for the University of Warsaw, which is the most prominent university in the country. Last year, before the invasion this would have been hardly conceivable: the only foreign language of instruction was English.

In the long run, I hope that the offer targeted at Ukrainians will help to raise new voices in Poland — ones that do not belong to the ethnic majority. I also hope that after their graduation, my students will acquire cultural awareness and social tools to participate actively in Polish public life.

Finally, I think it is worth mentioning the importance of (so-called) intercultural school mentors, who are employed to support migrant children. These people are often themselves of Ukrainian heritage, who have already lived in Poland for some time and know the language. But there are many Poles among them, too. In one of the primary schools in Warsaw, where my mother works as a psychologist, they organize hours of group therapy for Ukrainian kids. Although there is a language barrier, they use art therapy and music therapy to establish contact.

Kushnir: In the summer, in his article for *Forum* Andrzej Szeptycki mentioned the growing "Ukraine fatigue" in Poland. Patrice McMahon raised a similar issue in *The Conversation*. Will Poland exhaust its support to Ukrainians any time soon?

Kwiecińska: The fatigue exists; we all are humans, and we all get tired. Also, unlike many countries to its west, Poland has never had well-functioning and centralized mechanisms to accommodate waves of migrants. It is no surprise that Polish civil society has gotten tired, as it carries on its shoulders many functions of the state.

When migrants or refugees arrive in, for instance, Germany or the UK, they know where to go and which steps to take. In Poland the migrants often feel lost. The state's provision of care and services is not coordinated, and that puts additional strain on local volunteers.

Notably, the other thing is that political support for Ukraine has remained invariably strong since 1989. All the major political forces in Poland wish to have a reliable neighbour to the east and develop mutually beneficial relations. In light of today's war, there is no doubt that Poland will help Ukraine with arms and tanks, as well as promote Ukraine's interests internationally.

A dangerous trend that I have observed is the activation of far-rights who disagree with the state's policy of accepting Ukrainians and try to capitalize on social fatigue. They purposely nurture anti-Ukrainian attitudes, as they did against migrants from Syria and Afghanistan. They want to increase their public support, which is relatively low today, by attacking Ukrainians. Luckily, the far-rights have not been successful so far.

Another dangerous trend is that the government has lagged in creating centralized mechanisms and policies to accommodate Ukrainians. The most crucial issue where the state needs to step up is housing. The dearth of places for Ukrainians to stay is tremendous. For instance, the population of the city of Rzeszów grew by 50 per cent in the last half-year. In Warsaw, hundreds of thousands of arriving migrants and refugees have seriously undermined the real estate market: even before February 2022 it was hard for Poles to find an affordable residence in the capital, but now it is almost impossible. Therefore, I think the state should loosen the real estate tension and prioritize the provision of shelter to Ukrainians, especially in big cities.

One more domain where the state should step up is the creation of language classes for Ukrainians. For the smooth integration of a sizable wave of migrants into Polish society, these migrants must know how to communicate. Mastering the language opens doors to employment, education, and comfortable living conditions in a new place.

Kushnir: Why do you think Poland supports Ukraine so much?

Kwiecińska: Above all, Poland seems to perceive Ukraine as its *alter ego*. Poles look at Ukrainians and see themselves from the past. Massive armed revolutions against Russian rule started in Poland already in the 19th century. The revolutionaries failed, but they took the risk and demonstrated courage. Then there was a war in the 1920s, a more successful one. On the level of cultural memory, Poles understand what is going on in Ukraine today and why Ukrainians have chosen to fight.

Another reason behind the support of Ukrainians is the human factor. Poles simply sympathize with people who are suffering, being displaced, or have lost their property. Not to mention that many Polish families have histories of surviving the Second World War with its destruction and atrocities. Poles understand what it means to live in utterly destitute conditions caused by Russia.

Kushnir: Considering the ongoing adaptation processes and support from the government and civil society, how do you see the future of Ukrainian migrants in Poland? In your opinion, how many of them will declare Poland to be their new homeland and decline to return to Ukraine after the war?

Kwiecińska: Today, with the war being far from over, I note that some Ukrainians have taken a courageous decision and returned home. After the fighting ends, some of the Ukrainian shelter-seekers will probably leave Poland. That being said, many of them will indeed remain.

For Ukrainians to settle permanently in Poland, they need to change the perception of their new surroundings from "shelter" to "home." They came here because they wanted to feel safe and that safety was granted by the Polish state and society. Today, their feelings toward Poland are framed by how much the state and society agree to integrate them. Ukrainians could become active members of their new communities if Poles agree to treat them that way.

The most recent challenge for many Poles resides in their unpreparedness to look at Ukrainians as equals. At this moment, the majority of Ukrainians are performing low-qualified jobs and are considered a cheap labour force. With this, Poles have no issues. However, as just a deeper social integration starts, the reaction of the Poles may be less favourable. This will likely be the end of Poland as a state with a homogeneous society. Not all Poles will find it normal to listen to non-Polish voices. To this, we should add and counter the possible irritation when Ukrainians will use their right to find a decent job, get an education, or pursue their desires and dreams in Poland.

Another challenge that I see for Ukrainians is their experience of living in a bilingual society. Polish society has been formed as monolingual. Therefore, it may be hard for ordinary Poles to feel comfortable in a situation where one person speaks in one language and the other answers differently. In turn, many Ukrainians came to Poland believing that they would be able to speak Ukrainian and Poles would respond in Polish. Communication in Poland does not work that way. This leaves Ukrainians disappointed — especially those Russian speakers who used to think that Russian was a universal language and should be comprehended in Poland.

Therefore, if Ukrainians want to integrate, they will need to learn the language. Those Ukrainians who have serious plans for Poland have already started doing so. Those who are not ready to embrace that effort will probably return to Ukraine given the opportunity. The stress from migration can be bigger in their case than the stress caused by missiles.

Kushnir: From your perspective, will the majority of Ukrainians who currently are in Poland return to Ukraine or decide to stay?

Kwiecińska: I do not know. I wish them to stay. The contribution of Ukrainians to Polish society has been and will continue to be constructive. Moreover, I think it is necessary to make Polish society more diverse and open. At the same time, I am afraid that Ukrainians will leave Poland if they find it hard to integrate, if they are not helped with at least accommodation and language classes.

Kushnir: There is a growing belief among academia that the ongoing war is the painful, yet pivotal process of Ukraine's decolonization. Do you agree with this belief?

Kwiecińska: Yes, I do agree. Ukrainians took a step toward decolonization and now must endure the consequences. I am not sure there could be a less painful way, considering the genocidal politics of Russia, but I am sure that Ukraine will succeed. It is not only the army that is battling the former colonizer but the whole society.

I agree that the human cost of Ukraine's decolonization is very high, but I doubt that surrender could be a better option. I also agree with those experts who claim that to have the conflict resolved quickly the West needs to send more armour to Ukraine and make Russia withdraw its army.

Russia must be defeated, as otherwise we will see new atrocities, similar to those in Mariupol, Kherson, and Bucha. Civilians should not be tortured and killed because of their national loyalty. Ukrainian kids should not be kidnapped for forcible deportation and identity reprogramming. Those who have lived through twentieth-century history may experience a clear *déjà vu* today. To stop it, Ukraine must win this war.

As a historian, I want to emphasize that decolonization is a process that happens in our minds. Thus, all stakeholders should stop perceiving Central Europe as a playground between the West and Russia. People from the region have desires and needs, and such states as Ukraine have a right to choose which side to join. The US-dominated West is not a perfect place, but still, it should be the right and liberty of Ukrainians to decide if they want to part with it.

Kushnir: What circumstances should be in place to have the process of Russia's decolonization started? What kind of decolonization will it be? What will be its domestic and international outcomes?

Kwiecińska: That is a tricky question, as it concerns predictions that have always been hard to get absolutely right. Many experts [such as Olexiy Haran—*Ed.*] believed that Russia would not launch a full-scale invasion in February 2022 as it would be irrational to do so. Yet, the invasion was launched.

I wish for places such as Buryatia or Tatarstan to stop being subordinated to Moscow. However, such a development requires many other preconditions to take place. Above all, Russia must lose against Ukraine. If it happens, then Moscow's domestic grip will weaken and that may encourage Russia's provinces to rebel. There is a probability that Moscow has squandered so much of its power that claiming independence will become a formality. Another probability, a more troubling one, is that domestic conflicts and civil wars will erupt after the Russian Federation's provinces claim independence, vying for control over natural resources.

Western states should weigh all scenarios in getting ready for decolonization inside Russia; and if it takes place, make it as painless as possible. This means that today, as I see it, they should support liberal forces within Russia, the ones fighting corruption and advocating the rule of law. However, the West should also be aware that many Russian liberals find nothing wrong in shouting "*Krym nash*" [Crimea is ours] and supporting specific points from the imperialist agenda. It is important for the West to research whom to collaborate with.

One thing is clear to me: for domestic decolonization to start, Russia must lose the war. The death of President Putin, if such a miracle happens, will not change much in the nature of the regime. Putin's friends or aides will easily seize power and the continuity of governance will prevail. Moreover, their attitude toward Ukraine will likely remain the same.

The political core in Moscow needs to weaken for Russian Federation's provinces to become independent.

Kushnir: The same as Aliaksei Kazharski, you are known to be a consistent critic of the academic culture of Westsplaining. In your opinion, what are the major misconceptions that Western wannabe analysts put forward?

Kwiecińska: The primary misconception that the Westsplainers put forward is that Ukraine is a failed state. They argue that Ukraine is full of divisions, particularly between its eastern and western parts, which makes the effective rule of a single government impossible. However, I think that there is nothing wrong with having divisions. Every country has them. In Poland, for instance, a division runs between a more liberal west and a more conservative, even right-wing east. In Italy, there is a division between north and south; the way people speak in both parts is different. Yet somehow, no one is using Polish or Italian internal differences to conquer those countries.

It is normal to have diversity within one state. Moreover, it is the desire to achieve homogeneity that leads to the construction of a totalitarian state.

Another thing that the Westsplainers get wrong is Ukrainian nationalism and so-called Russophobia. It is unwise to claim that such political convictions do not exist in Ukraine. However, they are of a similar nature as the much less criticized Russian nationalism and Ukrainophobia in Russia. In times of war, making an argument that nationalist convictions are the root of the problem for Ukraine is nothing but victim blaming.

The Westsplainers often perceive Central Europe, and specifically Ukraine, as a playground between global powers. They deny the region a distinct identity. The whole of Central Europe appears to them as a uniform space squeezed between Germany and Russia.

Whenever the regional states take any side – for instance, to follow the US lead – the Westsplainers interpret this as an imposed move, not a sovereign choice.

Finally, the Westsplainers are very keen to project their post-nationalist conceptions on Ukraine and the region. It is very nice to sit in Berlin or in Florence, drink coffee, and philosophize in different languages on how Central European states should look and how to proceed with reconciliation. However, in Ukraine you may be killed because you are Ukrainian. This is where the post-nationalist utopia ends.

The war in Ukraine today resembles the one from the 19th century, when Europe was torn with national struggles and clashes for independence. It sometimes is hard for the Westsplainers as well as the multicultural societies they represent to understand why people in Ukraine want to fight for their nation-state instead of fostering the spirit of co-existence with Russians. They think that genuine freedom and security can be achieved only within the borders of a sovereign state an outdated one.

Kushnir: Has there been any improvement in the quality of Westsplaining recently?

Kwiecińska: Yes, I think that the Westsplainers made some progress. Many of them discovered Ukraine better. Overall, Central Europe started making more sense to them. Many revised their perception of the region as a playground.

That being said, those Westsplainers who were not ready to acknowledge their previous misconceptions became attached to them even more. They made Ukraine-blaming a part of the professional political agenda. They started proudly presenting themselves as non-mainstream voices. Here it is important to stress that such Westsplainers are not bewildered victims of Russian propaganda but experts who have made their educated choice to support the Russian position. We should not deny their agency but rather need to take them seriously.

CHAPTER 18

After Russia's departure from great power status, the world will once again become bi-polar

Alexander Motyl

Interview with Oleksandr Pankieiev and Ostap Kushnir, published 28 November 2022

> Alexander J. Motyl (PhD, Columbia University, 1984) is a professor of political science at Rutgers University-Newark, writer, and painter. A special-ist on Ukraine, Russia, and the USSR, among his recent books are *National Questions* (2022), *Ukraine vs. Russia: Revolution, Democracy, and War* (2017), *Imperial Ends: The Decay, Collapse, and Revival of Empires* (2001), and *Dilemmas of Independence: Ukraine after Totalitarianism* (1993); the edited volume *The Encyclopedia of Nationalism* (2000); and co-edited *The Holodomor Reader: A Sourcebook on the Famine of 1932–1933 in Ukraine* (2012). According to Academic Influence, Motyl was ranked among the "Top Influential Political Scientists 2010-20."

Pankieiev: Many experts predicted that Russia's defeat in Kherson would bring an end to Putin's regime. Kherson was liberated one week ago. Do you think we have crossed that point of no return in Russia's war against Ukraine, or do we need to watch for other signs?

Motyl: Well, it seems to me that Putin has already lost. So, it's important to keep in mind that he's been defeated, and Russia has been defeated. The war isn't over yet. But thus far, Russia has lost, as has Putin.

So, my first point would be to emphasize that I have been fairly certain about Putin's not surviving the war since about March or April. That is not to say I predicted the war; quite the contrary, I did not. But it seemed to me that starting a war would be a disaster for Russia, and I thought that for this reason Putin wouldn't do it. Well, he did, and it did turn out to be a disaster — a strategic miscalculation on an enormous scale. It would be hard to overestimate the gross idiocy of Putin in starting this kind of war.

And now, with every day, as the occupied territories are progressively being liberated, as discontent within the Russian army grows, as the number of Russian soldiers killed grows, as discontent and opposition even within Russia itself grows, albeit slowly, as increasingly larger numbers of people affiliated with the oligarchs, political or economic, are persuaded that Russia can't win—as all of these factors are multiplying, as Ukraine is not only resisting but liberating, as the West remains committed to helping Ukraine—Putin's own position is getting progressively weaker and weaker; his legitimacy is eroding, and his popularity is declining.

Inasmuch as his legitimacy is eroding, so too is the stability of the fascist system he constructed, within which he is the core—the linchpin. So too, that system is becoming progressively weaker, which means that Putin's weakness will have an impact on the stability of the system. And the fascist system's progressive weakness will have an impact on the Russian Federation's stability. Will a systemic crisis happen tomorrow? I don't know, it could. It's likely to happen within the next six months to a year, perhaps sooner.

Putin's departure becomes more and more likely. A year ago, the likelihood of Putin's departure was tiny. Today it has become significantly larger. But we can't predict how much larger; there are just too many imponderables.

Pankieiev: Apart from Putin and his aides in the Kremlin, how do you see the motivation for the collective ordinary Russians to support the invasion and commit war crimes in Ukraine?

Motyl: Well, "collective" potentially refers to two sets of individuals. One is the population in general, which has in fact absorbed many of the values propagated by the Putin regime for the last twenty years. I've written about this, and in one of my essays I've even used the term "collective Putin." Essentially, it's a stand-in for "political culture"—namely, the Russian political culture that *has been, is,* and because of Putin has likely *become even more* authoritarian, even less democratic than it normally would have been.

But there are differentiations. The "collective Putin" is significantly weaker in Moscow and St. Petersburg than in the provinces. So, if there is going to be trouble, if people are going to take to the streets, if people are going to engage in demonstrations or other kinds of actions, it's likely to take place in the big cities, because that is where revolutions, uprisings, and insurrections always take place. So, there won't be a revolution in Omsk or Tomsk, but there very well could be one in Moscow or St. Petersburg. Again—if Putin leaves, if there is disarray, if there is conflict, and so on.

Now, the second category to which the term "collective Putin" could apply would be the political and economic elites. And again, we see that whereas a year or two ago these elites solidly—almost uniformly—supported Putin, nowadays serious cracks have emerged. A recent study published by *Meduza* shows that many economic and political elites are persuaded that the war is lost. We know from insiders that there's fragmentation within the political elite. People are dissatisfied with Putin. We know that the General Staff and FSB are at loggerheads as well.

Thus, it's not clear that there is today a "collective Putin" within the elites. I'm not even sure that his closest associates, people like Naryshkin and Lavrov, are all that committed to Putin. If given the opportunity to throw him to the wolves and save themselves, I do not doubt that they would do just that. They are not ideologically committed to him; they're not personally committed to him. And they would easily betray him if and when the need for that to happen arose.

We often hear: "Well, what happens if Putin goes, won't things get worse?" What we know from Russian history, what we know from Soviet history, and what we know from comparative studies is that in the immediate aftermath of a dictator's departure—for whichever reason or reasons—one of two consequences is very likely. The first is a power struggle, and that makes perfect sense because the dictator has *defined the political system*. This is especially so with Putin: he is the core of that system. If and when he goes, that system will be without its core, and it could easily implode.

It won't be obvious to any of us who the successor will be, and it won't be obvious to the Russians, either. During a power struggle, however, the attention that is paid to Ukraine will automatically decline, and the war will become somewhat less important.

Furthermore, based on historical experience the winner of such a power struggle is usually a little more committed to openness, democracy, and some kind of liberalism. I want to underline "some kind"—we're not talking about pure democracy, pure liberalism, but rather a bit more. We saw that with the "Khrushchev Thaw" following Stalin and with Gorbachev's glasnost and perestroika following Brezhnev. And it makes sense for the immediate successor to try to be different from the predecessor. Because a transition is an ideal opportunity to blame the problems on the person who preceded you. Because someone will have to take the blame for Russia's war on Ukraine; someone will have to take the blame for 100,000 or 200,000 dead Russians. Someone will have to take the blame for the sanctions, for the continuing collapse of the economy. And who better to take the blame than your predecessor?

But for that to work, you need to be able to position yourself as someone who is different, who is more democratic, more liberal, who is promising a new Russia, a "new deal," a "new economic program." So, I am somewhat optimistic that in the aftermath of Putin's departure there will be a good chance that the winner or winners of the power struggle will be people who are more normal, so to speak.

Pankieiev: Some speak about the "collective Putin" and that removing him from power would not bring any significant changes but could even worsen the situation in Russia. What are your thoughts about it? How will Russia after Putin look?

Motyl: Very many Russians have absorbed an ideology that has its roots in the Soviet Union and, more importantly, within Imperial Russia. However, this mindset has become more virulent, more dangerous, because it's been attached to a *fascist imperialist* ideology under the regime that Putin has constructed. And it's a regime that brooks no compromise: you're either with us or you're against us.

The attitudes of this "collective Putin" towards Ukrainians have historically been very negative, both in Imperial Russia and the Soviet Union, which committed genocide against Ukrainians on several occasions. These attitudes were more or less absent in the official discourse during the Yeltsin and Gorbachev periods, but they have been central to Putin's rise to power, his ideology, and the degree to which Ukraine plays a key role in this ideology. So, you have an accumulation of cultural predispositions that are destructive of and certainly negatively attuned towards Ukrainians.

For Putin and for the people in the "collective Putin," Russia's ascendancy necessitates Ukraine's elimination. The two cannot coexist in their heads. Ukraine either has to be absorbed or it has to be destroyed. In order to justify a genocidal war, the regime — and, to some degree, the people in general — has to demonize and dehumanize Ukrainians. After all, the Russians are bombing hospitals, they're bombing theatres, they're destroying kindergartens and daycare centers. They've already destroyed a significant portion of the Ukrainian population.

How can one possibly justify that? Well, one needs to say that Ukrainians are Nazis, that they are Satanists, that they're drug addicts, that they're evil. We can see this even in statements by the so-called Patriarch Kirill, we see this in statements by that crazy former prime minister Dmitry Medvedev, we see this in statements made by other propagandists like Solovyov, Simonyan, Skabeeva, and others. They positively hate Ukrainians. They see them as vermin. What the Jews were to Nazi Germany, Ukrainians have become to the Russians.

Now let's just look at the war itself. From almost the very first day, the war started going badly. The expectation was that Russia would be marching in full uniform down Khreshchatyk Street within a few days of the invasion. And instead, it was clear from about the third, fourth day, or possibly even earlier, that that wasn't going to happen.

And then there was the withdrawal from Kyiv, Sumy, Chernihiv; then there was the withdrawal from Kharkiv, then there was the withdrawal from western Kherson. Then there's also the destruction of the *Moskva* ship and the Kerch Bridge to Crimea. All of these cumulatively translate into enormous frustration for the Kremlin elites, for the Russian population, and especially for the soldiers. And in this kind of brutalized environment, where they're told that they are fighting Nazis, vermin, inhuman people, it's very easy for them to translate their frustration, their anger into violence—a violence that is directed against men, women, and children regardless of age, regardless of position. Hence, these mass rapes; hence, the torture.

Pankieiev: There is some talk in the West about leaving the possibility of ending the war through diplomatic negotiation and signing a peace deal at the end. Russia sometimes signals the need for peace talks as well. What is your opinion about this scenario, and how dangerous can it be for Ukraine to negotiate peace with Russia at this stage?

Motyl: Well, it would be stupid and dangerous. After all, Ukraine is winning, so they should keep on winning. And then, at some point perhaps negotiations might make sense. But it's also dangerous because there's no way that one can believe anything the Russians say. They are constantly lying, they have constantly lied, and they will continue to constantly lie. If something is said by a Russian official, one has to assume the opposite is true. That's really the best way of interpreting their statements. So, if they say peace, they mean war. If they say negotiations, they mean capitulation. There is no way in which agreement can be reached with people who are unreliable and who are not credible. One must assume that whatever peace treaty the Russians sign would be treated as a scrap of paper by them from the very beginning. So that is point one.

Point two, I am not so sure that the mood in the West is all that supportive of negotiations. There are people, there are factions, there are groups who are urging Ukraine to negotiate. But the key country, the United States, has said that it's up to Ukraine. And the US indisputably sets the tone in this, as well as in so many other things.

Moreover, just yesterday the NATO Parliamentary Assembly decreed that Russia was a terrorist state. How do you sign a peace treaty with a terrorist? Well, you don't; that's just the reality. Moreover, this resolution is indicative of the general mood within the West. I'm not so sure that people will be pushing Ukraine very hard.

And the final point I want to make is this: Putin, when he formally annexed Luhansk, Donetsk, Zaporizhia, and Kherson oblasts — and when, of course, they went through with the referendum and the Duma approved it — he created an impossible situation for himself and for whatever possible peace talks that might at some point take place. According to the Russian logic, these regions are now formally part of Russia. There is no mechanism within the Russian constitution for de-annexing territories.

Of course, Russia is a fascist state, and Putin doesn't care about laws. So, if he wanted to very badly, I'm sure he could push this "peace talks" ruse through. But for this to happen, either Putin would have to destroy a sizable portion of the Russian elite, or they would have to destroy him. In any case, he's created an impossible situation because, formally, there's nothing to talk about.

Ukraine says these territories are Ukrainian. Russia says no, they're Russian. How do you produce a compromise? Before that happened, there was at least a thinkable compromise. It was at least possible, as some people said, that Russia would retreat to the boundaries of February 23rd, Ukraine would get reparations, and then Donetsk, Luhansk, and Crimea would be left for the future. But now, what is there to compromise about? Nothing at all.

Therefore, the only way that change can occur is for Putin to go. If and when he goes, then there will be an opportunity for a new relationship that makes possible an end to the war. Right now, though, it's pretty much impossible.

Pankieiev: The full-scale invasion of Ukraine on February 24 of this year dramatically changed the perception of Ukraine and Russia in the West, and particularly in the EU. How will those changes define postwar politics and diplomacy in the region and the world? What will be the role of Ukraine?

Motyl: Well, the perceptions have indeed changed, that's true. And that is very important. First of all, they've changed at the level of the mass population. People actually know where Ukraine is, whereas half a year ago they had no idea.

They've also changed in the sense that Ukraine is finally on the mental map of the Western policymaking community. Policymakers finally understand that Ukraine matters to their security, to their prosperity, to their lives.

As to what happens after Russia's defeat in the war—as you can see, I'm assuming that's a done deal—the major factor that will determine Ukraine's position in the new European architecture will be the fact that Ukraine will have won—that it will have defeated a country that is much stronger. That it will possess an army that is going to be Europe's strongest, and in fact may be one of the world's top five or top ten armies. So, suddenly Ukraine becomes important not just on the mental map; it becomes important in a geopolitical sense as well.

Of course, one of the major downsides for Ukraine will be that enormous investments will be required to bring the economy back to some degree of normality. And that will be an Achilles heel for Ukraine for a while. But the military balance will have shifted significantly: Russia's army will have been defeated; Ukraine's army will have become victorious. And Ukraine will therefore be able to play a much more significant role in the politics—not so much the economics but the politics—the geopolitics of the West.

That Russia will become significantly weaker politically, militarily, and economically means that its geopolitical role will also be significantly diminished. It's possible that Russia may even experience collapse or descend into civil war. But whatever the scenario, the fact that Russia will become significantly weaker will have implications for Asia. Because if you were China, would you really want to have an alliance with a weak, mendacious, and irresponsible country? It doesn't make any sense.

As a final point, with Russia's departure from great power status, the world will once again become bi-polar. There will be the United States and China. The second-tier power will be Europe, while Russia will find itself on the third, fourth, or even on the fifth tier. That will change geopolitics as well, because the United States and Western Europe will be closely allied.

One of the important things that we learned from the Cold War is that bi-polar systems are less conducive to war than multi-polar systems. One of the reasons we have wars today is precisely because of this multi-polarity. So, if Russia goes out of the calculation, then we come back to a more stable international political arena. And that would be good for everybody — especially, of course, for Ukraine.

Kushnir: What developments on the Russo-Ukrainian battle and diplomatic fronts do you expect will happen during winter 2022/23?

Motyl: Well, when it comes to Europe and the United States, the US has ample reserves of energy, so we will stay warm, and of course Canada will as well. Europe may face some shortages, but as you know, the Europeans have taken some serious steps in the last few months to guarantee sufficient supplies of oil and gas. So, my guess is that there may be some problems, some difficulties, but the Europeans will manage. They'll have to drink a little more Jägermeister to keep warm. But I don't foresee a crisis.

It's obviously more complicated with the Ukrainian population. I can't even begin to imagine what it's like when you have no electricity, heat, or water, especially if you're living in a 10-storey building. In that sense, living in a village is preferable because at least you can burn wood to keep warm.

But it's often said, and I think I agree, that Ukrainians will manage simply because they have no alternative. They're also fired up, they're angry, they're willing to take a lot. It will be a difficult winter. But as I said, and as many Ukrainians have said, there is no alternative. So, they have to survive.

It's similar to 1947 in Germany, which was known as the *hunger-winter*: it was especially cold, there was very little food, the economy was in shambles, and the country, as you know, was destroyed. The winter was very tough, but the Germans somehow managed. Well, if the Germans could manage in '47, I'm sure the Ukrainians can manage in 2022 to 2023.

In terms of the battlefield, the winter will be equally harsh for all the soldiers on the front lines. The difference is that Ukrainian soldiers will be fighting on their own territory and will therefore have more access to supplies, warmth, food. Their logistical supply lines are shorter, and they may be able to get some assistance from local inhabitants. None of that will apply in equal force to the Russians on the front line. They will have a far harder time supplying themselves with the necessities for surviving the winter. And then one needs to consider that the performance of the Ukrainian army and Ukrainian logistics has been exceptional. That's unlikely to change in the next few months.

In contrast, the performance of the Russian army and its commanders and logistical supply networks have been poor, sometimes even catastrophically so, and it's likely that that too will continue throughout the war. It seems to me that, other things being equal, Ukraine will have an advantage in the winter, and it will be able to convert that advantage into further territorial gains. As long as it continues to get significant Western military support, of course; that is the *sine qua non* of all these discussions.

CHAPTER 19

Participation of LGBTQ+ people in the war effort cannot be ignored

Maryna Shevtsova

Interview with Ostap Kushnir, published 14 December 2022

> Maryna Shevtsova (PhD, Political Science, Humboldt University, Berlin) is a 2021/26 Senior FWO Fellow with KU Leuven (Belgium) and formerly an MSCA-EUTOPIA Co-fund fellow at the University of Ljubljana (Slovenia, 2021/23), a Swedish Institute Post-doctoral Fellow at the University of Lund (2020), and a Fulbright Scholar at the University of Florida (2018/19). Her recent publications include the edited volume *Feminist Perspectives on Russia's War in Ukraine: Hear Our Voices* (2024) and the monograph *LGBTI Politics and Value Change in Ukraine and Turkey: Exporting Europe?* (2021). In 2022 Shevtsova received an Emma Goldman Award for her engagement in feminist research and human rights activism.

Kushnir: In your opinion, what major gender-based challenges in social and political life has Ukraine faced, resolved, or failed to resolve since the beginning of the war in 2014?

Shevtsova: When it comes to legislation, Ukraine has been on the right path and demonstrated good progress. This has happened not without the help of its Western partners. Immediately after Euromaidan in 2014, Ukraine reoriented itself toward integration with the European Union, which was accompanied by technical, economical, financial, political, and other kinds of support from the outside. This also additionally empowered civil society, activists, and individual MPs to push forward for further updates.

Even before Euromaidan, in 2012 Ukraine had adopted anti-discrimination legislation that was important for gender equality. After that, Ukraine adopted a law on prevention of and combating domestic violence; its implementation became a challenge for the country because of the existing stigma related to this kind of crime. In particular, Ukrainians had never been at ease with reporting domestic violence to the police.

Thanks to the EU, US, and Canadian funding and guidance, and also facilitated by local civil society organizations, police officers in Ukraine have completed numerous training and educational sessions since 2014. Special teams have been created and trained to communicate with victims and survivors of domestic violence; and special shelters have been built. These steps are limited and remain utterly insufficient for a large country such as Ukraine; nevertheless, they have been taken.

Then, in 2017 Ukraine introduced a new official position, the Government Commissioner for Gender Policy. That position not only became important for increasing legislative effectiveness, it sent a powerful symbolic message by the sole fact of its existence.

Yet, if one looks at Ukraine's overall performance with respect to gender equality, it was ranked 74th among 150 countries in the Global Gender Gap Report 2021 compiled by the World Economic Forum (WEF). This is a relatively respectable position in the middle, though I believe that the country could do much better.

Ukraine also did comparatively well, ranking 27th in an assessment of gender aspects of education. For one thing, national secondary education and higher education are highly feminized areas. Many Ukrainian women possess graduate degrees, which make the country one of the world's leaders in this respect. On the other hand, Ukraine's system of education is largely underfunded, which prevents all women who are willing from enrolling in post-secondary studies and sometimes casts doubts on the quality of their acquired knowledge.

However, unlike the education indicators, Ukraine does only moderately well in gender aspects of economic participation: its position was 44th in the world in 2021. One of the major reasons for this resides in a 23-per cent gender pay gap. In other words, women in Ukraine earn 23 per cent less than men for doing the same job.

As paradoxical as it may sound, in a 2020 nationwide survey almost 80 per cent of Ukrainians said that gender inequality was not among the major problems of their country. A general idea prevails among the population that Ukraine has achieved a certain functional balance and does not need feminist revision of realities or the introduction of additional measures to improve the balance even more.

Next, in the *political aspect* of gender Ukraine is not doing well. In women's political empowerment, the country was ranked 103rd in the WEF's Global Gender Gap Report 2021. The low ranking was assigned notwithstanding the fact that Ukraine introduced a new law on quotas requiring all political parties to have at least 40 per cent women in their election lists. This law unquestionably increased female participation at all levels of decision making, from municipal to national. As of today, Ukraine has a historically high number of women in its parliament, the Verkhovna Rada, as well as women ministers in the cabinet. However, compared to other countries this share—around 20 per cent across all institutions—is not that impressive.

Another achievement that should be mentioned is that the Soviet-era list of professions banned for women was revoked in 2018. This cancellation opened the path for legal employment of women who were *de facto* working in banned positions, earning much less money, deprived of rights protection and the possibility of official registration, or being forced to agree to being paid "under the table." One of the direct outcomes of the cancellation was a significant increase in women's participation in the military, from around 14,000 before 2018 to more than 50,000 today (of whom around 5,000 are now at the front line).

In sum, Ukraine has been steadily improving with respect to gender equality since 2014, but many challenges remain to be addressed. One of them is putting the Istanbul Convention into practice. A convention that aims to prevent domestic violence was ratified in 2022, in partial fulfillment of the requirements for EU candidacy. That ratification was a significant milestone. For many years, feminist activists had been promoting the importance of the convention for Ukraine but could not overcome the resistance, especially from religious institutions. However, as shown in the events of the recent summer, when there is a political will, the opinion of religious institutions stops being pivotal.

Kushnir: In her article for *Forum*, Tamara Martsenyuk stated that as of September 2022, "Ukrainian society generally supports egalitarian ideas as to engaging women in the armed forces on a par with men, as well as having a professional army of those enlisted voluntarily." Do you agree with this statement?

Shevtsova: I read this statement by Tamara, that Ukrainian society supports a professional army which is equally accessible for all willing men and women because it is no longer based on obligatory conscription. If my reading is correct, I fully agree with this statement.

Overall, from what I observe in social media and across civil society, there is no resistance to the fact that women who want to join the army and occupy various positions there can do so. I think that society is ready for women in the army, including women commanders.

However, when it comes to obligatory conscription—and in light of recent rumours that the borders of Ukraine will be completely closed and women will be forced to join the military—I have observed clear discontent and angry opinions across society. People do not accept obligatory conscription for women. There still exists a common perception, when it comes to gender roles, that women have to take care of children and family, while men are supposed to go and defend the country.

Another thing is that mothers who decide to join the army are not treated well after their return. Society is inclined to blame such women for leaving their children behind and neglecting their family duties. This puts additional mental pressure on female soldiers. This pressure is not there for men who go to the battlefield and leave their close ones behind.

Kushnir: How do you see the contribution of Ukraine's LGBTQ+ communities and individual activists to the war effort? In general, how has the Russian invasion changed gender roles and perceptions in Ukrainian society?

Shevtsova: We are now witnessing history in the making. With the escalated Russian invasion, Ukrainian public opinion was believed to approach the position of gender scholars who had argued that war would cement conservative values. It was widely believed that militarization would lead to the traditionalization of society and reinforcement of traditional gender roles. However, as many sociologists report today, the case of Ukraine is more complex.

Above all there is a general recognition of the role of women in the present war effort. President Volodymyr Zelensky even changed the salutations in his public addresses: he now says "Dear *zakhysnyky* and *zakhysnytsi*," using the word "defender" in both male and female form.

Similar processes are taking place around the LGBTQ+ communities. Since 2015 many LGBTQ+ individuals have been serving openly in the Ukrainian army, and experienced soldiers have been coming out. An official organization has appeared in Ukraine, the LGBT Military, whose members regularly participate in pride and equality marches in Kyiv.

Today, when the scale of the war has expanded grievously and many people are dying on the battlefield, the issue of coming out has become pivotal for many LGBTQ+ individuals. They are doing so in large numbers, and it is a chain reaction—the more people come out, the more others are willing to do so. To be sure, not the least factor in coming out is the desire to be honest with oneself. All LGBTQ+ soldiers know that they can die at any moment, and this discourages them from hiding. Thus, they think that "if I die tomorrow, at least I will die being myself."

Comings-out of people in the military are becoming more public and taking place on social media. I think this is a game changer for a large part of Ukrainian society. A sociological report from Nash Svit demonstrates that attitudes toward LGBTQ+ individuals have improved immensely. Over 63 per cent of Ukrainians today agree that there should be equal rights for LGBTQ+ people.

In the summer of 2022 a petition to the President of Ukraine to legalize same-sex partnerships collected 25,000 signatures, which means that it must be considered. He did so and promised that legalization of same-sex partnerships would be raised after martial law ends.

Today, the participation of LGBTQ+ people in the war effort cannot be ignored. They serve as soldiers and provide support as volunteers. For instance, the organization Insight, which caters to lesbian women and transgender persons, started receiving many requests for humanitarian assistance from women and mothers with kids after the full-scale Russian invasion began. So they even had to mobilize additional resources to help heterosexual women in need.

I know many LGBTQ+ organizations that help soldiers directly by sending equipment, food, and clothing, and the soldiers are aware of whom this aid comes from. They are aware of who runs fundraising and manages supplies. I also know many heterosexual families who stay in shelters created for LBGTQ+ people. Undoubtedly these wartime developments have converted social attitudes toward the LGBTQ+ in Ukraine.

Apart from that, there is a growing wave of Ukrainians who do not want to be associated with Russia. This encourages them to reject Russian homophobia and so-called "traditional values," which have little to do with genuine family values. Because of this, I suspect that more and more Ukrainians will strive to be different from Russians, which will make them become more liberal, pro-European, and accepting.

Kushnir: How do you see the probability of the introduction of registered partnerships for same-sex couples in the nearest future in Ukraine? What will be the impact of Ukraine's status as an EU candidate country on these and other legal processes?

Shevtsova: In Ukraine—the same as in other countries from the EU neighbourhood, primarily Moldova and Georgia—reforms in the sphere of gender equality became possible not least due to Europe's conditionality. The ratification of the Istanbul Convention is the most recent example. There was much resistance, many people were against it, but things changed when Ukraine's EU candidate status became at stake.

The paradox is that immediate ratification of the Istanbul Convention was not even a direct demand of the EU. Moreover, many of the Union's members—including Hungary, Bulgaria, Czech Republic, Latvia, and Lithuania—have not ratified it yet.

I think that society in Ukraine is overall ready for registered partnerships for same-sex couples. However, the probability is very low that this will happen during the active stage of the war. Both the president and the government seem to be reluctant to consider the issue today. In their turn, the interested individuals and activists understand that the right time for such major developments is yet to come.

After the war, when Ukraine is rebuilt with the help of the West, I find it highly likely that the appropriate changes to the legislation will be introduced. Same-sex couples will acquire the right to register their partnerships and marriages. After the war, the EU will possess very strong leverage over the Ukrainian government. For their part, civil society and active grassroots will contribute additional motivation.

Surely, if the war becomes protracted and social conditions deteriorate, Ukrainians may state their famous *ne na chasi* [not the best time] to same-sex partnerships and marriages and turn their attention to more critical issues. However, this is a worst-case scenario. Personally, I remain optimistic.

To sum up, if you ask me whether Ukrainian society is ready for legal changes in favour of same-sex couples, I will say yes. However, many Ukrainian politicians overestimate the homophobic sympathies of their voters. Last year, when I interviewed representatives of the liberal camp, they were saying things like, "I have nothing against it myself, but this is a political suicide—people are not ready." In my opinion, this is no longer the truth. Politicians are misjudging their voters, and for no good reason.

Kushnir: How is the EU supporting members of LGBTQ+ communities and women in need who fled the war? What challenges do Ukrainians face after crossing the EU's border?

Shevtsova: There is no universal answer to this question, as the support depends on specific cases. In the least accepting countries—such as Poland, Slovakia, Romania, or Hungary—the government does not support LGBTQ+ individuals at all. Unfortunately, these are the countries that Ukrainians fleeing the war need to enter first.

In the least accepting countries, the major burden of support rests on the shoulders of civil society. Such is, for instance, the case of Slovenia, where I am currently based. In Poland, the situation looks similar: crowdfunding, offers of shelter, organization of language courses, and other kinds of assistance are performed by the volunteers. The situation may be better in Sweden or Germany, where the government indirectly finances NGOs that work with queer refugees. However, when looking at Central European states, civil society shoulders the entire burden.

Concerning displaced Ukrainian women, what I hear from many volunteers in the EU is that their governments promise to act fast and effectively, but the support is often delayed. When a woman arrives in a given country, she has to endure long bureaucratic procedures that make the provision of immediate help almost impossible. Many women who are not lucky to find accommodation right away end up in very basic shelters. These women are provided with food and clothes, but their living conditions remain dire for months, up to the moment when the government funding arrives. The same applies to work permits—they are not issued immediately due to bureaucratic procedures, and therefore women have to wait for months before they are legally allowed to earn money.

That being said, Ukrainians should not feel ungrateful. The EU governments are trying to do their best to provide support. But in light of lacking mechanisms to cope with the waves of incoming Ukrainian migrants, much of the most-needed work is done by volunteers and private benefactors.

In Poland, where so many migrants have ended up, there is an issue with abortion rights. Being prohibited in the state, it is especially painful for women who got pregnant because they had been raped by Russians. A major political debate broke out recently about how to help these women. They are often so traumatized that it becomes a challenge for them to self-organize and move farther to the West, where abortions are allowed. For such women, the assistance of NGOs and activists is crucial.

We should also acknowledge that in many EU countries Ukrainian communities are supporting Ukrainian migrants. Apart from them, there are communities of other people who came from post-Communist countries and are willing to share the burden. Knowledge of Ukrainian or Russian certainly helps to establish communication in such cases.

On the other hand, there is a backlash in some EU media against Ukrainian women who allege abuses of their situation or who demand high social benefits to obtain a comfortable life in a new place. This backlash is rather unjustified. As a rule, however, Ukrainian women who arrived in the EU are willing to work even in the poorest conditions. They need money and do not know the language. This means that they are often exploited and underpaid.

Kushnir: How does the EU academic community perceive and help scholars from Ukraine?

Shevtsova: We have been discussing this a lot with my colleague sociologists, mostly women, and concluded that all of us have a bit of "impostor syndrome."

When the invasion started, many Ukrainian scholars were either collaborating with EU institutions or had connections there. For such people, it was comparatively easy to get a position at a new place. Not to mention that many EU institutions swiftly created new openings to accommodate the inflow of scholars. Of course, much depended on the country and the type of institution, but if Ukrainian scholars had connections and qualifications, they could easily find themselves in the EU.

That being said, there is a big cohort of people who cannot benefit from such favourable circumstances. Sometimes they lack degrees or qualifications that are attractive in the EU. For example, a friend of mine has a PhD in English language and literature and it took her a great effort to find employment. None needed her skills or wanted to hire her outside academia. My friend became so desperate that she considered cleaning jobs — though, again, she was denied the option as the employee would had to have paid her according to her background. Eventually, she ended up in a small German town with no university.

The situation is full of absurdities and paradoxes. On the one hand, there is a will and expression of solidarity with Ukrainian scholars in the EU. On the other hand, when it comes to a real-life situation, all institutions and academic communities want people who are familiar and qualified, who pursue attractive research and have dozens of publications. However, such people are neither in major need nor have major issues with employment.

Here in Slovenia, my university opened a position for Ukrainian scholars, and I already know that we will have trouble finding appropriate candidates. The lion's share of applicants will likely not have a background in the sociology of gender or will not know the language.

Another problem is that the scholars in social sciences — I do not know about other fields — are all placed in the basket of Ukrainian or Eastern European studies. This is quite a narrow field. Very few of the universities are represented in this basket and very few want to advance Ukrainian or regional studies. This means that scholars in need have limited places to compete for. At the same time, if Ukrainian scholars decide to move to a different field of research, they will need to compete there with more experienced colleagues.

Here we face one more absurdity. On the one hand, there is a very narrow bottleneck for Ukrainian social scientists to compete for a limited number of region-focused positions. On the other hand, even if Ukrainian scholars change their field of research, the EU's academia will still be unable to offer them positions.

Honestly, I think that it is not only the task of academia to help scholars. Having a huge influx of highly qualified and educated migrants, many of whom will stay in the EU for quite some time, governments should consider how to help them adjust to new realities.

Many incoming Ukrainians want to work, not sit on the sofa and enjoy migrant benefits.

I also think it is very counterproductive and even dangerous to have so many talented people in the EU who find that their potential and skills get wasted. This may lead to social tensions. Host populations will become irritated that their taxes are spent on migrants who cannot find jobs. In turn, Ukrainians who escaped the war and never thought of self-inviting themselves will become irritated with the impossibility of contributing to host societies. Not to mention that many Ukrainians believe that their husbands and children have put their lives at risk in Ukraine in order to protect EU citizens and Western values.

EU governments should seriously consider how to accommodate highly qualified Ukrainians and make them useful for their local economies. Actually, the solution should have already been invented in 2015, when the Syrian migrant crisis erupted. Unfortunately, I do not see that EU governments learned from their mistakes. This disappoints me a lot.

Kushnir: In your opinion, how many Ukrainians, especially high-quality specialists, researchers, and human rights activists will be comforted by the EU's living standards and decide to stay there after the war is over?

Shevtsova: A lot will depend on what the host countries will do to integrate Ukrainian migrants. However, in any case, many Ukrainian women and families will consider staying, to give their children a better future. The longer the war lasts, the higher the chance that Ukrainians will permanently settle in the host country after the fighting is over.

Once children feel good at a new place, like their school experience, and learn the local language, then they will not have enough motivation to come back. Their mothers will definitely notice that and do their best to find any jobs, even the lowest qualified, to make their children happy. Also, many new families will be created in the host countries between Ukrainian women and local partners.

I believe that the share of those who will not want to return to Ukraine increases with every month. However, there has not been a similar situation in the past to compare human behaviours. We are witnessing a unique experiment.

CHAPTER 20

The West either deals with Mr. Putin now on our own terms or later on his terms

Michael Bociurkiw

Interview with Jars Balan and Oleksandr Pankieiev, published 19 December 2022

> Michael Bociurkiw is an independent global affairs analyst, a Senior Non-resident Fellow at the Atlantic Council and a contributor to CNN Opinion. He has worked for the United Nations Children's Fund (UNICEF) and the World Health Organization, serving as spokesperson for UNICEF in Geneva and for the OSCE (incl. during the MH17 shoot-down over eastern Ukraine in 2014). As a journalist, Bociurkiw has reported for Forbes, Globe and Mail, Los Angeles Times, MSNBC, and Newsweek. His first book, *Digital Pandemic: How Tech Went from Bad to Good* (2021), focuses on the nexus of diplomacy, geopolitics, media and social media, and technology.

Balan: How do you explain the change in Russian war strategy following the events of early September 2022, when Ukrainians gained the initiative?

Bociurkiw: Russians changed their strategy because they had done very badly on the front lines. Russia was not set up against forces like Ukraine's, with their professionalism, their determination with Western-provided weaponry, and intelligence. Therefore, Moscow went back to its well-worn playbook used in Chechnya and Syria. They resorted to very violent tactics, and among those was the use of long-range weapons that could hit as far as Lviv or Yavoriv, close to the Polish border.

Later on, in October, they used Iranian-made drones that were sent in very large numbers to places like Kyiv. Because there were so many drones, they confused radars, anti-rocket artillery, and defence systems. All the Russians needed was for a few of these drones to strike in strategic places and cause maximum damage.

More recently, the Kremlin has resorted to striking Ukrainian power and heating plants. They have the benefit of knowing where many of the infrastructural objects are in Ukraine because they were involved in building them [during the Soviet era]. Also, Ukrainian informants let them know where the strategic objects are, so their ability to accurately target these is quite something.

The Russian strategy today seems to be inflicting maximum pain and inconvenience on the Ukrainian people at a time when winter is hitting. Moscow is aiming to cut power, heat, even water. These are war crimes. These are on top of the other acts of genocide that they have committed in Ukraine.

Around April I went with a group of journalists to Chernihiv and its outskirts. That was my first time going to places which the Russians had occupied and bombed quite badly. The experience of seeing the damage that they inflicted was jaw-dropping. I remember a small town outside of Chernihiv with a 500-pound bomb crater in it. We looked inside that crater and saw shredded teddy bears and toys. To us, that showed that a lot of kids used to live in that area. There was no military or strategic reason whatsoever for Russians to drop a heavy bomb in a place like that. Then we went to the sports stadium, which was also badly bombed. Next to it was a completely destroyed children's library. That was quite an eye-opener to go to these places.

What Russians are doing right now is basically weaponizing energy, weaponizing winter. Staying in Odesa for the last couple of months, I have been observing a very sad thing happening. People are at their wits' end. They are coping, but their life is very difficult with power outages and lack of water and heating. Also, I am very worried about small to medium-sized businesses. Odesa is known as a resilient, innovative, and high-energy city. However, I am concerned about coping mechanisms, about people's finances, as this war goes on for longer.

Balan: From your observations, what moods and attitudes dominate Ukrainian society today?

Bociurkiw: A really important point is that Ukrainians changed their attitudes towards the war four or five weeks ago, when the first missile attack happened in Kyiv and the downtown Shevchenko Park was hit. I think that what people felt before, in February—the fear of Russian attacks—turned to anger. Real anger. The attitude of Ukrainians became, like, "We are going to make it through this; we will make it all the way to victory, even if we have to live like this for two or three years." However, Ukrainians are expecting that their suffering and sacrifice will culminate in EU membership.

That being said, if you ask me what help is really needed right now from the West, it is to give Ukrainians more ability to close their skies to the Russian terror — to the missiles, to the drones. On Wednesday 23 November there were seventy or so missiles sent from Russia to various parts of Ukraine. Around fifty of them were shot down. The problem is that the remaining twenty were very accurately targeted and inflicted a lot of damage on critical infrastructure.

Balan: What are Ukrainian society's major needs today? You mentioned air defence capabilities, but this is on the military list. What about the people, what do they need?

Bociurkiw: I just came from Odesa and an immediate need there is for generators — small, medium, and big sizes. For private businesses and charitable organizations. Generators are becoming difficult to find in Ukraine. They also are becoming more expensive, from 500 to 1000 USD.

To give you an idea of how difficult things are, people are scrambling to buy firewood to heat themselves. And this is in Odesa, on the Black Sea shore! Now, imagine how it is up north. So, probably people would need warm clothing as well.

I think it is a good time for whomever is involved in providing humanitarian aid to go to Ukraine and do a rapid assessment. I am not sure if people here in Canada will like hearing this, but the feeling among Ukrainians is that they would welcome more assessment missions or visits from diaspora leaders. Canadians and other international partners should get a better sense of things on the ground. Also, assessments should not be limited to Lviv but spread further into the country.

Balan: Let us return to the issue of defence. Since the very beginning of the invasion, Ukraine has been pleading for the West to help them with the airspace. Is there any chance, in your opinion, that Ukrainians will get what they ask for?

Bociurkiw: What Ukrainians would welcome — and I think that Poland has been lobbying for that [on their behalf] — is the Patriot [air defence] missile system. However, there has been some opposition from German partners on that one. There have also been suggestions that Israel (who has a bit of a spotty record when it comes to helping Ukraine) provide their Iron Dome system. My understanding is that the Iron Dome is really great technology, but its transfer would require American approval. Also, active help from Israel to Ukraine will put it in a tough spot because Israel works with Russia in Syria.

Who is in a very good position to help Ukraine—and has played a key role in opening up the Black Sea to food exports in the "Black Sea Grain Initiative"—is President Recep Tayyip Erdoğan of Turkey. I think he has the respect of President Putin and has access to the Kremlin. He is also much respected by Ukrainians, by President Zelensky, and he made a visit to western Ukraine a few weeks ago with a big delegation. I think that Mr. Erdoğan could negotiate much more than arms supply.

In recent decades, Turks have really gotten deeply into Ukrainian investment. Before the invasion, Turkish Airlines were flying to more destinations in Ukraine than even Ukraine International Airlines. ONUR, a Turkish construction company, is one of the biggest construction contractors in Ukraine today. They are helping to rebuild the damage in places like Irpin. Turkey is also selling the Bayraktar drones to Ukraine, and I think they want to actually manufacture them on the ground. The Turks are very pragmatic; but I also believe that thanks to history they will remain trusted friends of Ukraine and very important interlocutors.

Balan: Do you see movement across the NATO countries, apart from Poland and Turkey, to support Ukraine? Europe is being pressured by all these war developments, inflation is on the rise, and the influx of refugees may become even bigger. Will NATO respond more pro-actively?

Bociurkiw: I was recently in London and the intelligent people asked me "why should we be funding this war effort while we are hardly able to cope with energy bills at home, and we are having inflation?" I just have one answer to that. The West, the civilized world, either deals with Mr. Putin now on our own terms, or we deal with him later on his terms. In between those two poles is a wide range of contingencies that could happen if he is not pushed back. It is also important that he should be pushed back entirely, with the de-occupation of Crimea and Donbas, and return to pre-2014 borders in Ukraine. If Mr. Putin is not taught a lesson, he will try again and go further.

Being in the region, Estonia, Lithuania, and Latvia are, I know, very worried about a Russian invasion. The same holds true for the

Nordic countries and Poland. So I think, if we are not going to see more action from NATO or the EU, there will be new micro-alliances happening with neighbouring states in order to help Ukraine defend itself, to push Mr. Putin back. The states in the region all feel vulnerable—and for a good reason, especially after what happened in recent weeks.

As we speak, the Russian invasion is spreading beyond Ukraine's borders. Missiles are landing in Poland and Moldova. I think Western leaders need to wake up to the fact that this is happening!

A lot of Ukrainians were surprised that the Russian invasion did not trigger more reaction or action from the West. They had been speaking about Russia's threat for many months. Today, you start to question yourself, how loud do you have to scream [to get a proper response?].

Let me say this again: Ukraine has the ability to protect its skies 100 per cent. Ukrainians do not need NATO aircraft patrolling, but they need the technology. Until that is acquired, no inch of their country can be regarded as safe. The technology transfer has to happen quickly. My concern is that without effective air defence, it is going to be very difficult for normal life to go on. The economy will not likely function to a level where it can continue to last through the war.

Balan: We regularly get reports about the demoralization of the Russian army. Do you think that the scenario of Russian soldiers putting down their guns and walking home is possible?

Bociurkiw: I think that we are witnessing a war where victory depends more on technology and tactics than on men on the front lines. Remember when this full-scale invasion started, everyone said, "Oh, my goodness! Ukraine is up against the second-biggest military in the world." So what? Russians are using outdated equipment. They have lousy training, bad morale, and tons of corruption.

The other thing is Ukraine has already destroyed much of Russia's weaponry and equipment. Russians, mostly because of corruption, do not have a well-formed military-industrial complex to restock. So, they go to their buddies in North Korea for ammunition or to Iran for drones. They are in a very bad spot right now, I think. This is recognized by Ukrainians, who continue to press on.

Ukraine has the benefit of much more Western intelligence now, with satellite imagery. I would not be surprised if Western special forces are on the ground in Ukraine providing support. In late November, what is interesting, the United Kingdom sent its helicopters over to Ukraine. I think these helicopters are equivalent to the Sea King vehicles, military transport carriers. It was the first time a Western country gave Ukraine manned aerial devices or equipment to fight back against the Russians.

As I understand it, these helicopters are used in the UK for search and rescue. However, they can also be adapted for patrolling the Black Sea and submarine surveillance, or for moving troops and equipment around. They are basically flying tanks, amazing pieces of equipment. The fact that the UK gave them to Ukraine was a big development, and I think we will see more of that.

In the big picture, what we have seen in this war is a bit of a lack of Western leaders growing the spine to stand up to Mr. Putin. They all know that he has the ability to use nuclear weapons. I think that scares them a lot, but the worst scenario becomes less and less probable because of what has happened in recent weeks. Xi Jinping, the leader of China, has probably told Mr. Putin in no uncertain terms, "Don't even think about using nuclear weapons."

However, Russians have a very dirty playbook of dirty bombs: biological, chemical, and others. We should also not forget that they occupy the Zaporizhia nuclear power plant, the biggest in Europe. The IAEA [International Atomic Energy Agency — *Ed.*] is very worried that a stupid mistake will cause an explosion there and we would all pay the price.

We know how careless Russians were with Chernobyl. Today, they could do a deliberate strike on the Zaporizhia NPP and blame it on the Ukrainians. On the other hand, they will have to retreat from the power plant, and on the way out they could do something worrisome. So we have to be very careful.

Balan: What about Western media? Has there been a noticeable evolution in the coverage they provide from Ukraine? Have they changed the way they work on the ground?

Bociurkiw: A lot of media institutions—and I find it a positive development—have invested for the long term in Ukraine. We now have, for example, a permanent *New York Times* bureau in the country. *Washington Post* and the BBC have really upped their presence, and then CNN—whatever people think of them—have set up simultaneous pop-up bureaus in Kyiv and Lviv.

Having an increased media presence at the beginning of the full-scale invasion and the weeks leading to it was a blessing for me. Not only could I spend a lot of time in the bureau and do my work there, go on air at a moment's notice, but also it was this camaraderie that was really important. We went with my colleagues through some dark days at that time. So, having the correspondents and producers in Ukraine and brainstorming on different stories was absolutely fabulous. CNN retains a presence in the capital still, and their correspondents have really put themselves at risk, Clarissa Ward and others going very close to the front line.

The amazing thing is that the correspondents not only learned a lot about the country but they want to come back time and time again and do more reporting. Whenever I reach out to producers, whenever my editorial assistant in London, Preeti Bali, and I do pitches, we almost always get a positive response: "Yes, let us know when Michael can come on air." Producers give us a lot of time. Even in recent days, with what we are competing with—the World Cup and the US midterms—Ukraine features very prominently in headlines. Everyone realizes this is a big story.

Balan: What is the sense in Odesa of the potential spillover of the war? Russians initially were talking about occupying all of southern Ukraine and uniting with Transnistria on the other side. Are the people of Odesa still afraid of the Russian threat?

Bociurkiw: I think people in Odesa do not expect a sea landing or anything like that today. In terms of Russian strategy, it was a paramount task to secure the land corridor from the Russian border to Crimea. I doubt Russians will have the ability to hold on to that, not to mention uniting with Transnistria. Instead, Ukrainians are looking to at least be in northern Crimea by the New Year. The passages to the peninsula will be the focus of action in the next few weeks.

Odesa is a very well protected city. It has three strategic ports. Again, these are the anchors of the Black Sea Grain Initiative, where Ukrainian grain, sunflower oil, and other agricultural products are now being exported to world markets. Russia recently agreed to renew the deal for another 180 days. However, if Odesa continues to be plagued by power blackouts, how are the ports supposed to function if there is no electricity? I have a feeling that Moscow did sign the renewal of the deal, but they knew that they were going to work in the background to degrade infrastructure and energy so that the port could not export anymore. That is the way the Kremlin works.

Balan: In the course of the war, many times already Ukrainians have surprised their Western partners with improvisation and uncanny military solutions. Any idea what could be next? What other tricks do Ukrainians have up their sleeve?

Bociurkiw: The recapture of Kherson was a big signal to the West that their investment is paying off and that Ukrainians know what they are doing. They are to be trusted, and they do not give up. Moreover, I think Ukrainians have been very careful with telegraphing military strategy. I frankly do not know their plans. That being said, if Ukrainians continue at this pace I cannot see Russians having much success physically on the battlefield.

Look at the bungled mobilization in Russia. The recruiters had to go to prisons and get convicts to send to Ukraine. They also recruited homeless people and derelicts. There is no lack of video on social media about whom Russia has deployed in Ukraine, their equipment and uniforms. Therefore, I do not think that the newly mobilized soldiers will make a big difference.

Ukrainians have a clear advantage in the war today, especially with the new kit that is being sent by the West. Also, the training has been very good. Ukrainians have the wind behind them, so to speak. A lot of experts have commented about winter and how it will slow the fighting down, but I think still that Ukrainians have the advantage of "going for it."

Pankieiev: Do you see that Ukraine right now may be missing some voice in the international arena?

Bociurkiw: A real area that I am concerned about in terms of Ukraine's ability to get its messaging out is the diplomatic posts. There have been across-the-board budget cuts since the start of the invasion. I know for a fact that many Ukrainian embassies and consulates are shorthanded. It is really important for them, for example, to more effectively use social media, get out to the media; however, they cannot do this without the proper resources. Today is totally the wrong time to be cutting the budgets of Ukrainian diplomatic posts.

Therefore, communication is an area where the worldwide Ukrainian diaspora can help Ukraine. I do not think they are of the mindset to actually come out and ask for help. So I think that diaspora leaders should go to the consuls and ambassadors and ask what they need and what help they expect.

Pankieiev: Many experts believe that it is worth trying to break the informational wall around Russia and influence those people directly. Is it something that you think is worth trying?

Bociurkiw: I think there are Russians who can be influenced and those who cannot. Do not forget that when the mobilization happened, most Russians were protesting against the mobilization — not against the war. That is an important point to reiterate.

I have never been a big supporter of sanctions. However, I think that if there are more sanctions put on Russians, it will bring positive effects in this unique situation. I think that if the livelihoods of Russians are affected, if they cannot make trips abroad or buy certain goods, then some constructive reaction may follow.

The primary area to target is the influential circle around Mr. Putin. They should not be able to travel to the Maldives, even to Turkey, to Dubai. I think the US administration, the UK, have to work harder at influencing the Gulf states to plug these gaps in the sanctions. I mean, I just transited through Istanbul airport and it is full of Russians and Russian-language signs. Russians are even able to use their credit cards there. It is getting a little bit more difficult, I understand, but they are still able.

An important thing to keep in mind — and I am reminded about it by correspondents who have served in Russia — is that only a small segment of the population has foreign travel passports or is able to travel. The majority does not. So, it is a very complex issue. At the same time, millions of Russian nationals live overseas and send their kids to elite schools there. A lot of Russian properties are probably still owned in places like Toronto's Bridle Path or in Vancouver. Are you trying to tell me this is not ill-gained wealth? Let us take a closer look there. I think that would also send a very strong message.

CHAPTER 21

In the EU, Ukraine is perceived as "the eastern edge of Western Europe"

Peter Vermeersch

Interview with Ostap Kushnir, published 12 January 2023

Peter Vermeersch is a professor of politics in the Faculty of Social Sciences at KU Leuven (Belgium), where he is a member of the Senior Academic Staff and connected to the research group LINES (soc. kuleuven.be). His academic interests are democracy in Central and Eastern Europe, ethnic mobilization and LGBTQ+ policies in post-Communist Europe, nationalism, and social movements. His work has been published in a range of academic journals, and among his books are *The Romani Movement: Minority Politics and Ethnic Mobilization in Contemporary Central Europe* (2006) and the co-edited volume *The EU Enlargement and Gay Politics* (2016).

Kushnir: How has the perception of Ukraine changed across the EU — and specifically in Belgium, the EU's core state — since February 2022?

Vermeersch: The perception of Ukraine has changed a lot across the EU. Though it is hard to generalize, Ukraine was largely unknown as a country before the invasion. It was a faraway piece of Eastern Europe — or, perhaps more clearly, the western edge of Eastern Europe. However, since the escalated invasion a lot of Europeans, and specifically Belgians, have started perceiving Ukraine as the *eastern* edge of *Western* Europe.

If you take a wider perspective, perceptions of Ukraine had already begun changing before the Russian invasion in 2022. After the Orange Revolution (2004–05) and later the Euromaidan (2013–14) and annexation of Crimea, it became clear to Belgians that Ukraine is something unique and worth observing. The connection and solidarity with Ukraine have been growing and intensifying over the years.

Certainly, in today's context Ukraine is seen as an ally in the opposition to Vladimir Putin's regime. This is the dominant perception. But in Belgium as well as in the EU in general, I do not think that the familiarity of Ukraine—its cultural commonalities as well as the need for solidarity with it—has been fully acknowledged.

On the one hand, across the European Union, although not as much in Belgium, there has been an established tradition to deal with Putin on certain issues, especially energy and economics. That has clearly ceased now, but it was strong enough to overlook the Euromaidan and the annexation of Crimea.

On the other hand, the EU has many times been excessively optimistic in its attitude toward Ukraine. This optimism stimulated wishful thinking in Ukraine about the possibility of its quick accession to the EU, which was not so close to reality. Even today, the EU continues portraying membership as a real possibility. Obviously, this is in the heat of the moment and carries a mobilizing effect. However, I am afraid that Ukrainians may feel disappointment in the future, when the war situation changes.

I think that Belgium has a particular role in radiating excessive optimism. Guy Verhofstadt, a current European parliamentarian and former Belgian prime minister, visited Ukraine personally several times to promote EU membership and support protest movements, including during the Euromaidan. Obviously this was done with good intentions, but it might have given a misleading impression about the ability of the EU to bring Ukraine into its fold in a short amount of time. The Balkans may serve as a good point of reference here, with the EU's enlargement toward that region never having been as smooth as many people there hoped it would be.

Kushnir: How do you assess the sensibility and effectiveness of the EU's current wartime policies toward Ukraine and Russia? Can anything be done differently, with higher effectiveness?

Vermeersch: It is a good question but a difficult one to answer. I know that a lot of people are complaining that the EU is not doing enough and that it will not be able to make a difference in the end. However, I have a slightly more positive view of this. You have to acknowledge how much the EU has done in terms of unifying its member-states' policies regarding Ukraine.

In recent times the EU has been through a series of crises: Brexit, the rise of anti-EU populism, tense relations between Poland and Germany, economic recession and energy troubles, the willingness of Hungary to continue doing business with Russia, and others. If you place the EU's policy on Ukraine against this background, a remarkably solid and unified stand of the EU has been achieved despite all internal disagreements. There has been a powerful response to the war in terms of economic actions, accompanied by a response on the energy front, which will definitely hamper the regime in Russia. The EU made a big gamble to play on the level of energy.

I should also stress that sensibility and effectiveness of the EU's policies can only happen when the population in the EU supports those policies. And this is what we can observe across the board today. For instance, in Belgium support of Ukraine as well as openness to Ukrainian migrants and refugees have not diminished since February. I am not saying it will last forever—there may be a point when politicians mobilize the population in the opposite direction—but for the moment there is unified support across the population for the EU's actions being taken toward Ukraine, as well as sanctions against Russia.

Kushnir: Do you think that the EU could have prevented Russia's invasion of Ukraine if different steps were taken before February 2022?

Vermeersch: Observing how Putin's regime operates and what kind of reality it constructs, I think no. The invasion was the result of decisions in Russia; it was not provoked by NATO or EU actions. We should not make a mistake or misjudgement here. The responsibility for the aggression lies with Russia.

The EU could have probably seen the invasion coming for quite some time. However, we know that it takes *faits accomplis* to understand the past and explain how the current reality has been influenced by what came before. Very few people predicted the invasion as it happened, but once the invasion happened many started claiming: "We could have predicted it." But if you could have predicted it, then you should contemplate the actions which you did not take to prevent it. That being said, I do not think that the EU could have dissuaded Putin's regime from the invasion.

A different issue is whether the EU made good political choices regarding Russia in the past. I think it did not. The energy deals were not properly balanced. In the pre-invasion reality, the EU as a global player excessively relied on fossil energy and made itself dependent on petrol states like Russia. That was counterproductive and hamstrung the EU.

Also, there was wishful thinking on the side of many EU countries that ultimately Russia would democratize thanks to its thriving economy. The influx of money and technologies as well as the friendliness of EU energy policies were supposed to soften the regime. However, it turns out that if you are dealing with a corrupt petrol state, the money you invest is not fairly distributed. Thus, the influx of money neither makes the regime more democratic nor helps to protect human rights or allows the opposition to function. This is where the EU jeopardized a couple of chances.

It is important to stress that with respect to Russia, political gamesmanship had a bigger effect on the current situation than the EU's generous symbolic support to Ukraine. For example, during the Euromaidan protests a lot of cheerful statements were made about the bravery of the people. Nevertheless, the EU still continued to be dependent on fossil fuel energy from Russia.

Taking an even wider perspective, I think that the EU should have acted on Eastern Europe, including Russia, much earlier. In the 1990s, a sort of Marshall Plan was needed for the post-Soviet countries to become more democratic, build a different future, and acquire new opportunities.

The EU should have also drawn lessons from global warming much earlier and engaged in climate-friendly energy policies years ago. Today, that would have made the EU more independent from the petrol states, specifically Russia.

Kushnir: Considering that the Russo-Ukrainian war is happening in the EU's "backyard," same as the Yugoslav wars in the 1990s, what solutions from the postwar reconstruction of the Balkan states can the EU use to assist Ukraine after the fighting is over there?

Vermeersch: It is an interesting question. To begin with, the conflicts are very different. They are taking place in different times and geopolitical realities. One cannot copy-paste solutions just like that. But there are a number of lessons to be drawn.

Cleaning up after war takes a lot of time. The fighting in the Balkans ended two decades ago, and the cleaning up there continues still. In a literal sense, war damage needs to be physically removed. The damage must also be removed in a metaphorical sense, from societies. People are not easily forgetting their own injuries and victimization, as well as the crimes committed against their country overall.

Furthermore, certain aspects of political thinking and societal mobilization may remain rooted in the frameworks of the past war. As long as you cannot escape from it, then the conflict continues even if there is no fighting. Therefore, my first caution is that time will be a crucial element.

Speaking of Russia, there will be questions raised about what the regime did to the mentality of its population. It is pretty clear to me that within the context of today's Russia, public opposition remains a very tricky thing. It is really hard for many Russians to speak against their government, as the risks of persecution are real. So it is normal, to some extent, that you do not see much anti-government activity.

That being said, the overall passivity of Russian citizens against Putin and his regime has only increased over the years, alongside the strengthening of that regime. This is something that Russian citizens will eventually have to take responsibility for and think very hard about how they arrived at that connivance. The postwar situation in Russia will probably be more difficult than in Ukraine.

You also need to look to the root of the problem to understand why the fighting erupted. The conflicts in the Balkans in the 1990s were very much seen as conflicts of identity. These were Serbs against Croats, Serbs against Bosniaks, one group against the other. In this light, the danger of the ongoing war is that it may be predominantly perceived as a conflict between Russians and Ukrainians. However, in my opinion it is never a good idea to reduce a major international war to a conflict of identities. Instead, it is always important to keep in mind the political motivations of power holders who mobilize populations to the idea that the fighting is about identity. This nuance gets lost very quickly in a war situation. Therefore, it is crucial to remember that the Russian invasion of Ukraine is not simply a sort of identity fight, but Putin's decision to start that fight and present it as one about identity.

Kushnir: Apart from that, what social and political challenges do you think Ukraine will face after the fighting is over?

Vermeersch: Predicting is a tricky business. When thinking about what happens when the fighting is over — and let us hope it will be over very soon, with Ukraine's victory and territorial restoration — you will face another situation. In it, disappointment will set the tone on many sides.

On the side of the EU, there may be disappointment that the conflict will not be over after the fighting stops. Quite the opposite, it will become more difficult and complex to understand. What you have now is clarity of the battlefield, which will likely disappear when you have no battlefield anymore. It will become shrouded in politics, negotiations, internal friction, and pettifoggery.

On the side of Ukraine, there may be disappointment about the promises of the EU. Expectations in Ukraine are very high today. It was very powerful footage when people waved EU flags in the liberated Kherson. However, genuine membership is a long shot. The internal division in the EU about Russia has not dispersed entirely, and Hungary is still recalcitrant against Europe's unified stand.

Also, the role of populism needs to be taken into account. In a few EU member-states, populism has been infamously sympathetic to Russia and has probably enjoyed generous support from Putin's regime, especially on the right wing. The EU is now discovering and severing all these connections.

Russia was using right-wing extremists across the EU to create division and confusion for quite some time. In the face of the ongoing war, this activity seems to have stalled. The extremists can no longer exploit and rely on pro-Russian sentiment — and currently the huge support to the Ukrainian side nurtures an anti-Russian standpoint. However, this may change. In future, the extreme right could mobilize on the grounds of "Why should we continue our support to the refugees from Ukraine?"

Among the radical voices on the left-wing side, the question may sound differently: "Why should we continue to support the war effort in Ukraine, purchase weapons, and endure sanctions when we need to take care of our own labour forces and inequalities?"

What I am saying here is that more divisions may appear in Europe in future, and the probability of such divisions will only increase after the fighting stops. As we know from the Balkans, the conflict does not get resolved as the moment the belligerents lay down their arms. And even if the conflict gets resolved, it does not mean that we will immediately have a shining example of democracy. In a future peaceful Ukraine, there may still remain a lot of informal ties, Russian influence under the radar, and internal problems.

Therefore, the major social and political challenge after the fighting is over will be dealing with disappointment. Things will not immediately be as good as Ukrainians and the EU hope them to be.

Kushnir: Do you think that the EU's "Marshall Plan" for Ukraine will be put into practice?

Vermeersch: There will definitely be some investment. When you consider that the EU itself emerged as an economic organization and has traditionally been good at raising economies, investment in postwar Ukraine looks like a logical step. On the other hand, providing military support is something that the EU has never been comfortable with.

The problem with economic aid is that it alone will not be sufficient. Above, I mentioned many other efforts that will be needed to make postwar Ukraine function—in particular, reconciliation and justice. To that you have to add efforts to find out how a new geopolitical balance in Europe will work. Relations with Russia, as well as what happens inside of Russia, will be important for achieving the success of the EU's economic investment in Ukraine. By relations with Russia I mean answering questions about to what extent will the EU become independent from Russia's fossil-fuel energy, and to what extent will Russia become marginalized.

In addition, much effort will be needed to remove all the land mines and eliminate other war damage in Ukraine. Like in the Balkans, this will not be a matter of simple economic support. It is also about structures and the distribution of responsibilities between politicians.

The case of the Balkans demonstrates that it would not be very wise for the EU to make Ukraine overly dependent on external funding. In the long run, this may even provoke resentment against the EU, as happened in Bosnia. The state has been so much under the umbrella of international organizations that it hardly had a chance to make its economic system sustainable and independent. For decades, politicians in Bosnia worked with a layer of international presence, and eventually they mobilized against it. A similar situation, if it happens in Ukraine, would not be very healthy.

Therefore, as the EU's "Marshall Plan" will be put into practice I am not sure what it will look like exactly. Also, I cannot clearly say whether this plan will be sufficient to transform postwar Ukraine into a state where everything is better than before.

Kushnir: How do you assess the chances for Ukraine to gain full-fledged EU membership in the future? You have mentioned already that as a goal it is a long shot. But when do you think it will happen? How do you see the process of Ukraine's European integration?

Vermeersch: This process cannot be approached outside of the logic of how the EU's enlargement has developed so far. Therefore, a quick enlargement and incorporation of Ukraine are not much of a realistic prospect, even though sympathy for Ukraine remains really high. The EU has drawn lessons from the previous history of its enlargements, especially from their flaws.

Also, you need to keep in mind the regulations that are in place. To become a full-fledged member of the EU, any country has to meet demanding preconditions. These preconditions will not change and none will treat Ukraine exceptionally.

Another issue is the political will within the EU. The resolve to be on the side of Ukraine during the war may be great; however, the resolve to accept Ukraine as a full-fledged EU member after the war—not that much. We need to be realistic here. I do not think that the political will be as high in the EU after the war as it is today, in the midst of it.

Kushnir: What will be the long-term impact of the war on EU-Russian relations?

Vermeersch: Since the beginning of the war we have seen a complete break between Brussels and Moscow. The war came as a wake-up call for many EU leaders and I think there is no way back.

It is hard to speculate what Russia will look like after the war. Will it be without Putin? Will it abandon all of its claims over Ukraine? However, in any case, we will not be going back to the situation that existed ten years ago. The suspicion toward Russia has risen and cannot be reversed.

With respect to energy dependence, I would like to be optimistic. The EU member-states are doing almost the impossible now. They are changing their energy policies to move away from the petrol-state Russia. There is no going back to the pre-invasion volumes of oil and gas imports. I think that this will be the biggest long-term effect on EU-Russia relations.

CHAPTER 22

Russia has failed to subordinate Ukraine

Alexander Vindman
Interview with Oleksandr Pankieiev, published 14 March 2023

Alexander Vindman, a retired US Army Lieutenant Colonel, was the director for European Affairs on the White House's National Security Council. Before that, he served as the Political–Military Affairs Officer for Russia for the Chairman of the Joint Chiefs of Staff and as an attaché at the US Embassy in Moscow. While on the Joint Staff, he co-authored the National Military Strategy Russia Annex and was the principal author of the Global Campaign for Russia. He earned an MA from Harvard University, where he serves as a Hauser Leader, and a PhD from the Johns Hopkins School of Advanced International Studies, where he is currently a senior fellow. His best-selling memoir is called *Here, Right Matters: An American Story* (2021).

Pankieiev: What are your main observations of Russia's one-year escalated invasion of Ukraine? What conclusions can we draw from it?

Vindman: Well, the most important conclusion is that Russia has failed in its project of subordinating Ukraine, destroying Ukraine as a sovereign independent state. It is no longer feasible for Russia to win through military force.

The biggest potential risk to Ukraine's sovereignty is a multi-year war in which Russia uses its resources as a country of 140 million people to grind down the Ukrainian population, which is significantly smaller.

But it's highly unlikely that Russia has the [necessary] power for a multi-year war when it has been such a disastrous war for Russia from the military perspective—and economic costs as well as politically Russia has been isolated. But from a military standpoint, the way wars are won, it's been a complete disaster for Russia.

The biggest thing is that Ukraine will survive, and Ukraine will survive as a sovereign independent state. It's no longer the thinking that Western Ukraine is Western-oriented and everything on the eastern side of the Dnipro is Russia. The best Russia could hope for is limited objectives and to freeze the war and retain some control over the four regions that Russia annexed since last year. But that's still not a likely notion.

So my biggest takeaway is that Russia has fundamentally lost this war already, because its project was to eliminate Ukraine as an independent state. Ukraine is one.

The question is, then, details. What does Ukraine look like? What are the boundaries of Ukraine? How severely damaged is Ukraine? Could it reconstitute as a prosperous state that could integrate with the West? And how much of the damage that Russia has suffered will fundamentally undermine Russia as a regional power?

Pankieiev: Looking back now, can we say that it was predictable and preventable? The West and the US, particularly, knew about the planned invasion months ahead. What was not done? Or what was done wrong?

Vindman: Too much has been wrong, frankly. I think there was a lot of equivocation and political hedging, which *suggests* that the US was aware that war was coming. I think actually the fact is that the US ultimately determined that war was coming much later than what they're trying to present now.

It wasn't until the negotiations and diplomacy failed in January that the US finally realized that war couldn't be averted. Up until that point, there was still plenty of senior leadership in the US that were saying, well, this could be a demonstration, this doesn't necessarily mean full-scale war. So I think we got that wrong.

And it was clear the telltale signs of full-scale war were present in October, November, increasingly clear through December and January. I was writing about a full-scale war in December and then laying out the way that Russia was going to conduct a full-scale-war—not a limited war with limited objectives for just the Donbas but to seize, capture, and destroy Ukraine as an independent state.

I think part of the consequences of this kind of thinking, this equivocation about whether the war was coming, influenced the ability to provide Ukraine support. Because the thinking from policymakers was: "Well, if this is not a war, if this is just a demonstration, wouldn't giving Ukraine military arms precipitate the war that we're trying to avoid?"

In fact, if we had recognized that war was definitely coming and started to provide significant support to Ukraine before the first shots were fired, it [w]ould have sent a signal to Russia that the US, the West, the Euro-Atlantic Alliance as a whole, were going to be there for Ukraine. And maybe even [they could have] played some sort of role in deterring the war.

Instead, we were completely reactive. The US, as a policy, was entirely reactive, not providing really anything in terms of significant materiel. We provided limited numbers of javelins, anti-tank systems, and air defence systems. Somewhat modest: nothing that was going to change Russia's calculations about whether to conduct this war. Everything else came very slowly afterwards — and reactively, mainly because of some misplaced fears about Russian escalation that never materialized.

We're still getting it wrong, frankly. The West is still wrong about this war, over-ascribing the risks of escalation and the possibility of a direct confrontation between Russia and NATO. Or not having a concrete strategy around what we want [from] this war or where we want this war to end — that we want Ukraine to win, that we want Russia to lose, and that *it's important to the rules-based international system that Russia loses this war*, in order to preserve what our grandparents fought for in World War II: a system in which strong states don't prey on weak states and use military force to acquire territory.

We don't have a complete strategy; we have something far more rather amorphous about supporting Ukraine — "for as long as it takes" but not "whatever it takes" yet.

Pankieiev: How would you evaluate the current level of military help Ukraine receives from its Western partners? Is it what Ukraine needs now, or is it still insufficient to liberate the occupied territories?

Vindman: Unfortunately, I think we've continued to under-resource Ukraine. If Ukraine is, in fact, fighting for the rules-based international system that has enabled the US, Canadian, and European democratic prosperity, we should be giving Ukraine all the resources it needs.

Ukrainian soldiers are dying on the battlefield, Ukrainian civilians are suffering, and the least we should be doing is resourcing Ukraine to defend itself, to liberate its territory, to impose a cost on Russia for this illegal barbarous war. We're not doing anywhere near enough; we keep moving in the right direction, but it's very slow, it's very plodding. It's a very unsure policy, in which we provide Ukraine support and then, based on the reaction from the Russians, we determine that there isn't a risk of escalation, and then we go to the next level of support.

That's not the way that this war ends quickly. That's a recipe for a long drawn-out war, a war that lasts years—instead of giving Ukraine all the resources it really needed from the beginning, where Ukraine could have terminated Russia's theory of victory, which is this campaign of grinding down the Ukrainian armed forces. We could have provided the long-range artillery, the tanks, the armoured personnel carriers earlier. We didn't do that. We're still resistant to providing air power and unmanned drones. It's a bit of negligence, I think, on the part of the Euro-Atlantic Alliance, where for really a negligible contribution of resources we could end the biggest threat to the international system since World War II.

And I guess the last thing I'll mention about this is that the US has poured in tens of billions of dollars of resources to help Ukraine win—even in this limited, insufficient manner—but [nevertheless] it's tens of billions. And some of the US industrial base is shifting to be able to continue to support Ukraine and rebuild the depleted stocks of military materiel, which the US will need—either to fend off Russia but mainly focused on China. We now are learning what sort of war we will probably face with China also. But if that's what the US is doing, then the rest of the Euro-Atlantic Alliance has done far less.

I mean, even the Canadian government has really kind of supported Ukraine on the cheap. As a portion of Canada's gross domestic product, or defence budget, it seems like a lot. But it's not retooled, it's not saying "okay, we need to invest much more resources into defence in this very critical moment." It's all under the assumption that "while this war could end in the next six to nine months, why should we retool, why should we put large defence orders? Why should we take resources away from other economic activities?" That is a mistake.

I tend to think about the fact that the US defence budget is, in fact, somewhat bloated. If you asked me before this war started, "Do we spend too much on defence?" I would say yes, but not in this crisis moment.

In this crisis moment we need to make sure that we're properly resourcing not just the fight in Ukraine but also deterrence in China. I think that we need to do at least as much, if not more. But the same thing goes for the rest of NATO; the Alliance needs to step up and contribute in a much bigger way.

Pankieiev: US President Joe Biden, when asked whether President Volodymyr Zelensky needs F-16 fighter jets, replied, "He doesn't need F-16s now" and that there is "no basis upon which there is a rationale, according to our military now, to provide F-16s." What is your opinion on this? Is it true that Ukraine does need any fighter jets to conduct successful offensive operations this year?

Vindman: It's smoke and mirrors—seemingly applying some analysis to something that's illogical. It's the ability to say, "Well, our military experts have looked at this, and have judged that there are other systems that Ukraine needs. And for efficiency purposes, we shouldn't be talking about F-16s, we should be talking about other systems"—that is invalid.

There is no world in which you're giving Ukraine more advanced aircraft—even though it might take six months to get there—giving Ukraine a better opportunity to take control of its skies, that doesn't make military sense. I think it's a bit of strategic negligence to say that we don't need to make this investment, where it takes a long time to build the military base for support—and they're one of the most advanced aircraft in the world. Training pilots, training mechanics and engineers, and providing a logistical base for operating a sophisticated Western platform—that takes a long time, and we're not making those investments now. We should have done that months ago, six, nine months ago. And [now] we would have been in a position where Ukraine would have trained pilots, would have these resources.

Eventually, Ukraine is going to transition to Western-made equipment, to an entirely Western-equipped force. It may not be F-16s, it could be Swedish Gripens, it could be Tornados, it could be any number, it could be Rafale fighters. It doesn't have to be the latest, fourth-generation-plus fighter, but it should be something far more advanced than Soviet-era MiG-29s. So I think it's unfortunate that the rhetoric hasn't changed, because the reality has changed.

And even Biden, within that same speech, will say, "We're going to give Ukraine everything it needs"; this rhetoric shows a little level of urgency, commencing with the crisis, but the actions don't. So it's really troubling that we're still in the place where we're saying, "Well, they don't need this, we're not going to give them this" — when we know at this point, looking at the way the support to Ukraine has unfolded, we know that we're gonna get there. It'll just be a matter of time.

We said that tanks would cause World War III, but we gave them tanks. We said all these different things and we completely blew past them. When I talked to the Biden Administration, when I talked to the National Security Council way back in the days before [all-out] war and after it started, *I told them that they are going to do things that they think are impossible.* They will ultimately provide Ukraine with all the support it needs, it's just a question of when. And they have slowly moved in that direction — but frankly, just too slowly, with a high degree of risk that is unnecessary. Because a long war is not just damaging to Ukraine, it's also damaging to the United States. It's damaging on the basis of the fact that the Russians can incrementally escalate or the Chinese could see some opportunities to step in and embarrass the US and support an authoritarian regime. It is too close for comfort, when the stakes are so high, to provide, you know, this kind of really quite slow, insufficient support.

Pankieiev: It's also a hybrid war, and information plays a huge role in this. I remember months ago, before the full-scale invasion, Jens Stoltenberg and many other officials repeated many times that NATO and the US would not be fighting "for Ukraine." This also contributed to Putin's decision to invade Ukraine. It seems like the West is making the same mistake right now.

Vindman: Well, it's longer than just this period, frankly. This is, let's say, a microcosm of the broader relationships that the US has had with Ukraine and the Russian Federation since 1991 — namely, [an attitude of] primacy towards Russia and stability in the relationship with Russia, averting a crisis with Russia, and preserving the possibility of a long-term cooperative relationship with Russia. All at a cost to Ukraine.

It's a mistake that in the short term we do things that minimize the risks, without recognizing how those decisions in the short term stack up into a very acute crisis in the long term. We keep buying down the risks in the short-term, while in a way breeding impunity and with Vladimir Putin believing that he could get away with it.

That's the story of 23 years for Vladimir Putin [since he succeeded Yeltsin in 2000]: at almost every turn he's suffered nearly no consequences. And he was trained to believe that: "Why couldn't I conduct this war? What [have I got to lose]? The Ukrainians are going to fold, the West might render some punishments for a short period of time. Why not?" We see the same thing playing out now in the Biden Administration. It's shifting to kind of—frankly, more of a consistent relationship with Ukraine, but still way too slow.

Pankieiev: We are witnessing an ongoing heavy battle for Bakhmut. What is happening there now? What is the strategic significance of that location if Russia gains complete control of it?

Vindman: It's troubling. I think they're going to start to get more and more criticism. I've been talking about this for probably six weeks, maybe eight weeks, and I'm very concerned about what's going on in Bakhmut.

Bakhmut itself is not strategic. It's only taken on a strategic significance because Volodymyr Zelensky has put a lot of his own credibility on the line with regards to saying that we're going to hold Bakhmut, we're going to win here.

From a military perspective, I mean, not everything is that black and white; there are concrete tactical, operational reasons for areas. If they're transit hubs, if they're rail networks, if they're controlling terrain for a region, they might have a significance of their own or a piece of ground that allows you to conduct follow-on operations. But Bakhmut doesn't really hold any of those, you know—minor, let's say—tactical advantages. In general, it's not that important.

But it's turning out to be a strategic fight between Russia pouring all sorts of resources to take the city and Ukraine defending at all costs. I think it's a mistake.

Where Ukraine was successful for much of the war up until this point is that they traded space for time, inflicting massive casualties on Russians and then sapping Russia's ability to conduct offensive operations—we call it forcing the Russians to culminate, where they can't conduct any more offensive operations and have to shift to defence. And then Ukraine is able to pick and choose where to fight.

That was the recipe for success in Siverskodonetsk, Donetsk, and Luhansk. Those tough fights, in which Ukraine ultimately withdrew but Russia had no ability to continue to fight, allowed Ukraine to pivot to a very successful offensive in Kharkiv and a very successful offensive in Kherson.

For some reason, the Ukrainian military—but its political leadership in particular—has decided that they want to fight in Bakhmut and hold it at all costs. The problem I see with this is that while Ukraine is inflicting significant casualties on Russia, it's also taking significant losses. And that's a problem, because eventually, when Russia does run out of steam and can't conduct any more offensives, Ukraine may also run out or not have sufficient capacity for a counteroffensive.

And that's troubling. To me, unless the Ukrainians are absolutely sure they could win and preserve combat power for an offensive in the spring and summer, to me this doesn't make a lot of sense. And I think there's an element of pride—you know, that Ukraine has lost too much and too many people have been sacrificed to let the city go. But it's troubling, because I think Ukraine is taking some significant losses around Bakhmut.

Pankieiev: What is your prognosis of how the war will develop this year? What should we expect from Ukraine's planned offensive operations this spring and over the summer?

Vindman: I was more confident about this, you know, some six weeks ago or two months ago, and I looked at it as campaign cycles. Russia would run an offensive that would peter out, wouldn't really achieve anything, or maybe small tactical gains like, you know, taking Bakhmut. And Ukraine would then seize the opportunity afterwards, when Russia switches to defence, to liberate large chunks of territory—again, like Kharkiv, like Kherson.

My assessment was, up until recently, that you'd be in one of these campaign cycles—Russian offensive, Ukrainian counteroffensive—and then Russia would basically not be in a position to continue to fight this war without another mass mobilization. And then Putin might choose to negotiate in order to hold what he has, hold some portions of the Donbas, or hold on to Crimea, because Ukraine would be successful.

With the way things are shaping up in Bakhmut, it introduces an element of risk and doubt that we may not have a full "Russian offensive – Ukrainian counteroffensive" campaign cycle. If we don't [manage the counteroffensive this time], Russia has the breathing room to do another call-up and conduct another offensive. And then Ukraine hasn't gained anything, it hasn't liberated territory as it did in the summer and fall of last year.

Right now, I still think the leader of the Ukrainian Armed Forces, [Valerii] Zaluzhnyi, is probably going to eventually conduct a similar operation to what he did in Eastern Ukraine, in the Donbas last year: withdraw and make sure he has the means to conduct an offensive later. I think if that's the case, the way I see this playing out is that by late summer Ukraine will liberate additional territory. And then we could start to hear much more substantive conversations from the Russians about negotiations. But that's where I think this is going to fall out.

There's a small chance that this just drags out for another campaign cycle, another six to nine months, and deep into 2024. And that becomes quite risky, because we'll see another Russian mobilization, we'll see too little support coming in from the West, and none of this equipment is not going to come in a large formation – like armoured formations that have the ability to penetrate through Russian lines. Instead, they're rather piecemeal, with small dribs and drabs of equipment coming in to stabilize the lines. And if this extends through 2024, then there are also some questions emerging about Western support. Will the US continue to support Ukraine in the same way? Will the rest of the Euro-Atlantic Alliance continue to support it in the same way? So I think, again, it's too close for comfort.

The US, as a world leader in the arsenal of democracy, should be providing more support. Ukraine should be very thoughtful in its strategy and determining what works, and we could start to see a winding down of the conflict towards the end of the year. That's a bit of an optimistic view, but it's feasible, it's realistic, that we could start to see that.

And then there's the other side of the coin, where we don't do enough and Ukraine isn't successful at the strategic level. And we see this war extend through another year.

Pankieiev: In your essay for the *Foreign Affairs* magazine, you discussed the possibility and impossibility of liberating Ukrainian territories. Do you still think it is possible, and what is needed to achieve it?

Vindman: I laid out a course of action in which Ukraine had a very difficult road to liberate Crimea. I laid out a scenario in which, if everything worked out well, they would be able to do that. But my ultimate conclusion was that it might be too costly an operation, even back then.

The reason is that considering it just as a military problem, there are not that many ways to get to Crimea; it's a peninsula with limited access. And so the Russians know exactly where the Ukrainians are coming from. Ukraine doesn't have an amphibious capability to be able to attack across the water. That would be very challenging.

The purpose of the article was mainly focusing on arming Ukraine with all the resources Ukraine needed to make Russia's position on Crimea untenable, as well as destroying the Kerch bridge and making sure that Ukraine has all the resources to really punish significant portions of Russia's military infrastructure. It's a possibility, although I think it's not the most likely course of action. Other analysts are more rosy and optimistic, but I think it's a stretch.

And if this battle of Bakhmut—which is, again, not strategic but has taken on a strategic significance—doesn't play out in Ukraine's favour and Ukraine doesn't have the strength to threaten the land-bridge—basically, from Zaporizhia to Melitopol and Mariupol—then there's no conversation about Crimea, period. Ukraine has to be successful in starting to roll back some of Russia's occupation, holding some of Russia's forces in place and attacking to basically break Russia's land-bridge to Crimea, as well as destroy the Kerch [Bridge] in order to have any chance of liberating Crimea.

Pankieiev: But it seems like Russia is considering that this scenario is possible, because recent imagery from satellites, and also some videos, show that Russia has constructed some trenches on the [Crimean] shoreline.

Vindman: That's true. I think the fact is that it doesn't take a huge application of resources, it's actually pretty modest, to put up trenches and fortifications on Crimea and not necessarily rely on a huge amount of force to defend them, because they are fortifications on top of a water obstacle. So you don't need a lot of manpower to defend those. But every little bit helps.

Russia has also fortified the entire front line behind the advance troops in the same way. So it's a relatively modest application of resources. The biggest challenge that Russia has is trained troops, and being able to man those defences. Once Russia shifts to defence, that's going to be a challenge for Russia.

Pankieiev: If I am correct, you also don't exclude the possibility of tactical nuclear strikes by Russia. How likely is Russia to use nuclear weapons, and what can it achieve if it uses them?

Vindman: So there are a lot of reasons why Russia won't use nuclear weapons in Ukraine. But the one time that it makes sense for Russia would be Crimea. That's the point I was making. It's not that it's likely or significantly more likely, because the use of nuclear weapons is strategic in a global context, not strategic in just a Russia-Ukraine war context.

The use of nuclear weapons would isolate Russia in a way that it hasn't been isolated thus far — from its last remaining relationships, with China and India. And it would potentially precipitate all those limits on US and Western support, could potentially be limited… It could introduce the possibility, although remote, that NATO gets directly involved, because the use of nuclear weapons that close to a NATO territory may necessitate NATO establishing a no-fly zone to make sure that there was nothing, no accident of a strike on NATO territories. So I think there are a lot of reasons that Russia wouldn't go down that road.

But in my scenario Ukraine is successful: it destroys the Kerch Bridge, threatens or destroys Russia's land-bridge, and then starts to posture forces for an attack on Crimea. That concentration of forces and along the front line — it takes a lot of force to break through into Crimea — that concentration of forces is also a lucrative target for nuclear weapons, tactical nuclear weapons. So out of all the periods of time, that's where it might make sense from a tactical level. It might make sense for Putin given the fact that Crimea is his kind of crown jewel. It would be deeply embarrassing to him if he lost Crimea. So the chances are higher but not significantly higher because on the other side, the use of nuclear weapons would be extremely costly to Vladimir Putin.

And he could even [afford to] lose Crimea. He could lose Crimea and go back to pre-2014 [borders] and still survive. His regime is not really that threatened; he's still popular, could use all of the law enforcement, the security services to repress the population, keep control. Whereas using nuclear weapons would actually destabilize and threaten Putin's regime. So I think, on that basis, my conclusion is that he wouldn't use nuclear weapons, but the highest chance would be around a Crimea scenario.

Pankieiev: What are other resources and options that Russia has left to continue the war?

Vindman: Russia doesn't have inexhaustible resources; it's a country of 140 million people, but it's a country that has somewhat modest capabilities. This is not the Soviet Union mobilized for World War II, you know, full mobilization. It's not a country of 320 million people — it's a country of 140 million people, much smaller than the aggregate Soviet Union and much weaker in terms of economic resources.

Even that population of 140 million people is a bit of a mirage. It somehow implies that it's three times the size of Ukraine and therefore has three times the manpower, but that's not true. Estimates are, for instance, in the United States that at any given moment only about 23 percent of the military-age male population in the US is adaptable for military service: they're healthy, psychologically fit, and reach the basic aptitude standards. If that's the case in the US — with a much healthier society — we are talking about a fraction of that available in Russia, let's say, 10 percent of the military-age male population is useful for military service. So that means that it's a pretty limited resource, it's a perishable resource.

Russia started this war with, on paper, a military of 800,000. The attacking force is closer to about 150,000, but it cycled through, at this point, somewhere in the ballpark of about 300,000, 350,000, maybe 400,000 troops, and that is a lot. Many casualties — we're talking about well over 100,000 killed and severely injured, out of the fight; It's probably closer to 150,000, maybe even 200,000 now (the numbers on this are tough). So that's why Putin had to do a call-up of 350,000 troops.

They don't have an endless supply of military-age males. They're using penal battalions to fill the ranks of the Wagner Group.

Not only is it a problem just actually conscripting those people, but when Russia tried to do the mobilization back in the spring for 300,000, three times as many people left the country. That is a pretty costly decision: you've basically lost somewhere in the ballpark of a million people. Some of them have been mobilized into the force, a lot of them have already been killed, and half of that 300,000 is already out of the fight. And then a huge number has left the country because they have no interest in serving. Imagine that Putin did the same thing for another 500,000 and another 1.5 million left the country because they did not want to serve. How many times can Russia go through that, with this relatively modest amount of military-aged males, before it runs out of military capacity? So it's not endless.

Nor is it a guarantee that just because Russia calls these personnel, it's going to be successful. With those 300,000 troops that Russia called up previously, it was able to stabilize the lines, [but] it didn't really enable offensive operations. Russia is still fighting for the same territory it's been fighting for from the beginning. The Ukrainians haven't been able to take territory, but Russia's made [only] very tiny gains. So, another 500,000 troops may not necessarily be as meaningful in terms of allowing Russia to annex additional territory. But it's also at a huge cost—in manpower, in internal stability—so I think it's increasingly hard for Putin to make the decision to move in that direction.

Pankieiev: What are your most realistic scenarios for how the war could end? Are there any possibilities of a revolt among the Russian military or political elites against Putin's regime?

Vindman: To me, as a strategist, this is the beginning of the end of Putin and Putinism. I think that could play out over the course of years, not months. I think the fact is that ultimately the costs—economic costs, the isolation, the manpower, the folly of this campaign against Ukraine—are going to wear down Putin and Putinism. Nothing acute, not a coup, not mass protests; I don't see the signs of that.

But ultimately, Putin is going to pay the cost for this. Again, I think that could be over the course of the next year and a half, maybe, because he's up for reelection in 2024. Maybe, if this war was over relatively quickly, I could see him putting in somebody else, as he did with [one-term president Dmitry] Medvedev, who would be the face of Russia, to normalize relationships. The longer this war goes, the less likely he is to step down; that means Russia is isolated for longer, for another six years, if Putin remains the head of state. At least from a conceptual standpoint, I think it would be hard for him to maintain power after this disastrous war.

I need to think about this a little more, because I was thinking about it consistently at the beginning of the war, the cost for Putin. I haven't really reassessed the risks more than a year into the war. But if I had to make a judgment call, I don't see any real domestic risks right now for him. He's still quite popular; there is no real sign of popular discontent, with mass protests. That was the hope behind large sanctions on Russia, which were supposed to suppress GDP by 15–20 percent; instead, only 2.5 percent of Russia's GDP has been impacted.

This next year will be different, because part of the reason that Russia was able to weather the sanctions was oil prices. Russia will not enjoy those oil prices in the middle of [this] mild winter. Oil prices are low and will get lower when it warms up. So, the ability to cushion the sanctions is not going to be there. There might be something, socio-economic protests that could emerge; the costs of all these tens of thousands of casualties might wear down [the economy]. But right now, given the fact that Putin's security apparatus is really untapped — they haven't had to do mass repressions, they haven't had to suppress mass protests — I think there is no real significant risk from popular discontent yet.

And the idea of a coup also seems remote, because although these elites don't have the ability to travel in Europe and send their kids to elite universities, they're still at the top of a rotting system in Russia. They know that to maintain their hierarchy, they need to continue supporting Vladimir Putin, so I don't think that will change either. So the idea of a palace coup seems remote — only in the case of an extreme scenario, like Putin wanting to go nuclear and then the elites recognizing that that could be the end of them also.

CHAPTER 23

Russia's disinformation goes nuclear

Polina Sinovets, Khrystyna Holynska, and John V. Parachini

Essay[1] published 23 March 2023

Polina Sinovets (PhD, Odesa Mechnikov National University) is a founder and the current head of the Odesa Center for Nonproliferation at the Odesa Mechnikov National University. She is the author and co-author of works on nuclear weapons policy in the US and Russia, nuclear deterrence, strategic stability, and European security, which have been published in the *Bulletin of the Atomic Scientists*, NATO Defence College's Research Papers series, and the War on the Rocks platform, as well as editor of the collective volumes *Ukraine's Nuclear History: A Non-Proliferation Perspective* (2022), *Arms Control and Europe: New Challenges and Prospects for Strategic Stability* (2022), and *Russia's War on Ukraine: Implications for the Global Nuclear Order* (2023).

Khrystyna Holynska (PhD, Kyiv Shevchenko National University; MBA, Kyiv School of Economics) is an assistant policy researcher at RAND and a doctoral candidate at the Pardee RAND Graduate School (USA). At the KSE she headed the defense and security policy research startup KSE StratBase and was an assistant professor of public policy and governance. Holynska has also been a strategic analyst at the Hague Centre for Strategic Studies (Netherlands) and a research associate with the Center for Global Security Research at the Lawrence Livermore National Laboratory (USA). In October 2023 she participated in the New Security Leaders Program of the Warsaw Security Forum.

John Parachini (MA, Johns Hopkins University, MBA, Georgetown Univ.) is a senior international and defense researcher at RAND, and a member of the Pardee RAND Graduate School faculty. He recently served in the Office of Chemical and Biological Weapons Affairs at the US State Department's Bureau of Arms Control, Deterrence, and Stability. He has testified before both houses of Congress and published in specialized journals as well as the *Washington Quarterly, Los Angeles Times, Newsday, USA Today,* and the *International Herald Tribune*. Parachini has taught at Georgetown University, USC's Washington Policy Center, and CUNY's Baruch College.

Prior to the escalated invasion of Ukraine, the political and military leadership of the Russian Federation alleged that Ukraine was

---

1. Funding for this research was provided by the US Department of State.

planning to regain its nuclear status and that it would be receiving the help of Western countries (Putin 2022a). This claim was repeated on 9 May 2022, almost three months following the 24 February incursion, during the closely watched Victory Day speech by Russia's President Vladimir Putin (2022b). He declared that Russia could not tolerate Ukraine becoming a nuclear state in its "near abroad" and was forced to take steps to prevent it. These false accusations have been repeatedly refuted by Ukraine, the US, and other Western nations; nevertheless, Moscow continues to disseminate them to Russian and international audiences. Essentially, this should be regarded as one of numerous forms of Russian disinformation that are designed to justify its unprovoked invasion of Ukraine and maintain domestic and international support for an illegal military operation that has been floundering.

Russia continues to push false narratives

Russia perpetuates three types of false narratives on nuclear and radiological weapons in Ukraine: (i) Ukraine has nuclear weapons aspirations; (ii) it has ready technical capabilities to produce a nuclear or radioactive device of some sort; and (iii) it is benefitting from Western assistance. These three allegations are examined below in greater detail.

(i) Political will to acquire nuclear weapons

First, by distorting statements made by Ukrainian leaders Moscow alleges that the political will exists for Ukraine to return to its nuclear status. It is true, of course, that Ukraine's leaders have repeatedly expressed dissatisfaction with the 1994 Budapest Memorandum on Security Assurances, which formalized the new state giving up the Soviet nuclear weapons on its territory and declaring its non-nuclear status. Russian media has recently picked up on such statements and often quotes them out of context to suggest that Ukraine is seeking nuclear weapons capability. To be sure, as far back as 2003 respectable Ukrainian publications aired discussions of nuclear status being the only way to protect Ukraine from foreign aggression—primarily, Russia. Russian media emphasized that the first Ukrainian President, Leonid Kravchuk, who was directly involved in the negotiations on the 1994 Memorandum, said in a series of interviews that Ukraine gave up its nuclear arsenal under immense pressure.

Russian media repeatedly refers to Ukrainian President Zelensky's speech at the 2022 Munich Security Conference. In this speech, he expressed concerns that Ukraine had given up nuclear weapons for nothing as the security guarantees received from other countries, including Russia, might have never materialized (Zelenskyy 2022). Russian media published headlines, misinterpreting these words as if Ukraine had threatened the world with nuclear weapons.

Russia's misleading and distorting narratives are based on extracting these quotes from Ukrainian and Western media to give them a patina of legitimacy. Countering false claims and putting circumstances in context takes time and energy to set the record straight. Ukrainian and Western leaders' refutations of false claims about Ukraine's nuclear ambitions sometimes make them seem defensive and divert attention from Russia's aggressive behaviour towards neighbouring nations that are charting independent and democratic political pathways.

(ii) Technical capabilities

Russian military and intelligence leaders alleged that Ukraine currently has or can quickly regain the technical capabilities to create a weapon of mass destruction: if not a nuclear bomb, then at least a radiological bomb. During Russia's Security Council meeting on 21 February 2022, Russian Minister of Defense Sergey Shoigu listed the arguments for how Ukraine could acquire such capabilities quickly, especially if it had extensive Western aid (Regnum 2022). On 3 March 2022, the Director of the Foreign Intelligence Service of Russia, Sergey Naryshkin, claimed to have evidence of Ukrainian efforts to build nuclear weapons (RFIS 2022). Russia's political and military leaders have talked about some old Soviet capabilities, such as the Tochka-U missile, which could carry a nuclear payload. The explosions at the Zaporizhia nuclear plant and the physics campus of Kharkiv university were also discussed in Russian media. Russia alleged that Ukrainian forces attacked these facilities to hide any traces of the development of nuclear capabilities (Reuters 2022). On the contrary, multiple credible sources revealed that the Russian military was responsible for the attacks on the Zaporizhia nuclear power plant, not Ukrainian forces.

These allegations are nothing new. Russian concerns about Ukraine's developing nuclear capabilities were repeatedly voiced in 2014 during Russia's annexation of Ukrainian territory. After

Russia's first invasion of Ukraine, TASS published an interview with experts claiming that Ukraine would be able to develop nuclear weapons in ten years (ITAR-TASS 2014). In a contradictory and condemnatory fashion, Russian media also criticized the idea that Ukraine would even be capable of developing it. Instead, many Russian outlets snidely asserted that Ukraine could not produce a nuclear weapon and could only create a radiological weapon or so-called "dirty bomb." Russian media called this type of weapon a "poor man's atomic bomb" and emphasized the ease with which Ukraine would be able to convert its existing limited capabilities to develop it. In 2015, the Russian publication Military Review discussed the history of the dirty bomb concept and concluded that Ukraine would be highly capable of creating them on its territory (Volodin 2015). There is no evidence that the Ukrainian military or energy authorities have ever pursued the development of radiological weapons in any form.

(iii) International support

Finally, the third line of argumentation centers around the claim that the West, both politically and financially, incentivizes Ukraine to develop nuclear weapons as a means to threaten Russia. An article in a Russian military journal, Military-Industrial Courier, talked in 2018 about how China might supply the technology and Saudi Arabia might provide money for the research that can enable Ukraine to develop a "dirty bomb" or even a nuclear weapon.

A possible reason why these claims may seem plausible to Russian audiences is that Russia and Ukraine have a long history of joint work on nuclear capabilities during the Soviet era. Ukrainian research institutions, particularly the above-mentioned Kharkiv institute, played a crucial role in developing Soviet weapons. Russian media openly acknowledged the contribution of the Kharkiv institute in their publications on the topic. A design bureau in Dnipro (Yuzhmash, today "Pivdenne") was also central to the Soviet intercontinental ballistic missile program. Russia's disinformation narratives claim that Ukraine's missile production capabilities serve as evidence of its ability to produce launch vehicles for nuclear warheads. This ignores how producing missiles is fundamentally different from producing nuclear weapons. The Russian claim that missile production equalled an intentional effort to also load the missile with nuclear weapons was pernicious conjecture on their part.

Russian leaders make the strategic argument that they cannot accept Ukraine as a nuclear-armed neighbour because nuclear weapons launched from its territory would strike Russia in a few minutes. The Levada Center's polls show that, over the past years, the fear of imminent global war has been increasing among Russians. Ukraine is portrayed as a Western proxy, deprived of any decision-making ability and yet capable of inflicting a devastating nuclear strike on Russia.

Why these narratives lack grounds

Political will

Ukrainian rhetoric on dissatisfaction with the Budapest Memorandum and renunciation of its nuclear status can be tracked throughout Ukraine's history as an independent state. Some of the statements that have received considerable media attention in Russia can be attributed to extremist political groups originating from fringe individuals and organizations that lack legitimacy, both in Ukraine and abroad. Despite numerous attempts to enter mainstream politics, these groups have little electoral support among Ukrainian voters. Therefore, their rhetoric cannot be rightfully interpreted as representing the majority opinion, nor, moreover, can it serve as evidence of Ukraine's national political objective.

In instances where statements have been made by legitimate Ukrainian political and community leaders, a closer look at the timing of such statements shows that in most cases they were made in response to increased threats from the Russian Federation to Ukraine's sovereignty and territorial integrity. For instance, Russia's construction of a dam in the Kerch Strait in close proximity to Ukraine's territory was one of the early incidents which forced Ukrainian leaders to question the support guaranteed by the Budapest Memorandum.

The annexation of Crimea in 2014 led to even more frequent claims that renunciation of Ukraine's nuclear status was a mistake, as it did not increase the country's security. Since 2014 Ukraine has asked for consultations on the Budapest Memorandum four times. They never happened, because Moscow repeatedly blocked the meeting.

Furthermore, Russia's military buildups over recent years provided Ukrainians rational reasons to express regrets about the renunciation of Ukraine's nuclear status; some of these regrets were expressed by members of the Ukrainian parliament. However, the many attempts to revive the Budapest Memorandum through consultations occurred during Zelensky's presidency, which underscores the current Ukrainian government's commitment to its non-nuclear status. While the Ukrainian government is upholding its commitment, it wants Russia and the other parties involved in the Memorandum to uphold their commitments.

Ukrainian presidents Poroshenko and Zelensky made desperate pleas to revive the international assurance mechanism and expressed disappointment that it had not been working properly. Trust in the Budapest Memorandum was explicitly stated even in the Military Doctrine of Ukraine, adopted in 2012 — before Russia's first invasion of Ukraine (Yanukovych 2012). The military and national security doctrines that were passed after the territorial integrity of Ukraine was violated did not express such hope. Notably, even despite the Russian annexation of Ukrainian territory, these documents do not refer in any way to revival of the country's nuclear status.

Technological capabilities

Russian claims that Ukraine has—or could easily get—the technological capabilities to quickly build nuclear—or at least radiological, weapons—ignoring the fact that even if it wanted to build one, Ukraine would need to make an extraordinary effort to produce a nuclear weapon. Ukraine's civilian nuclear energy facilities do not possess the necessary technology for producing the fuel required for building a nuclear bomb. Neither does it possess any existing stockpiles of highly enriched uranium. To make a weapon, Ukraine would need to import the necessary enriched uranium or plutonium from another country. After Ukraine eliminated its nuclear arsenal and infrastructure by 2001, 234 kilograms of enriched uranium remained in Ukrainian labs. Then, in 2010 during the Nuclear Security Summit Ukraine decided to give up that nuclear fuel and transferred it in 2012 to the US as a sign of goodwill.

Ukraine does engage in the extraction of natural uranium (which usually consists of 0.03 percent of the mined ore) and processes it into uranium concentrate. However, it does not have the capability to enrich uranium and purchases the nuclear fuel used in its own nuclear power plants from international suppliers. Ukraine has fifteen reactors (13 VVER-1000 and 2 VVER-440) that operate with uranium fuel, enriched up to the level of 3–3.5 percent. It was provided to Ukraine by Westinghouse and Rosatom before the war. These suppliers can use either Ukrainian uranium, enriched to the needed level, or buy it in an already enriched form from an enriched uranium supplier such as the French company Areva.

There was never a uranium enrichment capability in Ukraine during the Soviet times; this was one of the technical reasons that Ukraine gave up the nuclear weapons it inherited from the collapsed USSR. In 2009, when the issue of energy independence from Russia first became relevant for Ukraine, the initiative of President Yushchenko to introduce uranium enrichment for non-military nuclear energy purposes was discouraged by Western partners. Partly due to Iran's example of using a civilian nuclear program as cover to develop uranium enrichment capability that is also applicable to weapons programs, uranium enrichment is today of great international concern. If a country can enrich uranium for nuclear reactors, then it has the potential to sooner or later also enrich it to highly enriched uranium or weapons-grade material.

Therefore, since Ukraine does not have any enrichment capabilities to obtain weapons-grade uranium, it would need to establish new capabilities, thereby violating IAEA safeguards. According to many expert assessments, Ukraine would need thousands of centrifuges to produce sufficient highly enriched nuclear material for a nuclear weapon. But Ukraine has signed and ratified the Additional Protocol [to the safeguards agreement], which gives the IAEA expanded rights to conduct inspections in order to verify a country's legitimate retention of nuclear material and verify that there is no prohibited radioactive material. Given that, it would be extremely risky for Ukraine to launch a covert nuclear program, and extraordinary effort would be required to initiate a new enrichment program now without being detected. Moreover, to do so Ukraine would need to violate international export controls on the highly enriched material clandestinely, but today it is highly likely that such an effort would be detected. Since Ukraine is focused on obtaining conventional weapons to help it counter the Russian invasion, it is highly unlikely that it would risk Western support for its conventional defences by embarking on a long-term risky effort to develop nuclear weapons capability.

Russian false narratives alleging Ukraine's radiological weapons capabilities highlight that Ukraine uses nuclear power and produces spent nuclear fuel that could be dispersed with conventional explosives, creating a so-called "dirty bomb." While theoretically possible, handling radioactive material and dispersing it with conventional explosives is very complicated, which partly explains why it has never been done. Highly radioactive spent reactor fuel is stored in a water-cooling pool to lower its radiation level and eventually packed in heavy concrete containers for lasting storage. Even if some amount of spent nuclear fuel is obtained clandestinely, handling highly radioactive material remains a formidable challenge. To keep a human being safe, one kilogram of lead covering is needed for each gram of gamma radiation-producing material. Thus, a bomb containing 5 kilograms of gamma-radioactive material would weigh 5 tons.

Last but not least is the danger of a nuclear reactor blowing up, which could lead to the dispersion of radioactive material over a territory of unknown size. Given Ukraine's experience with and continuing custodianship of the Soviet-era reactor at Chornobyl, Ukraine is not likely to risk another nuclear industrial incident of this type on its territory. However, Russia's military attacks on the Zaporizhia Nuclear Power Plant entail a serious possibility of creating just this type of radiological incident. Ukrainian reactor management officials moved 200 metric tons of spent fuel containers at the reactor so that they could be monitored by overhead satellites, in order to detect any attempts to move them further, which would require special transport capabilities in order to do so safely.

International support

Russia's narratives on Ukraine building a nuclear or a radiological weapon to target Russia include a reference to external support. This false argument plays the most to the fears of Russia's domestic audiences. Western leaders explicitly and repeatedly refute this claim. While some Ukrainian extremists have argued that nuclear capability would protect it from Russia, Ukraine's elected leadership has been extremely cautious about not stoking Russian fears.

Given the IAEA inspection provisions under the Additional Protocol, the cost of a clandestine nuclear program and the risk of it being detected are significant disincentives for Ukraine to pursue nuclear weapons capability today. Moreover, the international political costs of secretly pursuing nuclear capability after having committed not to do so would threaten Ukraine's relations with Western partners and would inevitably undermine one of the main pillars of the country's foreign policy since 2014. Notably, while a legislative bill on Ukraine's withdrawal from the Nonproliferation Treaty was registered back in 2014, it never received serious consideration.

In sum, underscoring once again, Ukraine accepted the obligations of the Additional Protocol's comprehensive safeguards agreement, which entails "the highest level of trust of the Agency to the state." The IAEA regularly checks all the nuclear facilities in Ukraine, including the Neutrons Source Facility in Kharkiv — which Russia often falsely claims is the main source of Ukraine's "nuclear program." SIPRI Research Associate Peter Topychkanov has stated that there have never been concerns associated with Ukraine regarding any prohibited nuclear activities (Topychkanov 2022). Neither the IAEA nor any other actor other than Russia have ever claimed that Ukraine was developing a clandestine nuclear program. Russia's false accusations about Ukraine's desire to obtain nuclear weapons capability are just part of its information warfare, which aims to justify the invasion and maintain support for its invasion of Ukraine with Russian domestic and foreign pro-Russian audiences.

Works cited

ITAR-TASS. 2014. "SMI: Ukraina mozhet sozdat' iadernuiu bombu za 10 let." TASS, 17 September 2014. https://tass.ru/mezhdunarodnaya-panorama/1447246.

Putin, Vladimir. 2022. "Obrashchenie Prezidenta Rossiiskoi Federatsii." Kremlin.ru, 21 February 2022. http://www.kremlin.ru/events/president/news/67828.

Regnum. 2022. "Shoigu: Ukraina khochet vernut' sebe status iadernoi strany." Regnum Information Agency, 21 February 2022. https://regnum.ru/news/3513734.

Reuters. 2022. "Russia blames attack at nuclear power station on Ukrainian saboteurs." Reuters, 4 March 2022. https://www.reuters.com/world/europe/russia-blames-attack-nuclear-power-station-ukrainian-saboteurs-interfax-2022-03-04.

RFIS. 2022. "Direktor SVR Rossii Sergei Naryshkin o Spetsial'noi voennoi operatsii na Ukraine." Press Bureau of the Russian Foreign Intelligence Service, 3 March 2022. http://www.svr.gov.ru/smi/2022/03/direktor-svr-rossii-sergey-naryshkin-o-spetsialnoy-voennoy-operatsii-na-ukraine-.htm.

Topychkanov, Peter. 2022. "'Ukraine bylo by kraine slozhno skryt' prakticheskie deistviia po sozdaniiu iadernogo oruzhiia.'" Kommersant, 10 March 2022. https://www.kommersant.ru/doc/5250345.

Volodin, Aleksei. "'Iadernaia derzhava' s kamennym toporom." Voennoe obozrenie, 14 May 2015. https://topwar.ru/74824-yadernaya-derzhava-s-kamennym-toporom.html.

Yanukovych, Viktor. 2012. Decree of the President of Ukraine No. 390/2012 "On the decision of the Council of National Security and Defence dated 8 June 2012 'On a new revision of the War Doctrine of Ukraine'" dated 8 June 2012. https://www.president.gov.ua/documents/3902012-14403.

Zelenskyy, Volodymyr. 2022. "Speech by the President of Ukraine at the 58th Munich Security Conference." President of Ukraine Official Website, 19 February 2022. https://www.president.gov.ua/en/news/vistup-prezidenta-ukrayini-na-58-j-myunhenskij-konferenciyi-72997.

CHAPTER 24

Russo-Ukrainian war is a clash between two national armies and two global world views

Agnieszka Legucka

Interview with Ostap Kushnir, published 4 May 2023

> Agnieszka Legucka is a professor of international security and an analyst with the Eastern Program at the Polish Institute of International Affairs (PISM), where she deals with the domestic and foreign policy of the Russian Federation, NATO-Russia relations, hybrid conflicts and threats, and Russian disinformation. In 2015/16 she served as rector for student affairs at the National Defence University of Warsaw. Legucka is a long-term coach of the SESNE program, which is part of the development aid of the Ministry of Foreign Affairs of Poland to countries recovering after armed conflict. She has thrice been awarded medals in recognition of her involvement in the national defence of Poland.

Kushnir: How would you define the Russo-Ukrainian war compared to other military conflicts of the 21st century? Is there anything outstanding or unexpected in its character?

Legucka: The Russo-Ukrainian war differs from other military conflicts in the last seventy years, the ones taking place after the end of WW II. The majority of these conflicts, as we calculated at the SIPRI [Stockholm International Peace Research Institute], were *intra*-state hostilities, fought within national borders. However, the Russo-Ukrainian war is an *inter*-state conflict engaging two sovereign entities.

Apart from this, the Russo-Ukrainian war is not an "ordinary" violation of international law but rather an act of aggression that could ruin the architecture of global order and security. Indeed, one of Russia's objectives well before February 2022 was to challenge the existing equilibrium and rise against the West. The war became instigated by and involves one of the members of the UN Security Council, a country with "great power" ambitions, which hinders seeking for peace via diplomatic means.

On the eve of the full-scale invasion, many experts were skeptical about the probability of Russia resorting to ultimate aggression against Ukraine and breaching international law, yet it happened. Since then, the conflict has involved not only Ukraine and Russia but the whole global community.

Another issue that came unexpectedly is that the West, perceived as weak by both the Kremlin and Beijing before the invasion, became more united in order to counter the aggression. This unity happened not only within the EU but in the transatlantic dimension too. The NATO countries understood that Russia, if not stopped, would likely go beyond Ukraine in its conquest. After February 2022, Ukraine started being regarded as a first step in the Kremlin's undermining of the European security architecture and global order. In this light, NATO countries became more open to Kyiv's requests.

Developments during the past year also fractured many myths that existed before the full-scale invasion. The first myth argued that the Russian army, regarded as the second-most powerful in the world, was invincible. Instead, Ukraine demonstrated that Russia could be stopped and defeated. The second myth argued that the West was weak, divided, and lacked resolve. Instead, the West became united as it never has been since the end of the Cold War.

The shattering of both myths sent a strong signal to Beijing: taking risks and applying power alone, without assessing the situation and own resources critically, do not necessarily lead to irreversible global changes. Exactly because Russia violated international law in Ukraine and jeopardized regional security, the US became very active in Europe. The analysts in Washington connected the dots very quickly and concluded that China, as a fellow "great power," might follow the Russian tactic and send troops to Taiwan. Therefore, for this reason alone Russia's overwhelming success in Ukraine became unacceptable to the West.

In sum, the Russo-Ukrainian war is a skirmish between two national armies on a local battlefield and a clash between authoritarian and democratic systems on the global level. This makes the war unique.

Kushnir: In your opinion, what have been the major successes of Ukraine and Russia today, more than a year after the full-scale invasion started?

Legucka: Ukraine can boast a few successes. Primarily, and most importantly, the country stood its ground against Russia and preserved its sovereignty.

Secondly, Kyiv created a powerful coalition of Western allies around its cause. The European Union, which had previously demonstrated only "deep concern" when addressing world crises, became more active and bold, even procured weapons for Ukraine in an unprecedented move. In turn, the US reinvigorated its status as a global leader. To my knowledge, 80 percent of the military ammunition and equipment that Ukraine possesses today has been provided by Western allies.

The third success is the evolved resilience of Ukrainian society in the face of Russia's blackmail. This includes the nationwide readiness to endure nuclear threats, destruction of energy infrastructure, displacement of people from Ukrainian territory, and other forms of blackmail. I have never seen such strong resilience in any other country at war.

Ukrainian resilience has become something that everyone in the West admires. It has two roots: the excellent leadership of President Zelensky and the grassroots social desire not to fall under Russia. In Poland I met a lot of Ukrainian refugees and migrants who spoke confidently about the forthcoming victory. Not only did they have little doubt that their country would survive, they believed in the victory of their army.

The resilience of Ukrainians is something that needs to be constantly highlighted. When I talk to German, French, or American experts, I feel their fear. These people are particularly concerned about Russian nuclear escalation. However, I feel nothing like that from my Ukrainian colleagues or ordinary citizens. Their fearlessness is a good basis for the authorities in Kyiv to wage a successful war. Ukrainians know why they are fighting. They perceive the Russian invasion as an existential threat. They built a unified front against this threat. This development, in my view, is another major success of Ukraine.

On the Russian side, the war has reinforced the authoritarian regime, social subordination, and loyalty of national elites to the Kremlin. This is something that neither Ukraine nor the West can ever experience. Putin has successfully deployed systems of repression and propaganda and divided Russian society into those who publicly support victory and those who conceal their criticism of the aggression. The unwillingness of ordinary citizens and elites to speak against the regime allows Putin to continue feeding the war and even, if needed, transform it into a protracted one. In other words, Putin successfully raised the level of connivance in his society—a unique Russian strength that is impossible to duplicate in democratic societies, which sooner or later start suffering war fatigue.

That being said, I do not see many other Russian successes, apart from Putin's strengthening his political course at the domestic level and amplifying war fatigue among Ukraine's partners at the international level.

Kushnir: How would you assess the current level of war fatigue among Ukraine's international partners?

Legucka: I think that the fatigue is slowly growing, at least among some groups of countries and political parties in the West. For instance, in the US many members and voters of the Republican Party are raising their voices against helping Ukraine, unlike the majority of people affiliated with the Democratic Party. Analysts speculate today that if a Republican candidate wins the next presidential elections in the US, then the attention to Ukraine will shrink.

In Western Europe, support for Ukraine remains high on the agenda, but its sustainability greatly depends on the position of Washington. If the US reconfirms its strong commitment to European security, then all the countries in the region will continue to stand behind Ukraine. However, even under the most favourable scenario, the support of Hungary will remain limited because that government and society are largely pro-Russian. In France and Germany, understanding of Ukraine's suffering and effort has always been rather strong, but the anti-American sentiment of people there risks sabotaging long-term transatlantic partnerships.

Apart from this, Western states are not only accumulating war fatigue in a "natural" way but also falling victim to Russian propaganda. It is not uncommon to find articles in Western media about the dire consequences if Russia's nuclear weapons were deployed. Also, many articles spread narratives of uncertainty—for instance, the possibility of escalated bloodshed if Ukraine liberates Crimea, the chaos in Eurasia if Russia collapses after losing the war, or the radicalization of Russian society and elites after Putin gets ousted.

However, when looking at public opinion in Poland and the Baltic states, support for Ukraine remains unwavering. Central European countries believe that Ukraine needs even more weapons and ammunition.

Kushnir: Speaking about weapons and ammunition, what kinds does Ukraine require from the West in order to succeed in the forthcoming counteroffensive, liberate its territories, and make Russia start genuine peace negotiations?

Legucka: The Western experts whom I talk to—specifically, those from the US—claim that Ukraine has not received enough weapons. For a successful counteroffensive, the ratio of weapons needs to be 3:1 in favour of the attacking side. On top of that, the attacking side should have a strong presence in the air, in order to successfully storm well-fortified positions from above, which is exactly the case of Russian entrenchments in Crimea and the Donbas. Instead, as it stands now Ukraine has received enough weapons to survive but not liberate its occupied territories.

From my talks and observations, Ukraine's readiness for a counterattack stems not as much from Western military support as from the bravery and tactical improvisation of its soldiers. Ukrainians have learned to capitalize on the bad logistics, chronic corruption, and poor training of Russian troops and conduct daring operations with shock tactics.

That being said, Russia's advantage in the current stage of the war is that they are on the defensive. Considering the existing deficit of weaponry, Ukraine will have a challenging time mounting a counteroffensive. Not to mention that little or no successes in 2023 will make it even harder for Ukraine to advance in 2024, when war fatigue will further grow in the West and elections will take place in the US. Thus, this year will be crucial for Ukraine.

In sum, I believe that Ukraine's victory will not be as much secured by military support from the West, which could be much stronger, as by innovative tactics and the high motivation of ordinary soldiers. But I could be wrong, as my analysis is based on open sources. A lot can take place behind the scenes.

Kushnir: You are known as a proponent of the "matryoshka"-style Russian disinformation theory. What exactly is this theory about?

Legucka: The general principle of the "matryoshka" theory claims that the true information about an institution, a person, or the truth behind facts is buried under layers of falsifications, distortions, and manipulations. Therefore, if all is hidden and nothing is clear, audiences will always live in uncertainty and question reality.

It is fairly hard to fight with "matryoshka"-style disinformation, especially the Russian variety. Western audiences regularly fell for it before February 2022. However, my latest hypothesis is that the West now acknowledges the threat and is learning to defend against it. At the same time, it must be noted that Russian disinformation has also evolved.

The major feature of current Russian disinformation in the West is the promotion of desirable messages at all costs, even if they occasionally confirm facts of aggression and crimes of the invaders. On top of that, Russia is expanding the geography of its disinformation activities. It has recently stepped up its information exchange with China. Media outlets associated with the government in Beijing are copy-pasting messages from Russian sources and spreading them further. Although many statements by Chinese officials include abstract reflections about the necessity to respect the territorial integrity of states, they never address the specific case of Ukraine's territorial integrity.

Recent opinion polls demonstrate that the lion's share of Western audiences does not believe Russia's messaging anymore. This does not mean, however, that Russia has stopped working effectively in the Western media space. It only means that Russia has become smarter. One way is that the narratives it popularizes today are not as much pro-Russian as they are anti-Ukrainian.

It is very important to understand that the evolved version of the Russian "matryoshka" relies on undercover activity a lot. Comments left by troll factories on the Internet are often favoured over publications in official media outlets. Also, Russia continues using "useful idiots" [a memetic reference, dating back to the Stalin era, to pro-Russian public figures in different countries] to spread its messages. A recent development is Moscow's engagement of its diplomats and their Twitter profiles to spread disinformation. For example, Russian Foreign Minister Sergei Lavrov is a well-used instrument of Kremlin propaganda.

Finally, one more aspect of the expansion of Russia's "matryoshka"-style disinformation is its aggressive penetration of Spanish-speaking media, particularly Twitter. For one thing, misleading messages written in Spanish are not always properly detected by English-language moderators or AI. For another, Russia relies on the Spanish language to rally the Global South to its cause—specifically, the countries of Latin America. It exploits the anti-US post-colonial narratives there and portrays the war in Ukraine as one more conflict between "white people," where a single great power (Russia) is fighting against another (the West).

Kushnir: How can ordinary readers or viewers defend themselves against Russian propaganda? What should they do to preserve informational hygiene?

Legucka: Today, even if one tries it is rather difficult not to be fooled or manipulated. All of us receive tons of information every day when scrolling through newsfeeds on social media. My advice is to follow a simple rule: whenever you encounter information on the Internet that makes you feel nervous or too emotional, start suspecting that something is wrong. I also strongly suggest that you do not spread such information any further.

The point is that the majority of Internet readers and viewers are rather lazy. Verification of sources and cross-checking of facts, which I recommend doing regularly, are not common practices. Therefore, to be on the safe side readers and viewers should approach disturbing news with caution; at the very least, they should avoid clicking on catchy images or uncritically forwarding such items to their friends.

Kushnir: What about cyberspace? How does Russia use it to attack Ukraine and the world?

Legucka: Russia uses all means at its disposal to conquer Ukraine. I have observed that the Kremlin orchestrates attacks in cyberspace before any conventional military advance. This was a regular practice before February 2022 and was epitomized on the eve of the invasion, when Russia tried to block the web pages of all Ukraine's ministries and online banking applications, aiming to disrupt communications and sow panic. They did not achieve much then.

In general, the effectiveness of Russia's cyber-attacks against Ukraine is not very high today. Since 2013, Ukrainian IT specialists have developed countermeasures to withstand them. Another issue is Russian attacks against NATO countries. The disruption of critical infrastructure and leaks of secret information are becoming more frequent there. The paradox is that *the more technologically advanced West needs to learn from Ukraine* how to defend its cyberspace.

Another paradox is that the initiative on the cyber-battlefield has shifted during the course of the war. At the beginning of the invasion, it was Russia who dictated the logic and dynamics of disruptive events. However, today Ukrainians are the ones demonstrating more audacity, attacking and hacking Russian targets, particularly media outlets. Many times already, Russian viewers have been unexpectedly presented with Ukrainian news from Ukraine, not to mention the broadcast of an anti-war speech by President Zelensky.

Kushnir: What is your opinion of current Polish-Ukrainian relations — specifically, in the security domain? What are your predictions for the future?

Legucka: On every level, since 1989 Polish-Ukrainian relations have never been better. The war became an unfortunate reason for this. Social and historical discrepancies that have always been difficult to address were cast aside. They have not disappeared — and I think that they will resurface as a problem for historians and politicians in future — but the security priorities of the present moment enhance our cooperation.

The government of Poland has delivered to Ukraine everything Poland could deliver. In terms of volumes of supplied weapons and intensiveness of personnel training, Poland is third among all Ukraine's allies, following the US and UK. Poland has also become a logistics hub for military assistance to Ukraine from all across the globe.

A new Polish-Ukrainian treaty is being prepared today to reshape and institutionalize the existing frameworks of cooperation as well as elevate them to a higher level, which was impossible before February 2022.

CHAPTER 25

Ukrainian universities engaged in war effort beyond expectations

Serhiy Kvit

Interview with Oleksandr Pankieiev, published 18 May 2023

Serhiy Kvit (DPhil, Kyiv Shevchenko National University; PhD, Ukrainian Free University, Munich) is the president of the National University of Kyiv Mohyla Academy (also 2007–14). He was the Minister of Education and Science of Ukraine in 2014–16 and head of the National Agency for Higher Education Quality Assurance of Ukraine in 2019–22. Kvit founded the Kyiv-Mohyla School of Journalism (2001) and has headed the Centre for Media Reforms and the Consortium for University Autonomy (2005–10). A former national champion of Ukraine in fencing, he was awarded Fulbright Scholar grants to Ohio University (2006–07), Stanford (2017–18), the Kennan Institute (Washington, 2009), and the DAAD German Academic Exchange Service (Cologne, 2010).

Pankieiev: How has Russia's full-scale invasion affected universities and the education process in Ukraine?

Kvit: Russia's destruction has been unprecedented. I am not speaking here of universities alone: Russians have wiped out entire cities and towns across Ukraine. If you add all this destruction to the distress caused earlier by the COVID-19 pandemic, Ukraine's system of education has had to endure a double strain.

For many, studying in conditions of war means a continuation of distance learning. At the National University of Kyiv-Mohyla Academy (NaUKMA) we introduced a hybrid approach—simultaneous face-to-face and remote interactions with students who are either physically present in Ukraine or connecting from Western Europe, North America, or any other part of the world. This approach relies heavily on online video broadcasts and streaming.

The consequences of the invasion are detrimental, but our educational system—especially higher education—is continuing to operate. I want to emphasize that wartime challenges have not had any significant effect on the quality of knowledge transmission. Our students and instructors remain very motivated and committed to their studies. In the past academic year, some members of the Kyiv-Mohyla academic community were participating in classes while being on territory occupied by Russians.

Another challenge to studying under wartime conditions is the threat of blackout. To mitigate it, the Kyiv-Mohyla Academy organized workspaces with autonomous power sources. Also, Starlink equipment (provided by Elon Musk) was installed to secure uninterrupted Internet access. Thus, today we at NaUKMA have the capacity to continue the educational process even under a blackout.

Regardless of the war, we are continuing our work and have developed different responses to new challenges.

Pankieiev: What is the role of Ukraine's universities in organizing resistance to Russia's aggression—specifically, that of the Kyiv-Mohyla Academy?

Kvit: The major challenge in coordinating resistance during wartime is that members of the academic community are dispersed across not only Ukraine but the whole world. This complicates efforts to communicate with them. As a matter of fact, however, most of our Kyiv-Mohyla Academy instructors are working on campus, in the centre of the capital.

Moreover, our community initiated resistance measures that are not directly connected with research or teaching. For instance, within the first few days of the escalated invasion we established a specialized logistics centre to deliver supplies to the front line. This was an initiative of our graduates, who left their studies at American universities and returned to Kyiv to manage the centre.

We have a lot of recognizable media projects, such as StopFake, which counters Russian propaganda by exposing it—in twelve languages—and the *Kul't* [cult] podcast administered by our professors Tetiana Oharkova and Volodymyr Yermolenko. The podcast is offered in two languages, English and French, and targets a worldwide intellectual audience. Apart from this, both students and instructors also work as journalists for international media. At the beginning of the full-scale invasion, it was crucial to help with translation and deliver objective information to foreign diplomats, military officers, and journalists, and members of our academic community did that—in six languages.

It is also worth mentioning that thirty-one different think tanks and research centres are based at the Kyiv-Mohyla Academy. Last year we even registered three new think tanks, which a specific focus on issues of national security and psychological support for civilians and soldiers in need. Our centre for mental health and psychological social support is one of the most advanced of its kind in Ukraine. Since the liberation of Bucha, such centres have been in demand and of great importance.

Also, we have a special IT unit that cooperates with Ukrainian authorities and contributes to the war effort in cyberspace. A special legal unit based at our law school has been assisting Ukraine's parliament, the Verkhovna Rada, since the first day of the full-scale invasion. A year ago, many questions suddenly emerged regarding the interpretation of international law, and this legal unit helped to explain why the Russian actions in Ukraine can be unequivocally defined as war. It also helped to prepare a draft of the Ukrainian parliament's appeal to the international community, in which the Russian invasion was condemned as an act of genocide against Ukrainians.

Many members of our community—students, graduates, instructors, and administrative staff—joined the Ukrainian armed forces, most of them as volunteers. Fourteen of them have died on the front lines, with one more body, whom we suspect to be that of a NaUKMA graduate, being in the process of genetic identification. We have the necessary expertise to conduct such identification.

The Kyiv-Mohyla Academy is in the process of registering a patent developed by scholars in our chemistry department. The patent describes how CO^2 can be used as a component of synthetic fuel in steelmaking. The discovered chemical process will not only increase the cost efficiency of the industry but prevent the emission of CO^2 into the atmosphere. It will also boost the competitiveness of Ukraine's steelmaking industry, which is especially important in the time of war.

Apart from the war, NaUKMA has also established new projects that are important for the development of the institution. For instance, the Faculty of Health Sciences will become a part of a future Faculty of Medicine. It will likely take two years to complete this project, which we are pursuing in collaboration with Dobrobut, one of the biggest medical networks in Ukraine. Our aim is to have the best medical faculty in the country. Another project is the establishment of an HR Department within the Kyiv-Mohyla Academy Centre for Quality Assurance. If we are successful, this department will become one of the first of its kind in Ukraine.

Pankieiev: What is the role of Russia's universities in the invasion?

Kvit: There is no role, because unfortunately there is no civil society in Russia. Russian universities have stopped their primary function of being educational institutions. In my opinion, a university should be an independent platform that cherishes freedom of speech and the expression of diverse opinions; it should be a network of intellectual activities and discussion platforms. This is not the case in contemporary Russia, where universities have lost their sense of existence.

Russian society no longer has any independent centres or mechanisms of critical thinking. From the point of view of political culture, the situation there has become much worse than in Nazi Germany during WW II. Professor Bohdan Osadchuk, who lived in Berlin during that war, told me once that even at the zenith of the Nazi regime Hitler did not control German media as firmly as Stalin did in the Soviet Union. Germany had always retained a strong tradition of freedom of speech, which allowed the public to look down on the Nazi journalists whom Hitler had installed in all media. Germans understood that Nazism was a temporary disaster for German political culture. Therefore, after the collapse of Hitler's regime Germans started to change their minds and political behaviour, because they could refer to alternative narratives and traditions that had always been around. On the other hand, Russians have never had alternative narratives or traditions. All of them have learned to submit to unified thinking and autocracy. Peter the Great, Lenin, Stalin, Putin, and other leaders have always promoted an *exclusive* authoritarian view of reality.

I am afraid that after the collapse of Putin's regime, Russians will start looking for a new Putin. That is why we need to encourage them to change their political culture. This will be possible if we help Russians create a new state within its national borders as well as build a new society with a true version of Russian history.

I believe that instead of a national history Russians today have adopted an imperial history. This is the cornerstone problem. All the people who have come to Ukraine to kill Ukrainians—all the soldiers and officers—are collectively referred to as Russians, but they are not. Chechens are not Russians, and neither are Buriats, Yakuts, or Volga Tatars. They are people who have Russian passports, but they are not Russians.

I used to be a professional athlete. I had the opportunity to travel across the Soviet Union. I remember very well, for instance, in Kazan or Ufa, in Tatarstan or Bashkortostan, the attitude to Russians and Communists. That attitude was very ironic, even derogatory. In this light, we should not accept Russia as something stable and immutable in the future. We need to work to change its political culture and help Russian peoples to discover their true history, their true identity. This may lead to the creation of a new country with different borders. If we do not do this, the old imperial problems will return to us over the years.

Pankieiev: When you say "we," what do you mean?

Kvit: "We" refers to Ukrainians, of course. If you look at Ukrainian history, we had to wait for and deal with recurring Russian invasions, many times. In their daily speech, Russians mostly say "to go to the Ukraine [*na Ukraïnu*]," not "to go to Ukraine [*v Ukraïnu*]," which is an illustrative and symbolic turn of phrase. It manifests the unconscious understanding of Ukraine as a territory that Russia needs to subordinate and keep in check. From the military point of view, Russians never regarded Ukraine as a fully conquered part of their territory (though they wished to) or Ukrainians as people they could trust, because they had constant problems with them. That is why many times in their history Ukrainians would suffer new invasions. To break this vicious circle, Ukrainians must dismantle the current Russian Federation—which is the latest incarnation of the Russian Empire. I want to make it clear: Russia is not a country of Russians but rather an empire—or a prison of nations, as Taras Shevchenko defined it.

Pankieiev: When the invasion started, the media landscape changed dramatically in Ukraine. The "United News" marathon news broadcast was launched on all TV channels. How would you define the national media landscape today? How are media functioning in the environment of a full-scale invasion?

Kvit: The "United News" marathon has different shades to it and has changed the media landscape in different ways. On the one hand, many TV channels, especially those loyal to the government, have continued to work with little change to their information policies. Those channels that were not necessarily loyal [to the ruling party] had to adjust to the new environment and limit their criticism. On the other hand, all the TV channels in Ukraine have felt the lack of resources and needed to reduce the scope and quality of their information products. It has been a real problem across the board. Last but not least, a few TV channels with a visible pro-Russian position were shut down, as they were no longer welcome by the Ukrainian public.

Speaking of civil society, it is very active. If Ukrainians want to obtain the information they are interested in, no obstacles will likely stop them. They will find the sources and means.

A very important point to highlight is that in times of armed combat, the nation should be united. This is why I think that some media discussions, especially on sensitive political topics, should be postponed until the end of the war. In this light, the "United News" telethon is providing a new experience to Ukrainians, who are receiving similar bits of information across the country. I also think that it is important for Ukrainians to trust their military command and generals. Our officers, unlike those of Russia, look very professional and competent, and the telethon helps to build up this trust.

At the same time, even under martial law restrictions, there remains a lot of hidden political struggle in Ukraine. Many powers are trying to influence the messages of the "United News" telethon.

Apart from TV channels, a variety of media outlets is also offering more diversity to interested consumers. Not that the "United News" is an exclusive source of information, but still more could be done to increase diversity.

Pankieiev: In Ukraine there are quite a few independent media personalities who are not associated with any specific outlet. What is their role in the wartime media landscape?

Kvit: Indeed, we have many well-known journalists, among whom I specifically like Vitaliy Portnykov and Larysa Hubina. We also have a lot of visible and well-known figures on social media who are brilliant experts with their own brands. The existence and activities of these people guarantee that freedom of speech unquestionably remains in Ukraine even in this time of war. I would even say that the reason Ukrainians have freedom of speech is because they demand it no matter what.

If there are any problems with freedom of speech, social unrest will follow. The major flaw of [former President] Viktor Yanukovych's policies, which led to his downfall, was that he did not understand the nature of Ukrainian political culture. The Ukrainian population needs to be heard. They are the ones to decide when to speak, what to say, where and when to say it, and how much. I believe that all political actors who are currently or will ever be in Ukraine's government should never forget this.

Pankieiev: Ukraine is experiencing a tremendous brain drain. Many Ukrainians are scattered around the globe in different countries, and there is a high probability that they will stay there. What effect will it have on Ukraine? How can Ukraine attract them back or engage them?

Kvit: I think that currently we are not dealing with a brain drain as such but with a potential brain drain. We do not know how events will unfold in Ukraine and what will happen with the Ukrainians who are abroad. My initial reaction to the situation is positive: it is very good that our people, including students and instructors, have the opportunity to find secure shelter and study at high-ranked foreign universities.

At the same time, the intellectual and demographic threat that looms is related to uncertainties that Ukraine will need to resolve. To what extent will postwar Ukraine be attractive for people who have left it today? How will the country and society change after the war? What reforms will be implemented to rebuild Ukraine? Will these reforms offer more opportunities for the young generation to live in and develop their country? In a word, I think that the extent of damage from the brain drain will depend on the postwar offers that Ukraine makes to its people.

We need to change the country, change our relationship to Ukrainian society, and continue implementing reforms. In times of war, as many examples from history show, mass migration and fleeing the battlefield are not unique, and Ukraine is no exception. Nothing irreparable happened. However, it may happen if we fail to change our country and society. I think that universities should play an instrumental role in designing and implementing these changes. Ukraine's universities should seek and find answers to the questions and uncertainties of today and the future.

CHAPTER 26

Ukrainian refugees are gradually finding their place in Irish society

Donnacha Ó Beacháin

Interview with Ostap Kushnir, published 1 June 2023

> Donnacha Ó Beacháin is a professor of politics in the School of Law and Government at Dublin City University, where he lectures on post-Soviet politics, unrecognized states, Irish studies, and foreign policy. He has been the principal investigator of two major EU-funded projects focusing on the post-Soviet space. Donnacha has twice (in 2012 and 2017) been awarded the accolade "Champion of European Research" by Ireland's National Research Support Network. His books include *The Colour Revolutions in the Former Soviet Republics* (with Abel Polese; 2010), *Life in Post-Communist Europe after EU Membership* (with Vera Sheridan and Sabina Stan; 2012), and *The Domestic Politics of Post-Soviet Unrecognized States* (forthcoming).

Kushnir: What are the reasons for the government and society in Ireland to support Ukraine so profoundly in its war effort, especially on diplomatic and humanitarian levels?

Ó Beacháin: Because of centuries-long anti-imperial struggles, there is a tendency in Ireland to identify with the underdog, those who fight against injustice. For example, during the 1950s and 1960s there was great sympathy in Ireland for the decolonizing struggles of nations in Africa and Asia against European powers. Up until the early 1990s, there was a very strong identification with the black majority population in South Africa; protests and boycotts against the apartheid regime occurred regularly at the levels of government and civil society. Today, there is a consistently strong identification with the people of Palestine.

Irish interest in Ukraine had peaked before—in 2014 with the annexation of Crimea and war in the Donbas—but then it subsided, as in most of Europe. Last year's invasion was different: Its brutal character shocked everyone. Irish people have always empathized with David in any struggle with Goliath, so the nakedly imperial and destructive character of Russia's invasion triggered a strong reaction in Ireland. People were appalled by the suffering they saw.

The invasion happened on the borders of the EU, of which Ireland is a part, and that spurred additional empathy and willingness to help. Within a very short space of time, Ireland accommodated tens of thousands of Ukrainian refugees. That also meant that Irish people could hear firsthand from Ukrainians about what was happening in their country.

The message from Ukraine, particularly as articulated by President Volodymyr Zelensky, carried extraordinary power and clarity. Irish people understood that the conflict concerned not only Ukraine but all of Europe, even the world. Moreover, Zelensky made a smart move to contact Ireland, as well as other members of the EU, directly and specifically. As with similar addresses to national legislatures, his message to the Irish Parliament back in April 2022 was carefully crafted for the local audience. For example, Zelensky made reference to hunger as a weapon and condemned Russia's interruption of Ukrainian grain exports through the Black Sea. That resonated in Ireland because of how hunger has been weaponized against the Irish people in the past. In general, the bitter experience of hunger unites Irish and Ukrainians, because both nations survived artificial famines while under imperial rule.

I had the honour of introducing President Zelensky to Irish university students last November, when he joined us via a video link from Kyiv to answer questions. During the discussion, he paid tribute to Ireland's warmth in taking in Ukrainian refugees and concluded by encouraging people to cherish their freedom. He compared freedom to good health—a person fully appreciates it only after it is threatened or gone. As you can imagine, Zelensky's words had quite a profound effect on the students.

Another thing to keep in mind is that while Ireland is politically active, it is militarily a neutral country. It has a very small army; Ireland spends less on defence than any other EU member in terms of per capita contributions as a percentage of GNP. Therefore, Ireland could not participate in Ukraine's war effort by providing tanks, for example. Instead, the government has concentrated on providing non-lethal military aid and supports people who have fled Ukraine. It is worth mentioning, however, that Ukrainian forces have been trained by Irish soldiers in things like de-mining and bomb disposal.

When President Zelensky visits Western Europe, he usually delivers a three-pronged message. He is looking for means of defence.

He is looking for sanctions on Russia. And he is looking for endorsements of Ukraine's EU membership bid. Ireland has been strong in responding to two of these three requests. Lacking on the military side, it has been at the forefront of advocating sanctions against Russia and supporting Ukraine's EU membership bid. This year, Ireland celebrates half a century in the European Union. It experienced the transformative effect that membership can have on a country and society. Therefore, Ireland is enthusiastic to bring Ukraine into the Union so that it can also enjoy peace, prosperity, and security.

Kushnir: How do you see the long- and short-term effects of the massive migration of Ukrainians to Ireland?

Ó Beacháin: They were and remain very welcome in Ireland. However, the unexpected influx—Ukrainians now constitute 2 percent of Ireland's population—has increased the already substantial strain on the housing system. Ireland had already been undergoing a prolonged housing crisis before February 2022; the national population was rapidly expanding and the government could not satisfy accommodation needs. Therefore, most Ukrainians who arrived in Ireland were placed in hotels, government-controlled buildings, or private facilities.

In the Irish media I pointed out that in 2008 the Georgian government built thousands of modular houses within months when people fled from South Ossetia. And those houses are still there, they are being lived in. The Irish government, for reasons that are not entirely clear, has been unable to complete a similar task. It is certainly not because of a lack of will; it seems that myriad bureaucratic problems have prevented houses being built quickly enough.

In cultural terms the Irish-Ukrainian interaction has been very positive. Most Irish people had very little interaction with Ukrainians before Russia's full-scale invasion last year. Today, Ukrainians are gradually finding their places in Irish society. Here in Dublin, I have several students taking my modules who last year fled Ukraine, including from Mariupol. They have integrated very well. Some Ukrainians will undoubtedly stay in Ireland after the war subsides, although I think that the majority will want to go back to Ukraine. I know some who have already returned. The long-term effect of Ukrainians staying in Ireland will be the strengthening of ties—above all, cultural connections—between the two countries.

Kushnir: Recently, in light of the 25th anniversary of the Good Friday Agreement, which put an end to the decades-long clash between the Irish and British, the Western media started discussing the probability of arranging something similar for Ukrainians and Russians. In your opinion, can the Good Friday Agreement provide a point of reference or guideline to end this particular war?

Ó Beacháin: The short answer is no. The ongoing Russian invasion of Ukraine and the Troubles in Northern Ireland are fundamentally different. The Good Friday Agreement was negotiated by two democratic and sovereign governments who shared a common goal of moving beyond destructive conflict. This was very different from what you have with Russia and Ukraine today. Russia, a pariah dictatorship, is bent on a genocidal campaign against Ukraine. During the late 1990s the governments in Dublin and London guided the parties in Northern Ireland toward an agreement which helped transition society away from armed conflict. Their mutual interest was to get away from zero-sum politics, which had dominated Northern Ireland for decades.

By contrast, there is no win-win scenario when it comes to Russia and Ukraine. Ukrainians must regain and retain all of their sovereign territory. Otherwise, the foundations of international law will be fundamentally undermined.

Moreover, 25 years ago important international actors were interested in resolving the conflict in Ireland. Bill Clinton's presidency, combined with bipartisan support within the US Congress and the mediating role of Senator George Mitchell, all helped produce the Good Friday Agreement. The European Union provided financial assistance to underpin the peace process. Everybody shared the same interest in ending the Troubles. As for the current war in Ukraine, there is no similar unity of purpose among the relevant actors.

Therefore, I don't see how the Good Friday Agreement can be used as a point of reference for ending Russia's invasion of Ukraine.

Kushnir: How has the perception of Ukraine changed in Ireland since February 2022? You have already mentioned a few details, but can you elaborate a bit further?

Ó Beacháin: The national and international perception of Ukraine, as well as Russia, has changed fundamentally. The Irish—and Europeans in general—have acknowledged that they had not listened to Ukrainians carefully enough. For years, the government in Kyiv and its supporters warned about the Kremlin's aggressive intentions. The Kremlin would characteristically depict these warnings as the product of Russophobia. But as you know, a phobia is an *irrational* fear of something. Looking at what has been happening during the last 18 months, there is nothing irrational about being afraid of Russia, especially if you are Ukrainian. It is Russia that has proved to be Ukrainophobic.

A lot of people in Ireland are now very familiar with the details of the war. Russia's invasion and Ukraine's heroic defence are daily news stories. Irish affinity with Ukrainians has blossomed. Before the invasion, many considered Ukrainians to be somehow outside the European club, the borders of which roughly overlapped with those of the EU. Today, Ukrainians are very much considered as "us" — indeed, "the best of us." Many people in Ireland understand that it is not just Ukraine fighting Russia but Russia fighting Europe with Ukraine being the front line. There has been strong Irish support for bringing Ukraine into the EU as quickly as possible, even though it is a very complicated process that requires unanimity and the political will of all participating governments. However, I think the emotional decision has already been made, which in some respects is the most fundamental thing. The politics will inevitably follow.

In turn, the perception of Russia has plummeted. Despite being a dictatorship, before the invasion Russia was still regarded as an integral part of the European economy. It was largely business as usual between the EU and the Kremlin, even after the annexation of Crimea. The completion of Nord Stream 2 provides ample evidence of this. However, everything changed after February 2022. This war was supposed to be a demonstration of Russian power. In fact, it has been the very opposite. Far from being a global political heavyweight as projected, this war has emphasized Russia's status as a resource-rich regional bully. Russia is increasingly weak and isolated. Its only firm allies — those who vote with Russia at the UN — are a small cabal of fellow dictatorships, the personal fiefdoms of Kim Jong Un, Bashar Al-Assad, and Aliaksandr Lukashenka. I think it will take a very long time for Russia to be considered as anything other than a brutal aggressor. It is not in the foreseeable future.

Kushnir: Is fatigue from the war growing in the region — specifically, in Ireland?

Ó Beacháin: I would not call it fatigue. Certainly, there is an increased familiarity with the war. And the longer a war persists — or indeed any issue, however grave — the greater the risk of people losing interest or simply being distracted by other problems, not least their own personal challenges.

In this sense, dictatorships have a comparative advantage over democracies when waging a war. Dictatorships can ignore public opinion to a large extent. For states like Russia, it matters little what people think because the Kremlin can throw its citizens into the military effort against their will. Democracies are different, they depend on popular opinion. People are not going to spend money on supporting Ukraine unless they are sure that such support is the right thing to do. If public opinion changes, political leaders will likely feel compelled to adjust the levels of assistance.

So far, there has been no diminishing of support for Ukraine — quite the opposite, as can be observed from the increased supply of ammunition and weapons. Political backing for Ukraine's EU membership bid has also augmented over time. But the risk of fatigue exists. Vladimir Putin's biggest potential weapon is Western collective indifference. The longer the war continues, the greater the risk is that apathy might set in.

Hearing of so many atrocities can desensitize people. It is easy and understandable to get dispirited when one gets a seemingly endless stream of horror arising from Russia's invasion of Ukraine. This is why, I think, Ukraine is so persistent in planning a counter-offensive. It needs to show results because otherwise, people in the West might conclude that the war has reached a stalemate, and this could affect the amount of military and financial support they are willing to provide to Ukraine. Ukrainians know well that Russia will not return occupied territories through negotiation and that any final settlement — be it negotiated or imposed — will reflect the realities on the battlefield. If Russia is not forced out of Ukraine, it will consolidate its territorial gains and freeze the conflict indefinitely.

The Ukrainian government has been very astute in how it interacts with its partners. For example, in the US President Zelensky was very conscious of the need to express gratitude for the support already provided. If Americans felt that Ukraine was somehow ungrateful, that would play into the hands of those in the US — and they are not few or without influence — who believe that support for

Ukraine should be radically reduced, if not halted altogether. Thus far, President Zelensky has pulled off remarkably well the delicate balancing act of conveying appreciation while simultaneously requesting more assistance.

Kushnir: To summarize, what have been the major achievements and failures of Ireland and the EU in addressing the war?

Ó Beacháin: Let us look at the failures first. Ukraine was not provided with enough weapons at the very beginning. *There is a strong argument that if Ukraine had received what it asked for in a timely manner, this war would have ended already.* During President Zelensky's visit to the US, a Ukrainian journalist, Olga Koshelenko, put a very good question to the host, President Biden. She asked, more or less, why, instead of drip-feeding supplies to Ukraine—some ammunition now, some later—Americans would not supply the defending army with everything the US had to give at once, so Ukraine could liberate all territories sooner rather than later. Biden did not answer that question satisfactorily.

However, the decision to drip-feed the Ukrainian army is not one confined to the US. The EU stockpiles very little weaponry and ammunition. For decades, following the collapse of the USSR, European states complacently believed that they would never be attacked. European democratic societies put pressure on their governments to redirect money to much-needed domestic services such as health and education. They saw defence as a distraction that was not worth the investment. The EU was therefore ill-prepared for Russia's full-scale invasion of Ukraine—a big failure that it continues to grapple with.

Another failure was the lukewarm reaction to the annexation of Crimea and the resulting acquiescence to war in the Donbas. Sanctions were very weak then. The EU put a lot of effort into trying not to provoke Putin, with the result that far from being punished for aggression, Putin was emboldened. All this caution did not avert war—it made it much more likely. Moreover, Europe's reliance on Russian energy encouraged Moscow to believe there would be no meaningful or effective response to a full-scale invasion of Ukraine. So, when Putin launched his murderous assault in 2022, he seems to have expected that the EU would tolerate it, as it had acquiesced to his conquest of Ukraine's territories in 2014.

The EU's reaction to the events of February 2022 was extremely slow. Many decision-makers could not predict how the war would evolve. There was a widespread expectation that Ukraine would be militarily defeated within days, and therefore some felt that the losing side should not be armed unnecessarily. Only when Ukrainians stopped the invasion and repelled Russia's best units did the EU start mobilizing. Notwithstanding the confusion and divisions within the EU, it eventually managed to get a grip and start acting cohesively with a clear direction. But it did so very slowly.

Today, there are still people in the EU who would probably prefer a stalemate or a frozen conflict to Russia's defeat. I said earlier that there is no win-win situation to this war. A Russian defeat is necessary to protect Ukraine's sovereignty in perpetuity but also as a matter of justice, to punish those responsible for all the atrocities.

But, again, this necessity still appears unacceptable for many. You may remember that in August 1991, just three weeks before Ukraine declared its independence, the senior George Bush travelled to Kyiv and tried to persuade the Ukrainian people to stay in the USSR and give Mikhail Gorbachev a chance. Bush did so because he supported the status quo. Western decision-makers preferred the continuation of the Soviet Union to an unknown alternative, even though the demise of the USSR meant independence for so many nations that had been forcibly incorporated into the Bolshevik empire. Instead of wholeheartedly supporting Ukraine's independence, many in the West feared the unpredictability of change. They could only see risk, a chain of events that might spin out of control. I think that until last year, a similar logic applied in dealings with the Kremlin. The desire not to attract Putin's ire eclipsed any impulse to help Ukraine.

As for achievements, the EU and the US have provided Ukraine with unprecedented economic support. Moreover, promises have been made to play a leading role in the postwar reconstruction effort. If you add to this the enthusiasm about helping Ukraine join the European Union, the growing isolation of Russia, and diminishing dependence on Russian energy, you end up with several breakthroughs that would have taken a much longer time to accomplish if not for the war.

CHAPTER 27

More than a year into the escalated war finds Ukraine with a stronger voice in Western media

Marta Dyczok

Interview with Oleksandr Pankieiev, published 16 June 2023

Marta Dyczok is an Associate Professor in the Departments of History and Political Science at Western University, a fellow at the University of Toronto's Munk School of Global Affairs, and an adjunct professor at the National University of Kyiv-Mohyla Academy, as well as president of the Shevchenko Scientific Society of Canada. Previously she was a Wilson Fellow (2005/06) and a Harvard Shklar Fellow (2011). She is the author of seven books, the latest being *Ukraine not 'the' Ukraine* (2024) and *Ukraine Calling: A Kaleidoscope from Hromadske Radio, 2016–2019* (2021), and of book chapters and articles, including in *Europe-Asia Studies*, *Demokratyzatsiia*, and *Canadian Slavonic Papers*.

Pankieiev: What was the role of media in Russia's decision to launch the full-scale invasion of Ukraine last year? Can we say that narratives which Russia had produced for decades heralded its forthcoming aggression? Could we have predicted and prevented the aggression if the indicators were interpreted correctly?

Dyczok: The media, and especially those spreading propaganda, were used to prepare public opinion for a large-scale invasion. Media messages were deliberately framed to present Russia's aggression as something justifiable.

The big question is how effective that propaganda was. And here, it depends on which audience we are looking at. Within Ukraine, obviously it was not effective. Very few Ukrainians bought into such justificatory narratives. It is difficult to measure within Russia, on the other hand, because they do not have a free society where public opinion can be surveyed accurately. However, fourteen months into the war, support for the aggression apparently remains high, and presumably it was high when the aggression started. Beyond the battlefield, the perception depends on whether the countries are democracies or not, and whether they belong to the so-called Global South or the "wealthy part" of the world. Public opinion in different countries is very different.

The countries of Europe, the United States, Canada, and Australia—the democracies—remain united, but they have not been monolithic in condemning Russia's invasion. Media narratives do appear in these countries—the ones spread by Tucker Carlson are the most obvious examples—that criticize support for Ukraine as being over-commitment. There are also media outlets that uncritically repeat Russia's messages. However, they do not significantly influence public opinion or make it less favourable for Ukraine.

It is interesting to observe the degree to which Russian narratives resonate across the Global South, in countries that Ukraine has traditionally not partnered with. India, Brazil, South Africa, and many others are now very much in Ukraine's focus. When assessing their media landscape, we need to differentiate between messages and propaganda that were coming out a year before the invasion—pre-existing ones—and those following the full-scale invasion.

In my class on Russia's war against Ukraine, a student from India came to see me during office hours. We talked about disinformation and propaganda, the international dimension of the war, and the role of NATO. He believed the narrative that Russia was fighting against NATO and that all the bloodshed was the US's fault. From his perspective, the war was nothing else but "great power" politics, where the United States was trying to weaken Russia.

His belief was not so much shaped by Putin's latest disinformation as by the perspective from India itself. That perspective contends that the US is an imperial country, while Russia—heir to the Soviet Union—was a traditional ally in the anti-colonial struggle. This is the lens through which the student was seeing the situation. And he was a 21-year-old individual, doing a degree in Canada, with full access to every world media, and a participant in my course, where I had been laying out "here are the narratives, here are the facts."

Many analysts overlook the impact of Putin's narratives in the Global South, which is conditioned by pre-existing beliefs. The ability of media to directly shape public opinion in real time is complicated. And here we need to address questions about media effects. Do media have the ability to shape public opinion?

The issue of media effects concerns not only Russia, Ukraine, and the war. This is merely a current example that we are particularly interested in. However, if we look at Canada's southern neighbour as another example, there is a lot of debate about how the media influences public opinion there. When the previous POTUS called out a major outlet as "fake news" and many people believed it, then their belief is likely shaped by existing perspectives on media and on politics. The messages that come through to such people resonate with their established value systems.

This is where scholars should step up and contribute more actively to media proficiency and the education system. Otherwise, people will continue holding on to misleading beliefs. Some colleagues whom I respect and like, used to repeat Russian narratives when speaking about the war — I found it shocking every time and engaged in conversations with them. And then we have examples of really well-known scholars, such as John Mearsheimer, who have been blaming NATO since 2014 for the outbreak of the armed conflict. He has not changed his position yet, regardless of the information that is available to him.

We need to forfeit the naïve thinking that providing people with information will automatically make them see the truth. It is not that simple. People have been developing their value systems and mental maps for years. Those who are not informed about Ukraine and Russia will buy into the narrative that Ukraine has always been a part of Russia. There are a lot of gaps in their education, including gaps in the history courses they take.

Ukrainian issues have very modest coverage in the European history courses that are taught across Canadian and American universities. Even if Ukraine is covered, it is presented as a part of Russia, part of the Soviet Union, and part of the post-Soviet space. Ukraine is often denied its own voice, its own agency. If people are taught history that way, then they will think in corresponding terms. This is why controversial statements by Russia's President Putin about Ukraine do not provoke criticism; instead, they only add a compatible new layer to what people already believe in.

Pankieiev: What have been the goal and targets of Russia's propaganda in Ukraine during the last ten years? Has something changed since 24 February 2022 in Russia's information strategy?

Dyczok: I do not think there have been many changes; accents might have shifted slightly. However, the portrayal of Ukraine as not an independent state or being full of fascists and Nazis who should be exterminated has persisted. At the same time, it is interesting to observe the new messaging coming out of Russia today. A recent example is related to the drones over the Kremlin: "Ukraine is trying to assassinate Putin." This is such a departure from what we saw last year, in February or March of 2022. This actually acknowledges that Ukraine can go on the offensive. However, what remains in the media is portraying Ukraine as an evildoer: "Ukrainians are trying to kill us, and this is terrible."

I am also curious to see what messaging Fox News is going to be doing about Ukraine [following Carlson's departure]. My best guess is that there will be a shift. But again, as I think of it, I see a complex picture. It is not only about standards in reporting about Russia or Ukraine, it is also about Fox News' relationship with Donald Trump and Moscow. It is about the audience and its interests. Those people who are following the Trump story are not really following the Ukraine story. Those who are following the Ukraine story and the war are not necessarily focusing so much on Trump. However, I think that we should not compartmentalize, because everything is very interrelated.

Pankieiev: How has the media landscape in Ukraine changed since the full-scale invasion? How is Ukraine balancing between upholding the values of freedom of speech and wartime realities?

Dyczok: The first major change in the landscape is that there are now less media in Ukraine. Renat Akhmetov, a media tycoon from before February 2022, basically gave up all of his holdings. A big player went off the field. A lot of journalists became unemployed and the amount of media contracted.

The other important change is that the major TV channels started working together. This is quite an interesting phenomenon, as instead of competing they pooled their resources and launched "United News" joint information "tele-marathon" broadcast. A discussion continues on who got excluded from that collaboration, but the fact remains that all the major TV channels started informing society as one. Initially the information marathon was very popular, but that popularity decreased over time. Some questions have also been raised about state interference with editorial policy in the news coverage.

The main issue in terms of access to information in Ukraine right now is that the state does not always respond to queries from journalists. I would not call it censorship, but journalists may pose questions and receive no answer. Information is not always being properly provided from government sources.

In terms of media freedom, just recently Reporters Without Borders released their annual Press Freedom Index. I was quite impressed to see that Ukraine's ranking went up, even in the conditions of war, from 106th position in 2022 to 79th in 2023. It is quite a dramatic increase, which I think is unprecedented considering the active fighting.

What usually happens in wartime is the state takes over the control of information. This is to a large degree understandable because information is a crucial component of the war effort. The state cannot be releasing all the details on everything because that would contradict the national interest. If we look at the obvious examples, in Great Britain in WW II, for instance, the BBC operated as a mouthpiece of the state to keep up morale. This is normal. Another example is the Iraq war, when the US limited the amount of information provided to the media, while journalists actually got attached to military units — a revival of the old concept of embedded journalists. We do not see that in Ukraine, although unquestionably the state regulates access to information or the mobility of journalists in the war zones. At the same time, this has much to do with guaranteeing journalists' safety and securing legitimate state interests by not showing the world everything that is happening on the front lines.

There was an article in *Open Democracy* recently where the author claimed that the Ukrainian authorities restricted freedom of speech and journalists were complaining about it. The complaints that I am hearing and reading about — legitimate complaints, in my view — are that the state does not always provide full information. And journalists want full information.

At the same time, I think it is understandable that the government in Kyiv does not release casualty statistics. For morale reasons, Ukrainians do not want to be reporting how many of their nationals lost their lives. However, they are regularly reporting on how many Russians were killed. This is again understandable because of similar morale reasons.

Mobility restrictions in war zones are not a simple matter, either. There was a case when journalists started reporting from the liberated Kherson before they were given permission to go there and, when asked to leave, filed complaints. It is, again, a sort of understandable tussle between journals trying to obtain information and the state trying to protect larger national security interests. I am not sure that this case can be defined as suppression of freedom of speech, although some people are presenting it as that.

A good move for Western media outlets would be to turn to Ukrainian journalists for information because they are the ones on the ground. They are the ones who know the story and context. They are the ones who have the language skills and the experience. I think that greater cooperation between Ukrainian journalists and Western media outlets will be mutually beneficial.

Notwithstanding, another piece of positive news is that Western reporting on Ukraine has become better because many Western journalists arrived to work in Ukraine. People like Luke Harding, Isobel Koshiw, Mark MacKinnon, and Yaroslav Trofimov know the story. However, others who parachute in, write something, and leave, their reporting sometimes leaves a bit to be desired.

Pankieiev: When we read Western media today, can we say that understanding of Ukraine and the Russian aggression has improved compared to one year ago?

Dyczok: In my opinion, there has been a dramatic shift. I have recently started exploring the way in which the Ukraine-Russia story was reported before the full-scale invasion and after. One of the major changes is that the Ukrainian voice in the media became much stronger.

Media reports before 24 February 2022 were about what and when Russia's president had said. Afterward, journalists started to cite Ukrainian sources and statements of Ukraine's president. There was also a real shift in the way that the story got framed. The shock and horror of the actual war, the number of journalists who went to Ukraine and saw the atrocities as well as their encounters with ordinary people and local journalists — I think all that greatly impacted their thinking. Also worth mentioning is the excellent job Ukrainian organizations have done on fact-checking.

Another striking change is the way Ukrainian place names are now being reported. They are spelled and pronounced directly in the Ukrainian language — not Russian, as was commonly done before. Today, I almost never hear or read "Kiev" or "Kharkov," but Kyiv and Kharkiv, and journalists are now pronouncing names like Avdiivka, Bakhmut, and Kherson. This is very significant.

However, there are still media outlets and journalists that continue to repeat Russian narratives. Therefore, I would say that the overall Western media picture is "more Ukraine," "more accurate Ukraine," and "more agency to Ukraine" — but not completely, not always fairly.

Pankieiev: What is the role of President Zelensky in shaping the image of Ukraine for the global audience? Does he have the same impact inside Ukraine?

Dyczok: His impact is different domestically and internationally. Internationally he is a superstar. His charisma and communication skills are among Ukraine's most powerful weapons. In May 2023 Zelensky was at the Hague, and despite not having had a day off for more than four hundred days and leading a country at war, he still displayed a sense of humour. Speaking to the International Criminal Court, he said: "We all want to see another Vladimir here." This is invaluable in shaping public perceptions of Ukraine outside of Ukraine.

The fact that Zelensky is Jewish and the fact that he was elected president by 73 percent of the [voting] population of Ukraine is also very significant. The old Putin narrative that Ukrainians are anti-Semitic was blown out of the water. Only small extremist circles continue to accept that as a credible narrative.

One of my PhD students, a grandchild of Holocaust survivors, said that his views, as well as those of his peers in the Jewish community, changed radically after 73 percent of Ukrainian [voters elected] Zelensky, who is a Jew. When they look at statistics on anti-Semitism in Ukraine and see that it is one of the least anti-Semitic places in the world, their perception of the country becomes more favourable. They understand that many of their earlier views were false.

The skill with which Zelensky is able to interact with international media and international leaders, as well as his skill in messaging and effectively communicating — all of this has been vitally important. And we see how warmly he is received when travelling abroad.

I used to be quite critical of Zelensky. I was unimpressed with him and skeptical about his competencies as president. Many worrying incidents occurred during his election campaign — Zelensky's refusal to meet with journalists, the whole fiasco with the debates, and others. Today, I think that his lack of political experience has worked in his favour. He does not have the arrogance of a lot of political leaders, including some of Ukraine's previous elites.

It is a little harder for me to judge Zelensky's image within Ukraine. My perception is that there are a few controversies involving the President, but for the most part Ukrainians are trying to pull together in wartime and not spill too much to the public. That being said, if major issues with governance appear, then they *are* raised in the Ukrainian media. Stories about corruption or poor political decisions that do not work, journalists do report on them. However, the criticism tends not to be so much of Zelensky and his team but rather of the issues. Apart from that, I also observe a vibrant discussion in the Ukrainian media about how governance should be conducted, including the above-mentioned discussion that "We are not getting access to the information we need."

In other words, people do criticize Zelensky within Ukraine. However, my vantage point is that such people are in the minority. They do not want to create unnecessary disruptions during the war. That being said, once the fighting settles down they will likely commence more assertive arguing and criticism.

Pankieiev: Since the full-scale invasion, do you see any changes in Russia's propaganda and disinformation campaign in Canada?

Dyczok: On the contrary, it has not stopped. The Canadian government has taken steps to shut down official Russian propaganda channels which were allowed to freely function earlier. However, a recent report discloses how Russia continues to lobby individual journalists, media outlets, and academics to push through its false narratives. What surprises me is that some academics and journalists in Canada easily agree to become accomplices in the Russian disinformation campaign. I do not understand why anybody would choose to do so as professionals or experts in their area.

Pankieiev: In your home department at Western University (London, Ontario), you established a new course last semester titled "Russia's War Against Ukraine." What was the idea behind this course and how was it received by students? Do you see a need for similar courses at other universities across Canada?

Dyczok: I have not seen anything like this at other universities, but that might just be because I have been too busy to do a thorough search. I designed that course because I kept receiving many emails and phone calls from students and former students who asked me to explain what was happening, why it was happening, and where this all will lead to. My Political Science department agreed to the proposal, my university was also very responsive, media-related people paid attention, and this is how the course started. Because the new course was listed as a Special Topics course, it did not receive the full kind of advertising that regular courses do. And yet I was very pleasantly surprised at the enrollment—475 students signed up for it, including retired professors and staff members. It was a very diverse class. However, because it was taught online, I only got to meet my students in person if they decided to come to my office hours. The course was a lot of work, but I am really glad I did it.

CHAPTER 28

Equipping Ukraine for the long haul: Some initial thoughts

Frank Ledwidge

Essay published 21 June 2023

> Frank Ledwidge is a Senior Lecturer in Military Strategy at the University of Portsmouth, and he also teaches at the Royal Air Force College (UK). He is a former UK Military Intelligence Officer and also worked with the Organisation for Security and Co-operation in Europe investigating war crimes and torture cases. Ledwidge is the author of several books, including *Losing Small Wars: British Military Failure in Iraq and Afghanistan* (2011) and *Aerial Warfare: A Very Short Introduction* (2018).

Background

The focus of Western assistance so far during this phase of the Russo-Ukrainian war has been to deal with the acute problem of defending Ukraine and retaking its territory. Notably, the nature, scale, and effectiveness of equipment delivered has been constantly increasing. It is strange now to remember that there was a controversy even over the transfer of anti-tank missiles—or even helmets (in the case of Germany). Meanwhile, medium-range cruise missiles such as the UK's Storm Shadow are today being provided and used.

The war is not going to end in 2023. It will go on to 2024 and likely beyond. Whenever this phase ends, the threat from Russia will persist. There is no doubt that Russia will rebuild its forces. Commensurately, the Kremlin's ambitions to neutralize Ukraine and retain or retake Ukrainian territory will remain.[1] The challenge of building sustainable combat power in Europe in the next decade applies to all European powers. This is especially so since the United States will inevitably focus more on the "pacing challenge" of China (Neuhard 2022; Garamone 2023). In other words, to put it bluntly, Europe will need to step up in order to defend itself as the US ramps down its direct and leading involvement on that continent. The US

---

1. "NATO's generals reckon that Russia could rebuild its land forces in 3–5 years. Ultimately, conditions would be ripe for Putin or his successor to have another go" (Economist 2023).

focus on China is likely to persist into the late 2020s and beyond. Indeed, there is a significant probability that there will be a major conflict in the Western Pacific during that period. For Ukraine, the implication is clear. First, it will need to sustainably rearm. Second, it will need to make a serious effort to integrate with European powers.

This essay will not deal with the complex questions concerning various combinations of security guarantees to Ukraine or paths to NATO membership. Whatever form NATO's arrangements with Ukraine takes, the country will need to rearm in an affordable, sustainable, and above all effective manner. The purpose of this short paper is to outline some ideas as to how its armed forces should or could look in the medium and even longer term.

Hitherto, understandably Ukraine's long-term defence needs have been largely ignored in the rush to provide immediate defensive equipment (Gressel 2022). It will take several years for decisions — whether on policy or procurement — to bear fruit in terms of ensuring the beleaguered country's continuing military capability. Consequently, those decisions need to be made now.

This paper will briefly address three combat domains: land, sea and air; space and cyber domains give rise to a different set of problems. It should be recalled that equipment is not the same as capability. *Capability is a function of many factors aside from equipment, especially training and support.*[2] The focus here will be on equipment, as it takes longest to generate and will require the most intense discussion and debate. The paper will conclude with a brief discussion of one highly controversial possibility: the idea of Ukraine choosing to consider the option of developing nuclear weapons.

Rearming the Army

On land, notwithstanding the vast influx of Western weaponry, the great bulk of Ukrainian equipment remains ex-Soviet in design (IISS 2023). In due course, as attrition takes its toll, this equipment will be

---

2. Capability is the product of equipment, personnel, training, and support, among other factors. Ukraine's integration of NATO doctrine and practices is beginning at an informal level, with extensive training programs taking place throughout Europe and the United States. Serious consideration should be given to establishing a cross-fertilizing theoretical and field training centre of excellence, with the goal of capturing and integrating real-time lessons from the current war.

"flushed out" of Ukraine's arsenal. The current situation has given rise to an unsustainable and extremely difficult logistical challenge with multiple repair and supply chains.[3] Preparations must begin now to ensure that as time goes on, in order to reduce as far as possible the logistical burden, a very low number of variant types of equipment are supplied. This is as much the case with vehicles, such as basic transport, trucks, or all-terrain cars, as with higher-end materiel such as tanks or the equally essential armoured fighting vehicles (AFVs). The reality is, as hinted above in the assumptions, that cost of maintenance will be a factor in the relative suitability of all the different types of military equipment.

Let us deal first with the "flagship" element of the battlefield: tanks. The initial best option would be the Leopard 2 tank, which comes in several variations (A2–A7, as matters stand). On the face of it this would seem to offer the best option, with about 2,000 in service or storage in Europe alone (Statista 2024). Hitherto, European nations and Canada (one of several non-European nations that make use of it) have shown themselves reluctant to part with significant numbers. Further, the issue of multiple variants in service only increases the logistical burden.

However, another option exists. There are over 2,000 extremely effective and fully combat-proven US-made M1A1/2 Abrams tanks in storage in the United States (IISS 2023). These particular tanks are extremely expensive to maintain and run (Schogol 2023) — rather more so than other Western tanks (all of them are complex, of course). Nevertheless, while it would take many months to make the stored tanks battle-worthy, maintaining this capability could be an enduring major US commitment to the Ukrainian army. It would also give Ukraine the option of common maintenance facilities with Poland, which has also purchased the Abrams (AP 2023). Further, as to artillery, clearly now the vital arm of service, Ukrainian ground forces need a single reliable platform, while the United States has about 850 M109 self-propelled 155 mm guns in storage (IISS 2023); these systems are unlikely to be used in any other context. The same applies to the US-made and also combat-proven Bradley AFVs, of

---

3. For example, there are at least twelve foreign artillery systems in Ukrainian service, each with a different supply chain and many with different types of shells and charge bags. There is an equal number of ex-Soviet types (Cancian and Anderson 2023).

which there are about 2,000 in storage (ibid.). Taken together these vehicles would provide a very sound and more than adequate basis for an effective combined arms ground force—which, if well-supplied with artillery, would be modern and enduring enough to challenge and defeat Russia well into the 2030s. Over a period of 2–3 years, adequate supply of these weapons systems could be accomplished in whatever numbers are required. The advantage of the US-centred approach is that it would give Ukraine a tank, AFV, and artillery combination from a common source and equipment with which Ukrainian troops will have some familiarity.

Moving across to the key issue of long-range rocket artillery (Multi-Launcher Artillery Rocket Systems—MLRS), it will take several years for the orders of new missile systems such as HIMARs to come into service (Lopez 2022), but there may be an interim solution just to the West. Poland is soon to receive HIMARS and Korean Chunmoo MLRS (Adamowski 2022). One option may be developed for the Polish lend-lease of some of these systems. Clearly such a decision would present something of a risk for the government in Warsaw; however, these investments are designed to act as deterrents against Russia, and their use by Ukraine would only act to supplement that objective.

Rebuilding the Air Force

So far, Ukraine has been most effective in its operation of decades-old ex-Soviet Ground-Based Air Defence (GBAD) missile systems. Through attrition, the numbers and effectiveness of these relatively old systems will diminish. Indeed there is good evidence that at the time of writing (June 2023) Ukraine is already suffering from shortages of these weapons.[4] Transfers of newer Western anti-aircraft systems are (at the current rate of supply) inadequate to provide sufficient cover (Watling, Bronk, and Reynolds 2022). The rate of supply will need to be increased in the short term and reliably maintained in the long term. Resourcing this will be extremely expensive. Anti-aircraft missile systems must continue to be Ukraine's main effort in securing its air defences. This is an area

---

4. The daily UK Defence Intelligence review reported on 5 June 2023 that depleting Ukraine's supply of anti-aircraft missiles is the main objective of Russia's spring missile onslaught on Kyiv and other parts of the country. See Ministry of Defence (2023).

where Ukraine has a real edge and it is important that it continues to leverage its success (Grieco and Bremer 2023).

Prior to the announcement of the removal of the US's objection to supplying F-16s, there was much debate as to whether they were the right aircraft to meet the country's requirements (Losey 2023). Whatever the decision of history is in that respect, one thing is certain—they are a significant improvement on what Ukraine has hitherto deployed. Depending on the way in which Ukrainians deploy the aircraft and their success in doing so (it is unlikely that we will see any significant effect before the spring of 2024), a long-term solution to Ukraine's future air power needs will need to be determined.

It may well be that their experience of the F-16 will make the decision a simple one. In terms of numbers, a wing (48 aircraft) of late-model F-16s (F-16 C/D) might be appropriate. However, another—or indeed, depending upon the resources available, a supplementary—long-term option might be the excellent Swedish Gripen, about 30 of which will be available by 2027 (Defense Express 2023). Many air power experts consider these to be ideal for Ukraine, as they are built for rough airfields and for so-called *dispersed operations*, which means taking off and landing on highways (SAAB 2020). Further, they are specifically designed for combat against Russian forces.

Whichever aircraft forms the basis of Ukrainian air power into the future, none of them will be of any use without effective weapons to fire. The best options here are probably the AMRAAM air-to-air missile, common to the NASAMS anti-aircraft system, or the Spear air-to-ground missile (Bronc 2023). A reasonable number of well-armed such jets, 30–50 F-16s and/or Gripens, could provide an affordable yet valuable contribution to Ukraine's arsenal. This would need to be supplemented by a modernization of the adequate and well-organized radar system that is already being deployed and used. Integrating this system into NATO's wider defence network will be vital.

Increasing maritime power

While less well-reported than the ground or air campaign, the maritime element of the war is essential to the state's survival as a viable economic concern. Ukraine will continue to develop capabilities to challenge Russian naval power on the surface or under the surface (Rowlands and Kaushal 2023). Russia's submarines present a particular threat in this regard. However, nothing at or near the sea provides a better deterrent capability to submarines than submarines.

Of all the categories of equipment so far mentioned, this would be by far the most expensive. Ukraine will not be able to afford to buy submarines of adequate quality, along with the supporting infrastructure, including training. However, with some innovative thinking NATO and the West could provide such a capability.

For example, Sweden is due to decommission two of its old but still highly effective Gotland Class submarines. A plan for them to be purchased by Poland appears now to have been shelved (Dura 2019). Indeed, Poland is now tendering for a new submarine (Reuters 2023). Might it be feasible for Poland or another NATO state (preferably a Black Sea littoral state—Romania?) to acquire second-hand submarines and share them with Ukraine? These need not be necessarily Swedish; many other capable submarines will become available globally and could be loaned and jointly crewed with Ukrainian naval personnel. Poland could share its planned new submarines in this way as well; it is possible. Such an arrangement is in place vis-à-vis Australia and the UK (Ministry of Defense 2022). Legal complications may arise with respect to deployment considering the Montreux Convention, but they are by no means insurmountable. Submarine capability such as this would be a significant deterrent against Russian aggression, offering a real possibility of Russia losing control of the Black Sea.

Aside from manned submersibles, options are rapidly being developed around the world for unmanned submarines to work alongside conventional boats. One option that might be suitable for Ukraine in this regard might be the autonomous "Cetus" submarines currently being developed and soon to be deployed by the British Royal Navy (Royal Navy 2022). These are envisaged as primarily surveillance platforms. They are relatively cheap, at about £15.7m each. Of course, we have seen Ukraine deploy maritime drones in assaults on Russian bases in Crimea (Pancevski and Lovett 2023), and the Ukrainian navy will have their own ideas about how to proceed in the development of maritime drone technology.

On the surface and rather more conventionally, a flotilla of well-armed patrol boats will be an essential component of the future navy of Ukraine, alongside its mine-sweeping and clearance capability, which would involve surface and subsurface crewed and uncrewed vessels.

The emerging question of nuclear weapons

As discussions concerning the possibility of NATO membership intensify, there are signs of an emerging discourse in Ukraine (and elsewhere) as to the possibility of Ukraine re-acquiring nuclear weapons capability (Zhdanov 2023). This has not yet emerged into the mainstream, and it may not do so. Whether it does or not will largely depend upon the nature and reliability of security guarantees that Ukraine will or may receive from its allies. Advocates take the view that nuclear weapons represent the ultimate guarantee.

Ukraine possessed nuclear weapons inherited from the former Soviet Union for four years. The state disarmed in 1994 in exchange for security guarantees in the form of the "Budapest Memoranda on security assurances," signed by the three nuclear weapons states and guarantor nations of the US, UK, and Russia.

In view of the events since 2014, Ukraine has reason to doubt such assurances (Grant 2015). Nuclear weapons are the ultimate assurance, provided that the concept of deterrence works. There is little doubt that Ukraine has the technical knowhow to achieve this. However, the dangers are very clear. There would seem to be equally little doubt that Russia would have, to put it mildly, severe objections to such an approach. These are likely to take the same form as Israel's objections to Iran's alleged nuclear programme. Consequently, the development of a nuclear weapons capability by Ukraine would need to be secret and—like Israel—if not deniable, then never commented upon. In the case of Israel, but not in the case of Ukraine as matters stand, there are delivery systems (missiles and aircraft) that can be relied upon.

Conclusion

Apropos Israel, one potential model for Ukraine's future defensive posture is that Middle Eastern state—particularly inasmuch as it is strongly supported by the US, both financially and technically, and with a strong security guarantee dating formally from 1963 (Noring 1995). Clearly there are major differences in the two cases, not least the deep history that the US has vis-à-vis Israel. However, the effective result may be similar, provided Ukraine can sustain its democracy: a very well-armed and militarily capable state relying to a greater or lesser extent on outside assistance.

Time will tell whether this will be an appropriate model. Whatever the shape of Ukraine's relationship to Europe, the United States, and NATO more widely, it is very clear that the country will remain a bulwark of European defence against Russia. This imposes a duty upon Western states, the discharge of which will be essential to European security. This will cost a very great deal of money. However, as with any good investment, the return will vastly outweigh the outlay.

Works cited

AP (Associated Press). 2023. "Poland signs deal to buy 2nd batch of Abrams tanks." Defense News, 4 Janurary 2023. https://www.defensenews.com/global/europe/2023/01/04/poland-signs-deal-to-buy-2nd-batch-of-us-abrams-tanks.

Bronc, Justin. 2023. "Regenerating warfighting credibility for European NATO air forces." Royal United Services Institute, 22 February 2023. https://static.rusi.org/whr_regenerating-warfighting-credibility-nato_0.pdf.

Cancian, Mark F., and James Anderson. 2023. "Expanding equipment options for Ukraine: The case of artillery." Center for Strategic and International Studies, 23 January 2023. https://www.csis.org/analysis/expanding-equipment-options-ukraine-case-artillery.

Defense Express. 2023. "Gripen for Ukraine: Sweden reveals how many 'spare' aircraft it has." Defense Express, 15 February 2023. https://en.defence-ua.com/news/gripen_for_ukraine_sweden_reveals_how_many_spare_aircraft_it_has-5754.html.

Dura, Maksymilian. 2019. "Poland to acquire second-hand submarines from Sweden? Head of the MoD confirms the negotiation's in progress," Defence24, 11 November 2019. https://defence24.com/poland-to-acquire-second-hand-submarines-from-sweden-head-of-the-mod-confirms-the-negotiations-in-progress.

Economist. 2023. "Ukraine's fate will determine the West's authority in the world." *The Economist*, 25 February 2023.

Garamone, Jim. 2023. "DOD is focused on China, defense official says." DOD News, 9 February 2023. https://www.defense.gov/News/News-Stories/Article/Article/3294255/dod-is-focused-on-china-defense-official-says.

Grant, Thomas. 2015. "The Budapest Memorandum and beyond: Have the Western parties breached a legal obligation?" EJIL Talk, 18 February 2015. https://www.ejiltalk.org/the-budapest-memorandum-and-beyond-have-the-western-parties-breached-a-legal-obligation.

Gressel, Gustav. 2022. "More tortoise, less hare: How Europeans can ramp up military supplies for Ukraine in the long war." European Council on Foreign Relations, 4 November 2022. https://ecfr.eu/article/more-tortoise-less-hare-how-europeans-can-ramp-up-military-supplies-for-ukraine-in-the-long-war.

Grieco, Kelly, and Maximilian Bremer. 2023. "Air defense upgrades, not F-16s, are a winning strategy for Ukraine." Defense News, 25 January 2023. https://www.defensenews.com/opinion/commentary/2023/01/25/air-defense-upgrades-not-f-16s-are-a-winning-strategy-for-ukraine.

IISS (International Institute for Strategic Studies). 2023. *The Military Balance* London: Routledge.

Lopez, Todd. 2022. "Latest U.S. support for Ukraine targets long-term security investment." Department of National Defense, 22 September 2022. https://www.defense.gov/News/News-Stories/Article/Article/3173752/latest-us-support-for-ukraine-targets-long-term-security-investment.

Losey, Stephen. 2023. "Which fighter jet is best for Ukraine as it fights off Russia?" Defense News, 7 March 2023. https://www.defensenews.com/air/2023/03/07/which-fighter-jet-is-best-for-ukraine-as-it-fights-off-russia.

Ministry of Defence. 2022. "Australian submariners to join Royal Navy crews as UK and Australia deepen defence ties through AUKUS agreement." Gov.uk, 31 August 2022. https://www.gov.uk/government/news/australian-submariners-to-join-royal-navy-crews-as-uk-and-australia-deepen-defence-ties-through-aukus-pact.

———. 2023. "Latest Defence Intelligence update on the situation in Ukraine – 05 June 2023." X, 5 June 2023, 6:43 a.m. https://twitter.com/DefenceHQ/status/1665595205309833219.

Neuhard, Ryan. 2022. "The new US National Security Strategy: Four takeaways for Asia policy." Foreign Policy Research Institute, 21 October 2022. https://www.fpri.org/article/2022/10/the-new-us-national-security-strategy-four-takeaways-for-asia-policy.

Noring, Nina J. 1995. "John F. Kennedy Administration: Memorandum on the U.S. Israeli Security Guarantee." In Foreign Relations of the United States, 1961–1963. Vol. XVIII: Near East, 1962–1963. Washington: Office of the Historian.

Pancevski, Bojan, and Ian Lovett. 2023. "Russia says drone boats attack Black Sea Fleet in Crimea." The Wall Street Journal, 21 April 2023. https://www.wsj.com/articles/russia-says-two-drones-attack-crimea-another-crashes-near-moscow-d1f59bb5.

Reuters. 2023. "Poland to launch submarine purchase programme soon – minister." Reuters, 24 May 2023. https://www.reuters.com/world/europe/poland-launch-submarine-purchase-programme-soon-minister-2023-05-24.

Royal Navy. 2022. "Royal Navy orders first crewless submarine to dominate underwater battleground." United Kingdom Royal Navy, 1 December 2022. https://www.royalnavy.mod.uk/news-and-latest-activity/news/2022/december/01/20221201-royal-navy-orders-first-crewless-submarine-to-dominate-underwater-battleground.

Rowlands, Kevin, and Sidharth Kaushal. 2023. "Tackling the underwater threat: How Ukraine can combat Russian submarines." Royal United Services Institute, 7 March 2023. https://www.rusi.org/explore-our-research/publications/commentary/tackling-underwater-threat-how-ukraine-can-combat-russian-submarines.

SAAB. 2020. "Gripen Designed for Dispersed Air Basing System." SAAB, 6 August 2020. https://www.saab.com/newsroom/stories/2020/august/gripen-designed-for-dispersed-air-basing-system.

Schogol, Jeff. 2023. "How Ukraine might maintain its Abrams, Challenger, and Leopard tanks to fight Russia." Task & Purpose, 27 January 2023. https://taskandpurpose.com/news/ukraine-us-british-german-tanks.

Statista. 2024. "Leopard 2 tank inventories in European and NATO countries 2021." Statista Research Department, 2 February 2024. https://www.statista.com/statistics/1361760/leopard-tank-inventories-in-europe-and-nato.

Watling, Jack, Justin Bronk, and Nick Reynolds. 2022. "The Russian air war and Ukrainian requirements for air defence." Royal United Services Institute, 7 November 2022. https://rusi.org/explore-our-research/publications/special-resources/russian-air-war-and-ukrainian-requirements-air-defence.

Zhdanov, Ihor. 2023. "Will Ukraine's own nuclear weapons be a sufficient guarantee of its security?" LB.ua, 3 June 2023. https://en.lb.ua/news/2023/06/03/20672_ukraines_own_nuclear_weapons.html.

CHAPTER 29

Russians are going into Ukraine to kill Ukrainians and to be killed themselves

Marci Shore

Interview with Oleksandr Pankieiev, published 23 June 2023

> Marci Shore (PhD, Stanford University, 2001) is a professor of history at Yale University. Her research focuses on the intellectual history of 20th- and 21st-century Central and Eastern Europe. She is the translator of Michał Głowiński's *The Black Seasons* (2005) and the author of *Caviar and Ashes: A Warsaw Generation's Life and Death in Marxism, 1918–1968* (2006), *The Taste of Ashes: The Afterlife of Totalitarianism in Eastern Europe* (2013), and *The Ukrainian Night: An Intimate History of Revolution* (2017). In 2018 she received a Guggenheim Fellowship for her current book project, a history of phenomenology in East-Central Europe.

Pankieiev: What does the Russo-Ukrainian war tell us about the nature of "evil" in the contemporary world? How should one understand social and political "evil" today?

Shore: I would not put the word *evil* in scare quotes. Postmodernism has brought us not only a skepticism about the ontological reality of truth but also a skepticism about the ontological reality of evil. I appreciate many of the insights of postmodern philosophy. I am not, though, a skeptic about the existence of evil.

Twenty years ago, when I was teaching at Indiana University, the historian Tony Judt gave a lecture there. Reflecting upon 20th-century Europe, he said, "We are unwise to laugh too quickly at those who describe the world as a conflict between good and evil. If you can't use the word 'evil,' you have a real problem thinking about what happened in the world." That has stayed with me.

I've been thinking about evil a lot in the past several years: watching the Trump administration wrench children away from their parents at the border and toss them in cages; reading Stanislav Aseyev's account of his captivity in *Izoliatsiia*, a prison complex with torture chambers in Donetsk (Aseyev 2021); listening to Roman Protasevich give his gruesome confession-extracted-by-torture on Belarusan television in 2021. I became preoccupied with analyzing that confession, which I then wrote about in an essay titled "This is what evil looks like: Towards a phenomenology of evil in postmodern form" (2021).

What makes today's evil—and today's neo-totalitarianism, let's call it—different from the evil and totalitarianism that I study in the 20th century is the *obnazhenie*: nothing is hidden; everything is laid bare. We're watching it all in real time, over the Internet. Imagine it was 1942 and we had a live stream into the gas chambers. This is not just a technological difference; it's an existential difference. Evgeniy Prigozhin openly calls himself "Putin's butcher." Kremlin propagandist Margarita Simonyan publicly declares that Russia is blackmailing the world with starvation: "*vsia nadezhda na golod*" (our only hope is in famine). Protasevich's television personality-interrogator, Marat Markov, plays his role with a gleam in his eye. He knows it's all a performance. And he knows that the audience knows. And he takes obvious delight in the performance *qua* performance.

Pankieiev: What is the best way to make the atrocities of war more comprehensible to Western audiences? To what extent are appeals to shared values and collective security effective?

Shore: The only way to make the atrocities more comprehensible is through stories about individual people. Anything not about actual human beings and their real lives is an abstraction.

With respect to shared values, I am very wary about attempts to ground an argument for support for Ukraine in the longevity of Ukrainian history or the richness of Ukrainian art or the world-historical quality of Taras Shevchenko's poetry. It's true that Ukrainian history has its own deep roots and Ukrainian culture its own moments of brilliance—but to argue for support for Ukraine on that basis is a trap. It's a trap because it implies that the right of children not to be buried under rubble or mothers not to be shelled while giving birth or teachers and bakers and farmers not to be tortured with electric shocks is somehow contingent upon a history of national self-consciousness or a kinship with the creators of great literature. The right not to be slaughtered and tortured must be contingent upon nothing. That right must be *a priori*, universal, and absolute. What Russian soldiers are doing to Ukrainians is morally reprehensible not because Ukrainians are heirs to a rich culture but because they are human beings. Any argument that suggests that human rights are contingent upon cultural accomplishments is a moral trap.

Pankieiev: How will the war influence Europe's cultural environment in general and its intellectual historiography in particular?

Shore: In case anyone still harboured any doubts, it's now very clear that there is no such thing as the End of History.

It's also the case that—as at other moments of historical extremity, what Karl Jaspers called a *Grenzsituation*—remarkable writing and thinking and artistic creation have emerged from Ukraine in the midst of war. These essays and paintings and poems will comprise a new chapter of intellectual history. Aseyev's account of his captivity, *The Torture Camp of Paradise Street* (2023), will be read alongside Viktor Frankl and Tadeusz Borowski and Henri Alleg.

Pankieiev: How do we achieve the de-Russification of Ukrainian studies in Western academia? What is the most effective way to change the perception of Ukraine, pull it out from the shadow of Russian intellectual thought, and restore its *actorness* as a historical phenomenon and a modern state?

Shore: Slavic studies, including Russian studies, is already a relatively marginal field—I say this as a Slavicist who was trained after the Cold War, when political interest in the former Communist bloc was already waning. I do think that this war has inspired more curiosity about Ukraine; and I think there will be more Ukrainian language and literature and history courses in the future. But again, the scale is modest: we're talking about very small numbers of courses. Even at a university like Yale, there is a very limited number of courses in Russian history and literature being taught. When Ukrainians worry that everyone is reading Pushkin and no one is reading Shevchenko, I try to point out that, at least in my own country, barely anyone is reading Pushkin either. The problem involved in coaxing Americans into understanding Ukraine is not that Americans are too dazzled by Russia but that we are too self-absorbed: for most Americans, things happening in other parts of the world do not feel quite real.

Pankieiev: Maria Zolkina and Serhiy Kvit, whom the *Forum* interviewed in the past, argue that for the war to come to its end, Russians need to confront and revise their imperial past, their expansionist ideas. To what extent do you agree with such arguments?

Shore: A few thoughts about imperialism and decolonization. With respect to present-day Ukraine and Russia, it's very difficult to disentangle the legacy of Russian imperialism from the Soviet experiment. Sofia Dyak, a sociologist from Lviv, gave a lecture at Yale this fall. She spoke about decolonizing and how for Ukraine, part of decolonizing has to be *self-decolonizing*. The Soviet experiment was not only imposed from outside; it came from inside as well.

For me, one of the most interesting questions about decolonization is the one related to the Hegelian master-slave dialectic: when we think about Ukraine and Russia, how did it happen that subjectivity has emerged on the part of the colonized and not on the part of the colonizers? The Ukrainian novelist Volodymyr Rafeyenko described Russia as an "anthropological catastrophe," and that is perhaps the best short description I've heard. Imperialism is part of the problem; totalitarianism is part of the problem; intergenerational trauma is part of the problem; and a terrifyingly high tolerance for domestic violence is part of the problem, as is a failure to look with eyes wide open at the Stalinist terror of the past. Sergei Lebedev has written with merciless precision about this.

My intuition is that the deepest roots of the pathology in Russia have to do with a failure of subjectivity. Russians are going into Ukraine to kill Ukrainians and to be killed themselves *for nothing*. Part of the reason surely has to do with a history of imperialism and a sense that Ukraine is and/or should be part of Russia—but that only gets us so far. For me, the more profound question is why are Russians getting in line and doing what a sadistic tyrant tells them to do? As Andrey Kurkov points out in his war diary, most of the Ukrainian civilians Russian soldiers are killing in Ukraine are Russian-speakers—that is, they are slaughtering precisely the people they allegedly came to protect (Kurkov 2023). Putin's regime is also presiding over the destruction of Russia; it's shameless nihilism—and a chilling failure of ordinary Russians to think, or to conceive of themselves as subjects with a responsibility to think.

Works cited

Aseyev, Stanislav. 2023. *The Torture Camp on Paradise Street*. Transl. Zenia Tompkins and Nina Murray. Cambridge, MA: Harvard Ukrainian Research Institute.

———. 2022. *In Isolation: Dispatches from Occupied Donbas*. Transl. Lidia Wolanskyj. Cambridge, MA: Harvard Ukrainian Research Institute.

Kurkov, Andrey. 2023. *Diary of an Invasion*. Dallas: Deep Vellum.

Shore, Marci. 2021. "This is what evil looks like: Toward a phenomenology of evil in postmodern form." *Social Research: An International Quarterly* 88 (4): 773–94. https://doi.org/10.1353/sor.2021.0046.

CHAPTER 30

Russia's undue influence on Western scholars and scholarship

Hiroaki Kuromiya
Essay published on 30 June 2023

> Hiroaki Kuromiya taught Ukrainian, Russian, and Soviet history at Indiana University, USA, until his retirement in 2021. He is the author of *Freedom and Terror in the Donbas: A Ukrainian-Russian Borderland, 1870s–1990s* (1998), *Stalin: Profiles in Power* (2005), *Conscience on Trial: The Fate of Fourteen Pacifists in Stalin's Ukraine, 1952–1953* (2012), *Zrozumity Donbas* (Understanding the Donbas; 2015), and other books.

On 19 May 2023 the Russian government announced "personal sanctions" against 500 "American citizens," including banned entry into the country. Several friends promptly informed me, some with condolences and others with congratulatory notes, that I was among the handful of American university professors blacklisted by Moscow. (Strictly speaking, like some others on the list, I am not an American citizen but a US "resident alien.") We join a small number of our colleagues who were sanctioned earlier, in 2022.

Having examined the blacklist, Anders Åslund noted that among them are a large number of members of think tanks, and he adds, "Surprisingly, few university professors have been included. Does the Kremlin think that it has successfully [muzzled] them? What do those intellectuals not sanctioned have to say in their defense?" (2023). On the one hand, Åslund is perhaps unfair to the scholarly community: universities are not think tanks, and academics do not necessarily engage in current political affairs. On the other hand, it is hard to ignore the fact that few Russianists were sanctioned, while most of those who were banned are Ukrainianists. Regardless, Moscow's sanctions on certain individual scholars do afford an important opportunity for our scholarly community to confront uncomfortable issues that it has largely failed to address.

* * *

For those of us who have devoted years to the study of Eastern Europe and non-Russian regions of the former Soviet Union, it appears rather odd that only now does the field of Russian studies speak of "decolonizing" the discipline. It is never too late, of course, but this only emphasizes both the complacency with which the field has operated until now and the persistent imperialist outlook that Russia and the Soviet Union have imposed on the discipline over the last century. The field has too long been sanguine about the imperialist and Russocentric views of such Russian literary luminaries as Alexander Pushkin, Fyodor Dostoevsky, and even Joseph Brodsky. In historical studies, as I have noted elsewhere, as late as 2000 the hugely popular Russian history textbook by Nicholas Riasanovsky, *A History of Russia*, published by Oxford University Press, calls Kyiv-Rus' "Kievan Russia" (2000). Almost all textbooks still use such expressions as "Peter the Great'" and "Catherine the Great." It appears that the field has consciously or unconsciously swallowed whole Russian imperialist propaganda without even being aware of the biases and falsehoods in its narrative. There is every reason to believe that Moscow has been happy with this state of scholarship.

In the wake of the war unleashed against Ukraine in February 2022, many academic institutions publicly denounced Russia. This only serves to highlight the inconvenient fact that very few did so in 2014, when Russia annexed Crimea and opened a camouflaged war against Ukraine, particularly in the Donbas. As the author of one of few Western scholarly books on the Donbas, I find myself bringing to bear my historical analyses on the current situation in Russia and Ukraine. Moreover, being placed on the banned list, I cannot help but wonder whether my recent book on Stalin's secret wars of subversion, camouflage, and disinformation in China and Japan has possibly struck a nerve in Moscow (Kuromiya 2022).

Of course, I regret not being able to work in the Russian archives and to visit friends and colleagues there any more. I am grateful for the time I was able to spend there and for the exchanges I had with Russian scholars in the past. I readily admit that access to Russian archives and Russian experts has been critical to my work. At the same time, in the current situation few of us would dare to travel to Russia. Nor can we expect to reap much reward anymore from the Russian archives and libraries and experts. That being so, it seems a good time to reflect on our work in Russia and Ukraine over the past three decades, since the opening up in the 1990s of formerly closed [Soviet and imperial] archives.

* * *

Not long ago Western scholars spoke of an "archival revolution" in the study of Russian and Soviet history, but it has turned out to be illusory. Not only does Moscow still jealously guard its archives, it releases archival documents carefully and selectively so as to steer historians' views in its desired direction. After three decades of archival work, I now am certain that we have been naive in our belief that we've had good access to Soviet-era archives. We should be aware of Moscow's careful, purposeful, and adroitly selective release of archival documents, which is meant to manipulate the research of experts.

Take the example of Stalin and his era, which I have studied throughout my professional life. Much has been written on the Soviet dictator, yet we still know precious little about many aspects of his policies. Some policy documents were destroyed or never kept, and much was likely never put to paper. Numerous relevant documents are still kept under a tight seal in the Communist Party Archive, the Presidential Archive, military archives, archives of the Foreign Ministry and Federal Security Services, and elsewhere. Even the "open" files of Stalin and the Politburo in the former have numerous pages that are still classified. Moreover, apparently in fear of unauthorized or accidental access, the Russian government has removed some sensitive files from Moscow to distant locations. Although some classified documents may prove to be not so significant, one can safely assume that many of them are, and that that is why Moscow keeps them secret.

In this regard, we ought to take seriously Åslund's trenchant remarks quoted above. To illustrate, in a book published in 2014 by a distinguished university press, Western scholars of Stalin take his speeches and writings at face value, claiming that in the interwar period it was "rather simple" for foreign countries to organize subversive activity in the Soviet Union and that recruiting "spies and saboteurs" was also easy for them. Providing profuse citations of Soviet archival documents but citing not a single example of such alleged spies and saboteurs, the book touts "widespread infiltration" of the USSR by "enemy agents." This seems to justify Stalin's fears of foreign spies, and in doing so implicitly legitimates Stalin's Great Terror. However, this is pure Soviet propaganda, and if granting selective access to former Soviet archives has led Western specialists to this sort of conclusion about Stalin, then Moscow could not be happier. I published a critical review of the book at the time and am not aware of other, equally critical reviews. It is difficult to understand the lack of a principled rebuff by the profession. This example reflects the unfortunate state of scholarship on Soviet history.

Although books published during the Cold War got Stalin wrong in many respects, scholars seemed in general to be more aware of the limitations of their grasp of the subject, principally because there was no meaningful scope of access to the Soviet archives. Paradoxically, greater access to the archives seems to have led—to use Natalie Z. Davies' famous epithet—to "fiction in the archives," namely, a naive repetition of Russia's disinformation and propaganda.

True, we have to acknowledge that the new archival era in Russia in the 1990s contributed to the elucidation of not a few dark episodes of Soviet history by both Russian and Western scholars as well as, more generally, to a better understanding of Soviet history. Ukrainian studies has certainly benefited from greater access to the archives in Russia. Yet now, as before, many scholars privately express fear of being denied entry visas to Russia and publicly speak of Russian "visa support" as if it were a prize. Scholars from the free world are prone to fall, wittingly or unwittingly, into traps that Moscow has deliberately set up. Moscow believes that Western scholars are easily influenced and manipulated through "soft power" (including access to people, documents, and lavish treatment). Recently, Pavel Ivlev openly cautioned of this danger (Zhigalkin 2023). The same can be said of Beijing. If we scholars—as critically minded individuals who enjoy the privilege of academic freedom and often lifetime employment as well—prove to be so vulnerable, one has to wonder what our raison d'etre is.

This depressing state of affairs reflects the overall parochial insularity of Russian studies. Those who have worked in Ukraine, other former Soviet republics, and Eastern Europe are generally better placed, because they can view Russia from different perspectives, and their access to the archives in these countries has been far greater and less restrictive than in Russia. Their contributions to Russian and Soviet studies are likewise more significant than is usually acknowledged. For them, today's call for "decolonization in Russian studies" is long overdue.

* * *

For the foreseeable future, at least, the forecast for Russian and Soviet studies in the West seems bleak. Meanwhile Ukrainian studies, notwithstanding the war, are far better placed. All the same, without freer access to the archives of the empire, our scholarship will suffer.

We have to take appropriate measures. We cannot be naive about Russia's covert and adroit efforts to manipulate Western experts. As far as archival research is concerned, undoubtedly the now-independent former Soviet republics will assume a far greater role than has been the case up to now. Scholars of Russia will have to study non-Russian languages and trek to non-Russian lands in order to study Russia. Ukraine, which Moscow is trying to destroy by force, will assume the utmost significance. As far as I am concerned, I can say that I received my most critical training in understanding Russia and the Soviet Union not in Russia but in Ukraine, in the 1990s and 2000s when the Ukrainian archives became far more open to researchers than the Russian archives. Access to the former KGB archives in Ukraine from the mid-1990s opened new and strikingly revelatory perspectives on history, and it was in Ukraine that I learned to read Soviet-era documents critically. All the same, the fact remains that it is Russia—not the other former Soviet republics—that retains many documents which are critical to comprehending the history of Ukraine, Russia, and the Soviet Union.

Scholars can work around this to some extent by exploring archives in the West and in former Soviet Bloc countries such as Poland and Bulgaria. For instance, after years of searching for many documents in Russia, I found copies of some of them in Ulaanbaatar in Mongolia. A few years ago, in Taipei (Taiwan) I found two original letters that Stalin had written to Chang Kaishek in 1939 and 1941, whose copies in Moscow have been kept hidden. I published them in the original language for the benefit of all scholars (including Russian ones).

No one knows how and when Russia's war against Ukraine will end. Regardless, I would tend to agree with Sergei Radchenko, a historian originally from Russia and now teaching in the United States, who wrote in May 2022: "Why Russia needs to be humiliated in Ukraine: Too little was learnt from the collapse of the Soviet Union" (Radchenko 2022). Although this remark may sound insulting to Russians, in fact it is not. Every normal nation experiences humiliation. China constantly speaks of its historical humiliation at Western and Japanese hands. Those who saw the chaotic scenes of Saigon in 1975 know the humiliation the United States suffered in Vietnam. Russia claims its own humiliation in 1991—parroting President Putin's line that the collapse of the USSR was the greatest geopolitical catastrophe of the 20th century—conveniently forgetting that Russia actually wanted to be free of the Soviet Union at the time. Stomaching humiliation and starting over demands political courage; ignoring its lessons and blaming others for the humiliation is easy but dangerous. Russia's war against Ukraine demonstrates just such a lack of courage among Russian politicians. Russia's unqualified defeat may ultimately be the best outcome not just for Ukraine but also for the future of the Russian Federation and Russians themselves. The same might be said for the future of the academic fields of Ukrainian, Russian, and Soviet studies.

Works cited

Åslund, Anders. 2023. "Kremlin's new sanctions are openly campaigning for Trump." *Kyiv Post*, 22 May 2023.

Kuromiia, Khiroaki. 2021. "'Sovetskomu Soiuzu pridetsia voevat' s Iaponiei': Dva pis'ma Stalina Chan Kaishi (1939 i 1941 gg.)." *Klio* (St. Petersburg), no. 171: 28–31.

Kuromiya, Hiroaki. 2022. *Stalin, Japan, and the Struggle for Supremacy over China, 1894–1945*. London: Routledge.

Radchenko, Sergey. 2022. "Why Russia needs to be humiliated in Ukraine." *The Spectator*, 15 May 2022. https://www.spectator.co.uk/article/why-russia-needs-to-be-humiliated-in-ukraine.

Riasanovsky, Nicolas. 2000. *A History of Russia*. Oxford University Press.

Zhigalkin, Yurii. 2023. "'Zhalkaia igra Kremlia': Kur'ez – tak v Amerike vospriniali sanktsii Rossii." Radio Liberty, 27 May 2023. https://www.svoboda.org/a/zhalkaya-igra-kremlya-kak-v-amerike-vosprinyali-sanktsii-rossii-/32430295.html.

CHAPTER 31

We value Canada's support of Ukraine's future membership in NATO

Yuliya Kovaliv

Interview with Artem Mamadzhanov, published 10 July 2023

> Yuliya Kovaliv has been Ukraine's Ambassador to Canada since March 2022, following appointments as Deputy Head of the Office of the President of Ukraine in charge of economic policy and IFI, Chair (2016–17) and Deputy Chair (2019–21) of the Supervisory Board of Naftogaz Ukraine, Deputy Secretary of the National Investment Council of Ukraine, and member of the National Reform Council. In 2015–16 Kovaliv served as the First Deputy Minister for Economic Development and Trade, and in 2014–15 she headed the National Regulatory Commission for Energy and Utilities. She holds an MA in Economics from the National University of "Kyiv-Mohyla Academy" and an MPA from the National Academy for Public Administration under the President of Ukraine.

Mamadzhanov: Earlier this year, in your presentation at Carleton University you mentioned global repercussions that stem from the war: growing food insecurity, erosion of international order, and challenges to nuclear safety. How does the situation look today? Have new repercussions emerged?

Kovaliv: It is a crucial question. Russia's illegal invasion of Ukraine revealed a lot of disturbing and "engineered" developments in the world. Not only did Ukraine and its resilience become visible and acknowledged, many areas were noticed where global action and improvement are needed. Moreover, a handful of international institutions that were established after the Second World War to preserve peace, work on global prosperity, and address climate change are no longer as functional as planned. The illegal Russian invasion showed the weaknesses and gaps in the international order that we will all need to address—food security and nuclear safety being only some of them.

I would specifically like to mention Russia's recent destruction of the Kakhovka water dam. It is an example of the environmental damage that the war has brought not only to Ukrainians but also to broader ecosystems. It was a terrorist attack *against climate*. It has already changed many areas in Ukraine and will have an environmental impact far beyond the country's borders.

As we look at human rights, unfortunately the institutions created to protect them—including reputable ones such as the International Red Cross—do not actually work. Russia continues to hold and torture many Ukrainian prisoners of war in unknown circumstances. Fifteen months into the fighting, these people have not been attended to by any monitoring mission. Soldiers and prisoners whom we managed to exchange and bring home look as if they were deprived of food and tortured. You can readily find their pictures on the Internet. Then, there was the horror of Olenivka, an unthinkable crime when Russia deliberately destroyed the POW camp and killed over forty prisoners of war. In this context, we see that regrettably, institutions such as the International Red Cross—with a mandate to oversee and monitor the circumstances in which all the prisoners of war are kept—do not work.

The fates of Ukrainian children, their illegal deportation and adoption, also remain an unresolved problem. It is a part of the *crime of genocide*, and Ukraine is working to bring to justice all suspects and perpetrators. The International Criminal Court is also investigating.

Many dimensions of this war have been shown to the world and have become a global concern, but Russia has not stopped. This brings all of us to face new challenges. Therefore, the need remains crucial for strong support of Ukraine and quicker decisions on supplies of weaponry. *Ukraine needs to win this war. Its victory will be not only of one country against Russian occupiers but of all the democratic world against tyranny.* Democracy is something that Ukraine shares with Canada and many other countries. And democracy is being seriously challenged now in the global context. The victory of Ukraine will help to sustain democracy.

Mamadzhanov: Which fields of cooperation, apart from defence, are the most essential between Ukraine and Canada today? What do you think are the priorities for cooperation?

Kovaliv: Defence, defence, defence, and weapons. Unfortunately, Putin listens only to the language of power. We all saw the failure of the previous attempts to negotiate a ceasefire or find diplomatic engagement with him. Putin has one ambition on his mind, which can be best defined as "Russia means the big Russian Empire." His attempts to colonize other countries need to be stopped—once and forever. In turn, Russians need to realize and understand that respect for the sovereign borders of other countries is paramount.

Ukraine is an independent state and a part of the European family. I am sure that following Russia's illegal invasion many more people in the world, and especially in the West, realized how different our countries are, how different our cultures are. They have come to understand Ukraine better; our country has become closer to them. All these changes can be observed in the decisions of the European Union to grant Ukraine candidacy status, or in the promising talks about Ukraine's NATO membership on the eve of the Vilnius summit. And, of course, increasing weapons supplies and ensuring the military victory of Ukraine are now high on the Western agenda.

That being said, since the fighting is ongoing Ukraine also needs financial support. Its economy has shrunk, which is an inevitable development during wartime. The Canadian government's robust support to stabilize Ukraine's national budget is hard to overestimate. It has allowed the authorities in Kyiv to provide and cover the basic needs of many vulnerable people, including seniors, internally displaced persons, and all Ukrainians who have lost property, houses, and all their possessions. Another important contribution of the Canadian government, of course, is the humanitarian help for de-mining activity.

In the future, we also hope that the Canadian government will participate in drafting security guarantees for Ukraine. Our ultimate goal is full-fledged NATO membership. However, before that happens the country still needs to be protected, which will become an essential engagement for all partners around the world.

Mamadzhanov: Ukraine is investigating different options to secure financial compensation from Russia for all the damage it has caused. What help do you expect from the Canadian government in that respect?

Kovaliv: First, we believe that Russia has to pay for all the damage inflicted on Ukraine. The figures are really high. The latest estimation of the World Bank is 411 billion USD. All the Russian sovereign assets around the globe should not only be frozen, as they are right now, but transferred to Ukraine so that the country can rebuild itself.

We value Canada being the first to introduce national legislation that allows the seizure of Russia's sovereign assets and their transfer to Ukraine. Today the Canadian government is taking a look at two cases of Russian assets in light of that legislation. We also greatly value Canada's strong voice, among other Western partners, advocating that all Russian sovereign assets should be seized. In particular, Canada is consistently trying to influence those countries which harbour a huge number of Russian assets on their territory. This is really important.

In the future, we will also appreciate the engagement of Canada's private sector in rebuilding Ukraine. There is a huge need and a lot of room for various activities — an enormous endeavour, and active participation of Canadian businesses will be very welcome. From our side, we will try to provide the private sector with mechanisms of de-risking in Ukraine, including war insurance, some concessional financing, and government support. This is a field where we are also working closely with the federal and provincial governments in Canada.

Mamadzhanov: How has Canada been helping Ukraine with its ongoing counteroffensive? Has this help been sufficient or can anything else be done?

Kovaliv: Above all, we greatly value Canada's help. Last year, it was valued at over C$1 billion. This year, Prime Minister Justin Trudeau recently announced another C$500 million in military support alone.

Canada participates in all the important international arrangements that deal with the supply of weaponry to Ukraine. Canada is a loyal and constant partner, including in the Leopard tank coalition and the fighter jets coalition. Also, it is a vocal advocate of providing Ukraine with air defence, armoured vehicles, artillery shells, and other weapons. We value this a lot. However, if we look at the realities in Ukraine, if we talk with our Minister of Defense and ordinary soldiers, it is clear that demand for weapons remains high. To that we need to add time pressure. Therefore, it is also important that all the commitments already made are delivered as soon as possible. I would say Ukrainians needed more weaponry yesterday, if not even six months ago.

For months after the invasion started, the question of providing Patriot air defence systems was a hot topic. Today, they are irreplaceable in covering the skies of Kyiv and other major cities, in protecting civilians from ballistic missiles fired from Russia. But the provision of the Patriot took a while. It took a while for Ukraine to convince its international partners. The same goes for Leopard tanks. I hope these lessons will be learned. Right now, Ukraine is in urgent need of fighter jets. We hope to get them as soon as possible.

Mamadzhanov: On 11 July a NATO summit will take place in Vilnius, Lithuania. What can you say about Canada's position on Ukraine becoming a member of the alliance? How would you assess Canada's efforts to bring Ukraine's army up to NATO standards—for instance, under the Operation Unifier training program that was launched in 2015 and recently extended till 2026?

Kovaliv: Canada was among the first countries that started training for Ukrainian soldiers in Ukraine back in 2015. Their program helped to train over 30,000 soldiers in accordance with NATO standards—before the escalated invasion commenced. During the first weeks of active fighting in this hot phase of the war, Canadian training helped Ukrainians to save lives and stop the Russian offensive. Today, we greatly value Canada's decision to continue this program, in particular through joining efforts with the UK and Poland. It's also worth mentioning that this program was expanded to engineering and other areas which are of significant importance for us.

If we look at it in detail, the change in Ukraine's armed forces from back in 2014-15 and up until now has been immense. We have built one of the strongest armies on the European continent. Our army has acquired real battlefield experience. Our army has learned how to use NATO standard weapons—and uses them very effectively. Considering this, we believe that becoming a NATO member is important not only for Ukraine but for other European countries as well. With its strong armed forces and experience of this war, Ukraine will become a pillar of the eastern flank of NATO. This is why all of Ukraine's neighbouring Eastern European and Baltic countries are very vocal when discussing how much NATO security will be improved after Ukraine joins the alliance.

We hope that the forthcoming NATO summit in Vilnius will be historic and that its participants will learn from the mistakes of the 2008 Bucharest summit. Ukraine hopes to get a clear signal on NATO membership. We believe that this signal is also essential for all NATO members.

We do know that decisions can be adopted rapidly by the alliance. We welcome Finland's recent accession to NATO and that Sweden is on its way. We also know that the illegal Russian invasion of Ukraine significantly reshuffled the security architecture on the European continent and beyond. Considering these circumstances, we believe it is really important for Ukraine and NATO to deepen their collaboration and do it fast.

We are looking forward to the NATO summit in Vilnius. We value Canada's consistent support of Ukraine's future membership in the alliance. We cherish high hopes for next week.

CHAPTER 32

Kremlin plans on a long-term engagement, on a long war

Bo Petersson

Interview with Ostap Kushnir, published 10 July 2023

> Bo Petersson is a professor of political science at Malmö University (Sweden), where he is one of the founders of the research platform Russia, Ukraine, and the Caucasus Regional Research (RUCARR). He is also during 2022/24 a part-time researcher at Södertörn University, Stockholm. His special areas of interest include legitimacy, authoritarianism, national identity, and political myth, and he has throughout his academic career specialized in Russian and post-Soviet politics. He is, inter alia, the author of *The Putin Predicament: Problems of Legitimacy and Succession in Russia* (2021), *National Self-Images and Regional Identities in Russia* (2001; 2nd edn 2018), and *Stories about Strangers* (2006).

Kushnir: In March 2022, in your article for *Forum for Ukrainian Studies* you mentioned that "the signs [of the forthcoming invasion] were there for all to see, but we did not read them correctly." What signs do you see today in Russian politics?

Petersson: This is a tricky question, because wisdom often comes with hindsight. Before the invasion we, the Western analysts, did not take the time to reflect on the patterns of what we had been observing for years, and instead we rushed ahead with conclusions based on individual pieces of evidence. That was a mistake. Unfortunately, there is no guarantee that we will not make similar mistakes in the future as well.

That being said, one of the obvious signs that have been there since the full-scale invasion started—and especially *after* the largely unsuccessful initial weeks—is that the Kremlin has planned on a long-term engagement, on a long war. There will be no quick fix. Unfortunately, we are talking about time horizons that stretch several years ahead.

Of course, there are also signs that Putin and his henchmen are not always on good terms. Some of the underlings, especially the hawks, disagree with Putin's course of action and have become more and more vocal recently. The opposition to Putin includes such odd and rebellious hardliners like Evgeniy Prigozhin, but not only him.

So, if you ask me about signs, those are probably the two that I would feel most inclined to mention.

Kushnir: Are there any signs that Russia is seeking a common language with external actors and wants to change its foreign policy from confrontation to cooperation, especially with the EU?

Petersson: Such signs are few. At any rate, Russia is certainly not trying to build more conciliatory and peaceful relations with all external actors. If that is any indicator, the bombing of Kyiv in the midst of the visit of the delegation from African countries, on 16 June 2023, was quite an obvious sign that the Kremlin is not inclined to talk seriously about peace.

Putin has stopped referring to Western countries as "partners" as he used to do. It is quite clear that his regime became more oriented towards China and other more sympathetic countries. I am not sure, however, that the Chinese are entirely happy with such a change. There are signs that they, for instance, tacitly support Prime Minister Mikhail Mishustin, who has been low-key about the war. We are yet to see what might come out of this, but it is an interesting observation.

Kushnir: How would you assess the change in Western expertise on Russia following the full-scale invasion? Have there been any tectonic shifts in how analysts approach the aggressor state?

Petersson: Indeed, there have been some shifts. One of the most obvious is that the Russian regime has been reconceptualized. Before the invasion, Russia was approached as a paradigmatic case of a hybrid political system. *Electoral authoritarianism* was a breed and brand that was attributed to Russia. Recently, most serious analysts in the West have concluded that the "hybrid political" approach is no longer applicable. Today's Russia is discussed as a *closed authoritarian state*. The analysts started researching it differently, in a new way. So, that is one obvious change.

The other change is that, belatedly, the Western scholarly community has acknowledged that the expertise on Ukraine needs to be developed and improved. Thus, Ukraine must not be approached merely as a former Soviet republic or an appendage to Russia. There have been very serious decolonization debates across the globe during the past year. Several leading Western universities have decided to invest substantial funds into the study of and research programs on Ukraine as an independent actor. This is, of course, a very welcome development.

Kushnir: More than a year into the war, support of the regime among the Russian citizens, as well as their trust in the Kremlin's leadership, remain rather high. What are the sources of legitimacy of Putin and his regime?

Petersson: From the very outset of his first presidency, Putin and his spin doctors have been very skilled and successful in cultivating certain key political myths to the benefit of the regime. There are a couple of potent political myths that should be particularly highlighted.

First, there is the idea that Russia allegedly always has been a predetermined and preordained great power, regardless of what takes place within its borders or in the world. As a great power, Russia is argued to have inherent rights to spheres of influence and domination over adjacent countries. Secondly, there is a myth about a cyclical and detrimental recurrence of times of trouble, or *smuta*, that will unavoidably harm Russia unless precautions are taken. The prevention of a *smuta* from happening — and, thus, securing stability across the country — can only be achieved under the leadership of a bold and wise leader, ostensibly such as Putin.

Added to these two early political myths that the regime capitalized on, another myth started circulating with increased intensity after the return of Putin to the formal presidency in 2012. It was about the depraved and demoralized West that had always been attempting to destroy and rupture the Russian way of life and was increasingly continuing those efforts. Therefore, to withstand all Western misdeeds, resourceful action was needed — again, under Putin's God-given (according to some of his most ardent followers) leadership.

These political myths exemplify the narratives that the Putin regime has been very successful in communicating to and cultivating among the domestic population. It was very clearly argued that Putin is the only conceivable president and guarantor of Russia's remaining a great power, avoiding the *smuta*, and preserving its identity against the malicious onslaughts of the West.

Intimately connected to these myths is the very intense use of the narrative about the Great Patriotic War. According to the propaganda, the fight against Nazism from the 1940s has never been concluded for Russians, and they therefore need to relive and resume it, in connection with the Russo-Ukrainian war, through rivalry with the West, which is backing Ukraine. Given the Kremlin's rigid control of traditional mass media, this narrative is largely unopposed and has great nationwide reach, as well as, obviously, significant impact.

Another reason behind the seemingly successful legitimation of Putin's regime is the limitations in data collection. Even a reputable solid sociological institution like the Levada Center is not immune to the fact that surveys in Russia are undertaken in an authoritarian context. People either tend to avoid answering questions and keep their private thoughts to themselves or answer questions in a manner that they think the interviewers would like to hear. Therefore, the high support ratings for the war and the Russian leadership are interesting phenomena to study, but they also are most probably inflated and should be read with caution.

Kushnir: How would you describe Putin's perception of Zelensky? Can we say that the President of Ukraine has become a personal nemesis of the President of Russia? Is there a collision of two models of charismatic leadership?

Petersson: I would not say that there is a collision. It is rather that Putin became eclipsed by Zelensky on all fronts and can do little to change the situation. It is pretty much the same story as it used to be in the contestation between Putin and Alexei Navalny a few years ago. *The Putin whom we observe today is a tired and old man.* Just like Navalny before his long-term imprisonment, Zelensky, as an energetic and charismatic leader, sharply contrasts with this version of Putin. Putin is no longer the person that he seemed to have be some ten years back in time, when he was the macho man, the achiever, the goal-getter. Incidentally, he consistently avoids referring to Zelensky by name, just as he used to in relation to Navalny.

I would therefore not say that we have a competition between different kinds of charisma. Instead, we have the formerly charismatic figure of Putin looking increasingly weary, old, and fragile — nowhere near the man he used to be.

Kushnir: To what extent do you think that Putin started a "waiting game" against the West and Ukraine? Will the growing war fatigue make democratic societies less supportive of fighting Russia "as long as it takes?"

Petersson: I'm afraid that you are right. No matter how horrible the war is, public opinion and politicians in the West get accustomed to it being part of the everyday. And something that is part of the everyday is nothing to be so much concerned about. The fatigue grows. Moreover, other news appear and eclipse the war. The peculiar feature of the media reality is that apparently, only one major topic can be on air at the same time. We see this feature manifesting these very days. The big news is about the last minutes of the world's richest people on their underwater trip to the wrecks of Titanic, not Ukraine's struggle.

Therefore, I think, a very deliberate "waiting game" is being played by the Kremlin. The stakes are high, not least due to the impending presidential elections in the US in 2024. There is a tangible risk that Donald Trump will become elected president again, or someone pretty much like him. This development risks having detrimental consequences for Ukraine's war of defense.

Kushnir: Do you think that this strategy of waiting will work for Putin in the long run? Are there any signs that such a strategy is failing?

Petersson: I prefer not to think that it will work out in the long run, because that would already be defeatist thinking. What I am sure about is that the "waiting" has become a deliberate strategy. Hopefully, the West will not fall into the trap.

Kushnir: What war-provoked changes do you think will take place in Russian and Ukrainian societies in the future?

Petersson: This is probably the most difficult question that you have asked me so far. If we as analysts are prone to go in the wrong direction anywhere, it is in predictions about the future. However, from what is discernible right now, concerning the signs that we discussed in relation to the first question, Ukrainian society will get even more firmly integrated into the West.

At the same time, Russian society and the state will become weaker and weaker. The benefactor of all this will probably be

China. By continuing the war, Russia will deplete its resources, making China relatively stronger. Also, the US will face some decrease of resources due to its backing of Ukraine.

Kushnir: A few analysts whom I spoke to earlier said that following the war, Russians would likely revisit their self-identification, myths, and expansionist mindset. To what extent do you think this is possible?

Petersson: I think this development is desirable and very much hoped for. However, I do not see the signs of it happening. Maybe after a regime change there will be a chance. The 1990s are not that long gone, after all, and we observed very abrupt and drastic changes in post-Soviet Russia after the Communist regime crumbled. So indeed, why could not this happen again?

Let us not give up hope. But, as I said, I do not see the signs right now.

Kushnir: What has surprised you in Ukraine's response to the Russian invasion? What lessons can other countries in the region learn from Ukraine's case?

Petersson: What impressed and surprised me the most, and not only me, was the resilience of Ukraine and the Ukrainians, the strength that they put into the resistance. Another surprising point was the professional leadership at the highest state level. In less than two years, Zelensky has grown with the task to a stature of almost Churchillian dimensions.

Concerning the lessons for other countries of the region, well, they are not that easily translatable. Very few former Soviet republics have the advantages of size that Ukraine has. The strength of Ukraine's resilience that I mentioned is not least attributable to having a vast territory. So, maybe Kazakhstan and other Central Asian countries can learn some lessons from the Ukrainian experience, but probably not countries such as Estonia, Latvia, Lithuania, Moldova, or Georgia. In the potential case of Russian aggression, they risk being overrun quickly. Therefore, these smaller countries need to find or consolidate secure havens in the West before any aggression happens.

CHAPTER 33

Russians cannot perpetuate their myth of Russia if they lose control over Ukraine

Jade McGlynn

Interview with Oleksandr Pankieiev, published 20 July 2023

> Jade McGlynn is a Leverhulme EC Researcher in the War Studies department at King's College London, as well as a research fellow at the KCL's Centre for Grand Strategy and a senior associate at the Europe Program, CSIS. McGlynn holds a DPhil from the University of Oxford, where she previously worked as a Lecturer in Russian. She is a frequent contributor to international media, including BBC, CNN, DW, *Foreign Policy*, *The Times*, *The Telegraph*, and *The Spectator*.

Pankieiev: Your book is titled *Russia's War*—not *Putin's War*, as many frame it in the West. You examine the role of ordinary Russians in the aggression against Ukraine. What is the main message you are trying to convey in your book by exploring this dimension?

McGlynn: I would like to emphasize two points when answering this question. One is that the aggression against Ukraine is not Putin's venture only. And if we—we being the West—believe that the catastrophic genocidal war will be easily solved if we get rid of one person, then we are going to fall victim to misconceptions and design wrong policies. The second point is that we need to understand what kind of war the Russians are watching; we need to look at the propaganda. I do not like the argument that people back the war because they are zombified. It does not make any sense. There are 60 million daily users of Telegram [social media] who have access to all forms of channels, including oppositional, and yet of the top 30 political channels an overwhelming majority of 24 are very pro-war.

In my book I wanted to make the argument that the Kremlin's propaganda functions not only because it has a platform. Of course the situation in the media is rigged, to put it mildly, in favour of advocating the war effort, but such narratives also need resonance. Above all, the narratives are about meaning-making. They need to make sense and resonate with how people view their lives, the world, themselves as Russians, Russia's history, Russia's international role, and, of course, Ukraine and the West. And that is why the propaganda works.

Pankieiev: You write about Russia's liberal opposition and the reaction of some of its representatives to the aggression. What are your main conclusions about their stance on Russia's war against Ukraine?

McGlynn: One of the first things to say is that typifying the Russian liberal opposition is a difficult task because they are really incoherent. There is, for example, the feminist anti-war resistance, who I think are incredible. The work they do is incredible. They seem to "get" the calamity behind the war, to put it bluntly. But others — in particular, certain members of the Alexei Navalny team — are less supportive. They remove Ukraine from the narrative almost entirely. That was something else that came out of my research.

If you look for references to Ukraine on the Navalny Telegram channel there were very few, much less than is the average for other Russian Telegram channels, during the first three months of the invasion. They removed Ukraine from communication or tried to insert themselves into the war.

In March 2022 there was a moment when the opposition used the negotiations around Ukraine to try to ask Western governments to include releasing Navalny from prison as one of the Kremlin's concessions. As much as I would like to see him released — someone who should have not been imprisoned in the first place — Navalny's case cannot be inserted into such discussions.

Such actions by some of the Russian democratic opposition replicates the Kremlin's denial of Ukrainian agency, demonstrating Ukrainophobia, solipsism, and a kind of self-obsession. They invariably present themselves as friends of Ukraine but that isn't always the case. Moreover, it is incredibly offensive to see some aggressively rejecting criticism from Ukrainians using arguments like "Oh, well, you must be Putin bots, because you are fighting us and we are anti-Putin." But Ukrainians are *literally fighting*.

Having said all that, I do not want to condemn the Russian opposition. They are not a monolith and many have made incredible sacrifices to undermine Putin's regime. I do not think I would have the bravery to protest in Putin's Russia. I would not also have a smidgen of the bravery that Ukrainians have shown. This is more about some of the Russian opposition getting a sense of perspective. Their struggles—as awful as they may be—are not comparable to the struggles that Ukrainians are enduring.

Pankieiev: I recently watched a short video feature, produced by Dozhd, where Russian journalists discussed the issue of collective guilt in the context of war. It was really interesting to see that half of them felt no collective guilt at all. However, the other half did. Eventually, the discussion shifted toward issues of imperialism, and by the end of the video all of the participants acknowledged that they were imperialists. That conclusion did not come easily to them and really convicted them. In this light, how would you see the issue of collective guilt in Russia or the absence of such?

McGlynn: I will probably disappoint you because I do not really believe in collective guilt. Instead, I think that some form of *collective responsibility* exists. For guilt or culpability, individuals should be tried for their own actions.

What I wanted to look at in my research was how different people facilitated the horrendous events, facilitated the aggression. They were doing it in various ways, sometimes consciously and sometimes unconsciously, because not taking action is also an action. Moreover, I agree that the imperialist mindset contributes significantly to these people's actions. However, on top of that there is something specific about Ukraine in Russia and for Russians, in their *geopolitical mind-map*. The narrative or the autobiography that Russians have written for themselves depends on being able to control Ukraine. It depends on being able to show that Ukrainians want to be with them and that Russia is the legitimate heir to Kyivan Rus'. It seems to me that Russians cannot perpetuate their myth of Russia if they lose control over Ukraine.

Pankieiev: You have been following Russia's media narratives about Ukraine since the beginning of the full-scale invasion. Is it true that the media outlets outside the capital are practically silent about the war? How can you explain this?

McGlynn: The relative silence of the regional media about the war is not really my finding. I have mostly looked at the federal broadcast channels and Telegram. The regional media is something that Paul Goode at Carleton University examined. And what he found was that the war—obviously, they call it a "special military operation"—did not come up very much in the local news; they obviously tried to avoid it.

I just finished a small research project, looking at what media and news outlets wrote about and what kind of information Russians consume from television. I have observed—and it is very interesting—that since October 2022 a major shift has happened from political discussion programs to a variety of series [*serialy*] and films. I have observed a lot of escapism on the television, but news and real-time events are no longer in the focus.

I think that the war has not gone how the Russians wanted it to. Clearly, there is an awful lot of cognitive dissonance about the fact that the Ukrainians did not meet the Russians as liberators, to put it mildly. There also seems to be a large element of avoidance. Because if you have to start facing questions about the poor progress of the invasion in Ukraine, you need then to find the answers to why. And to be fair, for the majority of ordinary Russians there is not really any benefit in facing those questions. They would have to *do* something with that information afterwards. Finding answers and accepting them are not pleasant prospects for Russians.

Pankieiev: What do you think about the response to the war in different regions of Russia? Is there a chance that any region could put up an organized resistance to Moscow—for instance, Dagestan?

McGlynn: In my research I mainly focused on ethnic Russians and do not have much expertise in regional politics. However, from the research of other scholars I know of some interesting phenomena. For example, there appears to be comparatively high levels of support for the war in Kalmykia. But the reasons for that support are different when compared to other regions of Russia. Kalmykia has a cultural legacy of martialism or militarism. It is also an awfully poor region, where joining the army with its decent salaries could also lead to a major improvement in one's circumstances. On top of that, the region is run by a madman—I recognize that it's not a very academic term—in the form of the governor.

Turning to the North Caucasus in general, I find it very hard to comment because all regions there have different dynamics. Firstly, they are not densely populated by ethnic Russians. Secondly, there is a different history and social set up there, one which is very hard to read from without. So I am not in a position to provide reliable insights into what the true direction of public opinion in the North Caucasus might be.

Pankieiev: What are your thoughts about Evgeniy Prigozhin and his role in Russia today? What has changed after the march of his Wagner Group mercenaries on Moscow?

McGlynn: I am still not entirely sure what happened. The idea that Aliaksandr Lukashenka came in to negotiate does not seem very plausible. And then we had Putin speaking harshly in the morning when the events started and becoming more relaxed in the evening of the same day. I still have a lot of questions on that scale.

One thing that looks very interesting, and perhaps the one I feel most confident talking about, is the way in which Wagner fighters were greeted, especially in Rostov. The fighters were cheered! It surprised me. In this light, the UK Foreign Secretary paradoxically concluded: "Oh, it is evidence that there is no support or support for the war is breaking." I am really wondering how he arrived at that conclusion. Because it is odd, isn't it? Cheering for Wagner does not suggest that people love peace; I mean, they are warmly greeting war criminals who massacred civilians in Bucha and committed all manner of atrocities…

However, to come back to the point, I would not conclude that Prigozhin himself is very popular. He has been associated with many scandals, like providing school dinners that gave the pupils food poisoning after his company won a tender, and others. But I think that the role he plays is the one of a *muzhik*—a normal bloke, a guy from the people. His anti-elitist and anti-corruption ideas are easy to comprehend, for instance, "We would have won this war if not for the incompetent generals." These ideas and their presentation appeal to ordinary Russians because they allow people to keep their national pride, allow them to explain reality. I think these sorts of narratives will increasingly take hold. As a matter of fact, they have been around for a long time among some of the nationalists, particularly those who did opposed the war because it would weaken Russia, not out of any particular sympathy for Ukrainians.

Prigozhin seems to be influential—and here we come back to my answer to one of the earlier questions—because his narratives resonate with people. Prigozhin's tirades acquire popular legitimacy partly because he tells the truth about the war. Obviously, it is a kind of distorted truth — one that has passed through his own lens, through his knowledge and understanding — but it is broadly the truth. It appeals to people, especially after they've listened to so many Kremlin propaganda lies, disconnected from reality.

Pankieiev: Some time has already passed since you published your book. Have you discovered any new perspectives and facts on the Russian war against Ukraine that made you reconsider something that you wrote earlier?

McGlynn: No, nothing new was discovered in terms of the broad argument. Definitely, reading through the text again, because it was written kind of quickly I wish I could slightly change the turn of some phrases. But these are more editing issues. The content of the book, on the other hand, is something that I have been thinking about and researching since 2014. Ultimately, the discoveries that I made — or my research showed up over the years — came to fruition in different ways in 2022. The events of 24 February became the final piece of a puzzle that I have been sorting through for a while.

One of the things that I want to highlight about the book — one that many people in the West do not pick up — is the Ukrainophobia that can extend to some of the Russian opposition. Western readers fail to pick up on the controversies of Lev Kopelev, an otherwise exemplary Russian dissident and human rights defender who actually participated in the Holodomor in Soviet Ukraine. I think it is a shame. I would like to discuss that point more. It is a shame that people in the West do not want to start a conversation that needs to be had. Too often, when discussing the Russian opposition a reduction is made that if they are anti-Putin, therefore they must be pro-Ukrainian. This is not always true.

Pankieiev: How would you characterize the general attitude of Russians, both opposition and ordinary citizens, to Ukraine and Ukrainians? What is the impact of years of propaganda — or, if I may, zombification — on the formation of existing attitudes?

McGlynn: I really do not think that the process of zombification was crucial. I am cautious about that term. Instead, what came through to me and to a handful of my liberal Russian friends is that ordinary people have an inflated idea of the supremacy of Russian culture.

In today's Russia, this inflated idea could be one real reason behind the dismissiveness toward Ukrainian culture and some of the anger toward Ukrainians. There should be critical engagement with the continued feting of somebody like Kopelev and how he can be a hero even though he took part in the Holodomor. As Daria Mattingly has shown in her work, he enforced the famine of the 1930s at a time when others in his position tried to help the victims or at least to avoid doing such a murderous job.

The dismissive was towards Ukrainian suffering can also be observed among many Westerners. We have yet to explore the extent to which Ukrainians have been perceived as expendables in history. This is one of the things that I am always taken aback. I am a Russianist by training, but obviously I have had to study Ukrainian history in depth as a necessary counterweight to reading a lot of Russian propaganda about it. Very often throughout Western histories of the region, Ukrainian security and lives are presented as expendable. Ukrainian culture is represented as second-class or rural. This attitude has also impacted decision-making, if you think of the Treaty of Versailles and other similar events.

Hopefully that will change now with Ukrainians fleeing war greeted so warmly in Western Europe, and now that finally Ukrainian culture is being celebrated or even just discovered by some who know little about Ukraine. But the other attitudes will persist and it is important to acknowledge them and shine a light on them because Ukraine and Ukrainians aren't expendable and giving in to those who think they are will only bring more misery and death on all of us.

CHAPTER 34

UK can become a special platform for rebuilding Ukraine

Andrii Zharikov

Interview with Ostap Kushnir, published 27 July 2023

> Andrii Zharikov (LLM in international trade law, University of Essex; PhD, Aston University) is a senior lecturer in law at the University of Portsmouth, its School of Law's Departmental Director for Postgraduate Research, and the university's Academic Lead for the #Twin4Hope Initiative between the UK and Ukraine. He is also a fellow of the Higher Education Academy and of the Chartered Institute of Arbitrators in the UK. Previously he practiced law in Ukraine and was involved in various projects in banking and finance, international trade, dispute resolution, and corporate law.

Kushnir: How has the perception of Ukraine changed across the UK since February 2022?

Zharikov: I think it has changed considerably and positively. For a long time Ukraine was viewed simply as another post-Soviet republic without any deeper insight into its identity and culture. In February 2022 people here in the UK started researching more about the country. Their awareness of its history and traditions has grown to a much higher level since then. People have built a background in regional politics and now better understand the reasons for the ongoing war.

The experience of active fighting, even though it comes with great suffering, has put Ukraine on the world map and introduced it to the general public. There was little interest in Ukraine before the Russian invasion. But now the situation has drastically changed. If you go on the streets of any British city and ask anyone about what is happening in that part of the world, you will hear some very knowledgeable answers.

Kushnir: In your opinion, why has the government in London decided to become one of the major supporters of Ukraine, especially in regard to military equipment and training?

Zharikov: It is an interesting question. I am sure that no governmental support would be possible if the UK public did not back it up. And public opinion has grown very strongly pro-Ukrainian since February 2022. There are a few reasons behind it.

Above all, from my observations British people simply do not tolerate any injustice or unfairness — and the situation around Ukraine is clearly not fair. The sole fact of an unprovoked Russian invasion cries out for sympathy for the Ukrainians, who were forced to defend themselves and got stuck in fighting.

Another reason behind the public demand to do something for Ukraine stems from the personal grief of British people. The war in Ukraine is reminiscent of their WW II history. Many British cities were bombarded, and the whole nation had to stand and resist alone. People then volunteered to join the military and protect their homeland. So I see some parallels here.

Lastly, there is the role of individual politicians. As you know, Boris Johnson was head of the government back in early 2022. At that time, he had been facing some problems with domestic policies, with a couple of scandals linked to him. Therefore, I think Johnson used the Russian invasion as an opportunity to prove that the whole course of his previous actions had been relevant. Also, he wanted to score additional points by becoming active in the international arena and advocating the cause of Ukraine. As one of the biggest proponents of Brexit, he also wanted to show that stepping out of the EU had been a good move. Finally, supporting Ukraine was simply the right thing to do in his view. Considering all these variables, Johnson decided to act and eventually grew into the leader of the entire international movement of Ukraine's allies.

Kushnir: How many Ukrainians moved to the UK after the full-scale invasion started? How are they integrating into British society?

Zharikov: The numbers are relatively modest if you compare them to the big continental European countries like Germany and Poland or to countries that neighbour Ukraine. The official statistic puts it at fewer than 200,000 people. The real number may be even smaller, as it is hard to trace those who have since left. Generally, I do not think that the British migration measures designed to help Ukrainians have been comprehensive or ideal. They came quite late in the day, looked like rather rushed decisions, and have not worked well in practice.

There are two schemes for how Ukrainians can get to the UK. The first is the *family scheme*, where refugees need to obtain an invitation from a UK citizen who is their family member. The second is the *sponsorship scheme*, where any UK citizen who meets the requirements — primarily, has a bedroom to spare — can become a sponsor and welcome Ukrainians at his or her place. Both of those schemes, as I mentioned, have flaws. They were criticized by the United Nations as ineffective and even traumatic. On the sponsorship side, the state often failed to complete a thorough examination of households of UK citizens who wanted to become sponsors. Therefore, it sometimes happened that vulnerable Ukrainians ended up in places where proper living was impossible. In the worst cases, Ukrainians were forced to engage in illegal activities, which made them subject to criminal prosecution.

We rightly think that the UK has become one of Ukraine's greatest friends. This might hold in the context of actual military cooperation, but not that when considering social programs. In terms of basic support, like finding sponsors or learning English, Ukrainian refugees have been mostly left to themselves. There is no government-led system that introduces refugees to the new culture, language, and lifestyle. The options for accommodation have been limited, too. Even some social expenses, like education for schoolchildren, have been outside the bounds of government supervision and have put extra strain on Ukrainian newcomers. In general, I think that the social programs could have been much better designed. In other European countries, Ukrainian refugees enjoy higher levels of support, including being able to receive humanitarian aid.

There was one extraordinary step that the UK government adopted, though: special regulations were passed to ensure that refugees from Ukraine, unlike any other refugees, have the same rights as UK citizens. This means that Ukrainians are able to get a job without a work permit, apply for loans with banks in the UK, enjoy local tuition rates when studying at UK universities, use the National Health Service, and benefit from other support programmes.

Kushnir: Apart from the government, how are Ukrainians approached by the ordinary British? The UK has been known to the world as a migrant-wary country, and today it faces a massive influx of Ukrainians. How do ordinary people treat the newcomers?

Zharikov: Indeed, immigration has always been a sensitive issue in British politics. Until recently, whenever someone started speaking about immigration, it would usually be perceived in a negative light. However, the case with Ukrainians is different. These refugees are welcome. The British public does not see them as a menace. I think there is an implicit understanding that most of the Ukrainian refugees are women and children.

As I mentioned earlier, there has never been a sort of support in the social adaptation of the refugees or, for example, an initial welcome package. To compare, the member states of the European Union are much more generous than the UK.

So in terms of social attitude, Ukrainian refugees are fine and welcome. In terms of actual support, this is where the UK needs to improve — and today it is doing so.

Kushnir: As a coordinator of your university's cooperation with the Odesa National Polytechnic University under the Twinning Scheme, can you shed more light on the recent intensification of partnerships between the British and Ukrainian academic institutions? Why has this intensification taken place, how are the partnerships evolving, and where do you think they will lead?

Zharikov: The Twinning Scheme was initially designed as a response to the unprovoked Russian aggression and an attempt to mitigate the damage inflicted on Ukraine's academic institutions. It is a government-led initiative, which above all anticipates matching UK-based universities with partners in Ukraine. Apart from providing help in enduring difficult times, the Twining Scheme also aims to deepen interstate academic cooperation in future.

I am employed at the University of Portsmouth, and we were matched with the Odesa National Polytechnic University. I cannot explain why the scheme administrators made such a decision, but I think it is because both universities are located in port cities and the University of Portsmouth was once a polytechnic. Today, we are trying to provide our colleagues in Ukraine with immediate support in terms of continuing their teaching services and research activities. We are laying a foundation and establishing links for enhanced cooperation in the future. When the war is over we will likely conduct more joint teaching and research, including student and tutor exchanges.

For the moment we have received external funding for several projects that aim to improve Ukraine's economic and social standing during and after the war. The expected outcomes of these projects entail designing recovery solutions at the national and — above all — local levels. I am not speaking here of academic recovery only, as the universities are also used as mechanisms and mediums. For example, we have projects which focus on providing support to vulnerable categories of people who are affected by the war and have been internally displaced. We have projects which explore the potential of 3D printing in order to produce special equipment for those Ukrainians who lost parts of their body in the fighting. We also have projects that deal with the safety of nuclear facilities.

In a word, the Twinning Scheme covers a wide area and funds a variety of projects from many disciplines. That being said, its core aim is to design solutions that will help Ukraine to come up stronger after the war is over.

Kushnir: In your opinion, what current needs of Ukraine and its society does the UK have the resources to address? What kind of support do you think Ukraine would appreciate the most in the circumstances it finds itself right now?

Zharikov: At the time of this chat, I think that military support is of the utmost priority. Without military support it is very difficult to expect the end of the war in the near future. Therefore, it is a very positive development that the UK became the leader of a pro-Ukraine military coalition. The government in London not only provides training and equipment, it also advocates and lobbies for Ukraine's needs in the international arena. The UK has a long-standing reputation for being one of the world's powerhouses and diplomatic centres. Therefore, the word of London weighs a lot in terms of influencing other countries and coordinating their military assistance to Ukraine.

As for social and economic issues, the UK could become — and is working on this — a special platform for rebuilding Ukraine through managing investments and financial arrangements. London is a global centre of finance and trade. In late June 2023 the Ukraine Recovery Conference took place there. This is a very positive development. I think London is growing into a comprehensive platform that can consolidate different actors—commercial, governmental, public, private, and others—to help Ukraine rebuild its society, economics, industry, and infrastructure.

Kushnir: In the future, regarding international arbitration, what will be the most challenging war-related cases between Ukraine and Russia, or between companies that are registered there?

Zharikov: I think that most cases will address the domain of international investment arbitration, not commercial arbitration. Simply speaking, there will be a necessity to assess and investigate the damage or destruction of facilities and other property during wartime. There will be a necessity to find those responsible for these actions and decide on how the compensation will be recovered, what kind of compensation it will be (monetary or other), and what legal mechanisms will be put into practice. I suspect that cases will be filed not only against Russia but possibly against Ukraine too, for their failure to protect certain assets that are considered to be international investments. So we need to be prepared for this.

Obviously, the majority of international arbitration cases will likely be against Russia—specifically, against the actions of the Russian government. But I can also see some cases against Ukraine, similar to the issues which arose after 2014 when Crimea was annexed. A number of foreign investors accused Ukraine, not Russia, of the loss of or damage to their property, though they had varied success with their claims. To summarize, after the war is over the majority of cases will concern investment disputes between private investors and the countries engaged in fighting.

Kushnir: Overall, what legal challenges and developments do you expect to encounter between Ukraine and Russia in future?

Zharikov: The obvious ones will be on the issue of war reparations and compensation. Less obvious will be issues that are not yet high on the agenda—for example, the status of Russian citizens who would choose to stay in Ukraine.

For Ukraine there will be an urgent call to change much of its legislation and accommodate the needs of people who left the country as refugees. This will include, for example, sorting out the issue of citizenship of internationally displaced persons. Many

Ukrainians will have assimilated into their host countries to such an extent that they will feel it would be much easier to stay there instead of returning to their homes. I think that dual citizenship will become one of the priority legal matters to be addressed.

There will also be the problem of improving national legislation in order to attract more foreign investment and rebuild the country faster. It will overlap with the necessity of harmonizing Ukrainian legislation with that of the EU and meeting the requirements to be able to accede to full-fledged membership.

Overall, I am sure that in the legal landscape there will be a lot of matters to address after the war is over. Some of them will be more urgent, some less. As I see it, in the next few years Ukraine will become a completely different country in terms of legal regulations.

Kushnir: Do you think the initiative to redirect Russian frozen assets, both of state and private stakeholders, for Ukraine's postwar reconstruction will work? What are the legal obstacles?

Zharikov: It is complicated. As far as I understand, some countries are not politically willing to endorse this initiative because it would set a precedent that could be used against them or their allies in the future. A solution may reside in finding a legal tool to execute the redirection of the Russian frozen assets within the confines of existing legislation. Setting up new legislation that relies on a new precedent is a dangerous route here.

Nevertheless, Ukraine's partners and allies continue exploring opportunities for compensation using frozen Russian assets within the means and tools they possess today. I cannot tell whether such efforts will suffice, because some countries are quite reluctant to proceed consistently. Their reluctance stems not only from the fear of legal complications but also in the absence of political will.

Overall, the redirection of Russian frozen assets in order to fund the reconstruction of Ukraine will take time to discuss and execute. It might happen that Ukraine's case will become not about Ukraine only but will also lead to the creation of a mechanism that will address similar transgressions in the future. At the moment, heated debates are taking place on this issue. My guess is that it will take a number of years to finally set everything up.

CHAPTER 35

Ukrainians need to win the war as quickly as possible

Mychailo Wynnyckyj

Interview with Oleksandr Pankieiev, published 12 September 2023

Mychailo Wynnyckyj (PhD, University of Cambridge, 2004) is Vice-President for Research and Graduate Studies and Director of the Doctoral School at the National University of "Kyiv-Mohyla Academy," where he also teaches in the Sociology Department and the Business School. In 2023 he was appointed Deputy Minister of Education and Science, responsible for higher education. Previously he served as Head of the Secretariat of Ukraine's National Agency for Higher Education Quality Assurance (2019–22). Originally from Kitchener, Ontario, Wynnyckyj has lived permanently in Kyiv for over two decades. His latest book is titled *Ukraine's Maidan, Russia's War: A Chronicle and Analysis of the Revolution of Dignity* (2019; Ukrainian transl. 2021).

Pankieiev: What are the main changes you have observed in Ukrainian society since Russia's full-scale invasion began? How has the war affected Ukrainian identity?

Wynnyckyj: The changes to Ukrainian society that I have witnessed since the start of Russia's full-scale invasion have been massive. We have seen grassroots activism, unparalleled patriotism, popular resistance, and impressive resilience in the face of physical, economic and psychological hardship. Yet, your question reflects the primary interest of western observers: identity.

Because of the widespread myth that Ukraine is a supposedly "cleft" country with an apparently Ukrainian speaking western region and a supposedly Russian speaking east, the question of identity has consistently gained traction in both journalist and academic literatures. The vision of the east-west divide in Ukraine was emphasized by Huntington and many others; then popularized by scholars of Ukraine's electoral politics who consistently linked voting preferences to language and ethnicity. In the same vein, Russian propagandists claim that Ukraine is an "artificial culture": supposedly "created" by Lenin (according to Putin's latest narrative) and/or by marginal nationalists conspiring with western powers to undermine the "unity" of Great Russia. In reality, Rus'-Ukraine existed well before anyone had ever heard of Muscovite-Russia, but facts need not concern those who propagate simplistic narratives I suppose.

The "cleft nation" myth is just a continuation of the "little Russian" idea (according to which Ukrainian was seen as a quaint rural dialect of the Great Russian language and culture) that had been propagated by both imperial and Soviet authorities for over a century. In fact, Ukraine is as much a cleft nation as Germany, with its differences between Berlin and Munich, or as the US with its Texans and New Yorkers. New Yorkers are not "Little Americans" and Bavarians are not "little Germans". Yet this was the logic put forth by multiple Moscow-led governments: Russification was the aggressive policy of the imperial authorities in the late 19th century and then was revived in the USSR under Stalin. During brief periods in the 1920s and then again in the 1970s, Russification became lighter, but it never entirely disappeared. The fact that we survived these consistent policies of russification is testament to the resilience of the Ukrainian nation. These policies led to an accentuation of regional differences in language, but as seen in 2022 and beyond, they never really divided the nation to the extent many observers seemed to believe.

During periods of Ukrainization—or, if you like, de-Russification—a latent foundational identity seems to have consistently bubbled up. After Ukraine's declaration of independence in 1991, the Kyiv government introduced soft policies that emphasized the use of Ukrainian in education, in the media, in government relations, but the overall context respected language diversity, educational needs of minorities, and a linguistically diverse media landscape. As a result, many people from the diaspora arriving in Kyiv even ten years ago were shocked by the predominance of Russian in the city. Bilingual conversations where one party spoke Ukrainian and the other responded in Russian were normal. Though uncomfortable for non-natives, this bilingual reality made Ukraine unique, and I would argue – resilient to nationalist (both Russian and Ukrainian) extremism.

With the full-scale invasion, the tolerance for Russian speakers in Kyiv has significantly reduced, but patriotism has not degenerated into intolerance. Russian-speakers are not ostracized, persecuted, or in any way harmed. However, communicating in Russian in Kyiv today is comparable to speaking a foreign language in any other European capital. If you live in Paris, it is expected that you speak French. If you do not, you are a foreigner. This is common sense. Today, in Kyiv, if you are not speaking Ukrainian, you are treated like a foreigner—not ostracized but nevertheless kept at a distance. Your question asked how the war has affected Ukrainian identity, and this linguistic shift is one obvious effect.

However, Ukrainian identity remains inclusive. For example, the Crimean Tatars are unquestioningly considered Ukrainian—particularly since 2014. From the perspective of history, particularly considering events (battles) that took place in the 17th and 18th centuries, this inclusion of Tatars into the Ukrainian nation is questionable, of course. But recently, a sort of general consensus has formed concerning the Tartars according to which they are included in the wider Ukrainian political community. The same holds for other "people of Ukraine" that are of Jewish, Russian, and Polish descent, as well as representatives of various other ethnic groups. Centripetal nation-building processes have certainly accelerated since the full-scale invasion.

With respect to changes in everyday life, these in my opinion, have been much more significant and interesting than changes in identity. Ukrainians have lived through massive and wide-scale stress. Not surprisingly, people's daily routines changed significantly during the early months of the full-scale war, but then they seemed to have subsided into a "new normal". February to around June of 2022 was a period of shock. Massive relocation and readjustment took place. There was a lot of anger in the society. That initial period was followed by one of elation. During the summer months of 2022 the Ukrainian Armed Forces pushed back the Russians from Kyiv and Chernihiv oblasts, and then intensified operations in Kharkiv and around Kherson. Those early military victories demonstrated that a return to pre-invasion routines was possible, and so between August 2022 and May 2023, we see a third phase: gradual "normalization". Despite the difficult winter, with blackouts and periodic missile attacks, in areas not directly adjacent to the front lines, many people returned to their everyday lives: earning a living, attending school, relaxing in the evening and on weekends.

Interestingly, during this third period, a certain amount of resentment crept into the public discourse; I would even say that some became excessively judgmental of those Ukrainians who decided to stay away from Ukraine for longer periods. Questions started being asked about what these Ukrainians remained abroad? Obviously, the question was irrelevant if one had lived in Zaporizhia or Kharkiv because those areas were regularly targeted by Russian artillery or S300 ballistic missiles. However, if a refugee was from Kyiv, where an air defensive dome was established, or from Lviv or Ternopil, where missile attacks were infrequent, continued migration out of Ukraine came to be resented. Why have such people left the country, and why were they not coming back?

In early 2023 the Russians continued launching missiles at Ukrainians. People adjusted to the occasional air raid sirens and gradually normalized their lives as much as possible. They understood that they had a country to build and an economy to run. They donated large sums to the armed forces, provided help in multiple ways to those in need, and volunteered in civil society organizations. But what about those four or five million Ukrainians who had left the country? What were they thinking? I find myself hearing such rhetorical questions with increasing frequency.

Pankieiev: In one of your Facebook posts you mention the emergence of a new "territorial patriotism" and "heterarchic" structures in Ukraine. What exactly are these structures?

Wynnyckyj: Observing contemporary Ukrainian society is absolutely fascinating. Indeed, what is most interesting given my current involvement in government, is that society at large seems to be structured completely differently from the state. By definition, government is hierarchic. Having spoken to some of my western colleagues, it seems "chains of command" are ubiquitous in all governments. A basic requirement of a civil service seems to be that it is organized as a clear hierarchy with set procedures, chains of decision-making, signatures, etc.

However, this way of structuring government represents a total mismatch with the way in which Ukrainian society seems to organize itself. This mismatch became very clear during the first days of the invasion. At one point I tried to capture the spontaneous self-organization that became the hallmark of Ukrainians' resilience with an analogy: Ukraine is a beehive. If you look at how bees live, you will see that they are the least hierarchical society possible. On the one hand, a hive can include from 10,000 to 30,000 bees and a queen. On the other hand, the role of the queen is not to give orders or instructions. Every bee seems to know what to do. This is exactly the way in which Ukrainian society structured itself during the early period of the Russian invasion: situational leadership, *spontaneous sociability*, improvised action.

My initial observations of these phenomena were complemented in 2022 by the outstanding work of my PhD student Artem Serdiuk. I thought the "beehive" we were observing was something uniquely Ukrainian, but Artem demonstrated that spontaneous sociability seems to be a natural human reaction to stress. The major difference between hurricanes, tornadoes, and floods and the Russian invasion is that the former are short-term events whereas the latter has already lasted over 500 days. So Ukrainian spontaneous sociability may have a long-term socializing effect that may yet transform into new institutionalized structures. I hope so…

What I have observed in Ukraine — and continue to observe in the current phase of societal normalization — is that people tend to be most effective when they organize themselves in non-hierarchical structures. Though the term is not mine, I am calling this *heterarchy*. It signifies a specific network of relations within and between social groups and social hierarchies. Leaders emerge, but they are situational figures. These leaders take temporary responsibility for a particular task or project. I have seen this phenomenon in the resilience of the Territorial Defense Units, in the amazing effectiveness of Ukraine's Special Forces — basically, in every place and group where the war effort has been successful.

My current position in government, as Deputy Minister of Education, provides me with an actual opportunity to bring heterarchy into a traditionally hierarchical environment. I am convinced that Ukraine can potentially become an example for other countries and societies. As part of this war, we have demonstrated how heterarchy can be more effective than traditional institutional hierarchy in achieving results. Now the question is whether this amazing reaction to crisis can be institutionalized in more routine decision-making.

Pankieiev: What are the main institutional and structural challenges that the state of Ukraine is now facing? How can they be overcome?

Wynnyckyj: The main institutional and structural challenge is money. Ultimately, the Ukrainian economy is recovering from the shock of 2022, but recovery is very slow. The country has lost over 10 per cent of its population—probably closer to 15 per cent—because of emigration and flight abroad. The country is accumulating enormous debt. We continue to hope for a quick victory because, quite frankly, the resources that are being consumed by the war are astronomical.

Assuredly, Ukrainians are extremely grateful to our international friends. However, as I often repeat: this is our war to win. Unquestionably, we have a lot of help, but at a very basic level it is still our fight, our soldiers, our land, our families, and so it is our responsibility to win as quickly as possible.

Pankieiev: You and some other scholars have argued that the paradigms of oligarchy and "patronage politics" should no longer be applied to analyze Ukraine. Could you elaborate more on this?

Wynnyckyj: Thank you for raising this point. I've already mentioned one stereotype that exists about Ukraine – namely, that it is a country with internal identity cleavages. Recent months have proved that to be false. The other stereotypical image of Ukraine involves its somehow being controlled by "oligarchs" that rule through endemically corrupt means. As with the identity stereotype, I argue that the "corrupt oligarchy" meme is equally wrong.

Firstly, oligarchic structures can only be effective if they are based in monopoly. Once an oligarch corners a market, they can use their acquired power to establish a symbiotic relationship with the state that allows for long-term institutionalization of relations (what is referred to as "state capture"). Institutionalized oligarchy involves permanent subsidies, control of state policy for the benefit of a particular (monopolized) business sector, financing of media to influence voter preferences etc.

In today's Ukraine, there remain no industry sectors to monopolize. The metallurgical sector has been destroyed, as have coal mines; the energy sector has been severely damaged, and in some cases nationalized. The agricultural sector is too big to monopolize. There was once a businessman who tried to monopolize it, Oleh Bakhmatiuk, and at one point he actually came to control over a million hectares of land. But having achieved this amount (still only

1/40 of Ukraine's total agricultural land base), he understood that it was impossible to manage farming on such a grand scale. Since his failure, no one has seriously tried to corner the agricultural sector. The IT sector is also impossible to monopolize. My point is that a by-product of Russia's war has been the de-monopolization of Ukraine.

That being said, the state—headed, as we know, by an extremely media-savvy president—has gained full control over traditional media. I think that the current state monopoly on media is a temporary phenomenon, required to coordinate the war effort. Moreover, in response to the monopolization of traditional media, the circulation of information and news has moved to the Internet. And that sector is impossible to monopolize.

So put simply, my argument is that oligarchy in Ukraine is in the past. It started dying after 2014 and reached its complete demise in 2022. Contemporary Ukraine is a country of small, medium, and some large businesses, but it is an economy permeated by competitive markets. We still have problems with overregulation and petty corruption, but whereas once (e.g., during the Kuchma and Yanukovych regimes) we could legitimately claim that power rested with an oligarchic few, today what is left of the national economy—destroyed by the Russians—is certainly neither cornered nor controlled by big business, and certainly not by "oligarchs."

Pankieiev: You once wrote that "empires fail when they run out of (human) resources." Do you think that Russia will fail in this way?

Wynnyckyj: I am not a Russia expert. One thing I do know from history is that no empire lasts forever, and borders are not permanent. The history of the second half of the 19th century, the 20th century, and more recent events during the 21st century, have shown us that the future of human political organization lies with the nation-state. Nation-states may come together in unions like the EU, but they retain their identities and fundamental elements of sovereignty as nation-states.

The Russian Federation is not a nation-state. It is an empire that subjugates multiple nations. Eventually, like all empires, it will splinter into smaller political entities. I do not know what kind of entities these will be. And certainly, I am not going to predict when and how the disintegration will occur, but the end-result seems inevitable. What is most worrying to me is that most western policy-makers seem to be unable to imagine a disintegrated Russia. We seem to be observing a repeat of ostrich-like head-in-sand approaches seen 30 years ago when Sovietologists could not imagine a world without the Soviet Union. Alexei Yurchak wrote a wonderful book about those days, *Everything Was Forever, Until It Was No More*. I think we are on the cusp of repeating that title-phrase with respect to Russia. Urgently, we need to be planning for a post-Russia space, but even suggesting such a development seems to be taboo in many western diplomatic and academic circles.

Pankieiev: After more than a year and a half into the active fighting, what possible scenarios to end the Russo-Ukrainian war do you see?

Wynnyckyj: I know that many Ukrainians are hoping for a dramatic end to hostilities – a "victory day" that we will celebrate for generations to come. After the liberation of Kharkiv oblast and the city of Kherson, maximalist optimism swept the country. At present however, a decisive and quick victory seems increasingly unlikely. Frontal war seems likely for some time. Eventually, we may see the conflict simmer down, switching from a hot war — an extremely hot war — to a "warm" conflict with periodic skirmishes and air raids. I don't see it cooling to the point of a frozen conflict, but at some point in time the front line may stabilize. Unfortunately, Ukraine does not currently possess the military and economic resources required to sustain a long-term counteroffensive. On the other hand, Russia's forces are incapable of advancing further into Ukraine either.

I have no doubt that by the end of the year, the front line will shift further south and east from where it is today. I am not sure we have the capability to fully de-occupy our territory by the end of 2023, but recent advances have been encouraging. On the other hand, we should not forget that 2024 is an election year in the United States and will likely be an election year in Ukraine. Both of these elections suggest a likelihood of war intensity decreasing at least temporarily. What happens after 2024 in Ukraine will greatly depend upon what happens in Russia. I don't believe that the Kremlin regime is stable enough to last beyond 2025–26, but again – I am not a Russia expert...

No doubt, the war will end in victory for Ukraine. Eventually. This will entail not only the liberation of currently occupied territory, but also the disintegration of the Russian Federation. The permanent existential threat for Ukraine and Ukrainians will be removed. However, I lack the optimism to say that this will happen soon. Although I'd like to say the war will last no more than several more months, more likely we'll need several more years to achieve full victory. By victory, I mean the neutralization of Russia as a permanent existential threat to Ukraine.

Pankieiev: How has the war affected the education system in Ukraine? What major reforms and developments are underway today?

Wynnyckyj: The COVID pandemic health-related lockdown (lasting almost two years) was extended by another year and a half in Ukraine due to the invasion. Many students, teachers and professors have been working in an online format for over three years already and enough is enough. The extended shift to online has clearly affected the quality of education, which seems to have deteriorated on multiple levels. Primary education was particularly affected.

For many months now homeschooling has become the norm. Because of the shock of 24 February 2022, massive numbers of children and their mothers left Ukraine and enrolled in schools in Western Europe and often simultaneously continued distance learning. We now need to bring these children home, and where possible (not in Kharkiv, Mykolaiv or Zaporizhia, but elsewhere), to return them to classroom learning.

First and foremost we need to ensure safety – the safety of all students and teachers. This means ensuring that every school and university throughout Ukraine is equipped with adequate shelter facilities, and that staff are trained in emergency evacuation procedures. This is nothing new to the world—Israel, for example, has all schools equipped to withstand terrorist attacks, air raids, and bombings. Ukraine has no other option but to effectively recreate the Israeli security system in this respect. This is something of a high priority for the current government. Our donor friends support that effort and can help a great deal with its financing.

Higher education institutions, alongside the necessity to improve safety measures, are continuing to undergo reforms that began in 2014. That year, new legislation was adopted then to increase the autonomy of universities, in particular with respect to awarding academic qualifications. The centralized and Ministry-controlled "candidate of sciences" system was replaced by the Western-type PhD system where degrees are awarded by individual institutions, rather than the state. In parallel, we implemented 3 cycles (bachelor, masters, PhD) of higher education harmonized with the European system; quality assurance was separated from the Ministry and delegated to an independent agency; programming came to be based on competencies and learning outcomes... Indeed, there have been a great many changes in higher education since 2014. During the last three years, however, the reforms dynamic was interrupted by COVID and Russia.

Ukraine faces a huge challenge with its displaced universities. Since 2014, 31 higher education institutions have been relocated from their original campuses to different places. Paradoxically, many of those universities can no longer be called displaced. They have been accepted in new environments and have localized. For example, the Donetsk Stus National University relocated to Vinnytsia in 2014, and I personally doubt that most of its staff and students will return to Donetsk when Ukraine liberates the Donbas. Some employees may return, but I am not sure about the whole institution. They have now become rooted in Vinnytsia. At the same time, the academic community of Mariupol State University, which was displaced in 2022, remains very united and determined to go back to their home city as soon as the opportunity arises.

On a system-wide level, the differences between top-grade and mid-level universities in Ukraine is stark. Such "quality pyramids" exist in other countries of the world. In the United States, for example, the top universities are Harvard, Yale, and Stanford, but the quality difference between Ivy League and non-elite schools is not as great as in the Ukrainian case. In the UK, there are Cambridge and Oxford at the top, and then the mid-level. In Canada, there are the Universities of Toronto, Alberta, and McGill at the top, many provincial universities below. In each case, a quality education obtained at mid-level institutions is not dramatically different from that of top-rated universities.

When I refer to the top Ukrainian institutions, I include the Kyiv Sikorsky Polytechnic Institute, Kyiv Shevchenko National University, Kyiv-Mohyla Academy, Lviv Franko National University, Lviv National Polytechnic University, Kharkiv Karazin National University, and several others. Some of the top schools are located in smaller cities, such as Ivano-Frankivsk with its powerful

Subcarpathian University or Sumy State University. However, once one goes beyond the top institutions, the difference between the top and the mid-level universities is dramatic.

Therefore, the task of the ministry at this point is to try to flatten the pyramid without diminishing the quality of the top-level universities. In some cases this may involve merging universities; in other cases, giving them greater autonomy. Throughout the system, we need to invest in building managerial capacity among university leaders. We need to improve our instruments for tracking performance and analyzing large amounts of data. In a word, there are many reforms that need to be done from the governmental level. However, without the support of individual faculty and students in university communities all of these transformations will remain unrealized.

My dream—which I think is not just mine but is shared by the current Ministry leadership—is to grow pride among Ukrainian professors and students with respect to the institutions they belong to. Ukrainian universities objectively provide excellent education, but their academic communities lack institutional pride. Low salaries, poor infrastructure, insufficient research funding, and perceived problems with teaching quality (often not reflective of reality, but nevertheless stereotypically perceived)—when we add all these variables together, we find few enthusiasts who are truly proud of their institutions. We need to change that!

Ukrainian universities must become places of identity. Our task is to awaken the same pride of community that Ukrainians demonstrated during the last year and a half fighting as a nation.

CHAPTER 36

Losing intellectuals on the front lines is a disaster for Ukrainian culture today

Iryna Tsilyk

Interview with Oleksandr Pankieiev, published 25 September 2023

> Iryna Tsilyk is Ukrainian filmmaker and writer; she is a member of the European Film Academy and of Ukrainian PEN International. She graduated in film studies from the Kyiv Karpenko-Karyi National University of Theatre, Cinematography, and Television. Her documentary film *The Earth Is Blue as an Orange* won a directing award in the category "World Cinema Documentary" at the 2020 Sundance Film Festival. Tsilyk is also known for her feature film *Rock. Paper. Grenade*, which had its world premiere at the Warsaw Film Festival in 2022.

Pankieiev: After Russia's initial invasion of the Donbas in 2014 you made *The Earth Is Blue as an Orange*, a documentary film about the life of a family in Donetsk oblast—and also your husband served in Ukraine's army. How did these experiences affect or help you once the full-scale invasion happened?

Tsilyk: My husband served in the army for the first time in 2015–16, and then he rejoined the army again when Russia's escalated invasion began. As for my experience, I have always tried to be involved in different activities in the cultural field over the years of Russia's war in Ukraine. In the first years of the war, I used various opportunities to go to Donetsk and Luhansk oblasts, including taking part in literary readings. I made documentary films, and I also participated in events and classes for children living in the front-line zone. It was crucial for me to go there, to see everything with my own eyes—to meet people, talk to them, listen to their testimonies, and actually feel what is happening there—because, you know, in the first years of the war Ukraine was also divided into these parallel realities.

The east of Ukraine was under attack, there was a real war, and meanwhile my Kyiv—I'm from Kyiv—was completely peaceful, and many people in other Ukrainian cities also weren't aware of what it meant to live in a war zone. That is almost the same as what foreigners feel now towards Ukraine. They have deep empathy, but at the same time they can't imagine what it means to live in the reality of war. So when the full-scale invasion started, many things changed for all of us—for the whole of Ukraine, because suddenly we discovered that the "red zone" was everywhere. And of course, some regions feel much safer compared to southern and eastern Ukraine, but still there is no completely safe city or region in Ukraine.

My experience of being a filmmaker—a person who somehow reflects on everything around me—was useful. But at the same time I suddenly felt numb and speechless, because I had actually comprehended that being just an observer, I had completely another perspective. When you are in the middle of this reality, you suddenly lose all the possible tools you had before to express somehow what is happening and what it means for all of us. So, I somehow stopped filmmaking and used other artistic ways to reflect reality. For example, when time had passed, I started to write many essays and that kind of thing. Poetry is also a very special and powerful tool to reflect our bizarre state of being today. I feel that only now have I come back to myself and through filmmaking am trying again to find the proper way to talk about everything happening to us.

Pankieiev: This leads to my next question. How did the war affect the work of film directors, writers, and people who work in the field of cultural production? Does what is going on now differ entirely from before the full-scale invasion? You described that you, for instance, had to put some of your work on hold.

Tsilyk: The situation changed completely—but most of all in its scale. In the first years of the war, many people from my bubble were already involved in different kinds of activities helping the front, and my husband and some of my friends joined the army back then. But since February 2022 the circle seems to have widened. Almost everyone I know is somehow affected by this war. Most people around me are fighting or waiting for their spouses who are fighting. Some of my female friends have become widows already. One of my friends, who used to be a film editor before the war, joined the army and then was killed at the front line.

Last May, my husband was in a situation where he survived by a miracle. He and his unit were trapped in positions at Bakhmut, and they were under constant fire for five days. He already believed that he wouldn't survive, but he did. So I'm trying to say that I am an artist, filmmaker, and writer, and most people I know are artists too. So now, many of them have to take up arms and change their lives completely, which is a colossal tragedy. We live in times of so many tragedies, and no one is born to fight. I don't mean that artists are in a better class—that's not what I want to say. But the problem is that we are losing so many intellectuals, philosophers, writers, bright minds! You probably know some of these tragic stories—of how, for example, the Russian military killed the Ukrainian writer Volodymyr Vakulenko. His body was found in a mass grave. Another writer, intellectual, and volunteer—Viktoriia Amelina—was just a customer at a cafe when a Russian missile hit it and killed her. And so many have already been killed at the front. So what I'm trying to say is that it's so painful that most of these people—young people, cool, strong personalities—are not only losing their chance to build a house, to raise a child, but they're also losing all these chances to create some new senses and narratives. It means that losing intellectuals on the front lines is a disaster for modern Ukrainian culture.

And also there is another problem. Although many are still alive, they can't be active in *their field* when they're on the *battlefield*. I mean, all these filmmakers and writers can't make new films or write books, and that is why we also feel that we're somehow losing the chance to talk for ourselves, with our Ukrainian voices. At the same time, all these Russian intellectuals who fled to European countries have found some support and new opportunities. They're using all these new chances to talk loudly about themselves, their problems, and their pains, almost without focusing on the necessity to de-imperialize Russia; this is problematic from many angles and for many reasons.

Pankieiev: What about Ukrainian society at large? What changes have you observed in Ukrainian society? It's a broad question, but it seems like everyone notices different changes. Sometimes they are positive, and sometimes they are negative. What's your perspective on this?

Tsilyk: Ukraine is such a huge entity, and yet it's not homogeneous — because historically, various regions of Ukraine were under different influences. And of course, we are still having this journey from A to B, trying to search for our new identity, because we were oppressed for centuries. As I said previously, I want all these metamorphoses to happen faster, because we are losing many bright people. On the one hand, some processes need more time and it's impossible to quickly change our perspective on ourselves and our future in the context of European society. On the other hand, we sometimes feel frustrated that we lost these [previous thirty] years of independence, in which we should have been much more active in order to change so many things on different levels. We have had to walk this path in fits and starts.

I don't think that we could have avoided this war. It is such a painful but at the same time important turning point on the way to Ukraine's true freedom, its democratic future, and everything it can provide for us. For example, I look at myself, a person born in the Soviet time, a girl who in first grade was writing "Glory to the country of soviets!" And you know, I look back to all the metamorphoses I had in my life. I grew up in an entirely Russian-speaking community, in a family that had been affected by the Soviet regime, yet my grandmother didn't tell me a lot about all these traumas from the past. My great-grandparents were exiled to [the notorious Soviet island-monastery-turned-prison at] Solovki, but when I was a child, I never had a chance to think about this from the angle of a family that has been deeply traumatized. I took this journey only later, in the '90s when I started to search for my identity and fell in love with the Ukrainian culture and language.

So, I also needed time. Thus, I believe that it would not have been possible to fundamentally change me or Ukrainian society any faster. You know, I look around and sometimes feel exhausted and frustrated, because I often see so many people who are still affected by this Russian propaganda and all those influences. But at the same time we have changed a lot, especially in response to Russia's open aggression towards Ukraine. I look around and see people that have completely changed their attitude. Nevertheless, Ukrainian society is still very divided. When we have painful moments, we can be aggressive and cruel to each other — and the reasons for that are also clear. We have such a huge collective trauma! I also understand this, and I worry about it. We need to be connected and support each other in order to win this war. But I still try to be optimistic. We should be united in this fight, because I don't see any other choice. There's no way back.

Pankieiev: When you say that Ukrainians are cruel to each other, what do you mean?

Tsilyk: I mean that we are not tolerant of mistakes. We are all super-sensitive. We are very wound up. And sometimes, there is a feeling that this aggressiveness is still accumulating inside. And when we cannot punish the true culprit of our troubles, sometimes this aggression gets spilled over onto others—for example, our associates, family, friends, and other Ukrainians. And I'm very afraid of this, because we have to be united. Again, referring back to the history of Ukraine, when sometimes internal discord weakened our positions, I understand how important it is not to quarrel now. Because if we are working for the victory of Ukraine together, then we must not weaken each other. We must avoid crossing red lines among ourselves while we argue, discuss inner problems, and so on.

Pankieiev: Does our society today have any demand for a completely different intellectual and cultural product? What does Ukrainian society want to see now?

Tsilyk: Actually, for the last year and a half I've focused more on what demand has been coming from outside. Circumstances have developed so much in that direction that I started writing a lot for foreign media outlets. I am often invited abroad to give talks. Accordingly, I have observed how thirsty different countries and intellectuals from these countries are now for these new Ukrainian narratives—about what Ukraine is, who Ukrainians are, what happened in the past, and what we want from the future. It strikes me how little people know about us—and I also needed to realize this. If there is a demand, I always try willingly, as far as my internal resources allow, to be open to communicating with different audiences. For the last few years I have focused more on this field of cultural diplomacy and on conversations with foreigners.

    As for domestic demands, these are also no less important. But I guess what I mean is that it's hard for me to talk with any objectivity now. We also need to *tell ourselves*—not just foreigners—who we are, where we are going, and what happened to us in the past, because we have some new tools to rethink many things, all of which are essential processes. It's just a pity that now there is the demand, but often there is not enough supply, so to speak. Ukrainian literature, for example, is burgeoning with the same opportunities. I look around and see my colleagues writing, and this is all extremely important. They are writing a lot! They're trying to apprehend and comprehend these present moments and to think more globally.

This is also happening massively with Ukrainian poetry. I see how some strong poets are creating powerful, explosive things. On the other hand, cinema seems to be almost paralyzed — not entirely, of course. Documentary cinema is still doing well, but I am very sad to realize that there is no money for this now. Nothing like fiction films or animated films is being shot now, because they are very expensive. And I am sorry that we are losing in this field because simultaneously I see Russia allocating billions of rubles for its cinema. It will probably include some quite talented work, and we also understand that it will not only be stupid propaganda. This is big trouble for us, because we can't compete on an equal footing in this field. Meanwhile, Russia continues to spread its narratives all over the world — and this frustrates me terribly. It's why we here — I mean different Ukrainian artists — are doing what we can. Of course there are moments when we become apathetic and feel like we're hitting some walls that can't be broken through — including a lot of misunderstanding by our foreign colleagues, who often support us but unfortunately still don't understand *so much*. Some of them simply cannot give up the usual constructs, the usual views that they have about what Russian culture is, what Ukrainian culture is, and so on. All my colleagues are exhausted from this. But we must continue to work somehow.

Pankieiev: Regarding this "cultural exhaustion," you have mentioned language as part of identity. But all the characters in your documentary speak Russian. What is your opinion on the issue of language?

Tsilyk: I've already said that different processes happen at different speeds. And unfortunately some things don't speed up, no matter how much we want them to do that. A long time ago — in my life, in search of my own self — I concluded that language is an essential part of my identity because, in my case, it was like a return home, a return to that world to which I had not been invited but invited myself there. I started to speak Ukrainian in adolescence, and I finally switched to Ukrainian many years later, when I became pregnant. It was a crucial turning point for me when I realized that the next generation—in this case, my child—would be Ukrainian-speaking. I had been Russified and didn't want my son to be. And ultimately it worked: my son has a beautiful, amazing, native, true command of the Ukrainian language.

As for the film *The Earth Is Blue as an Orange*, of course I didn't choose the characters for this film based on their language. But there's an interesting thing… I always spoke to them in Ukrainian, and they spoke the way they were used to speaking. And I felt that Ukrainian was a very exotic language for them, at least for this family. That wasn't the case for the whole of Donetsk oblast, though; I have been to villages in Donetsk oblast where people do speak Ukrainian. It depends on different circumstances, but this particular family was totally Russian-speaking.

And interestingly, even after the start of the full-scale invasion, I would never have thought that these very people would also go in this direction. But they did. For example, the older daughter has completely switched to Ukrainian. The family tries to have all their communication in public or out in their city—they recently moved to Vilnius—only in Ukrainian, so that people don't think they are Russians. The mother, Hanna, speaks with me only in Ukrainian now. But you have to understand that they had to work hard for this. I was so surprised, because I hadn't expected this from them. I never pushed them to do it--well, except perhaps by my own example. We never discussed this topic, but at the same time they knew that I am generally very sensitive about it and how much I want more people in Ukraine to speak Ukrainian.

This is not just a choice of language—today, it is really a question of our survival as a nation. And so it was a kind of gift for me, too, that these people unexpectedly began to speak in Ukrainian. I mean, everyone achieves this at different speeds…but neither does it mean that we should sit back and do nothing to push Ukraine further along in these processes. Certainly the government and specific agencies should lay the groundwork, encouraging people to move a little faster in this direction. But at the same time, I don't believe in aggressive methods because, having many years of experience living in Ukraine and observing these processes, I see that the language of aggression does not work well—people go into their shells and take a protest posture. On the other hand, the language of positive examples entails a gentle, tender Ukrainization that is unfortunately too slow. I don't know the right way to do it, but as a Ukrainian artist, I am trying to do everything I can to facilitate. Let me say that my characters, whom I filmed back in 2018, do not deserve condemnation. I wish they had spoken Ukrainian then, but I'm glad they speak it now.

Ukraine's East is a very controversial region. I'm not justifying what was and is still happening to the people, but for so long this region had been under the *russkii mir* [Russian World], which has tried to expand its tentacles of total influence. But at the same time, it's also true that many people there think of themselves as Ukrainians, as part of Ukraine. Not everyone can change the language of communication so easily. But this last year and a half has pushed many people to switch to the Ukrainian language. Many people still do not consider it necessary, but something tells me that Ukrainization and other related processes are already well underway and so powerful. There is no way back from here.

CHAPTER 37

Sanctions are indirectly sowing divisions among Russians

Margarita Balmaceda

Interview with Oleksandr Pankieiev, published 26 September 2023

> Margarita Balmaceda (MA and PhD in politics, Princeton University) is a professor in the School of Diplomacy and International Relations at Seton Hall University. She is also a research Associate of the Davis Center for Russian and Eurasian Studies and of the Ukrainian Research Institute at Harvard University. She is the author of *Russian Energy Chains: The Remaking of Technopolitics from Siberia to Ukraine to the European Union* (2021) and *Energy Dependency, Politics and Corruption in the Former Soviet Union* (2008), and the editor of *The Ukrainian-Russian-Central European Security Triangle* (2000).

Pankieiev: At the outset of Russia's full-scale invasion of Ukraine, Europe was heavily dependent on Russian gas, and it was one of the factors that prompted Russia to decide to proceed with its war plans. What has Europe done since then to reduce its dependency? What measures have been undertaken in the energy security sector?

Balmaceda: I would identify three types of measures. First, de-carbonization has been expedited. A lot of the goals that were to be achieved in perhaps five years were achieved in one year. For instance, the overall average use of natural gas is down by at least 15%.

The second thing is that European countries have been attracting new types of energy, particularly liquefied natural gas (LNG). By the way, people in the US love to describe LNG as a panacea, but I don't believe it – it is rather problematic from an environmental point of view. The key thing is that Europe has significantly increased its LNG purchases, but it also needs to speed up infrastructure building in order to be able to receive and store it. For example, in Germany they have been talking about building LNG terminals for years. However, the first one was opened only now, and a second one is going to be launched soon.

The third thing that some European states have been doing is providing huge energy subsidies. They are not necessarily aimed at assisting a move away from Russian energy, but they intend to make it politically feasible to move away from Russian energy, by reducing the burden of the higher cost of alternative supplies on individual users and thus preventing a dangerous political backlash This is very important for a variety of reasons. For example, Germany invested about $200 billion in subsidizing energy so that users in Germany don't feel much impact. This is important, because it is a buffer between moving away from Russian energy and political dissatisfaction.

However, these subsidies were implemented differently in different European countries. And in some other European countries that buffer is not there at all. Moreover, the fact that the subsidization took place inconsistently is very problematic for the EU's cohesion. For instance, Germany subsidization of industry lead to tensions with other EU partners, which may interpret this aid as countering the EU principle of a common market and a level playing field for all. In sum, subsidies help prevent political backlash at the domestic level, but it's simultaneously very problematic.

Overall, people are very happy that Western Europe survived last winter—but the weather also helped. It was a relatively warm winter, and many specialists say that the real challenges may come next winter.

Also, in terms of indirect measures, some de facto nationalizations have taken place of infrastructure companies that were owned by Russian actors. In Germany, they had foolishly given Gazprom one of their most important natural gas storage facilities, in Rehden. So they had to take it under the direct control of the state. They also took back a very important oil refinery, the Schwedt oil refinery, that was owned by Rosneft under the direct control of the state.

Pankieiev: It is more than one year and a half into Russia's full-scale invasion of Ukraine. Russia has been subjected to numerous sanctions. What is your opinion about the sanctions that have been imposed on Russia? How effective have they been? And what is the measurement of their effectiveness?

Balmaceda: Some of the things that Russia complains about—for example, that its ability to export its own grain or fertilizers—those areas have been specifically excluded from sanctions. The point I want to make is that when we talk about sanctions, we can mean official sanctions but we can also refer to sanctions that create a different mood in private actors, who then might be more careful regarding their dealings with Russia. That is the case with Russian grain and fertilizer, for example. While these goods have been excluded from sanctions, even when quite a few Western companies continue to deal with Russia, shippers and insurers are often not eager to do that because of frequent problems with logistics related to being in higher risk and being in a somewhat unclear legal zone

But let's go back to the official sanctions: we are already seeing some impact. For example, in the past week, there has been a big devaluation of the Russian ruble. But the real impact of sanctions is never immediate. Suppose you think that the effect of sanctions will be that Russia runs out of money to continue attacking Ukraine, Russia withdraws from Ukraine, and the Russian people rise against Putin. That will not happen, especially in the short term. The impact of sanctions is more indirect and in the longer term — for example, in how members of the Russian elite will calculate their next steps. How will they align their loyalty? How will they determine the relative value of their relationship with Putin versus the relative value of their assets in Western Europe? As a result, divisions will be created among Russian actors. Thus, some of the divisions emerging between Russian actors will be an indirect effect of the sanctions.

But we also need to remember how Russian society and its political system work. The system almost always has a kind of plan B and can go into a "war economy" mobilization stance, and survive.

Pankieiev: In an interview for *Forum* last fall, Serhii Plokhy suggested that sanctions and military failures are forcing Russia to get closer to and more dependent on China, effectively helping China to emerge as a global power. Do you see a global shift happening like this?

Balmaceda: In the short term, China is supporting Russia diplomatically and economically. It may indirectly help Russia use the expanded BRICS grouping for diplomatic initiatives. It has also aligned with Russia in the UN. But in the long-term this will not be a beneficial support. Russia and China have a centuries-long relationship of tension and conflict. Furthermore, China is now deeply enmeshed in the world economy, and the Russian and Chinese economies are totally different in size. Russia is becoming increasingly dependent on China's technologies and banks, which is deepening its debt. As a result, Russia has a prospect of becoming a economic vassal of China.

Pankieiev: Russia's full-scale invasion has affected the countries of the Global South. Specifically, it is undermining food security in many African countries. Given that Russia is essentially weaponizing food in order to achieve its geopolitical goals, how do you think this particular issue can be addressed?

Balmaceda: The first thing that needs to be done is to take the Global South countries seriously. And I think that we are seeing their reaction to feeling neglected by Western states. Secondly, we need to consider their historical reversals. For example, looking at the case of India when one of its leaders was asked: "Why are you silent about this invasion? Why are you tacitly supporting Russia?" he replied, "Well, look at what happened during the Cold War when the US was arming Pakistan and left us nowhere, and it was only the Soviet Union that was supporting us." So, we need to be mindful of that.

And we also need to be aware of the domestic factors involved here. If you look at Africa, there's a very interesting interplay of food security issues, domestic authoritarian political issues having to do with the role of the military, coup d'états, and then the role of Russian mercenaries. The first thing that needs to be done is to think about these states' issues and grievances. And how can the Western world help so that these countries do not think about how they might get something from Russia?

For example, Russia says that it will donate grain and fertilizers, but well, we know that it's just empty words. The reality is that if you know something about development economics it doesn't help, because if you donate certain things you're disrupting the actual chains within the country, and using artificial pricing will not help. I think we need to work with the actual deep grievances of theses state and try to help them so that they do not fall into the embrace of these (dubious) promises by Russia. But we also need to work on the domestic side of things, because there's a dangerous interface between political corruption, coup d'états, reliance on the Russian military actors, and the food security issue.

Pankieiev: It's difficult to speak about the economy in Ukraine during the war. But what is your assessment of it right now? How is Ukraine coping?

Balmaceda: Some parts of the Ukrainian economy are working well. Many experts have mentioned the railroads and digital infrastructure, for example. Ukraine is also continuing to export steel despite its flagship steel factory, Azovstal, having been destroyed. But the reality is that Ukraine is highly dependent on Western support now. Namely, the European Union and the US gave Ukraine certain extensions on steel quotas so the produced steel could be exported, which is very important for Ukraine. We need also to make sure that foreign markets can access Ukrainian grain. That has brought up objections from Poland and other bordering states, which argue that Ukraine's grain has lowered domestic prices and presents unfair competition to their own farmers. It's a very difficult overall situation.

Pankieiev: Last winter, Russia targeted Ukraine's electrical grid system. Many believe Russia will also resort to the same tactic this upcoming winter. Is Ukraine vulnerable to it? Has something been done to offset the consequences of this tactic?

Balmaceda: Ukraine is better prepared, because some parts of Ukraine are trying to move to more localized energy sources, so that it is less reliant on the larger grid. Overall, there is a new protocol in place for rebuilding infrastructure that was destroyed by Russia. However, when you have massive bombardment, it is very difficult to repair the damaged system. You need access to the people who can go there and of course to the actual materials needed for the repairs. Currently there is dedicated help from some Western parties to rebuild Ukraine's damaged infrastructure, but political issues have sprung up. Because repairing infrastructure is expensive, political will in the US and the European Union is necessary in order to ensure a continued supply of support.

Pankieiev: And my last question is about the future. We know that wars end, sooner or later. What strategies do you see for rebuilding Ukraine after the war is over?

Balmaceda: In the past, Ukraine became one of the top net steel exporters through the export of (directly or indirectly) subsidized, high carbon footprint steel produced on the basis of ecologically problematic technology. It could do that because there were a lot of domestic subsidies, and the international barriers were not very high. But now there will be a whole new system of trade, started by the European Union with its CBAM system (the Carbon Border Adjustment Mechanism). They will scrutinize embedded carbon, so high carbon emissions from Ukraine won't stand a chance.

At the same time, moving to a de-carbonized world economy, or attempting to move towards it, makes some countries even more competitive than before. For example, China has already taken over the steel industry globally. And now, if there is a movement towards de-carbonized steel-making on the basis of green hydrogen, it turns out that China can also produce low-carbon hydrogen at a cost that is much lower than everybody else.

So, Ukraine will be rebuilding. On the one hand, rebuilding from zero after the destruction of some factories—Azovstal is again an example—allows Ukraine to move directly to better technologies. On the other hand, you have an international environment where some things and industries in which Ukraine was very competitive are being totally reshuffled. What do you do? Do you forget about steel? Or do you try to get investments to make de-carbonized steel from Ukraine competitive? And at the same time, I do not doubt that the same oligarchs, or their successors, will be there waiting for those subsidies.

So, it will be a different international environment, with new actors acquiring more importance because of the need for de-carbonization and new laws. And this will require Ukraine to rethink how it will be incorporated into the global economy. So, these are essential questions. And that's why we need to start thinking about it immediately, starting now.

CHAPTER 38

Evil must be called evil

Yevhenia Podobna

Interview with Natalia Khanenko-Friesen, published 30 September 2023

> Yevhenia Podobna is a journalist, chair of the editorial board of the "Suspilne" documentary program, a military correspondent, writer, and media coach. A graduate of Kyiv Shevchenko National University and the Drahomanov National Pedagogical University, she also teaches at the former's Institute of Journalism. In 2022, her book of stories about the war in Bucha and Irpin was published in Ukrainian. In 2020 her book *Girls Cutting Their Locks: A Book of Memories / The Russo-Ukrainian War* was published in English, and Podobna received the highest civic award in Ukraine, the Shevchenko National Prize.

Khanenko-Friesen: I would like to start with a conceptual question. How much has the field of journalism changed since the beginning of the full-scale war? What observations can you share as a scholar, professor, practitioner, and war correspondent?

Podobna: I will start by saying that there have been many changes. When discussing these changes, it is worth separating the Ukrainian and international contexts.

In Ukraine, in the effort to protect national media space, prior to Russia's full-scale invasion into Ukraine, channels that openly lobbied for Russian interests have already been shut down. Nonetheless, even since then the information field has changed a lot. Today, Ukraine does not have the same number of media outlets as it did before the Russian full-scale invasion. At the onset of the full-scale attack, in response to the government's call, television channels were asked to pool their resources within the framework of the "United News" marathon. Some channels were not invited in the United News marathon, as they were the supporters of the opposition prior to the full scale invasion. Channel 5, for example, was pushed to transfer their broadcasting to the Internet. Many other outlets were forced to reduce staff and volume of publications due to the fact that certain topics lost their relevance. Instead, bloggers, Telegram channels, and other similar social media channels have become very active, trying to take on the function of media, although these two means of mass communication function in very different dimensions.

Many Ukrainian journalists had to redefine themselves because the demand for generalists, as well as for narrow specialists, plummeted. Today, every journalist knows what a ballistic missile is and how it differs from an aeroballistic missile. The war became number one for everyone.

While in the last years before the all-out invasion we observed that some media reduced their coverage of the Russo-Ukrainian war to an absolute minimum, the situation then changed. For example, in the news programs of Channel 5, where I worked, there were three war stories covering the ATO JFO (Anti-Terrorist Operation – Joint Forces Operation). However, when many other TV channels delivered news, they would often include only one war story, hidden in between "more important" ones. The topic of war receded into the background because its active coverage led to a sharp drop in the ratings of TV programs. February 2022 then came as a watershed. The audience suddenly awakened its interest, started to read a lot about the fighting, and assertively sought information.

Paradoxically, it took the beginning of the full-scale invasion for it to become clear what it means to be a journalist and why this profession exists. In the first days of active fighting, informational chaos reigned. Nobody understood anything, and the audience was receiving atomized pieces of news about someone seeing or hearing something somewhere. This chaos was very actively used by the enemy, as they threw in and actively spread various misinformation and fake news via social media and Telegram channels. Regrettably, many people paid with their lives for this absolute lack of media literacy.

Turning our attention now to the international context, many outlets started paying attention to Ukraine. They began to dig deeper and understand better what was happening. That change made me very happy.

It is also very important that the international journalistic community has become actively engaged in discussing professional standards. If one takes the broadest perspective, all journalists in the world have one reference system—their ethical standards. The general rule is to follow the BBC handbooks in this respect. At their very first lecture in every journalism program students hear that pluralism of opinion should always be adhered to. Stories and articles in the media should always present the position of those who support something, those who oppose it, and those who remain indifferent. Unfortunately, during the ATO–JTO I often faced the condemnation of my professional activities. At international events, foreign journalists used to tell me and my colleagues that we were propagandists and scoundrels who purposely avoided covering the other side of the conflict. For me, this kind of accusation sounded like abuse of the profession. For me, there has always been a fundamental difference between the standard of presenting different positions and telling the truth. Evil must be called evil. All journalists must define for themselves whether they are routine communicators or socially responsible professionals. In addition to the fact that journalist stories and articles must meet the standard of pluralism of opinion, they also need to be accurate, up-to-date, and truthful. For me, no matter how unpleasant it may appear, the truth has always been paramount.

Toying with this standard of pluralism, many media outlets around the world became platforms for the spread of terrorist ideas and lies. For example, in one story foreign journalists could show the Ukrainian side, with factual information, and representatives of occupied territories or spokesmen of the Russians, who would say that 200 missiles and 300 MRL shells killed 500 children of the Donbas. For eight years we had been warning our foreign colleagues to be careful. If journalists deliberately spread lies, it was worse than if they did not adhere to the standard of pluralism. We used to ask them: "Why won't you popularize Osama bin Laden's ideas?" or "Why won't you give a word to the Taliban or other extremist organizations, representatives of totalitarian cults? They are also on the other side of the conflict, just like the Russians." Yet such discussions often led nowhere. Only today, when Russians themselves started hallucinating about mosquitoes as biological weapons, many foreign journalists understood that such things could not be broadcast. The world finally recognized that Ukraine was a victim and not a party to the conflict.

It seems to me that the most important thing in journalism is to tell the truth and call a spade a spade. Otherwise, the media distorts the reality that it talks about. In turn, audiences faraway from Ukraine do not understand the context.

In journalism there is a rule that can roughly be phrased as "check three times, publish once." According to this rule, each piece of news should be checked in at least three sources, preferably more. The information provided by the Ukrainian side can always be verified. Foreign journalists have the opportunity to go to the front lines and see everything with their own eyes, but this cannot always be done in the occupied territories. Thus, lies and fabrications from there are often broadcast simply to meet the "pluralism" objective and represent the position (no matter how dubious or suspect) of the other side.

Before the full-scale invasion, many foreign journalists had reproached us for not going behind the front lines and obtaining comments. They did not understand that Ukrainian journalists would have been imprisoned in the occupied territories, risking torture, rape, and beatings. Therefore, I am pleased today that many foreign colleagues are acknowledging the blind spots in their standards.

I am also very glad that there has been a large influx of journalists to Ukraine recently who finally saw the war with their own eyes. Previously, they had reported about Ukraine from Moscow, where many international correspondents worked. They reported about Ukraine through the prism of Russian propaganda, in which they had been immersed for quite some time, even if they were good professionals and good people by themselves. When they started coming to Ukraine and had to hide in shelters from shelling and missiles, the quality and content of their materials changed significantly. They began to write more truth.

Khanenko-Friesen: What is the importance of information and quality journalism in Ukraine's war effort?

Podobna: In the modern world, there is no such thing as a "pure war" or "noble war." The medieval skirmish was very much contact-based: an army of knights stood against an army of knights. The side which could destroy more heavily armed opponents won the victory. Today, wars are no longer fought in such a way. Today, the informational component has become crucial. Before an assault, the military implements a measure it calls "artillery preparation" — when all available large-calibre weapons are fired at the target area, into which the infantry then enters. In fact, Russia works in the same way in the information space. First, it pours phenomenal volumes of disinformation, propaganda, and fake news into the target area, and then brings in the troops.

The Russians have always invested a lot of money in informational preparation. They have produced hundreds of movies on themes of war. They meticulously readied the world and their own society for aggression. In addition, their propaganda has always been very flexible. When the Russians arrived in Kherson, they discovered that the local people hated them and tried to shoot them down from behind every bush. They quickly caught wind and started looking for an effective communication strategy to silence the Ukrainians' hatred. Thus, in order to change the public mood they began to disseminate leaflets about the "future with Russia" showing people in embroidered shirts.

In Volnovakha, where very heavy battles were fought, Russians entered the libraries in the first days of the occupation and threw away Ukrainian books. They like to abuse information, but they themselves are afraid of it. Russia is afraid of the truth like the devil fears incense. Therefore, the more truth there is in the information space, the fewer bullets there will be in the machine guns.

Khanenko-Friesen: How has the change from civilian to military journalism affected your personal projects and work?

Podobna: Apart from the increased volume of work, nothing else has changed. In 2014, when the invasion started some of my distant relatives from the Donbas—former relatives, I should say, since they decided to stay under the occupation—called me and complained in broken Russian that the Kyiv government had always suppressed their language rights. Thus, when I saw how my kinfolk changed under the influence of propaganda, how Ukrainian television towers were blown up, and how a bounty on the employees of Channel 5 was circulated on the Internet, I realized that journalists make the enemy feel afraid. Hence, I understood how important my professional activity was and that it should be continued.

My work as a war correspondent began with the Revolution of Dignity in 2014. Once every three days, if not more often, I had to be on duty on the Maidan. Compared to the number of events that were happening, there were too few journalists working in the city centre. Also, winter conditions significantly complicated the activities of all journalists.

For me, coverage of the Maidan events gradually evolved into coverage of the war. In fact, I have been reporting on military operations for eight years already. What happened in February 2022 was only a different understanding of war appearing in my head: the "safe rear" disappeared, there was nowhere to retreat, and "tomorrow" might never come. It became clear that I should engage in as much analytical reporting as possible, even if the literary quality of the material may suffer. No one else could do that besides me. No one else could see the facts and events that only I observed. No one else would cover many unpopular yet important topics. Thus, I decided to find my niche and work within it. That is how I started regularly recording eyewitness accounts—for history to remember, because people forget things quickly.

Khanenko-Friesen: Can you describe a bit more your practice of collecting eyewitness accounts? It is always hard to speak about war to people who experienced its cruelty. How do you do it; how do you abide by the principle of ethics in interviewing?

Podobna: Ethical issues become very acute when war takes place on your territory—when it is *your war*. Journalists can no longer work without feelings. Regarding the recording of accounts, as a journalist and for the purpose of reporting, I use the interview as both a tool and a genre. This differs from how book writers might be approaching interviewing. Such writers often see an interview as a tool to produce their own full written narrative account of what had happened.

If you try to define the way I work with eyewitnesses, it will be like *anthropological journalism*. I am interested in recording and unveiling a variety of human experiences. Currently, I am finalizing a collection of women's stories. It is very important for me to emphasize the diversity and multidimensionality of these stories, to create as broad a picture as possible. This collection will narrate women's experiences of war, peacetime life, the loss of loved ones and property, resistance to the occupiers, persecution, and being a victim.

In addition, as a journalist I am very careful about verifying information. I understand that people can unconsciously distort traumatic experiences. The mind gets confused when it tries to reconstruct events associated with major stress. I confirmed it myself! I was in Hostomel during the first helicopter assault by the Russians, in late February 2022. It was absolutely terrible. Afterwards, when I tried to establish the exact time of the beginning of the assault, I could not do it. Other eyewitnesses could not do this either—we all mentioned different times, and sometimes the discrepancies in our memories amounted to more than seven hours. As a result, we have established an approximate time of the assault, based on the metadata of photos and videos. Therefore, when recording eyewitness accounts I trust people's emotions and reflections but I always double-check the facts. Any traumatized person can very easily unconsciously give false information.

Another point is that I always take note of who is facing me. Among interviewees there are often people who simply want attention or just need to talk. There are also, unfortunately, people who pretend to be eyewitnesses, who present themselves as such. For instance, when collecting information about Ilovaisk, I was surprised to discover that with every new year more and more "survivors" appeared who had "experienced" the fighting there. Therefore, I had to ask these "survivors" relevant follow up questions, to verify their awareness of local geography, by asking for example about the village of Mnohopillia, or another neighbouring village within the vicinity of Ilovaisk. If an interviewee could not demonstrate the awareness of what communities were in the vicinity, then most likely it was a fake "eyewitness" sitting in front of me.

Before doing an interview, I try to learn as little as possible about the person but as much as possible about the context in which that person lived. When I was working on my previous book about Okhtyrka, which will soon be published, my interviewees were often confused about dates and events. During their assault on Okhtyrka, the Russians killed a child. This was a very important and iconic event, yet eyewitnesses named completely different places in which the killing happened. I had to turn to representatives of law enforcement agencies so that the investigative team could confirm the circumstances of the crime. The confusion appeared because on that day, the kindergarten "Sonechko" was shelled while the child, the girl Alisa, was killed near another kindergarten, "Rosynka." In people's minds, both kindergartens got merged into one. When I tried to clarify this, the interviewees looked baffled, and not all of them understood the importance of my picky questioning. I believe that history does not tolerate conjecture. If we allow such conjectures, then how will we differ from the Russians?

To try to summarize my practices, they stand on four pillars. First, I check the background of the person and confirm his or her relation to the event. Second, I formulate questions so that they uncover the broadest possible experience of this person. Third, I diligently check the facts and information presented by this person. Fourth, I formulate my questions depending on who is the person in front of me and how he or she feels.

In my mind, interviews should develop in real time, not follow rigid manuals. I am against lists of dos and don'ts with respect to the phrasing of questions. Many of my interviewees have already worked with journalists. After recording is over, I often ask them about their overall experiences of being interviewed; if something had been wrong during our conversation, if they had felt any discomfort. I am interested in their feedback to improve my practices in the future. Most people answer that they knew what they were getting into before agreeing to meet me. They could have predicted that my questions would be painful. In sum, people giving interviews understand roughly what they will be asked about, and manuals with lists of questions are superfluous in such cases.

An interesting thing I have discovered is that interviewees are more willing to talk about their experiences in the first few months after a traumatic event than after a year or more. I explain this by the fact that the more time passes, the more people try to forget and distance themselves from the trauma. For the first few months, they keep scrolling through the events in their head. Afterwards, they do not want to. Thus, my questions are forcibly dragging them back into the painful past with which they have already learned to live. Not to mention that after a year or two, people naturally forget many important details.

Before every interview, I emphasize that the person has a right to pause. Of course, most of the people who agree to meet me are very motivated to speak, they are unstoppable. Yet I make clear that at any moment every interviewee has the right to ask for a break. Then, we either go for a walk or agree to meet at another convenient time.

It is also no less important to clarify where the red lines run. I cannot know which topic will be painful for a person. Some interviewees are able to calmly describe how their legs were pierced with an awl or an awl was driven into their cheek. There are those who can tell in detail how the Russians scalped or ripped open the stomach of a man nearby. Someone can narrate how they held a severed head in their hands and smuggled it out of the occupation zone, because it was important to determine whose head it was. When telling such horrors, some people can maintain their composure and speak relatively easily. At the same time, the same people might categorically object to discussing their childhood, because, for example, their father left the family.

With some interviewees, I should be careful not to speak too much about their family in occupied territory. Personal safety has always been very important to me. Therefore, I have to double-check the risks of releasing the information that was collected during every conversation. Sometimes a person can be very open and trustful, while his or her relatives remain, for example, in Enerhodar. Therefore, everything that this person says must be published under a fictitious name. Sometimes, if my interviewees cannot realistically assess all the risks, I decide myself not to reveal their answers.

I avoid asking direct questions. Recently, I had an interview with a girl who escaped captivity. She told many details but did not want to touch upon the physical violence. She only briefly mentioned that she had been beaten very badly. When we started talking about her husband and family, about her conversations with relatives, about her family's attitude towards her after captivity, she immediately asserted that no one had raped her. She confessed that she would not have survived a rape. Therefore, my observation here is that even if the interviewees do not want to talk about something directly, they might return to that topic in the context of other questions.

A lot of people are willing to talk about being tortured, which came as quite a surprise for me. Also, it is very hard to interview relatives, especially mothers. I prepare for these interviews to last over two days, and I am often adversely affected after they are done.

Khanenko-Friesen: What are the parallels and differences between how Western and domestic journalists work in the Ukrainian information field?

Podobna: The biggest difference resides in the perception of events. Ukrainian journalists approach the war as "ours" while Western journalists report it as a conflict in a foreign country. We as Ukrainian journalists often feel pain when performing our professional duties, and our reports often appear more sensitive compared to what our Western colleagues produce.

I am very grateful to all the international journalists who decided to come to Ukraine. Their work is of paramount importance. They themselves may not understand how many lives have been saved because of their reporting. When the Western public reads the truth, when they see what is happening in Ukraine, they go to rallies at their parliaments. Under this social pressure, another package of aid gets delivered to Ukraine.

Honestly speaking, I do not believe in politicians. I believe in people. If there were no massive rallies in Western countries, if citizens did not show their parliaments that Ukraine needed support, then their support would be minimal. Doubtlessly, Ukrainians are very brave and courageous people, but we could never withstand Russian aggression without external help. The resources that Ukraine and Russia possess are simply incomparable. This is why foreign journalists who produce truthful reporting save lives — above all, the lives of Ukrainian children who cannot protect themselves.

At the same time, I would expect foreign journalists to be more open to information. They often come to Ukraine with certain attitudes, stereotypes, and baggage of knowledge — or lack of such. However, to really understand the country and its situation, they need to listen to people and be open to changing their wrong opinion, not clinging to it.

In terms of ethics, foreign and Ukrainian journalists also work differently. There are those who ask direct questions about everything they are interested in. There are those who constantly check with the interviewees whether they feel comfortable answering. Once I met a journalist who came to Ukraine to report on "nothing but the truth," but her approach was not particularly ethical. However, from the point of view of standards, that journalist was not entirely wrong: she honestly performed her duty in collecting important information and passing it on to her viewers.

Very often the acquisition and dissemination of important information is associated with ethical violations. For example, after [the young Ukrainian poet] Victoria Amelina was wounded [in the Russian missile attack on the pizzeria in Kramatorsk], journalists immediately posted about it in the media. In terms of standards, they did everything right: they promptly informed society about a serious injury of a public figure. However, her son did not know, and Victoria's family wanted to inform him about his mother's fate in person. Yet the media did it first, and the family was terribly traumatized by this development.

My most positive experience working with foreign journalists was with Czechs and Poles. These people were extremely ethical and competent. They filled me with love for my profession. On the other hand, I was offended by unexpected requests with very unethical wording from some other of my foreign colleagues. They happened to discover that I had worked in Bucha and Irpin and approached me to find a victim of sexual violence for them. That is, they asked me to find a woman who was raped and who would be willing to provide details about her unspeakable experience. Some of these journalists went as far as to ask for a woman who had been raped by both Russians and Ukrainians! I answered that the Ukrainian military did not rape the female citizens of Ukraine.

It also happens that people with a dubious reputation write to me and ask for help. Looking up their qualifications and publications, I often see that they sing Putin's praises and talk about the dire fates of the so-called "Donetsk and Luhansk independent republics." These people often brazenly demand that I take them to Bucha and show them the victims, because they want to write a big article. Moreover, such people get very offended when I refuse them and explain that they are not real journalists. They regularly publish unverified information. That is, the question here is not about their political position but about professionalism. The information spread by these people is not true.

Khanenko-Friesen: Have you had a chance to work or interact with colleagues who came from countries in the state of a so-called 'frozen conflict'? If yes, what has been your experience? Are there any similarities between what is going on in southeastern Ukraine and 'frozen conflicts' in their countries?

Podobna: I have a relatively extensive experience of such interactions. I visited Georgia and came close to the administrative border with occupied South Ossetia and Abkhazia. Of course, I could not get to the side that was under Russian control, but I could speak to people on that side of the barbed wire and get a good understanding of how the occupation took place.

Just like it did with the Ukrainians, Russia had declared that the Georgians were "fascists" prior to their invasion. This scheme became standard in both cases. It was not chosen on a whim.

Russian propaganda uses the trigger word "Nazi" when it defines enemies of their country for the European audience, which is still recovering from the traumas of WW II. At the same time, the propaganda uses a related but different specific word for its domestic audience, which is "fascists." That is, Russians depict Ukrainians and Georgians as "Nazis" to the West—which gets triggered by that word in the context of the WW II experience—but as "fascists" for the domestic audience, which easily catches on to the recognizable Soviet narratives.

When visiting Georgia and working there, I communicated with people who had fled from South Ossetia. I also spoke with people whose property borders the Russian demarcation line. Working in those parts of Georgia was a scary experience. Although no one was shooting, the atmosphere felt very tense and gloomy.

In Georgia, I met journalists from other countries in the region. By the way, Armenians and Azerbaijanis communicated very well, despite the fact that the "frozen conflict" nurtured political hostilities between their countries. Similar openness could be observed between journalists from Moldova and the so-called Transnistria. When I asked the latter where they were from and how they self-identified, I heard "From Transnistria and from Moldova." That is, Transnistria and Moldova were used as identity markers simultaneously.

The best connection that I established during my visit was with Georgians. They experienced much pain from their "frozen conflict" and could read our situation in the Donbas very well. However, Ukrainian journalists often felt confused about their attitudes. The majority of Georgians, both journalists and ordinary people, demonstrated absolutely no malice towards Russians. A huge number of Russians were bustling in their streets, but the Georgians claimed that those people were innocent even though aggression sometimes showed itself. For example, when I was shopping for spices at the market and tried to speak Russian, the vendor told me to go back to Moscow. I had to explain that I was from Ukraine and did not know

Georgian. As a result, the vendor's aggression changed to hugs and I got some spices for free.

Many Georgians are fighting for Ukraine today. They established a whole legion that is continuing their war against Russia. Unfortunately, a little country like Georgia could not stand up to the aggressor in 2008 on equal footing. The international community was sympathetic to the suffering of these people but chose not to take any groundbreaking action.

I understand that Ukrainian society—which experienced genocide, war, revolution, and other attempts to destroy it every few decades—should be constantly ready to withstand external aggression and therefore should learn from the experience of other societies. As a member of a Ukrainian delegation of journalists, I studied that experience in Georgia. I watched how people adapted to the war, how they looked for housing, and how they tried to preserve their property.

I also visited Azerbaijan but failed to get close to Karabakh. However, in Baku I was able to speak with many immigrants from that region. I also learned from them about ways for civilians to survive and adapt during active fighting. After all this communication, I realized that although military situations and frozen conflicts in Ukraine and the Caucasus had a lot in common, they were still very different. Namely, the scales and timeframes were different.

Then I decided to study how people survived the 'conflicts' on the Balkan Peninsula, particularly in Bosnia. Paradoxically, I found many more similarities there [than in the Caucasus] with what was happening in southeastern, northern and east-northern Ukraine. That being said, Ukrainians perceive their realities less confrontationally than the Bosnians did. And Ukrainians did not have so much hatred towards the aggressor.

Khanenko-Friesen: Taking into account the Bosnian experience, what might be the Ukrainian reality in future? How can the trauma of war be overcome? You once said that Ukrainians were fixated on their past—is that the case today?

Podobna: The main common characteristic of all the frozen conflicts I have ever seen and studied is that evil has never been punished. In fact, the way that the International Criminal Tribunal in The Hague addressed crimes in the former Yugoslavia is a sad reality for me.

I do not want Russians to be tried at the Hague—there will be no punishment for them! Many Bosnians were not able to overcome their traumas because following the ICTY rulings, both victims and perpetrators continued walking the same streets and living in neighbouring houses. Ukraine must not allow cases against Russians to be resolved in the same way.

The problem with all frozen conflicts in all countries was that key decision-makers—above all foreign ones—called for peace and negotiations instead of knocking out the aggressor's teeth. Incomprehensibly, they would frequently brush off the reasoning that a toothless aggressor would no longer be able to attack anyone—no other country or society.

I feel very offended by the common international belief that it is necessary for Ukrainians to sit down at the negotiating table and make peace with the aggressor. Every time I hear such a narrative, I use a simple analogy to explain to interlocutors from abroad that there are no good Russians today. I ask them to imagine that they were raped and brutally beaten, their hair torn—then, when the perpetrator was finished, his mother would approach with a smile and offer them tea. That mother would be innocent, for she did not offend anyone, and she might even condemn her child's actions. But would they drink tea with this woman? Hardly so. Then why are they forcing Ukrainians to do this? How could they force Ukrainians to forget about the atrocities?

I am very skeptical of any calls to seek peace with the Russians. Diseases should be treated, not ignored. If there is a tumour in the body, then applying a poultice will not help—the tumour must be cut out. If we are now faced with a Russian tumour that is metastasizing all over Ukraine, then it should be surgically removed, not ignored with the hope that one day it will subside.

If evil had been justly punished in all the previous frozen conflicts, then there would be fewer of them today. If Russia had felt serious consequences after its invasion of Georgia, it would not have invaded Ukraine. If the world had responded adequately to the annexation of Crimea, there would have been no invasion of the Donbas. Russia did what it was allowed to do. Moreover, Russia is the only country in the modern world that provokes conflicts regularly.

Thus, aggressors should not be appeased but hit back. Ukraine is trying to do this—and therefore, The Hague Tribunal is far from the best solution to prosecute Russian criminals.

When you look at how Ratko Mladić appears in those videos, you do not see an international criminal who has a guilty conscience. He lives in a comfortable cell and can even select his food from a menu. Many of his accomplices have already been released from prison. However, their traumatized victims, whose future was taken away, continue to stumble in the debris of their destroyed country. So which of the two is truly punished?

I am very skeptical about how international justice works today. Actually, it does not work. It neither prevents nor properly punishes crimes, as we have been shown many times. This dysfunctional justice gives perpetrators confidence. As for me, true punishment should reside in inflicting such grave suffering on perpetrators that their accomplices and sympathizers get terrified—not in socially isolating perpetrators in comfortable cells. In today's Serbia, many criminals are still considered heroes, and newspapers glorify them on the front pages.

I clearly understand that there will be no restitution for Ukraine in the international legal field. Therefore, for us, the only justice that exists is the one created by the Armed Forces of Ukraine on the battlefield.

Khanenko-Friesen: In sum, then, what are your key messages to Western audiences?

Podobna: The world must understand that if evil is not punished now, it will grow and spread further. If Ukraine does not defend itself now, then Poland, Moldova and the countries of the Baltic Sea will become the next targets. If the West presumes that Russia will never attack them because there are no conditions for it to do so, then it is worth realizing that Ukrainians thought the same way before 2013. At that time, no one thought that Kyiv would be bombed. But it was bombed today.

Western audiences should understand that the plans in Putin's head are simultaneously insane and ambitious. The world must finally hear and take seriously the narratives of Russian propaganda, especially those threatening to wipe out "unfriendly" countries across all continents. When such threats were first voiced against Ukraine in the 2010s, we laughed at them—up until Russian missiles flew at us. These missiles can fly farther still. People in the West, no matter how far away they live, must realize that Russia can reach them. Syria is located geographically far from Russia, but the sheer distance did not save it.

Ukrainian blood is being shed now, but not exclusively for Ukraine. I am not trying to exaggerate or sound dramatic here. Russians hate the West. For them, the West is a single collective enemy that is supposedly jealous of the achievements of their so-called "civilization." The Russians will keep on spreading their "Russian World" unless it is crushed on the battlefield in Ukraine.

Another message I would like to send is that people in the West should be ready to deal with different kinds of Ukrainians. As my colleague said, we are not a "museum of perfect people." The whole country should not be judged by the unworthy behaviour of a handful of its citizens.

I understand that the world is tired of Ukraine. It is tired of reading every day about the bloodshed and the need to send more weapons. However, we cannot win this war without external aid. Every vote of a person in the West—every rally, every newspaper article—everything brings us closer to victory.

I would like people in the West to be inspired by the example of Ukrainians and understand how much a single person can do. Because every person is powerful, every action counts. Sometimes a small rally at a parliament in Old Europe can save dozens of lives in Ukraine. It is very important that people in the West are not afraid to act for Ukraine—and above all for themselves.

My third message is that a genocide is happening in Ukraine. Russian lists of people to be exterminated, particularly in Bucha and Irpin, serve as the best evidence for me that the occupiers had a plan. They searched for specific people, Ukrainian patriots, and killed them deliberately.

I have often read how a person can become a wild beast in the conditions of war and how insensitivity can grow. I do not see this in Ukrainians. Once I asked a Ukrainian officer whose unit took Russian prisoners if they had tortured them. The answer was no; that officer said that torturing was below his dignity. He also added that if he was going to torture prisoners, how would he later embrace his wife with those same arms?

At the beginning of the war, my mother told me that she was afraid the Russians would kill me in two ways. The first was physical. She knew that I often got into difficult situations, under fire, where my life was in immediate danger. The second way was emotional. My mother was very afraid that the Russians would harden my heart, that I would become as callous as them. Two years after the full-scale invasion, I am still holding. Other Ukrainians did not turn into wild beasts, either. The Russians did not break us! They did not defeat us, regardless of all the atrocities they committed.

When I ask Ukrainians what punishment they want for the Russians, they often respond that the aggressors should receive exactly as much as they committed in Ukraine. No more, no less. Therefore, it would be very fair if the victims in Ukraine chose the punishment for their perpetrators. Then I believe there would be fewer perpetrators in other parts of the world.

When we talk about a civilized approach to punishment—one enshrined in international law—we must realize that by default, genocides do not happen in the civilized world. However, if genocides do happen, then they become a sign that relations between people have crossed the boundaries of a civilized world. A different approach to punishment is worth considering then.

CHAPTER 39

Russia selectively and deceptively manipulates Western media and public discourses

Vitaly Chernetsky

Interview with Oleksandr Pankieiev, published 6 October 2023

Vitaly Chernetsky is a professor of Slavic languages and literatures at the University of Kansas. He is the author of *Mapping Postcommunist Cultures: Russia and Ukraine in the Context of Globalization* (2007; Ukr. edn 2013), and his Ukrainian-language book on Ukrainian literature and cinema is forthcoming from Krytyka. His translations into English include Yuri Andrukhovych's novels *The Moscoviad* (2008) and *Twelve Circles* (2015). Chernetsky is a past president of the American Association for Ukrainian Studies (2009–18) and the current first vice-president of the Shevchenko Scientific Society in the USA, as well as president of the Association for Slavic, East European, and Eurasian Studies (ASEEES).

Pankieiev: You have been exploring the notions of postcolonialism and postmodernism in the historical and literary contexts of both Russia and Ukraine. How did Russia's full-scale invasion of Ukraine affect the reconceptualization of those theoretical frameworks?

Chernetsky: In the context of Russia, we have a throwback to pre-modern approaches to culture, state, and history — but in a very interesting fusion of selectively borrowed and applied concepts from various, more recent intellectual and technological global trends. Think about the world portrayed in Vladimir Sorokin's novel *Day of the Oprichnik*, which imagines Russia's near future that looks like medieval Muscovy of Ivan the Terrible time but with mobile phones, luxury cars, and the Internet. We have this strange hybrid of radically anti-modern developments and different elements of contemporary cultural philosophy they can choose from, as if at a smorgasbord.

Since Russia became aware of the ideas associated with *postmodernism*, around the early 1990s, there have been some interesting theoretical reflections. *Post-truth* is one of the very superficial ideas that became widespread and applied by people close to Russian government leadership. For them, there is no "truth and justice"; everything is language games. People can be manipulated, and everything is citational and potentially deceptive.

This very shallow caricature version of what postmodernism might be about was propagated and imposed very persuasively — taken on faith by the targeted consumers, as it were. It reminds me actually of Russia's illusory embrace of capitalism in the 1990s. It felt like they took the negative Soviet propaganda image of evil, ruthless Western capitalists and transformed it into a positive, trying to emulate not actual practices on capitalist economy but those propaganda images they had internalized.

On the other hand, there is also the turn away from postmodernist literature and culture, which is very reflexive and playful, toward a new type of more direct expression, new forms of realism. We can see that a *new drama* arose in several countries in the post-Soviet space, including Ukraine and Russia. The whole movement started as a pushback against this hypertrophied, on the one hand, but superficially understood postmodernism.

As for *postcolonialism*, Russia's paradox was that for a long time it completely ignored the discourse. And then, when some intellectuals discovered it in the early 2000s, they tried to adapt it to the idea that Russia was more of a victim of Western colonialist expansion than a perpetual rapacious colonialist offender in its own right. In this attempted adaptation, the narrative was cultivated (even though Russia was not directly colonized) that some semi-colonization had occurred in the 18th and 19th centuries. And then, notions of *self-colonization* or *internal colonization* were used to declare that Russian colonialism towards others was better, softer, and more enlightened than the supposedly more brutal and evil British and French versions. Russian scholars advanced a view that in their internal colonialist practices, the imperial elites were treating the ethnically Russian population of the Empire as badly, if not worse, than some of the other captive nations. This paradoxical, if not outright contradictory, interpretation became very entrenched.

They looked at other models as well — for instance, the Latin American model of *decolonial thinking* and *decolonial studies* as opposed to the postcolonial, which was more associated with the anglophone and francophone world. Today, however, the full-scale invasion of Ukraine has changed things dramatically. The world sees Russia as a resurgent neocolonial empire, very aggressive in its colonial practices. This also sheds light on its colonialist practices and ruthlessness toward the indigenous communities that still live within the borders of the Russian Federation—especially the indigenous peoples of the North Caucasus region, Siberia, and the Far North—and it has brought greater awareness to those issues.

Today we also see on the global stage that Russia is desperately seeking allies. It aggressively courts many countries in the Global South—at least, their intellectual elites and leadership. It selectively and strategically uses the language of anticolonial, postcolonial, and decolonial discourses to its advantage, and this is a very serious and troubling issue.

Many people from the Global South and Western academia whose research is focused on the Global South were deceived by this Russian rhetoric. They are obsessed with the idea that the 20th century was dominated by a "Pax Americana," and they are happy to see the American dominance, which they know how to criticize, destabilized; as such, they are willing to overlook the dangers of neo-authoritarian players on the global stage, like Russia and China. Anything that weakens the US and its global influence is good to them. In this sort of strange logic, they become supportive of Russia's and China's most horrible policies on the international stage.

Pankieiev: The need for decolonization of Russian studies and a reconsideration of how Russian history and literature courses are being taught at universities are increasingly discussed. What questions are on the top of the agenda in those discussions? What is your overall opinion about the need for decolonization of this field?

Chernetsky: There is an urgent need to rethink and reframe how Russian studies are conceptualized and taught, a need for a fundamental transformation. It requires deep, critical interrogation of many received ideas, stereotypes, and narratives that are entrenched in how they have been taught at the secondary and undergraduate levels. For instance, if you look at most syllabi on "Introduction to Russian History" or "Introduction to Russian Studies," or "Russian, East European, and/or Eurasian Studies" courses, the Kyivan Rus period is often presented part of Russian history without any awareness of controversies.

The projection of that is part of the uncritical absorption and recycling of the narrative that was brought by the early Russian émigrés to the West and was taken on faith by American, Canadian, and Western European students, who reproduced it in the teaching of this and various other periods, including the Soviet era, and in teaching Soviet culture. Even the periods of relative internationalism, such as the policies of indigenization pursued in the 1920s, for example, you would not see covered in most publications or courses taught by Western scholars. They were entirely Russo-centric — or even Moscow or St. Petersburg-centric. The prejudicial position was that everything interesting happened in the capitals, and everything outside was provincial, dull, uninteresting, and unimportant. Moreover, the approach itself is troubling in multiple respects — denigrating other cultures and dismissing them pre-emptively, if not appropriating their identity, history, and material culture outright. Addressing this is something I have been advocating, within the broader process of interrogating dominant paradigms and spotlighting the hidden presence of colonial attitudes in texts, in the works of visual arts, cinema, and in the cultural discourse. It needs to be made visible.

For example, this semester, I am teaching a course on gender, sexuality, and social justice in Eastern Europe, the former Russian Empire, and the former Soviet Union that I reformulated to make it *decolonially diverse*. And we were just discussing with students Chernyshevsky's *What is to be Done?* and the famous fourth dream of Vera Pavlovna, the utopian vision of society of the future. In our discussion, my students and I noted an avid embrace of colonialism there. The utopian society of the future has "New Russia" as well as other colonized territories.

Moreover, Vera Pavlovna asks the guide in the dream, "Is this where Odesa and Kherson are?" but the guide explains that it is not Odesa and Kherson and that it is a different territory that is being colonized now: "This was in your time, and now, look where New Russia is." We can tell that the lands described correspond to Central Asia, which was indeed actively colonized in the 1860s when Chernyshevsky wrote the novel. This is something that historically very few people paid attention to. But now, all of a sudden, this jumps at you from every page. I have written about this in a chapter on Empire for the new *Cambridge History of Russian Literature*.

In this chapter, I use the term *imperiality* by analogy with the term *coloniality*. *Coloniality of power* — a term in decolonial theory — is when somebody or something, a work of culture or cultural phenomenon, is not actively participating in a colonialist project but is still enabled by structures of power that are colonial in their origin, and this is something that endures even after overt official colonialism may be over. If we look at Russian culture, we have this situation with imperiality and coloniality in approaches fundamentally pervading it in the texts of both official and dissident writers, in texts both liberal and conservative; it is deeply present there. While it has become standard and common to talk about these things in the context of British, French, or Dutch imperialism, it has not been discussed with respect to Russian imperialism—which is important to change.

In terms of bringing voices forward, it is essential to confront and overcome *epistemic injustice*. It is a relatively recent term in philosophical discourse that comes from feminist philosophy but has broader application to racial and colonial injustice. Within the discourse of epistemic injustice, philosophers talk about one particular kind: *pre-emptive testimonial injustice*. It is when it does not even occur to those in positions of power—the privileged knowers, as described in this discourse—that somebody speaking from a different subject position, from a different situated experience, has anything of value to contribute. They pre-emptively dismiss viewpoints, experiences, and rich textured knowledge from that position because they think it is not interesting and does not contribute to anything. This is something that both Ukrainians and representatives of other cultures that were oppressed and marginalized within the context of the Russian and Soviet Empire, had been dealing with—an excessive epistemic burden. They and their cultures were oppressed, but on top of it representatives of these oppressed cultures carried the burden of expressing it to the dominantly situated. The dominantly situated, in turn, may well choose not to pay attention to those contributions to shared knowledge, as opposed to actively trying to change their attitudes. So this is a bigger problem.

We now see many Western Slavists and specialists in Russian, East European, and Eurasian Studies waking up to these problems, actively trying to rethink how they might approach and transform their teaching and research. However, quite many are still resistant, think of this as a temporary annoyance, and wish that those Ukrainians and all other pesky marginal people would go back to the dark, obscure mouse-holes they came from and not bother them in studying their *great culture*, because they all know that it is great. Then it becomes a circular reasoning — that it is great *because* it is Russian. So yes, it is a big problem, and much still remains to be done. Changes are happening, but we still have a very long road ahead of us.

Pankieiev: We hear much lamenting about the cancellation of everything Russian. What is your opinion about this?

Chernetsky: It is, again, an interesting case of Russian discourse selectively and shallowly appropriating from the Western media and public discourses. It is a frequent complaint of privileged people who are hetero, white, and mostly male, who have had unproblematic access as experts and opinion makers to the media, university lecturer podiums, and publications, whom people from disempowered or marginalized positions then challenge. It is this very selfish and dangerous precedent, them saying, "Woe is me, I'm being cancelled!" They thus create more noise and continue being very visible and vocal about it. But nobody can cancel them, as they dominate the discourse, sucking all the oxygen out of the room.

This tactic is mainly used by conservative, reactionary media personalities in the United States and elsewhere, and it has been appropriated by some representatives of the Russian cultural elite. They use it the same way as do some nefarious folks in the United States. Even while much anti-Americanism is happening in the Russian cultural discourse, we also see this use of what was occurring within the domestic United States debates, re-appropriating it and trying to use it strategically. For me, it is an entirely spurious and manipulative discourse. Whenever I hear anyone talk about "cancel culture," I immediately think something nefarious and problematic is afoot; it basically entails fighting a fictional enemy that they themselves have created. It becomes a way of whipping up emotions, being manipulative, and then projecting all this onto folks from historically marginalized positions, saying, "You are a nasty person, you hate me, while I am all fuzzy and innocent."

In all instances, this is a very pernicious discourse that needs to be called out. It needs to be resolutely rejected, as it absolutely has nothing to do with the actual situation of efforts to diversify culture and highlighting that within Russian culture there are problematic aspects, as well as the fact that in many cases, the overly visible presence of Russian culture in a given region — and invisibility of the cultures of other countries of that region—is the result of either ignorance by those in positions of power or their laziness.

A good example would be classical music. So many orchestras in the West to date have not even bothered to include even one short piece of Ukrainian music in the programming of their annual season. We are talking about a year and a half since the start of the full-scale invasion and soon to be ten years since the beginning of the war with the invasion of Crimea. And some of them just do not know—they claim—that good Ukrainian music exists. Yet we have everything here: if you want notes or scores, they are available. If you want Baroque, there is Baroque; if you want avant-garde, there is avant-garde—all those genres. It is just intellectual laziness on the part of orchestra management and artistic direction. Meanwhile, Tchaikovsky has not diminished, nor have Shostakovich or any other so-called great composer.

Similarly with Russian literature: just a couple of issues ago *The New Yorker* devoted a good five pages in its print edition to reviewing the latest translation of *The Brothers Karamazov* and explaining that while Dostoevsky may have been a nasty person, it is a work of genius that every self-respecting person must read and appreciate. In sum, there is absolutely no danger of Russian culture becoming invisible, obscure, or oppressed. This is a spurious discourse.

Pankieiev: What is the role of literature and art in Ukraine as a nation defending its land and identity and charting a path after the war?

Chernetsky: The cultural sphere, including literature and arts, cinema, music, and theatre, is very important. If we agree that a nation is an imagined community—in the sense that it is a community that actively imagines itself and tries to think about what binds it together—the shared cultural legacy is hugely important. This is why we must counter—both domestically within Ukraine and on the international scene—any and all dismissive, divisive discourses that denigrate Ukrainian culture and stereotype it as supposedly second-rate, of marginal importance. One of the sad consequences of colonialism is that many Ukrainians have also internalized this narrative. Although it has been 30-plus years since Ukraine regained its independence, valuing Ukrainian culture past and present as rich, innovative, and worthy of attention has not yet been embraced by all Ukrainians, including Ukrainians who consider themselves part of the intellectual elite or the decision-making groups. We see this happening within Ukraine, and we also see this happening on the global stage. Suppose we want people to support Ukraine more. In that case, it should not be just negatively defined by nasty things that others do to it. It also needs to be associated with cultural richness that can be shared with the world and can teach the world something.

Therefore, it is essential in the educational environment to make sure that Ukrainian cultural products are visible. There should be specialized Ukraine-focused university courses, thematic exhibitions, film retrospectives, etc. But we also need to ensure that Ukrainian content is present in academic courses, theoretical books and discussions, thematic anthologies, and art exhibitions that are not exclusively focused on Ukraine. Ukrainian culture has much to share on a wide range of topics. One of the classic examples is Taras Shevchenko's poem "Kavkaz"—a pioneering thoughtful articulation of anticolonial solidarity of the oppressed, written in the 1840s, a long time before these ideas were found elsewhere.

Speaking of postcolonial and decolonial theories, how much richer and more textured would they have been if the folks who articulated them in the mid-twentieth century had been aware of what Shevchenko wrote a century earlier! It would have been a very different story now. So, we are now belatedly catching up. Nevertheless, the world is now seriously paying attention, and we need to ensure that there is this recognition of how much Ukrainian thought and Ukrainian culture can contribute to the widest variety of topics, not just ghettoized, Ukraine-specific ones.

Pankieiev: As a translator, sharing Ukrainian culture is something that is important to you. What messages are you hoping to get to readers and the public through your work?

Chernetsky: Translation has been one of the most enjoyable parts of my intellectual work. And it became an essential creative outlet for me as well. I began working on translations more than 30 years ago when I had just started graduate school here in the US. It happened because I was excited about fun, innovative texts I knew in the original, and I wanted to share them with my American friends.

We have wonderful, talented people whom we enjoy reading, and this is worth sharing with others--this has been my approach ever since. I have participated in a lot of different projects. In most of my translations, whether it would be a few short pieces for an anthology of poetry, short fiction, or a novel, I try to meaningfully invest in building cultural bridges—in communicating ideas between cultures—so that more dialogue is happening.

As with all cultural work, one must know that the proper or deserved response might take time. For instance, the English translation of *The Moscoviad* by Yuri Andrukhovych, which I did more than 15 years ago, has been rediscovered and appreciated much more within the field of Slavic East European and Eurasian studies in the context of the full-scale invasion. I am now seeing this book assigned to university courses all over the English-speaking world. This is also the case with many other translations of various Ukrainian writers I have done. Fortunately, we see them now involved in this global exchange of ideas, opinions, and aesthetic experiences. They have a voice and a presence. In this sense, translation—in both the narrow and the broader sense—is a hugely important enterprise because it creates new relationships between creators and audiences and engages with new audiences who otherwise would not have had access to this kind of work.

Translation—when it is successful—in some way becomes a *co-creation of meaning*, because you are carrying the ideas of the original. You are making informed decisions on the most effective way to bring the riches of the original work to new audiences who might not know all the local contexts from which the work came. But you want to ensure that they still appreciate the many nuances of that work. So, it is both a science and an art. There is a delicate balance involved. And it is an inspiring and culturally rewarding activity.

Pankieiev: You, among others, have noted a positive change in the acceptance of LGBTQ people in Ukraine. What has been behind this, and do these developments suggest other changes in Ukrainian society?

Chernetsky: Since the start of the full-scale invasion, we have witnessed many segments of Ukrainian society thinking more about the war, about the aggression that Ukraine is heroically repelling and fighting as a war of values, mainly because the aggressor—contemporary Russia, at the state level—has embraced all the extremely right-wing, obscurantist, and oppressive ideologies and practices. It has propelled more Ukrainians to think of this conflict not as a conflict that is geographic or ethnic but as one that is based on values—and also that the Ukrainian nation is not defined ethnically but by the cultural values that we share and embrace. The fact that diversity—including the presence of the LGBTQ community within the diverse spectrum of the nation—is something that the Kremlin attacks so viciously in its official discourse has pushed many Ukrainians to rethink their attitudes.

Also, the fact that we have so many "out" queer Ukrainian folks fighting on the front lines, defending the country, has shattered many negative stereotypes that were strangely persistent and enduring. Thus, since the start of the full-scale invasion, we have seen a strong shift within Ukrainian society in terms of positive attitudes toward the queer community. There is now a solid chance of legal recognition and protection of same-sex unions through civil partnerships.

Ukraine is moving in a very progressive direction. We see the embrace of values of equality, diversity, and inclusion being taken seriously, and they have become understood, unquestioned, evident, and normal, especially for the younger generations of Ukrainians. In thinking about the values they defend and global cultural engagement, they see the aspirational model of what we want the future of victorious Ukraine to be, after the enemy is defeated and peace returns to the Ukrainian lands.

CHAPTER 40

Commitments to Ukraine in Budapest Memorandum are legally binding

Mariana Budjeryn

Interview with Oleksandr Pankieiev, published 7 December 2023

> Mariana Budjeryn (PhD, Political Science, Central European University) is a senior research associate with the Harvard Kennedy School Belfer Center's Project on Managing the Atom (MTA), a senior non-resident fellow at the Brookings Institution, and a global fellow at the Woodrow Wilson International Center for Scholars, as well as a member of the National Academy of Science Committee on International Security and Arms Control. Formerly she was a fellow at Harvard's Davis Center for Russian and Eurasian Studies and a visiting professor at Tufts University and the Peace Research Institute Frankfurt. She is the author of *Inheriting the Bomb: The Collapse of the USSR and the Nuclear Disarmament of Ukraine* (2023).

Pankieiev: How has Russia's full-scale invasion of Ukraine changed your understanding and view of the international security order? What pitfalls do you see now?

Budjeryn: One of the things that we probably knew before but has now come particularly into focus since the Russian invasion of Ukraine is the inadequacy of the global power structures as they were founded, incorporated, and institutionalized after the Second World War. This inadequacy has been laid bare when one of the core states of the international system, a member of the UN Security Council with veto power, has gone rogue. Great powers like to cut corners and bend the rules. But Russia has set to dismantling all the rules. We are witnessing the flagrant violation of basically every norm of international relations regarding the use of force and the conduct of war. And this is after WW II in Europe when we said *never again*.

That normative veneer has not been robust enough to constrain a power like Russia. Some people have always been sceptical about the role of such international rules, and they've said, "Oh, you know, international norms work until they don't." There's very little recourse to justice if powerful states decide to defy international norms. And in preventing something like this from happening — something like a full-scale invasion — we can't allow ourselves to be overconfident. That is not to say that international rules and norms have no significance in international relations, but we must adjust our understanding of how they work, in order to be able to prevent conflict.

Pankieiev: Last year, you published a book, *Inheriting the Bomb: The Collapse of the USSR and the Nuclear Disarmament of Ukraine*. At the outset of the full-scale invasion, the Budapest Memorandum was often referred to. Please tell us about the memorandum in the context of Russia's war against Ukraine.

Budjeryn: The research for my book was done before the full-scale invasion. When it started, I rethought my conclusions and analysis in the book, evaluating to see whether they had changed with the benefit of hindsight. We know that the future is unpredictable, but the past is even more unpredictable than the future. We re-evaluate the past in the light of current developments. And I largely stand by the conclusions I made in the book.

Regarding the Budapest Memorandum, we must be conscious that historical events must be evaluated in their own context. We might see them differently now. But to be fair to the people involved and truly understand their role, reasons, and consequences, we must put them in the context they were in at that time.

The Budapest Memorandum on Security Assurances, which Ukraine negotiated and signed with the United States, the UK, and Russia in 1994, was part of the broader deal that led to Ukraine's nuclear disarmament. There were also other components: compensation for the fissile material in the warheads and economic assistance. Ukrainian diplomats made concerted efforts to get the kind of robust security commitments that Ukrainian officials felt they needed in exchange for giving up this strategic asset. And what Ukraine was giving up then was not the third-largest nuclear arsenal or a fully-fledged nuclear deterrent. It was the *nuclear option*. Ukraine had a huge inheritance, but it did not amount to a nuclear deterrent that Ukraine was ready to put into service. Ukrainian officials made a concerted effort to get a fair deal for Ukraine, and we must give them their dues. It was challenging for Ukraine at that point to negotiate with two large nuclear powers, one of which, the United States, was the predominant political power in the world and the other one, Russia, while being rather weak in the early 90s, still held critical levers of influence over Ukraine—particularly energy supplies. Ukraine's energy supplies came from Russia: gas, oil, and fuel for nuclear power plants, providing half of Ukraine's energy mix. So there was enormous leverage on Russia's side and very little leverage on the Ukrainian side. Unsurprisingly, Ukraine did not get everything it wanted from the Budapest Memorandum, but it did get something. The fact that Ukraine negotiated a separate document that accompanied its accession to the Nuclear Non-Proliferation Treaty (NPT) was unprecedented. No other country acceded to the NPT with this kind of set of written security commitments.

The significance of the Budapest Memorandum was not in pledging some robust security commitments that Ukraine would not formally have in accordance with the UN Charter or with the 1975 OSCE Helsinki Final Act: not to use or threaten force against sovereignty, independence, territorial integrity, and to respect internationally recognized borders. Countries pledge all these things to each other just by virtue of being members of the UN and signatories to the Helsinki Act. What was significant about the Budapest Memorandum was the timing and the form: it recognized Ukraine's legitimate security concerns and linked security assurances pledged in the memorandum to its nuclear disarmament and accession to the NPT. The Budapest Memorandum is a part of the broader non-proliferation regime; it's registered at the UN and attached to Ukraine's act of accession to the NPT. It was signed by Ukraine and the three nuclear weapon states, the United States, the United Kingdom, and Russia, depository states of the NPT. And one of those signatories blatantly and brazenly breached its commitments pledged in the Budapest Memorandum—and more importantly, it breached the UN Charter. Thus, all the arguments that the Budapest Memorandum is not legally binding are moot. *The commitments in the Budapest Memorandum are legally binding* by other means, like the UN Charter, and Russia is part of the UN.

The Budapest Memorandum has political and historical significance. As with any international political document, you have to make something out of it. There's no automatic procedure. It doesn't matter how legally binding it is on paper; you must work at it. After signing the Budapest Memorandum in 1994, Ukraine as an independent state didn't leverage this document enough. Instead, it was something that Ukraine signed and put on the shelf. It said "guarantees" in Ukrainian translation, and that was good enough. It could have been more—a framework for military and defence cooperation with the signatories, whichever signatories Ukraine cared to pursue this cooperation with, likely the United States and the United Kingdom.

Before 2014, Ukraine was negotiating its identity and geopolitical course. Let's remember that someone like Yanukovych was popularly elected as president of Ukraine. Due to its political ambivalence and the lack of a concerted Western grand strategy toward it, Ukraine always had this "instrumental" engagement from the West. Without a long-term, sustained, and concerted strategy toward it, Ukraine found itself in geopolitical limbo.

The Budapest framework failed to be developed into something that could have been filled with more concrete, consequential measures of defence and security cooperation. After [Russia invaded Ukraine's Autonomous Republic of Crimea in February] 2014, the West—particularly the United States—should have taken the lead as one of the document's signatories [and security guarantors, but it did not]. The Obama administration took a "leading from behind" approach in terms of Ukraine and did not react stringently enough to the occupation of Crimea [and the war in the Donbas]. It dismissed Russia as a regional power and treated everything as if it was somewhere in a faraway country in Eastern Europe—about which we know very little, and frankly, we don't care, and we don't want to do something escalatory. That is why Germany and France were allowed to pursue negotiations [on the Minsk agreements]. However, the right thing to do would have been for the United States and the UK, as signatories of the Budapest Memorandum, to negotiate instead of the Normandy format. Maybe then, the Budapest format would have negotiated a more substantive and fair framework than the Minsk agreements, which could not have been implemented without compromising Ukraine's sovereignty.

In sum, the Budapest Memorandum was the best possible option under the circumstances in 1994. It undoubtedly could have been leveraged better—by Ukraine before 2014 and by the Western signatories after 2014. Today, its breach has very significant consequences for the credibility of the non-proliferation regime because it is a constitutive part of that broader non-proliferation architecture.

Pankieiev: At the outset of the full-scale invasion, Russia occupied the Chornobyl Nuclear Power Plant. The Zaporizhia Nuclear Power Plant is still occupied. What are the threats, and what are the possible solutions to prevent a nuclear catastrophe in Ukraine?

Budjeryn: One thing we can see from Russia's way of prosecuting the war, is that it is willing to defy the rules which, at one point, it had a hand in making. As the [self-proclaimed] successor state of the USSR, Russia is a founding member of the International Atomic Energy Agency, an international organization charged with the responsible development of civilian nuclear power and ensuring that civilian nuclear energy is not diverted to military applications. Now Russia has made the most blatant and almost unbelievable violations of these rules; using military force against civilian nuclear facilities is prohibited by international law and conventions of the IAEA, where Russia is a member of the Board of Governors.

Russia['s invading armies] occupied the Chornobyl NPP, which was decommissioned in 2000. But it remains a repository of a massive amount of radioactive material that needs special regimes and security procedures, requiring qualified personnel to attend to it. The negligence and ignorance of the Russian troops that occupied Chornobyl is mind-boggling: we know the reports of the Russians digging trenches in the Red Forest—one of the most contaminated places in the world—and the harm done to the Russian soldiers themselves.

But Russia's occupation of an operating power plant, the Zaporizhia NPP—the largest in Europe, with six reactors loaded with tons of hot, really active nuclear fuel—is an entirely new order of magnitude. And again, the Russian military forces have conducted themselves in brazen violation of any rules of war and nuclear safety and security protocols that apply to civilian nuclear facilities.

For instance, on March 4, 2022, when they were taking over the ZNPP, protected by only 200 men of the lightly armed National Guard of Ukraine regiment, the Russians shelled the power plant. They hit the training building and the building adjacent to the first reactor! There was no reason to shell and open fire from the tanks; there was nothing to hit [of strategic military value].

It was either a policy of intimidation or perhaps other things that they wanted to get through this assault that didn't have any military rationale. *The ensuing terror against Ukrainian staff once the*

Russians occupied the ZNPP is a qualitatively new story in the world of international security. We've always paid attention to threats to buildings and nuclear materials. The reactor's core has to be protected by a containment chamber, and you have to do everything to secure it from perhaps one or two bad people, earthquakes, or other things. But we never thought of how to secure a nuclear reactor from regular military forces of a hostile state power.

In any case, the people themselves, highly qualified nuclear engineers, are irreplaceable. It takes decades to train those people around a particular facility. They are not just any nuclear engineers; they are those who know how to operate this particular reactor — and these people became hostages. This is an unprecedented threat to nuclear security, because even if you can ensure that electricity and water keep flowing through the reactor's cooling systems, you still need experienced people to operate it. We would be in a major disaster if Russia removed all of these people from the plant.

We haven't made provisions for how to protect these people. Terrible stories are coming out of Zaporizhia. People who are suspected of passing information to Ukrainian Security Services — or being veterans of the ATO (war in the Donbas) or having a strong pro-Ukrainian position or refusing to sign a contract with Rosatom — are being taken to underground premises and tortured.

Pankieiev: One of the reasons why Western countries have been hesitant to provide advanced weaponry to Ukraine to defend itself is because they are afraid that Russia can resort to a nuclear strike. What is your opinion about those fears? To what extent are they real — or is Moscow bluffing, considering what we have been observing for over a year and a half of the war?

Budjeryn: One thing that can be observed is that there hasn't been a nuclear use in Ukraine. There is a combination of reasons why it did not happen. There has been caution on the part of Western governments, particularly the United States, in how aid is provided. For instance, aiming to prevent escalation, Ukraine is prohibited from using Western systems on Russian territory. These delays and limitations have cost lives, not just in the Ukrainian armed forces but also among civilians. It could have cost Ukraine this counteroffensive. But it might have influenced the Russian calculus. The aid is relatively incremental — not one significant flood that would create the context for some drastic response. And the drastic response might be nuclear.

Another reason why Russia might not have used nuclear weapons in Ukraine was simply the difficulty of achieving its political goals with nuclear means. It has long been said that nuclear weapons are good for deterrence: they're suitable for threatening retaliation, dissuading the adversary from striking first—that's the primary use these days of nuclear weapons. However, as war-fighting implements to achieve *political ends*, nuclear weapons are of little help.

There are three scenarios of how Russia could use nuclear weapons in Ukraine. The first is a demonstration over the Black Sea or Arctic, but there are very important reasons against it. It would show that you're refraining from using these weapons seriously. There is also a chance that nobody's impressed; maybe all you do is encounter negative fallout from breaking that taboo against nuclear explosions, and you've achieved nothing.

The second scenario is battlefield use along the front line. Both NATO and the Soviet Union, back in the '60s, had operational plans for it. It was nothing but a numbers game and logistics. The longer your logistics lines stretch to the battlefield, the harder it is to deliver thousands of conventional artillery shells to continue barrages against enemy fortified positions. Or, as the option, a handful of tactical nuclear weapons to achieve the same goals. Militaries usually hate that scenario because it complicates the battlefield and hampers the prosecution of conventional operations. They have to have special gear and training to operate in a theatre affected by nuclear use. It's not so easy.

Unfortunately, the third one—which most likely would have been the most effective—is the use of nuclear weapons against a city. Putin's mention of Hiroshima and Nagasaki in his September speech a year ago (in connection with the annexation [of illegally occupied territories]) was not without a reason. The precedent of Hiroshima and Nagasaki was a nuclear weapons state using nuclear weapons against a non–nuclear weapons state to induce its unconditional surrender. The way the United States did it, they staggered it. They hit one city, Hiroshima, and announced that more is coming if you do not surrender. Then came the second one, Nagasaki. That's a scenario where I think—at a critical moment, already stressed by war in a significant way—Russia would cross that line and would use a nuclear weapon against a Ukrainian city.

It might be a mid-sized city—Vinnytsia or Odesa, for instance—and then they would say that Kyiv is next if Ukraine does not surrender. And that would be a tough decision for the Ukrainian leader and the Ukrainian people. I cannot quote the source, but I have it on good authority that about a year ago, at the end of September or early October, US intelligence assessed that the chance of Russia using a nuclear weapon in Ukraine was about 50%—that's a flip of a coin…that's probably the highest probability of intentional nuclear use that history has known.

That is not to say that, you know, nuclear use is inevitable. It is not to say that Ukraine should stop fighting or the West should stop supporting Ukraine; quite the opposite. It is necessary to take these threats seriously and consider what to do in order to prevent Russia from crossing that threshold. Whatever was communicated to Russia a year ago—whether by the United States or by China or India, or all of the above—seems to have worked to dissuade Russia from using nuclear weapons. But we cannot be entirely complacent that that would last indefinitely. What we see now is that Russia is ramping up the manufacture of conventional missiles and shells. This is a sign that Russia intends to continue waging a conventional war.

Pankieiev: How do you see the war unfolding in the near future? What scenarios do you see for its end, and what order might be established afterward?

Budjeryn: By now it is obvious that Russia did not achieve a quick and glorious territorial conquest. The war is turning into a long and arduous slog. We know from the history of warfare that wars are either short, and there are very few of those, or else protracted over multiple years. And there's very little in the middle.

It's apparent that Ukraine and Russia are in a long war now. We won't see the Kharkiv counteroffensive or the Kherson retreat again. Those were exceptions rather than rules. So whatever happens now is unforeseeable. There will be a continuation of conventional operations on both sides with varying intensity. There could be internal destabilization in Russia, although it would be imprudent to count on that for the termination of the war. There could be some other things that occur in the occupied territories. It could be the butterfly effect—something small that triggers a cascade on the Russian side.

Barring that, we've reached a stalemate on the battlefield, where neither side can push through. We had a very good article from General Valerii Zaluzhnyi in the *Economist*, who observed that with the means that Ukraine has, it has reached the limit of what it can achieve on the battlefield. If there's some miraculous package of armaments from the West that comes at the right time and the right combination of things, I think Ukraine might have the potential for another counteroffensive next spring. Depending on what that achieves, then by about 2025, the parties might have to sit down. And again, it will not be predicated by pressure from the outside; it would be Ukraine's decision. Ukrainians are bearing a very high cost, and the leadership supported by the people might decide that they cannot keep pouring costs into this, mainly lives. Then, at that point, the critical question for Ukraine's Western partners will be not just reaching an armistice and ceasefire but how to redraw European security architecture that includes Ukraine and protects it in such a way as to prevent another round of escalation from happening again in the foreseeable future—prevent Russia from rearming, recovering from this, and re-launching another invasion.

The "permissive factor" of the war was that Ukraine was in a security vacuum; it was not part of NATO, it was not protected by any deterrent, conventional or nuclear—not its own nor one extended by an ally. Ukraine's military has only just begun recovering from decades of looting and neglect, so Russian perception was that Ukraine would be easy prey. But it proved to be stronger than anyone expected, certainly stronger than Mr. Putin had expected. However, the perception of Ukrainian weakness was conducive to his decision to invade. How do you ensure that he is disabused from that notion ever again? The West has to be humble about what it can do about Russia, other than containing it. But the West can do a lot with Ukraine, which is willing and able to be integrated into Euro-Atlantic political and security structures.

We must assume that Russia will be there for a very long time and that its regime will remain the same and have the same political aims. It's up to them to change it, and we have minimal impact on it—"we" meaning the Ukrainians, the West, and everybody else. Given that Russia is going to continue to be that kind of Russia, what is it that you do with Ukraine—and also with Georgia,

Armenia, or Moldova? How do we fill that vacuum, and with what type of instruments of power can we dissuade Russia and prevent it from waging war again?

Once the security part is settled, it will be easier to encourage investment in Ukraine for economic reconstruction. Because without that security component, without ensuring that the plant that you're going to build today is not going to be destroyed by a Russian missile tomorrow, nobody's going to invest in Ukraine. You can freeze the front, but Russia would still have the missiles. It can hit Ukraine over the front. How you prevent that will be a crucial question upon which the rebuilding of the economy and critical infrastructure will hinge. And after, Ukraine can continue to battle its own demons to develop an open, democratic, and well-governed state. Nobody has cancelled the dysfunctions that Ukraine has acquired over the past 30 years. They also proved to be a "permissive factor" for Putin. So there's still a lot of work to be done on the political front—with which EU accession will help. But a firm security foundation is the real key to Ukraine's future.

CHAPTER 41

The field isn't "Slavic studies" at all—it should be called "Russian propaganda studies"— and a few exceptions only confirm the rule

Ewa Thompson

Interview with Oleksandr Pankieiev, published 21 December 2023

> Ewa M. Thompson is a Professor Emerita of Slavic Studies at Rice University, Houston. She received her undergraduate degree from the University of Warsaw and her doctorate from Vanderbilt University, Nashville. She is the author of the groundbreaking book *Imperial Knowledge: Russian Literature and Colonialism* (2000; Ukrainian transl. edn *Trubadury imperii*, 2006) Her books and articles have been translated into Polish, Ukrainian, Belarusan, Russian, Italian, Croatian, Czech, Hungarian, and Chinese. She has published scholarly articles in *Slavic Review*, *Slavic and European Journal*, *Modern Age*, *Teksty Drugie*, and other journals, and she has done consulting work for the National Endowment for the Humanities, the US Department of Education, and other institutions and foundations.

Pankieiev: What is *decolonization* for you? How do you define it in the framework of current events, particularly Russia's war against Ukraine?

Thompson: The definition of *colonialism* is more complex because some people consider colonialism to be one thing, and another group of people considers it something else. My definition of colonialism is the *military conquest of a certain nation*. I emphasize the word nation here and the process of drawing out of that nation's economic, political, and cultural powers. In other words, you first have to have nations in order to have colonialism. The conquests of Alexander the Great were not colonialism because, in those days, people were thinking about belonging to a certain king, prince, or tribal leader—they didn't have this consciousness that they were members of a nation. But in the 18th century, nations began to congeal, some of them faster, some of them slower. Still, they were already groups of people who realized that they belonged together for linguistic, cultural, and other reasons.

To decolonize, you first have to look at the problems that colonialism caused. Colonialism means economic exploitation. The Muscovites have been trying to hide this, and persuade, the Russian population, that they supported those other nations that were part of the Soviet Union. But that's not true—it's just the opposite! Those nations that Russia conquered were primarily supporting the Russian efforts in the military area.

Colonialism also means political exploitation. Those nations were present on the international stage only through Russia. In other words, they were not present. Russia stole their voices; it was only Russia that could speak for them in the international arena. Then there is something that is sometimes described as *soft power*—a nation's ability (again we're talking about nations) to influence world affairs or some specific issue. For instance, Russia had enormous soft power during the Soviet period, and it still does have soft power, but this soft power is held at the expense of the nations Russia conquered. Soft power was taken away from conquered nations and handed to the victorious nation.

What does a nation-country need to do to decolonize its territory? Firstly, they need to stop economic exploitation and start building economic identity and independence. Secondly, they also need to start speaking for themselves in the international arena. They have to stop allowing the colonizer to tell the world about them. And I must tell you, the Ukrainians are doing a marvellous job. I look at them with admiration and envy. This is what decolonization means, as they say: "I am beginning to speak for myself, and I don't want Moscow to speak for me."

These are just general terms. How to do it in practice, of course, is something we all are thinking about. You begin to exist in the world when you tell the world about your identity. And Ukrainians have already achieved quite a bit in this area. They have already succeeded in teaching the world that they exist, which is the first and most important part of decolonization. You make the world listen to you, and you support your own native art, literature, and political writings. And of course, at the same time you build the economic power that has to stand behind those artistic and humanistic achievements.

Pankieiev: How did the field of Slavic studies in North America get colonized? Who, in your opinion, contributed to it? And how?

Thompson: This is one of my favourite topics. And of course, I'll be very politically incorrect. I spent my life in American academia. When I was a student in the 60s, American academia would absorb anybody who spoke Russian because very few people knew Russian. If Russia wanted to send its spies to America and make them go through universities, the opportunity was there. So, quite a few people came from the Soviet Union. Some of them were real refugees. Some of them were not. And these people began to build up what we can call "Russian studies" at American universities.

After that came some famous people. Some of them were born and raised in the United States—and were already taught by those from Moscow. Others came directly from the Soviet Union. And they taught American students about the Russian Empire, pre-Soviet Russia, and Soviet Russia.

I want to mention three people here who have done a lot of harm in falsifying the American vision of what Russia is. One of them is Nicholas Riasanovsky. He was a native Russian, spent his life in the United States, and wrote a history of Russia that had at least ten editions. The publisher was very respectable: Oxford University Press.

But if you look at the history of Russia—starting with the 18th century, when real colonialism began—it's unbelievable how he describes it. The partitions of Poland that gave Russia almost the entirety of Ukraine, Belarus, Lithuania, and Estonia and vast parts of Poland are described as "changes in the Western frontier." In other words, he omits the struggles, the complications, and the brutality of Russia and Prussia in cannibalizing Poland. These were the most critical events in the 18th century. Since Russia and Prussia dominated the discourse about Central Europe, European intellectuals never learned the facts of Central and Eastern European history. Therefore, this is how Nicholas Riasanovsky presented the 18th century.

And then, when it came to the aggression of Russia against Poland in 1939, he again described it as a "rectification of the Western frontier." In other words, the Nazis, when they started attacking Poland in 1939, were also wanting to rectify the frontier? This is the kind of vision of Central and Eastern Europe that Nicholas Riasanovsky left to American students. In sum, this is how Slavic studies were falsified from the beginning.

The second person I would like to mention is Steven Cohen, for many decades a political scientist and historian at Princeton. About five years before the disintegration of the Soviet Union, he published a book titled *Rethinking the Soviet Experience: Politics and History since 1917*, in which he argued that the Soviet Union is powerful and will last forever. And that it's a great country to be friends with.

The end of the Soviet Union came around 1990. Did Mr. Cohen apologize to the Slavic profession? Did he say "Sorry, I was wrong"? Not at all. He remained an authority. He moved from Princeton to New York University later on. And this is the kind of vision of Russia and the Soviet Union that he left as a gift to future generations.

And the third person is Dmitri Trenin. As a student and a young assistant professor, I remember seeing Trenin at various Slavics meetings in the 70s. And of course, he was a professor and writer, worked for the Carnegie Foundation, and later became head of it in Moscow. In 2019 he wrote a book saying that Russia is not at all an enemy of the United States and that the United States should not be afraid of Russia.

With this background, the people who graduated in Slavic studies in all those years in America were under the influence of mendacious and dangerous falsifications of Russian history. So that's one problem we've had, because we hired anybody who spoke Russian and had some competence in Russian history. These three people were in that category, and they were among the best—they were in the Ivy League circle! And they were the authority to many of us who were somewhere in the provinces. Truly, Slavic studies in America require a massive reform. How to do it is another issue, but this is how Slavic studies look. In other words, they're not Slavic studies—they're *Russian propaganda studies*.

Pankieiev: What are the main consequences of the colonization of Slavic studies that still prevail in academia?

Thompson: If you have a false image of a country, and if you do not realize that this country is very aggressive and uses not just free but also paid propaganda—you probably have a distorted vision of what's happening in the world. For instance, Patrick Buchanan, one of the famous American conservatives, says that Russia is such a conservative, good country, and Ukraine should just be put under the Russian boot. Even though people like him didn't study under

Cohen, Riasanovsky, or Trenin, they are the fruits of their efforts, and this is the kind of mind they worked to create. Thus, you have influential people who are very much unaware of the destructive role that tsarist and Soviet Communist Russia has played in Europe and the world.

Pankieiev: What are the main narratives in the current decolonization discourse? What is at the forefront of the discussion?

Thompson: What I have noticed in some of the attempts at decolonization is a hijacking of decolonization studies and using them as a support for some other studies, like feminist or sexual minority studies. Decolonization doesn't actually have much to do with sexual minorities or with other areas that may be of interest to some.

We've also seen a sudden change in the Association for Slavic, East European, and Eurasian Studies, which has existed all these years and has supported colonial attitudes towards Central and Eastern Europe. Recently, though, a convention of this association was dedicated to decolonization. Also, there appeared online some seminars dealing with that subject. So, there is a certain amount of change in the orientation of academic circles that previously were very much satisfied with making Russia the center of their study and completely ignoring nations like Ukraine. But I still haven't seen any serious attempts to reanalyze Russian literature, history, and to reinterpret Russian political attitudes. This is still to come.

Pankieiev: Are there any misconceptions about the decolonization of Russian history that you can see now in academia and public discourses? Some people say that it is not something we need to do, while others argue that it has already been decolonized.

Thompson: Those false statements have been made thousands of times. In order to undo the damage, you need a generation and you need many books. The fact that somebody will write an article, develop a theory, or lecture about something will not decolonize Slavic studies. If somebody says that we have already done it, this person doesn't realize the depth of destruction that colonialism has caused in those countries that Russia conquered and tried to make into its own.

There is also the fact that we're still struggling with the problem of language. Until recently, before the Russo-Ukrainian war,

Ukrainian as a language was basically nonexistent in Slavic studies. There were some places where émigré Ukrainians themselves gathered enough funds to introduce some Ukrainian courses. But generally, Ukrainian was completely omitted from Slavic studies per se. So, decolonization cannot be achieved by writing one book. The fact that we still do not have that done properly shows that we're far from decolonizing the discourse about Russia as a conqueror.

Pankieiev: What kinds of steps toward decolonization of the field do we need to take, particularly in how courses are being taught at universities?

Thompson: We need first to re-examine the history of Eastern Europe — what I call "non-Germanic Central Europe." It is a very delicate problem because some nations have different versions of the history of that area. And the worst that can happen is that those other nations, non-Russian nations, start quarrelling about how to present their history. You need to get some kind of get-together, some agreed version of this revised history before it is introduced in the academic world. But the first thing is simply courses; you must introduce Ukrainian, Polish, and Baltic history courses. And that means you have to reduce some courses in Russian history, although the new courses will of course hardly ignore or eliminate Russia's historical role in the region.

In many cases — maybe not regarding history but certainly regarding literature — there are courses that I would simply remove from view completely. Russian literature is not very good when you take away Tolstoy and Dostoevsky. Regarding the amount of literary works in existence, Russian literature is certainly smaller than British, German, French, or even Polish literature. And yet, we sometimes treat Russia as if it were as productive as France or Great Britain.

Furthermore, we need to remove certain courses that deal with trivial things, such as, for instance, Pushkin's poetics. There are many books on the subject, yet they say very little. Remove those courses and introduce courses in Ukrainian literature, Eastern European literature, or whatever the scholar is working on. And there has to be pressure put on university administrators to introduce those courses and remove certain others. Of course, the people who teach Russian will resist strongly, but that is the way it has to be done.

CHAPTER 42

Time is on Ukraine's side in this war

Mitchell Orenstein

Interview with Oleksandr Pankieiev, published 3 February 2024

Mitchell A. Orenstein (PhD, political science, Yale University, 1996) is a professor of Russian and East European studies at the University of Pennsylvania and a senior fellow of the Eurasia Program at the Foreign Policy Research Institute, Philadelphia. The most recent of his many published works are *From Triumph to Crisis: Neoliberal Economic Reform in Postcommunist Countries* (co-authored, 2018), *The Lands in Between: Russia vs. the West and the New Politics of Hybrid War* (2019), and *Taking Stock of Shock: Social Consequences of the 1989 Revolutions* (co-authored, 2021).

Pankieiev: Russia's decision to start its escalated invasion of Ukraine in 2022 was heavily determined by its calculations regarding Europe's dependence on its energy resources and presumed political influence in some EU countries. Nearing a full two years since the full-scale invasion, what is your evaluation of the EU's efforts to reduce its dependence on Russia in energy and other sectors?

Orenstein: I believe that the European Union has done a very good job of reducing dependence on Russian energy. The REpowerEU program, a medium- and long-term plan enacted in May 2022, had several successful elements. One was to diversify gas sources: build LNG terminals, reorient pipelines, and enable gas to come from different suppliers. Slapping a price cap on Russian oil was also instrumental. In the first winter, Europe also reduced energy usage by 15% or even 20% for some countries.

The medium-term objective is to increase reliance on renewable sources, which will significantly impact Europe. The expectation is to have 45% of overall energy through renewables by 2030, resulting in a new era for Europe where it can be more self-sufficient in energy.

All of these ideas were based on a longstanding history of cooperation on energy in Europe, since about 2006 or 2009. That's why they were able to move so quickly in 2022, and I believe that prolonged the war.

Ultimately, starving Europe of fuel was a Russian gambit to weaken Western support for Ukraine. Russia has failed to achieve its objectives on the battlefield in Ukraine. It was unable to capture Kyiv in three days, conquer the entire country, or achieve the very broad goals that Putin has made. Instead, Russia is now focused on holding on to the 17.5% of territory that it currently occupies and moving marginally beyond that. Therefore, Russia has used various gambits to try to shorten the war. Most of these can be put under the category of convincing the West that it doesn't really want to fight this war and persuading the West to stop supporting Ukraine and sue for peace.

I think that Russia expected that the West would give way because it did so several times before. We can look at the Minsk agreements in that light. Russia grabbed some territory. Europe wasn't interested in fighting, so Russia convinced European leaders to put a fig leaf over these conquests and reach some sort of agreement to stop fighting, while Russia's territorial gains remain intact. The same thing happened in Georgia in 2008. Nicolas Sarkozy came to represent the European Union and pushed through the agreement that there would be no more fighting, although it didn't solve Georgia's problems. Russia thought that more or less the same deal would be accepted by the West and underestimated the extent to which Western countries were shocked by Russia's full-scale invasion in 2022. This time, the reaction has been very different. Europe has become a very strong partner for Ukraine and has committed to taking Ukraine into the European Union. That's a really important step.

Essentially, Russia's gambit last winter had been to starve Europe of fuel and thus force Europe to realize that it's going to hurt its own economy, sue for peace, and say, "Ukraine, stop fighting, let's freeze this war." Europe, to its credit, did not do that. The EU members fought back and effectively won the gas war in Europe. This winter, as I understand, they are storing a lot of gas, which will enable them to get through it. The result of all that is that the war got lengthened. Russia's gambit failed: from the beginning it wanted a quick end to the war, and that has been denied.

Now we're in a situation where Russia has another gambit to win—this time in the US Congress. Russia is looking to convince some legislators somehow, primarily Republican ones, that they love Putin or that they're getting some benefit from Russia winning—that they don't like Ukraine—to hold up some deal for financing Ukraine, and then eventually Ukraine will have to sue for peace. We'll see how far that gambit goes. I hear different things about it from DC. The latest I heard sounded optimistic that the US will eventually provide these funds.

In any case, Russia is continuing to deploy more gambits. Russia is arguably responsible for inflaming wars elsewhere today in order to force the US to sue for peace or to get distracted by those wars—for instance, the war in Gaza and the conflict with the Houthis. Destabilization of the Middle East is a strategy to increase the price of oil and harm competitors. But in any case, the gas gambit in Europe failed for Russia, and hopefully it was only another of several failed gambits to end the war.

Pankieiev: To what extent has the EU's transition to alternative energy resources and the number of sanctions placed on Russia successfully reduced Russia's ability to finance its war efforts in Ukraine? Can we say that enough has been done to reduce Russia's capability to conduct its war in Ukraine?

Orenstein: Certainly not. The sanctions debate is complicated, because in any sanction situation some people always claim that the sanctions aren't working and that we should drop them. Usually, those claims are made because somebody has some sort of financial or geopolitical interest. And it is very easy to downplay the extent to which sanctions are working. I've recently seen apparently convincing arguments on both sides. Some people are saying that the sanctions are being broken and that they're very hard to enforce—that we're doing a terrible job and the Russian economy is doing well. And then other reports that I also highly regard say that Russian industry is in a horrible state. There are blackouts in Moscow, and Putin is very worried about the economy and can't pay for everything. There's a possibility of social discontent. I suspect that the answer is probably a little bit of both. There might be some truth to both of these perspectives.

And then there's a complicated question when assessing the effect of sanctions: What do we mean when we say the sanctions aren't working? One answer is that Russia keeps on doing what it's doing, so it's obviously not affected by sanctions. And that's often seen as a persuasive argument. But I would point out that military tactics also have not defeated Russia.

I see sanctions as an important tool. I think that on one hand, they're symbolic in the sense of cutting Russia off from the global economy. On the other, they're a very practical way of saying that we won't pay for the war effort. But it's clear that they are harming the Russian economy. I don't think there's any world in which you could really say that Russia has not been harmed—*it has been harmed*. Has Russia been harmed enough that it stops the war? No. However, the sanctions have substantially impacted arms production and Russia's ability to prosecute the war. So, sanctions are an important tool that has made a difference.

Pankieiev: In one of your published texts, you say that the logic of sanctions is to increase the chances of a political and social reaction from within that would challenge Putin. Evgeniy Prigozhin's mutiny ended with his assassination. Protests in Dagestan and Bashkortostan just a few days ago were immediately suppressed. What do you make of this? Do you see any real indications that Putin's regime is indeed crumbling?

Orenstein: Right now, it does look like Putin is not facing any substantial challenges. But the thing about social unrest is that we don't really know until it happens. In Russia, social change happens very suddenly after long periods of nothing much happening. It's very hard to assess.

The sanctions are having an impact on Russia's economy and output. One of the ways that sanctions work is by reducing the economic power of a country, reducing its resources, making it less able to fight the war, and particularly by reducing its arms industry—a lot of the sanctions are targeted against the arms industry. I think there's a fair case to be made that Russia has not been able to produce as many weapons, or of as high a quality, and that sanctions have probably had a substantial impact.

But then there's also the question whether sanctions make it more likely that average people will oppose the war? I think that under all these logics the answer is yes, eventually. The crux of the question is whether society and leadership are coming around to the position that this war isn't really worth pursuing. Unfortunately, the weakness of that argument is that Putin seems ideologically, even messianically driven to subjugate Ukraine. It seems crazy that he invaded the country and thought he was going to win. Today, it feels like he's backed into a corner and this is something he has to do for the purpose of his legacy. If he's not thinking rationally and this is a mission he's on, it becomes hard to imagine how he could change his mind. And how much social unrest would it take? In the Winter War of 1939/40 Russia lost about half a million troops, and at that point, Russia decided there was not much utility in fighting further. I don't know if the same number would apply in Ukraine, but it may be.

It's a conundrum to understand their strategy overall and when social unrest might occur. Both are hard to predict. But I do think that that is part of the rationale.

Pankieiev: Just a few days ago, Putin openly acknowledged that he is not planning to give up what he explicitly called "conquered territories." In that case, what kind of peace is there going to be if he's not going to give up those territories? That was the first time Putin was really explicit about the goals of his invasion.

Orenstein: It's obviously an imperial mindset, which many of us have been discussing for a long time. It's still striking to see the risks that Putin was willing to take, and the damage to people's lives and property, in order to achieve some sort of goal, which he presents as messianic or religious in character.

Putin seems to have settled on projecting an image of himself as Russia's saviour, who has to maintain Ukraine under Russian control and unite Belarus, Ukraine, and Russia.

Pankieiev: The United States have been one of the biggest supporters of Ukraine so far. Now the Republicans in Congress are blocking emergency funding for Ukraine. This year the US will also have presidential elections, and many pundits don't exclude the possibility of Trump getting elected. What is your evaluation of the situation for Ukraine if the US steps out of the game?

Orenstein: That's very hard to predict. Trump keeps saying, "Oh, I'll solve this problem really quick," and people assume that he means he's going to betray Ukraine somehow or he's going to pull out of NATO. I think that our experience with Trump's presidential term was different, though. Trump definitely had some type of affinity with Russia: he apparently had real estate deals that he wanted to happen there; he never personally criticized Vladimir Putin, which was very strange; and he seemed grateful to Putin for supporting his election campaign. While direct collusion was not proven in the famous Mueller report, it *was* found that Russia made efforts to aid Trump's campaign.

At the same time, Trump would argue—and did argue, and it is true—that he did more for Ukraine than Obama had done in terms of providing weapons. He provided the anti-tank missiles that Obama was afraid to provide, and his government was also strong on sanctions against Russia—all those claims are true.

How I understand Trump—and this is different from most people—is really grounded in my book *The Lands in Between*, which looks at "in-between-type" political actors, who want to have it both ways. They want to be "allied": they want to gain benefits from Russia and gain benefits from the West at the same time. I do think that some trades and bargains were made with Russia. At the same time, I don't think it would be fair to characterize Trump as a complete patsy to Russia or a complete ally of Russia. He also understood that his value as a broker in that relationship would be greater if the US was vigorously challenging Russia. Because if you're not a problem to Russia, why would they pay you anything? Why would they help you out? They don't expect to gain anything from you if you're giving them everything they want. Ideally, these actors want to win resources from both sides.

This is not unique to Trump. It's a game that's played by some politicians in Ukraine, and it's also probably played in all countries in Europe. You find a lot of politicians who are big NATO allies on the one hand, and on the other they are ready to make a deal with Russia easily.

So I think that Trump's in that camp; as a result, he's that in-between type of leader. We don't know exactly what he would do. Even after the fact, it's hard to know what he did in the 2016-20 period; it's not 100% clear yet. And I'm not sure that we know enough to know exactly whether he would sell out of Ukraine or not.

Similarly, people are saying that he was ready to pull out of NATO. He does say that, but Trump often adds "unless NATO countries do X, Y, and Z." He wants them to spend more money on defence—which would be rather positive for Ukraine overall. If Europe were spending more on defence, then Ukraine would be better defended.

Pankieiev: What kind of support does Ukraine need to win the war? And what kind of victory should it be?

Orenstein: The European Union has been very clear that it wants Ukraine to have 100% of its national territory controlled by Ukraine, and it wants Russia out. I think that is the objective for most people in Ukraine and in the West.

In terms of what type of support Ukraine needs, if I were more of a military strategist, I'd be looking at ways to move this beyond trench warfare and seek air superiority in the next stage. I think Ukraine has recently relied more on sabotage in the rear of the Russian lines, of knocking down supply lines. With the F16s arriving, the hope is that Ukraine can attain air superiority, at least in part of the country.

As for the other related question, I would be thinking about how to get around these lines. You could probably do that, but you'd have to go through Russia or the seas. What has been preventing getting around the lines is NATO's concern that its weapons are not used to launch any attack on Russian territory. The West is concerned about starting World War III with Russia.

The West has placed constraints on what Ukraine can do and perhaps it does need to operate within those constraints. But if you want to win the war, you might want to actually change the constraints and find some way out of the situation. The key thing would probably be air and naval superiority, and degrading supply lines.

I mentioned earlier that the war getting prolonged has not helped Russia. Has it helped Ukraine? I don't know. My intuition is that the longer this goes on, it's not really Russia that has time on its side. I think that time is probably on the side of Ukraine in this war, as long as it has solid backing from its Western partners.

CHAPTER 43

Invasion of Ukraine has proved to be a disastrous decision

Rajan Menon

Interview with Oleksandr Pankieiev, published 15 February 2024

> Rajan Menon is the Anne and Bernard Spitzer Chair in Political Science Emeritus at the City College of New York. He is also a senior research scholar at the Arnold A. Saltzman Institute of War and Peace Studies at Columbia University.

Pankieiev: This February marks ten years since the start of the Russo-Ukrainian war and two years since the start of its full-scale stage. Has this war made you fundamentally reconsider any notions or theoretical frameworks?

Menon: I've long believed that the US has been unwilling to allow any external power to establish itself in our hemisphere—the Western Hemisphere—since almost the founding of the country. But Russia has a certain proprietorial vision of the former Soviet states, especially Ukraine. I think that for historical, strategic, and cultural reasons, it's very difficult for Russian nationalists—and Putin is one—to conceive of Ukraine as an independent country. So I've never doubted that Russia wants to keep Ukraine within its sphere.

In 2008, when NATO opened its door in principle for Ukraine to join the alliance, tensions about where Ukraine would "belong"—to the West, the East, or Russia—became much more controversial. At the time, I was not a proponent of NATO enlargement, because I understood that when alliances intrude on what great powers think, rightly or wrongly, is their sphere of influence, there will be some backlash.

Where my thinking has changed with my fellow realists is on the following point. On 24 February 2022, when Putin invaded Ukraine, there was no evidence that Ukraine was any closer to joining NATO in 2022 than in 2008. Thus, I simply do not find the argument that he had to invade Ukraine to stop it from joining NATO to be credible.

I think that NATO could not have mustered the unanimity required to admit Ukraine. NATO did a disservice to Ukraine by promising that the door was open and they would be admitted and then keeping them waiting for 14 years. It was not a very smart thing to do. They either should have said yes and moved quickly or just said no and clarified things. My departure from my previous view concerns the question of what triggered the invasion. I do not think it had to do with Ukraine's prospects for joining NATO.

I also have an alternative theory that does not rest on evidence, but let me share it. Putin went into complete isolation during the COVID period. Very few people were able to see him. He demanded that documents be brought to him from the Russian archives. We know that he was reading widely about [the imperial rulers] Catherine II and Peter I. He was maybe thinking about his mortality, about his legacy. I think he wanted one of his legacies to be for Ukraine to be brought back into the Russian sphere. This is a hunch, but it's the only alternative explanation I can arrive at as to why the full invasion happened when it happened. Frankly, I was stunned. I did not think he would fully invade a sovereign country, but he did, and he expected a quick victory.

Pankieiev: In one of your essays you called Russia's war against Ukraine the war of surprises. I'm curious about the part that involves Ukraine. Why was Ukraine's resistance to Russia's aggression surprising to many experts in the West, particularly after Ukraine had two popular revolutions?

Menon: It did not surprise me that the Ukrainians would resist a Russian invasion. Generally, when you invade another people's country, you're challenging their right to exist, and there will be resistance. What I did not expect was how poor the Russian military preparations were and how hubristic they were in thinking they would march into Kyiv and install someone like Viktor Medvedchuk in place of Zelensky. And I underestimated the success with which Ukraine not only pushed the Russians from the gates of Kyiv by April but also cleared the Russian army from most of the north, including areas as far north as Chernihiv. So, the Ukrainians resisted — and in such a way that the Russian Army was turned back.

This resistance occurred successfully before Western arms started flowing into Ukraine in a major way. The Western assessment, for example from Mark Milley, then chairman of the American Joint Chiefs of Staff, was that Kyiv would be taken in 72 hours. He was not the only one saying this. To be honest with you, I thought the Russians would prevail because they had a massive advantage in everything. That's why their failure somewhat surprised me. Although I never expected the Ukrainians just to capitulate. I didn't expect, for example, [the Sudetenland,] Czechoslovakia, in 1938.

Pankieiev: One of Putin's miscalculations was that when he started the full-scale invasion, he thought it would be easy to take control of the regions of Ukraine where many people speak Russian. His Federal Security Service spent hundreds of millions to infiltrate those regions with agents and gain local population support. But as we see now, controlling those occupied territories is challenging for him too. News from those regions indicates that resistance and partisan movements within those territories are consistent and growing.

Menon: Just a couple of thoughts on this. Despite the reputation that he's now gained, Putin is not actually a person who takes big risks. The 2008 war against Georgia was not a risk. The 2015 intervention in Syria was not a risk, because he didn't put ground troops down. Crimea 2014 was not a risk either—it is geographically close to Russia and Ukraine's only Russian-majority province (two-thirds of the population and by some counts closer to three-fourths) with thousands of retired Soviet army personnel. I should also add Russia had a naval base on lease from Ukraine there at the time.

Putin's invasion of Ukraine has proved to be a disastrous decision. But from his point of view, it wasn't a risk, because all the intelligence that Russia had on the ground suggested the Ukrainians would welcome the Russian army, much like the Soviets thought the Afghans would welcome them in 1979. One of the reasons they assembled a small force relative to Ukraine's size was that they expected a quick victory. I have friends in the Ukrainian military who tell me that when they looked inside Russia's destroyed tanks and armoured personnel carriers, they found parade uniforms. Rumour had it that a few days before the start of the full-scale invasion, they even called Kyiv's swanky restaurants to make reservations to celebrate their quick capture of the city. There's no question that they were shocked at Ukraine's resistance.

Regarding Russophone Ukraine, this is a highly complex question, and many misunderstandings exist in the West about it. If you look at, for example, the election that Yanukovych won, the election results are pretty clear that the Party of the Regions did much better in the east and south than elsewhere. But the idea that there is a split Ukraine is vastly overplayed.

I've been to Ukraine four times since the full-scale invasion began. I just came back last December. I've been there many times before. I don't speak Ukrainian and have never presented myself as a Ukrainian expert. But I do know that I have talked to Ukrainian soldiers on the front lines in the east and in the south who spoke to me in Russian. I thought they were speaking to me in Russian because I don't know Ukrainian, but then I noticed that they were speaking to each other in Russian, yet fighting the Russian army. This idea that everybody in the east and the south is pro-Russian and waiting to be liberated is a myth, one that Putin believed and wanted us to believe.

And finally, which parts of Ukraine have been devastated the most by the Russian invasion? It's the very areas that Putin claims he is the saviour of! It's a very strange thing, but I think he fell victim to this notion of being a saviour.

I sometimes tell friends, only partly joking, that in a weird way, Putin has been unwittingly, that is, accidentally, one of the main contributors to modern Ukrainian nationalism. He has reformed and reframed a Ukrainian identity that is stronger than before. Let's assume that the war ends — now, I'm not predicting this, especially because American aid is now in doubt — with Russia retaining some proportion of Ukraine's territory. Whatever remains of Ukraine, and quite a bit will remain, will irrevocably lean Westward. Young Ukrainians will all learn English or European languages, with their entire outlook toward the West. In that sense, no matter the military outcome of the war, Putin has lost Ukraine. There's not going to be a Ukraine heading toward Russia. The defining characteristic of Ukrainian nationalism will be opposition to Russia.

Pankieiev: In your other essay, you say that it's time for Europe to get serious about its own defence. And we know why it's time. In the US, Trump's election is becoming a possible reality. What is the situation with Ukraine's security framework in this environment?

Menon: Trump has won the Iowa caucuses, he's won New Hampshire, and he will likely beat Nikki Haley handily in her own state, South Carolina. Trump's nomination is almost unstoppable. There is no question that the Republican Party, or large sections of it, are in his control. I could be wrong, but I don't think Congress will vote on the proposed military aid bill, where the border issue and Ukraine are tied together, until they know who's going to be the president. That's because the Republicans don't want to take a step without Trump.

We're talking about $40 billion or so of military assistance. Ukraine will fight on even if that bill doesn't deliver the assistance, but its ability to fight will be significantly diminished. It doesn't matter how brave Ukrainians are or how good their generals like Zaluzhnyi and Syrskyi are when you need artillery, armour, and air support to fight the Russians. If the aid doesn't come through, it's going to be a terrible thing.

And for all the talk that Putin's sending out feelers for negotiation, he's simply trying to play with the political climate. He won't make any serious decision on the war until he sees who will be the president in November. I hope it isn't true, but I think it will be Trump. I'd be delighted to be proven wrong. Because Trump's election is not only bad for Ukraine, it's terrible for the United States.

What does Trump's election mean for Europe? One can make the case that the future of Ukraine matters to the United States, but it matters much more to Europe, especially to the eastern flank of the EU. For example, despite all of the historic tensions between Poland and Ukraine, Poland has now been one of Ukraine's biggest supporters. If Russia dominates Ukraine, Russia becomes a neighbour of Poland. The same is true of Finland; they have a long border with Russia.

The problem is that if the United States aid does dry up and is still not 100% certain, Europe can only partially replace the United States as a supplier. The US provides more military aid (not economic aid) than all the European countries. Europe has to do some severe calculations on ramping up defence expenditure and boosting military industries, but it may not be able to do that in time. I think the lesson is that Europe's long dependence on the United States gave it the luxury of engaging in some form of military minimalism. If the US decides it is going to stop supporting Ukraine, Europe has a big decision to make. Does it achieve more strategic autonomy? I don't mean outside NATO necessarily; I don't mean that the US and Europe should stop being partners. But within NATO there has to be a much different division of labour, and Europe has to do more. Europe has the resources and technology for it.

Pankieiev: All wars end sooner or later. For Ukraine, it is crucial not only to end this war, but also to make sure that it won't be repeated again. What security frameworks are available for Ukraine now? And what are their pros and cons?

Menon: The ideal scenario for Ukrainians is to end the war by regaining all its territories back to the 2014 lines and by joining NATO. I understand that desire; if I were Ukrainian, I would want the same thing. There are two things about this. Despite the invasion, I'm still not convinced that NATO will achieve the unanimity it requires to admit Ukraine. Now, you might say, "This is different between 2008 and 2022, because Russia has now shown that it's capable of invading Ukraine." But you could turn that argument on its head and say, "Well, the lesson that the Europeans have learned is that Russia could actually invade Ukraine and Ukraine would invoke Article V of NATO's 1949 founding treaty, and Europe would be at war with Russia." Plus, you have people like Robert Fico in Slovakia and Viktor Orbán in Hungary. I'm not sure exactly what the Germans and the French feel. That's why I think that the question of NATO membership for Ukraine is not necessarily a done deal, but I understand why my Ukrainian friends, who don't like to be told this because it's news that they don't want to hear.

So, what does that mean? It means either a security guarantee for Ukraine by a collection of other powers (not necessarily all from Europe) or a security guarantee by some subset of European NATO members acting independently: Poland, Finland and others. Or it means that Ukraine opts for armed neutrality but reserves the right to train its forces and equip itself from any source it chooses, without restriction; of course, all those sources would be from the West.

And from this war I have learned two things. First, the Ukrainian army has a lot of morale, has outstanding generals, and has learned very quickly how to fight what was supposed to be the world's only other military superpower. I've also learned that the Russian army was different from what we thought it was. If you look at the battles of Avdiivka or Vuhledar, the Russians suffered enormous losses.

As an American, it's easy for me to say that Ukraine will be fine with armed neutrality. I understand entirely why Ukrainians wouldn't be willing to take that risk and why they believe that NATO is the only guarantee that works. I'm merely pointing out that it's not clear to me that even after the Russian invasion, the membership of Ukrainians in NATO will be signed, sealed, delivered, and tied up in a nice ribbon. Those are the alternative possibilities.

Pankieiev: But what about how the West actually wants Ukraine to end the war?

Menon: The West will be comfortable going back to the lines of 24 February 2022. When it comes to retaking Crimea, I expect some more ambivalence. The West is trying to balance two things. On the one hand, it is supporting Ukraine, but not to the point where Western weapons can be used to strike Russian territory. On the other hand, it is up to reducing the prospects of escalation.

I think escalation is not as big a danger as generally believed. But what I think doesn't matter. It's what people like Jake Sullivan, Biden, Blinken, and Defense Secretary Austin think. It seems to me that they're very cognizant of this risk. They believe that if Ukraine attempts to [liberate] Crimea, NATO will cross a threshold that makes escalation more likely. So, they are less keen on returning to the 2014 lines than the 2022 lines. Now, has anybody said this? Is there a document? Of course they won't say it. You can't be supporting Ukraine and saying that "our objective is only to return to the February 2022 lines" — why give Putin that gift? But I sense that that is what is going on in the minds of Western policymakers.

Pankieiev: What surprises are you expecting from this war?

Menon: Most people think that the Russians, having invaded Ukraine one time, will take what in Russian is called a *peredyshka*, a deep breath, and then invade again. Because they ran into resistance they didn't expect and lost their best equipment, any Russian leader, Putin included, will think long and hard before trying this again. Because one thing is clear: Ukraine is a formidable nation capable of defending itself. Whether it belongs to NATO or not, Ukraine's future defence ties will be in the West. Ukraine's going to have a Western-trained army. Its army is already substantially Western in orientation. It will have much more Western equipment. The proportion of Russian-Soviet equipment will diminish to almost nothing in 20 years. And so Ukraine will be an even tougher nut to crack. I don't know if this qualifies as a surprise, but my surprising conclusion is that while most people think it's only a matter of time before the Russians try again, I'm not so sure.

The other surprise is how wrong we were in how we judged Russia's capacity to fight. Our approaches to the assessment of Russia as a center and military power will have to be rethought. I think it's been sobering not only for us but also for them. To be honest with you, I'm not entirely surprised by this, because even back in the Soviet days, I raised questions about whether the Soviet Army was indeed as powerful as it appeared. I've also argued that Russia is not comparable to China or the United States, because it has a much smaller GDP. It primarily exports oil. If you look in your home or your office, how many products do you find that are Russian-made? I bet there are none. You find Korean automobiles, Japanese automobiles, Chinese equipment, etc., but you don't find Russian equipment. That is not the hallmark of an ascendant power.

And Russia has a growth problem. Oil and gas, which are its mainstays, will eventually, slowly be replaced by alternative technologies. So the question is, what will be their main export? I doubt that they're going to be exporting nanotechnology to Western markets. When I say this, people suggest I'm short-selling the Russians, insulting them or denigrating them. No, I'm not. I'm just saying to look around your house and your friends' houses. And tell me, do you see automobiles, washing machines, computers, coffee makers, or anything else from Russia? And the question is: why not?

≈ ≈ ≈

Index of Names

A

Abdullaev, Shamshad 50
Abkhazia 15, 337
Additional Protocol (IAEA) 216, 217
Afghanistan, Afghans 139, 150, 381
Africa, African 94, 119, 120, 121, 123, 235, 244, 280, 324.
 See also MENA, South Africa
African Union 123
AI xiii, 225
Akhmetov, Renat 246
Al-Assad, Bashar 239
Alexander the Great 365
Alexander, Tsar 24
Alleg, Henri 265
Amelina, Victoria 315, 336
AMRAAM 257
Andrukhovych, Yuri 91, 353
Arctic 361
Areva 215
Armed Forces of Ukraine 8, 32, 73, 106, 134, 341
Armenians 338
Aseyev, Stanislav 263, 265
Asia 94, 164, 235, 348
Åslund, Anders 267, 269
Association Agreement between Ukraine and the EU 100, 116
Association for Slavic, East European, and Eurasian Studies 369
Austin, Lloyd 385
Avdiivka 248, 385
Azerbaijanis 338
Azovstal 325, 326

B

Bakhmatiuk, Oleh 306
Bakhmut 10, 128, 201, 202, 203, 204, 248, 315
Baku 339
Balakliia-Kupiansk 129
Balkan wars xiii
Baltic states 11, 35, 39, 40, 41, 43, 45, 121, 223

Bandera, Stepan 91
Banderites 91
Bashkortostan 231, 374
Bavarians 302
Bayraktar 34, 180
BBC 183, 247, 328
Beijing 117, 220, 224, 270
Belarus, Belarusan 41, 43, 52, 82, 83, 84, 103, 114, 263, 367, 375
Belgians 187
Berlin 35, 88, 155, 230, 302
Biden, Joe 41, 133, 199, 200, 201, 241, 385
bin Laden, Osama 329
Black Sea 138, 179, 180, 182, 236, 258, 361
Black Sea Grain Initiative 180, 183
Blinken, Antony 385
Bolshevik 26, 27, 66, 93, 242
Borowski, Tadeusz 265
Bosnia; Bosniaks 191 193, 339
Brazil 244
Brexit 188, 294
Brezhnev, Leonid 24, 68, 69, 159
BRICS 323
Britain; British 74, 103, 108, 238, 247, 258, 293, 294, 295, 296, 346, 349, 370
British Royal Navy 258
Brodsky, Joseph 268
Brussels 12, 194
Bucha 97, 98, 152, 229, 289, 336, 337, 342
Buchanan, Patrick 368
Bucharest summit 278
Budapest Memorandum 13, 22, 210, 213, 214, 356, 357, 358
Bulgaria 172, 271
Buryatia 153
Bush, George 242
Byzantine Empire 103

C

Canada; Canadian xvi, 9, 10, 12, 14, 50, 52, 164, 167, 179, 197, 198, 244, 245, 250, 255, 274, 275, 276, 277, 278, 310, 348
Carbon Border Adjustment Mechanism 326
Carleton University 273, 287
Carlson, Tucker 244, 246
Carpathian Mountains 53
Cathedral of St. Sophia 71
Catherine II 53, 143, 380
Caucasus 288, 289, 339, 347
CBAM (Carbon Border Adjustment Mechanism) 326
Central Europe 153, 154, 155, 367, 370
Centre for Quality Assurance 229
Cetus 258
Chang Kaishek 271
Chechnya 87, 93, 94, 177
Chernihiv; Chernihiv oblast 30, 161, 178, 303, 380
Chernyshevsky, Mykola 348
China xiii, xv, 117, 164, 182, 198, 199, 205, 212, 220, 224, 253, 254, 268, 271, 280, 284, 323, 324, 326, 347, 362, 386
Chornobyl 117, 216, 359
Chornobyl Nuclear Power Plant 359
Clinton, Bill 238
CNN 183
Cohen, Steven 368, 369
Cold War xii, xiii, 26, 35, 117, 164, 220, 265, 270, 324
Communism xiii, 27, 72
Communist Party of Ukraine 27
Congress 27, 238, 372, 375, 383
Constantinople 44
Contemporary Ukraine Studies Program xvi, 1, 3
Convention on Preventing and Combating Violence Against Women and Domestic Violence 105
Convention on the Elimination of all Forms of Discrimination Against Women 105
Corsair 34
Cossacks 92
Council of Europe 105
COVID 227, 309, 310, 380
Crimea xii, xiv, 3, 5, 13, 15, 18, 23, 40, 43, 55–57, 89, 91, 100, 106, 115, 120, 129–31, 137, 138, 146, 153, 161, 163, 180, 183, 187, 188, 202, 204–6, 213, 222, 223, 235, 239, 241, 258, 268, 298, 340, 351, 358, 381, 385
Czech Republic; Czechia; Czechs 121, 172, 337
Czechoslovakia 381

D

Dagestan 288, 374
Davies, Natalie 270
Democratic Initiatives Foundation 138, 140
Democratic Party 222
Department of National Minorities 44
Dnipro 130, 195, 212
Dobrobut 229
Donbas Volunteer Battalion 109
Donetsk oblast 87, 313, 319
Donets–Kryvyi Rih Soviet Republic 93
Donetsk Stus National University 310
Dontsov, Dmytro 91
Dostoevsky, Fyodor 268, 351, 370
Dozhd 287
Drahomanov, Mykhailo 115
Dubai 185
Dublin 237, 238
Duma 162
Dyak, Sofia 266

E

Electoral Action of Poles in Lithuania–Christian Families Alliance 44
Ems Ukase 24
Enerhodar 335
English 50, 51, 53, 353
Eritrea xiii
Estonia 40, 41, 42, 43, 44, 45, 180, 284, 367
Estonian Council of Churches 44
Ethiopia xiii
Eurasia 223
Eurasian Economic Union 3
Euromaidan 3, 27, 56, 99, 100, 107, 109, 167, 187, 188, 190. *See also* Maidan, Revolution of Dignity
European Commission 145
Eurovision 76

F

Far North 347
Federal Security Service 381
Fico, Robert 384
Finland 31, 42, 278, 383, 384
First World War 26, 131. *See also* World War I, WW I
France 74, 222, 358, 370
Frankl, Viktor 265
French 50, 103, 215, 221, 228, 303, 346, 349, 370, 384

G

Galicia 26
Gaza 373
General Assembly, UN 34, 122
Georgia 23, 58, 99, 172, 284, 337, 338, 339, 340, 363, 372, 381
Ghani, Ashraf 139
Global Gender Gap Report 168
Global South 9, 12, 122, 123, 225, 243, 244, 324, 347
Gogol, Nikolai 51, 52
Goode, Paul 287
Good Friday Agreement 11, 238
Gorbachev, Mikhail 22, 159, 160, 242
Gotland 258
Government Commissioner for Gender Policy 168
Great Britain 74, 247, 370. *See also* Britain, UK
Great Fatherland War 99, 103. *See also* Great Patriotic War
Great October Revolution 68
Great Patriotic War 45, 65, 67, 68, 69, 99, 282. *See also* Great Fatherland War
Great Russia 25, 302
Great Terror 269
Grenzsituation 265
Gripens 199, 257
Groysman, Volodymyr 25
Grybauskaitė, Dalia 40
Gumenyuk, Nataliya 115

H

Hague 249, 340, 341
Haley, Nikki 383
Harding, Luke 248
Harmony 43, 44
Harvard University 310
Harvard Ukrainian Research Institute 2
H-Diplo 88
HIMARS 128, 131, 135, 256
Hiroshima 361
Hitler, Adolf 66, 94, 146, 230
Hohol, Mykola 51, 52
Holocaust 25, 56, 249
Holodomor 40, 290, 291
Hostomel 138, 332
Houthis 373
Hubina, Larysa 232
Hungary 172, 173, 188, 192, 222, 384
Huntington, Samuel 80, 301

I

IAEA (International Atomic Energy Agency) 118, 182, 215, 216, 217, 359
Ignatieff, Michael 52
Ilin, Ivan 100
Ilovaisk 333
Immortal Regiment 67
Imperial Russia 57, 160
Independence Square 100. *See also* Euromaidan, Maidan Revolution
India xiii, 205, 244, 324, 362
Indiana University 263
InfoSapiens 106, 108
Inokentijus (Innocent) 44
International Atomic Energy Agency 117, 182, 359
International Center for Defense and Security 44
International Criminal Court 41, 249, 274
International Red Cross 274
Invisible Battalion 106
Iowa 383
Iraq xiii, 119, 247
Ireland; Irish 11, 79, 235, 236, 237, 238, 239
Iron Dome 179, 180
Irpin 97, 98, 180, 336, 337
Islam 75
Islamic State 54, 116
Israel 116, 179, 180, 259, 309
Istanbul Convention 105, 169, 172
Ivan the Terrible 345
Ivlev, Pavel 270
Ivy League 310, 368
Izium 128
Izoliatsiia 263

J

Japan 88, 268
Jaspers, Karl 265
Javelin 34, 127
Jedinskis, Zbignevas (Zbigniew Jedziński) 44
Jewish; Jews 50, 56, 73, 75, 139, 161, 249, 303
Johnson, Boris 294
Joint Chiefs of Staff 134, 381
Judaism 75
Judt, Tony xviii, 263

K

Kadyrov, Ramzan 93
Kakhovka 273
Kalmykia 288
Kalush 76
Karabakh 339
Karachevtsev, Denys 76
Kazakhstan 284
Kazan 231
Kerch Strait Bridge 131
KGB 2, 21, 40, 72, 98, 100, 271
Khalkhin Gol 88
Kharkiv 24, 76, 89, 90, 128, 129, 130, 132, 134, 161, 202, 211, 212, 217, 248, 303, 304, 308, 309, 310, 362
Kharkiv Karazin National University 310
Kherson 128, 129, 130, 152, 157, 161, 162, 184, 192, 202, 247, 248, 303, 308, 331, 348, 362
Khersonsky, Boris 50
Khreshchatyk Street 161
Khrushchev Thaw 2, 159
Khvyliovyi, Mykola 115
KIIS (Kyiv International Institute of Sociology) 89, 106, 110
Kim Jong Un 239
Kirienko, Sergey 102
Kirill, Patriarch 44, 75, 100, 103, 161
Klaipėda 41
Kopelev, Lev 290, 291
Koshelenko, Olga 241
Koshiw, Isobel 248
Koshulynsky, Ruslan 25
Kramatorsk 336
Kravchenko, Volodymyr 3
Kravchuk, Leonid 210
Kuchma, Leonid 307

Kurkov, Andrey 266
Kyiv International Institute of Sociology 106. *See also* KIIS
Kyiv-Mohyla Academy 228, 229, 310
Kyiv Shevchenko National University 310
Kyiv Sikorsky Polytechnic Institute 310

L

Laruelle, Marlène 81, 101
Latin America 225
Latvia 39, 40, 41, 42, 43, 44, 45, 49, 172, 180, 284
Lavrov, Sergei 159, 225
Lebedev, Sergei 266
Lenin 25, 26, 27, 93, 230, 301
Leninopad 142
Leopard 255, 276, 277
Lesia Ukrainka 59
LGBTQ 8, 148, 170, 171, 173, 353, 354
Lithuania 39, 40, 41, 42, 43, 44, 45, 172, 180, 277, 284, 367
Little Russian 52
London 180, 183, 238, 250, 293, 297, 298
Luhansk; Luhansk oblast 3, 23, 57, 87, 89, 92, 93, 106, 125, 162, 163, 202, 313, 337
Lukashenka, Aliaksandr 83, 239, 289
Luxembourg Centre for Contemporary and Digital History 148
Lviv 177, 179, 183, 266, 304, 310
Lviv Center for Urban History 148
Lviv Franko National University 310
Lviv National Polytechnic University 310
Lyman 132
Lysychansk 6, 87, 128

M

MacKinnon, Mark 248
MacMillan, Margaret xii
Maidan Revolution 16, 55, 77, 139, 140, 331, 332. *See also* Euromaidan, Revolution of Dignity
Maistrenko, Ivan 94, 95
Maldives 185
Mariupol 24, 36, 73, 74, 152, 204, 237, 310
Mariupol State University 310
Markov, Marat 264
Marshall Plan 190, 193
Marzalik, Peter 40
Mattingly, Daria 291
McMahon, Patrice 149
Mearsheimer, John 245
Meduza 159
Medvedchuk, Viktor 380
Medvedev, Dmitrii 15, 64, 161, 208
Melitopol 204
MENA (Middle East and North Africa) 119, 120
Middle East 116, 119, 123, 373
MiG 199
Milley, Mark, Gen. 134, 381
Minsk 82, 146, 358, 372
Mishustin, Mikhail 280
Mitchell, George, Sen. ix, 10
Mladić, Ratko 341
Mnohopillia 333
Moldova 103, 172, 181, 284, 338, 341, 364
Molotov-Ribbentrop Pact 66
Monastery of the Caves 71
Montreux Convention 258
Monument to Liberators (Riga) 45
Moscow Patriarchate 43, 143, 144
MRLS 128
Munich 2, 16, 211, 302
Munich Security Conference 211
Muscovite Principality; Muscovy 53, 345
Museum of Historical Treasures of Ukraine 72
Musk, Elon 228
Mykolaiv 309

N

Nagasaki 361
Naryshkin, Sergey 159, 211
NASAMS 257
Nash Svit (Center) 110, 111, 171
National Anti-Corruption Bureau 141
National Guard of Ukraine 359
National Health Service 295
National Security Council 16, 200
NaUKMA (National University of Kyiv-Mohyla Academy) 227, 228, 229. *See also* Kyiv-Mohyla Academy
Navalny, Alexei 18, 282, 286
New Hampshire 383
New Russia 53, 89, 348. *See also* Novorossiia
New York University 368
New York Times 49, 182
New Yorkers 302
NLAW 34
Nordic countries 181
North Africa 119. *See also* MENA
North Caucasus 288, 289, 347
North Crimean Canal 138
Northern Ireland 238
North Korea 181
Norway; Norwegian 41, 81
Novorossiia 56. *See also* New Russia
Nuclear Non-Proliferation Treaty 357

O

Odesa 50, 89, 143, 178, 179, 183, 184, 296, 348, 362
Odesa National Polytechnic University 296
Oharkova, Tetiana 228
Okhtyrka 333
Olenivka 274
Olympic games xiv
Omsk 158
Open Democracy 247
Operation Unifier 277
Orange Revolution 3, 27, 90, 98, 99, 187
Orbán, Viktor 384
Organization of Ukrainian Nationalists 91
Orthodox 7, 43, 44, 53, 54, 72, 75, 99, 100, 102, 103, 104, 143
Orthodox Church of Estonia 44
Orthodox Church of Latvia 43
Osadchuk, Bohdan 230
Ostrovsky, Efim 43, 101
Ottoman Empire 116
Oxford University Press 53, 268, 367

P

Pakistan xiii, 324
Palestine 116, 235
Paris 303
Parliamentary Assembly 162
Patriot 179, 277
Pavlovsky, Gleb 101
Peter I 53, 380
Platt 49, 50, 51, 52, 54
Poland 11, 35, 41, 44, 94, 121, 147, 148, 149, 150, 151, 152, 154, 173, 174, 179, 180, 181, 188, 221, 223, 226, 255, 256, 258, 271, 277, 294, 325, 341, 367, 383, 384
Poles, Polish 26, 42, 43, 44, 52, 103, 147–52, 154, 177, 226, 256, 303, 337, 370
Polish Academy of Sciences 148
Poltava 51
Popasna 128
Prague 2, 5
Presidential Administration of the Russian Federation 102
Prigozhin, Evgeniy 264, 280, 289, 374
Princeton University 367, 368
Protasevich, Roman 263, 264
Protestants 75
Prussia 367
Pushkin, Alexander 59, 265, 268, 370
Putin-Verstehers 145
Pylypenko, Viktor 109

Q

Qatar 123
Quebecois 50

R

Radchenko, Sergei 271
Rafale 199
Rafeyenko, Volodymyr 266
Ramstein 123
Razumkov Centre 140
Red Forest 359
Rehden 322
Republican Party (US) 222, 383
Revolution of Dignity 3, 27, 77, 99, 331. See also Euromaidan, Maidan Revolution
RIA Novosti 97
Riasanovsky, Nicholas 53, 268, 367, 368, 369
Rice, Condoleezza 21
Right Sektor 25
Riurikide 52
Roman Catholics 75
Romania 121, 173, 258
Romanov 52
Rosatom 215, 360
Rosneft 322
Rostov 289
Rudenko, Oleksii 148
Rukh 140
Russian Army 97, 104, 380
Russian Empire 51, 52, 58, 59, 98, 114, 115, 116, 231, 275, 348, 367
Russian Orthodox Church 7, 44, 53, 100, 102, 103, 104, 143
Russian World, *russkii mir* 7, 25, 49, 54, 64, 75, 93, 98, 99, 100, 101, 102, 103, 104, 125, 320, 342
Ruthenian 53
Rwanda xiii
Rzeszów 150

S

Saigon 271
Sarkozy, Nicolas 372
Saudi Arabia 212
Schwedt 322
Scotland 148
Scythian art 72
Sea King 182
Second World War xi, 26, 31, 130, 151, 273, 355. See also World War II, WW II
Security Council, UN 16, 118, 122, 200, 211, 219, 355
Security Service of Ukraine 73
Serdiuk, Artem 305
Servant of the People 25
Shchedrovitsky, Petr 101
Shevchenko, Taras 26, 51, 231, 264, 265, 352
Shevchenko Park 178
Shoigu, Sergey 211
Siberia 40, 347
Simonyan, Margarita 161, 264
SIPRI 217, 219
Siverskodonetsk 87, 128, 202
Siverskyi Dinets River 87
Skabeeva 161
Slovakia 121, 173, 384
Slovenia 173, 175
Snyder, Timothy 73, 74, 81, 113
Sochi xiv
Solovets Islands, Solovki 316
Solovyov 161
Sorokin, Vladimir 345
South Africa 235, 244
South Carolina 383
South Ossetia 15, 237, 337, 338
Spear 257
Sputnik 43
Srebrenica xiii
Stakhiv, Ievhen 91
Stalin 6, 24, 25, 26, 27, 40, 41, 66, 67, 68, 72, 74, 87, 88, 94, 159, 224, 230, 268, 269, 270, 271, 302
Stalinism 27, 63, 100
Stand with Ukraine 148
Stanford University 310

Starlink 228
Steinmeier, Frank-Walter 145
Stingers 135
Stockholm International Peace Research Institute 219
Stoltenberg, Jens 200
StopFake 228
St. Petersburg 10, 21, 158, 159, 348
Stugna-P 34
Sudetenland 381
Sullivan, Jake 385
Sumy 30, 161
Sumy State University 311
Sustainable Development Goals, UN 105
Svatove 132
Svoboda 25
Sweden 42, 173, 258, 278
Syria 15, 87, 150, 177, 180, 342, 381
Syrskyi, Oleksandr, Gen. 383
Szeptycki, Andrzej 149

T

Taipei 271
Taliban 329
TASS 212
Tatars 230, 303
Tatarstan 153, 231
Teperik, Dmitri 44
Ternopil 304
Territorial Defense Units 305
Texans 302
The Conversation 149
Third Reich 88
Third Rome 103
Tishkov, Valery 101
Titanic 283
Tochka-U 211
Toler, Aric 40
Tomaševskis, Valdemaras (Waldemar Tomaszewski) 43, 44
Tomsk 158
Topychkanov, Peter 217
Toronto 2, 185, 310
Transnistria 138, 183, 338

Treaty of Friendship and Cooperation with Ukraine 22
Treaty of Versailles 291
Trenin, Dmitri 368, 369
Trofimov, Yaroslav 248
Trotsky 94, 95
Trudeau, Justin 276
Trump, Donald 17, 246, 263, 283, 375, 376, 382, 383
Turkey 180, 185
Turkish Airlines 180
Twinning Scheme 296, 297
Twitter 224, 225

U

Ufa 231
Ukraine International Airlines 180
Ukraine Recovery Conference 297
Ukrainian Armed Forces 37, 203, 303
Ukrainian Free University 2
Ukrainian Helsinki Group 115
Ukrainian National Republic 27
UK (United Kingdom) 11, 12, 36, 149, 182, 185, 226, 253, 256, 258, 259, 277, 289, 293, 294, 295, 296, 297, 310, 356, 358.
See also Britain, Great Britain
Umland, Andreas 81
UN 12, 34, 105, 122, 123, 219, 239, 323, 355, 357. *See also* United Nations
Union of Lithuanian Poles 44
United Kingdom 182, 357, 358.
See also Britain, Great Britain
United Nations 118, 122, 295.
See also UN
United News marathon 327
University of Alberta 2, 14
University of Pennsylvania 49
University of Portsmouth 296
University of St. Andrew 148
University of Warsaw 148, 149
Uzbekistan 49, 50

V

Vakulenko, Volodymyr 315
Valdai Club 17, 64
Vancouver 185
Verhofstadt, Guy 188
Verkhovna Rada 25, 169, 229
Vernadsky, George 53
Vienna 2
Vietnam 272
Vilnius 40, 275, 277, 278, 319
Vinnytsia 310, 362
Vladimir [Volodymyr] the Great 72
Volga Tatars 230
Volnovakha 331
von der Leyen, Ursula 145
Vuhledar 385

W

Wagner Group 206, 289
Ward, Clarissa 183
Warsaw Pact 22
Washington 12, 103, 117, 119, 133, 134, 183, 220, 222
Washington Post 183
WEF (World Economic Forum) 168
West Berlin 35
Western University (London, Ontario) 250
Westinghouse 215
Winter War 31, 375
World Bank 275
World Cup 183
World Economic Forum 168
World Press Freedom Index 9
World War I 114. *See also* First World War, WW I
World War II 6, 63, 64, 65, 67, 87, 91, 99, 103, 197, 198, 206. *See also* Second World War, WW II
World War III 200, 377
WW I xii, 7. *See also* First World War, World War I
WW II xi, xii, xvii, 1, 12, 13, 67, 88, 103, 219, 230, 247, 294, 338, 355. *See also* Second World War, World War II

X

Xi Jinping 182

Y

Yale University 53, 113
Yanukovych, Viktor xiv, 3, 98, 99, 100, 114, 214, 233, 307, 358, 382
Yavoriv 177
Yeltsin, Boris 160, 201
Yermolenko, Volodymyr 76, 77, 228
Yugoslav wars 12, 190
Yurchak, Alexei 308
Yushchenko, Viktor 142

Z

Zaluzhnyi, Valerii, Gen. 134, 203, 363, 383
Zaporizhia Nuclear Power Plant 117, 216, 359
Zhukov, Georgii, Marshall 88

UKRAINIAN VOICES

Collected by Andreas Umland

1. *Mychailo Wynnyckyj*
   Ukraine's Maidan, Russia's War
   A Chronicle and Analysis of the Revolution of Dignity
   With a foreword by Serhii Plokhy
   ISBN 978-3-8382-1327-9

2. *Olexander Hryb*
   Understanding Contemporary Ukrainian and Russian Nationalism
   The Post-Soviet Cossack Revival and Ukraine's National Security
   With a foreword by Vitali Vitaliev
   ISBN 978-3-8382-1377-4

3. *Marko Bojcun*
   Towards a Political Economy of Ukraine
   Selected Essays 1990–2015
   With a foreword by John-Paul Himka
   ISBN 978-3-8382-1368-2

4. *Volodymyr Yermolenko (ed.)*
   Ukraine in Histories and Stories
   Essays by Ukrainian Intellectuals
   With a preface by Peter Pomerantsev
   ISBN 978-3-8382-1456-6

5. *Mykola Riabchuk*
   At the Fence of Metternich's Garden
   Essays on Europe, Ukraine, and Europeanization
   ISBN 978-3-8382-1484-9

6. *Marta Dyczok*
   Ukraine Calling
   A Kaleidoscope from Hromadske Radio 2016–2019
   With a foreword by Andriy Kulykov
   ISBN 978-3-8382-1472-6

7. *Olexander Scherba*
   Ukraine vs. Darkness
   Undiplomatic Thoughts
   With a foreword by Adrian Karatnycky
   ISBN 978-3-8382-1501-3

8. *Olesya Yaremchuk*
   Our Others
   Stories of Ukrainian Diversity
   With a foreword by Ostap Slyvynsky
   Translated from the Ukrainian by Zenia Tompkins and Hanna Leliv
   ISBN 978-3-8382-1475-7

9. *Nataliya Gumenyuk*
   Die verlorene Insel
   Geschichten von der besetzten Krim
   Mit einem Vorwort von Alice Bota
   Aus dem Ukrainischen übersetzt von Johann Zajaczkowski
   ISBN 978-3-8382-1499-3

10. *Olena Stiazhkina*
    Zero Point Ukraine
    Four Essays on World War II
    Translated from the Ukrainian by Svitlana Kulinska
    ISBN 978-3-8382-1550-1

11 Oleksii Sinchenko, Dmytro Stus, Leonid Finberg (compilers)
    Ukrainian Dissidents
    An Anthology of Texts
    ISBN 978-3-8382-1551-8

12 John-Paul Himka
    Ukrainian Nationalists and the Holocaust
    OUN and UPA's Participation in the Destruction of Ukrainian Jewry, 1941–1944
    ISBN 978-3-8382-1548-8

13 Andrey Demartino
    False Mirrors
    The Weaponization of Social Media in Russia's Operation to Annex Crimea
    With a foreword by Oleksiy Danilov
    ISBN 978-3-8382-1533-4

14 Svitlana Biedarieva (ed.)
    Contemporary Ukrainian and Baltic Art
    Political and Social Perspectives, 1991–2021
    ISBN 978-3-8382-1526-6

15 Olesya Khromeychuk
    A Loss
    The Story of a Dead Soldier Told by His Sister
    With a foreword by Andrey Kurkov
    ISBN 978-3-8382-1570-9

16 Marieluise Beck (Hg.)
    Ukraine verstehen
    Auf den Spuren von Terror und Gewalt
    Mit einem Vorwort von Dmytro Kuleba
    ISBN 978-3-8382-1653-9

17 Stanislav Aseyev
    Heller Weg
    Geschichte eines Konzentrationslagers im Donbass 2017–2019
    Aus dem Russischen übersetzt von Martina Steis und Charis Haska
    ISBN 978-3-8382-1620-1

18 Mykola Davydiuk
    Wie funktioniert Putins Propaganda?
    Anmerkungen zum Informationskrieg des Kremls
    Aus dem Ukrainischen übersetzt von Christian Weise
    ISBN 978-3-8382-1628-7

19 Olesya Yaremchuk
    Unsere Anderen
    Geschichten ukrainischer Vielfalt
    Aus dem Ukrainischen übersetzt von Christian Weise
    ISBN 978-3-8382-1635-5

20 Oleksandr Mykhed
    „Dein Blut wird die Kohle tränken"
    Über die Ostukraine
    Aus dem Ukrainischen übersetzt von Simon Muschick und Dario Planert
    ISBN 978-3-8382-1648-5

21 Vakhtang Kipiani (Hg.)
    Der Zweite Weltkrieg in der Ukraine
    Geschichte und Lebensgeschichten
    Aus dem Ukrainischen übersetzt von Margarita Grinko
    ISBN 978-3-8382-1622-5

22 Vakhtang Kipiani (ed.)
    World War II, Uncontrived and Unredacted
    Testimonies from Ukraine
    Translated from the Ukrainian by Zenia Tompkins and Daisy Gibbons
    ISBN 978-3-8382-1621-8

23 Dmytro Stus
Vasyl Stus
Life in Creativity
Translated from the Ukrainian by
Ludmila Bachurina
ISBN 978-3-8382-1631-7

24 Vitalii Ogiienko (ed.)
The Holodomor and the
Origins of the Soviet Man
Reading the Testimony of
Anastasia Lysyvets
With forewords by Natalka
Bilotserkivets and Serhy
Yekelchyk
Translated from the Ukrainian by
Alla Parkhomenko and
Alexander J. Motyl
ISBN 978-3-8382-1616-4

25 Vladislav Davidzon
Jewish-Ukrainian Relations
and the Birth of a Political
Nation
Selected Writings 2013-2021
With a foreword by Bernard-
Henri Lévy
ISBN 978-3-8382-1509-9

26 Serhy Yekelchyk
Writing the Nation
The Ukrainian Historical
Profession in Independent
Ukraine and the Diaspora
ISBN 978-3-8382-1695-9

27 Ildi Eperjesi, Oleksandr
Kachura
Shreds of War
Fates from the Donbas Frontline
2014-2019
With a foreword by Olexiy
Haran
ISBN 978-3-8382-1680-5

28 Oleksandr Melnyk
World War II as an Identity
Project
Historicism, Legitimacy
Contests, and the (Re-)Con-
struction of Political Commu-
nities in Ukraine, 1939–1946
With a foreword by David R.
Marples
ISBN 978-3-8382-1704-8

29 Olesya Khromeychuk
Ein Verlust
Die Geschichte eines gefallenen
ukrainischen Soldaten, erzählt
von seiner Schwester
Mit einem Vorwort von Andrej
Kurkow
Aus dem Englischen übersetzt
von Lily Sophie
ISBN 978-3-8382-1770-3

30 Tamara Martsenyuk,
Tetiana Kostiuchenko (eds.)
Russia's War in Ukraine
During 2022
Personal Experiences of
Ukrainian Scholars
ISBN 978-3-8382-1757-4

31 Ildikó Eperjesi, Oleksandr
Kachura
Shreds of War. Vol. 2
Fates from Crimea 2015–2022
With an interview of Oleh
Sentsov
ISBN 978-3-8382-1780-2

32 Yuriy Lukanov
The Press
How Russia Destroyed Media
Freedom in Crimea
With a foreword by Taras Kuzio
ISBN 978-3-8382-1784-0

33 Megan Buskey
Ukraine Is Not Dead Yet
A Family Story of Exile and
Return
ISBN 978-3-8382-1691-1

34 *Vira Ageyeva*
Behind the Scenes of the Empire
Essays on Cultural Relationships between Ukraine and Russia
With a foreword by Oksana Zabuzhko
ISBN 978-3-8382-1748-2

35 *Marieluise Beck (ed.)*
Understanding Ukraine
Tracing the Roots of Terror and Violence
With a foreword by Dmytro Kuleba
ISBN 978-3-8382-1773-4

36 *Olesya Khromeychuk*
A Loss
The Story of a Dead Soldier Told by His Sister, 2nd edn.
With a foreword by Philippe Sands
With a preface by Andrii Kurkov
ISBN 978-3-8382-1870-0

37 *Taras Kuzio, Stefan Jajecznyk-Kelman*
Fascism and Genocide
Russia's War Against Ukrainians
ISBN 978-3-8382-1791-8

38 *Alina Nychyk*
Ukraine Vis-à-Vis Russia and the EU
Misperceptions of Foreign Challenges in Times of War, 2014–2015
With a foreword by Paul D'Anieri
ISBN 978-3-8382-1767-3

39 *Sasha Dovzhyk (ed.)*
Ukraine Lab
Global Security, Environment, and Disinformation Through the Prism of Ukraine
With a foreword by Rory Finnin
ISBN 978-3-8382-1805-2

40 *Serhiy Kvit*
Media, History, and Education
Three Ways to Ukrainian Independence
With a preface by Diane Francis
ISBN 978-3-8382-1807-6

41 *Anna Romandash*
Women of Ukraine
Reportages from the War and Beyond
ISBN 978-3-8382-1819-9

42 *Dominika Rank*
Matzewe in meinem Garten
Abenteuer eines jüdischen Heritage-Touristen in der Ukraine
ISBN 978-3-8382-1810-6

43 *Myroslaw Marynowytsch*
Das Universum hinter dem Stacheldraht
Memoiren eines sowjet-ukrainischen Dissidenten
Mit einem Vorwort von Timothy Snyder und einem Nachwort von Max Hartmann
ISBN 978-3-8382-1806-9

44 *Konstantin Sigow*
Für Deine und meine Freiheit
Europäische Revolutions- und Kriegserfahrungen im heutigen Kyjiw
Mit einem Vorwort von Karl Schlögel
Herausgegeben von Regula M. Zwahlen
ISBN 978-3-8382-1755-0

45 *Kateryna Pylypchuk*
The War that Changed Us
Ukrainian Novellas, Poems, and Essays from 2022
With a foreword by Victor Yushchenko
Paperback
ISBN 978-3-8382-1859-5
Hardcover
ISBN 978-3-8382-1860-1

46 *Kyrylo Tkachenko*
Rechte Tür Links
Radikale Linke in Deutschland,
die Revolution und der Krieg in
der Ukraine, 2013-2018
ISBN 978-3-8382-1711-6

47 *Alexander Strashny*
The Ukrainian Mentality
An Ethno-Psychological,
Historical and Comparative
Exploration
With a foreword by Antonina
Lovochkina
Translated from the Ukrainian
by Michael M. Naydan and
Olha Tytarenko
ISBN 978-3-8382-1886-1

48 *Alona Shestopalova*
From Screens to Battlefields
Tracing the Construction of
Enemies on Russian Television
With a foreword by Nina
Jankowicz
ISBN 978-3-8382-1884-7

49 *Iaroslav Petik*
**Politics and Society in the
Ukrainian People's Republic
(1917–1921) and
Contemporary Ukraine
(2013–2022)**
A Comparative Analysis
With a foreword by Mykola
Doroshko
ISBN 978-3-8382-1817-5

50 *Serhii Plokhy*
**Der Mann mit der
Giftpistole**
Eine Spionagaschichte aus dem
Kalten Krieg
ISBN 978-3-8382-1789-5

51 *Vakhtang Kipiani*
**Ukrainische Dissidenten
unter der Sowjetmacht**
Im Kampf um Wahrheit und
Freiheit
Aus dem Ukrainischen übersetzt
von Christian Weise
ISBN 978-3-8382-1890-8

52 *Dmytro Shestakov*
**When Businesses Test
Hypotheses**
A Four-Step Approach to Risk
Management for Innovative
Startups
With a foreword by Anthony J.
Tether
ISBN 978-3-8382-1883-0

53 *Larissa Babij*
A Kind of Refugee
The Story of an American Who
Refused to Leave Ukraine
With a foreword by Vladislav
Davidzon
ISBN 978-3-8382-1898-4

54 *Julia Davis*
In Their Own Words
How Russian Propagandists
Reveal Putin's Intentions
With a foreword by Timothy
Snyder
ISBN 978-3-8382-1909-7

55 *Sonya Atlantova, Oleksandr
Klymenko*
Icons on Ammo Boxes
Painting Life on the Remnants of
Russia's War in Donbas, 2014-21
Translated from the Ukrainian by
Anastasya Knyazhytska
ISBN 978-3-8382-1892-2

56 *Leonid Ushkalov*
Catching an Elusive Bird
The Life of Hryhorii Skovoroda
Translated from the Ukrainian
by Natalia Komarova
ISBN 978-3-8382-1894-6

57 *Vakhtang Kipiani*
**Ein Land weiblichen
Geschlechts**
Ukrainische Frauenschicksale
im 20. und 21. Jahrhundert
Aus dem Ukrainischen übersetzt
von Christian Weise
ISBN 978-3-8382-1891-5

58 *Petro Rychlo*
„Zerrissne Saiten einer überlauten Harfe …"
Deutschjüdische Dichter der Bukowina
ISBN 978-3-8382-1893-9

59 *Volodymyr Paniotto*
Sociology in Jokes
An Entertaining Introduction
ISBN 978-3-8382-1857-1

60 *Josef Wallmannsberger (ed.)*
Executing Renaissances
The Poetological Nation of Ukraine
ISBN 978-3-8382-1741-3

61 *Pavlo Kazarin*
The Wild West of Eastern Europe
A Ukrainian Guide on Breaking Free from Empire
Translated from the Ukrainian by Dominique Hoffman
ISBN 978-3-8382-1842-7

62 *Ernest Gyidel*
Ukrainian Public Nationalism in the General Government
The Case of Krakivski Visti, 1940–1944
With a foreword by David R. Marples
ISBN 978-3-8382-1865-6

63 *Olexander Hryb*
Understanding Contemporary Russian Militarism
From Revolutionary to New Generation Warfare
With a foreword by Mark Laity
ISBN 978-3-8382-1927-1

64 *Orysia Hrudka, Bohdan Ben*
Dark Days, Determined People
Stories from Ukraine under Siege
With a foreword by Myroslav Marynovych
ISBN 978-3-8382-1958-5

65 *Oleksandr Pankieiev (ed.)*
Narratives of the Russo-Ukrainian War
A Look Within and Without
With a foreword by Natalia Khanenko-Friesen
ISBN 978-3-8382-1964-6

66 *Roman Sohn, Ariana Gic (eds.)*
Unrecognized War
The Fight for Truth about Russia's War on Ukraine
With a foreword by Viktor Yushchenko
ISBN 978-3-8382-1947-9

67 *Paul Robert Magocsi*
Ukraina Redux
Schon wieder die Ukraine …
ISBN 978-3-8382-1942-4

68 *Paul Robert Magocsi*
L'Ucraina Ritrovata
Sullo Stato e l'Identità Nazionale
ISBN 978-3-8382-1982-0

69 *Max Hartmann*
Ein Schrei der Verzweiflung
Aquarelle von Danylo Movchan zu Russlands Krieg in der Ukraine
Mit einem Vorwort von Mateusz Sora
Paperback
ISBN 978-3-8382-2011-6
Hardcover
ISBN 978-3-8382-2012-3

70 *Vakhtang Kebuladze (Hg.)*
Die Zukunft, die wir uns wünschen
Essays aus der Ukraine
ISBN 978-3-8382-1531-0

71 Marieluise Beck, Jan Claus
Behrends, Gelinada
Grinchenko und Oksana
Mikheieva (Hgg.)
Deutsch-ukrainische
Geschichten
Bruchstücke aus einer
gemeinsamen Vergangenheit
ISBN 978-3-8382-2053-6

72 Pavlo Kazarin
Der Wilde Westen Ost-
Europas
Der ukrainische Weg aus dem
Imperium
Aus dem Ukrainischen übersetzt
von Christian Weise
ISBN 978-3-8382-1843-4

73 Radomyr Mokryk
Die ukrainischen »Sechziger«
Chronologie einer Revolte
ISBN 978-3-8382-1873-1

74 Leonid Finberg
My Ukraine
Rethinking the Past, Building
the Present
ISBN 978-3-8382-1974-5

75 Joseph Zissels
Consider My Inmost
Thoughts
Essays, Lectures, and Interviews
on Ukrainian Matters at the
Turn of the Century
ISBN 978-3-8382-1975-2

76 Margarita Yehorchenko,
Iryna Berlyand, Ihor
Vinokurov (eds.)
Jewish Addresses in Ukraine
A Guide-Book
With a foreword by Leonid
Finberg
ISB 978-3-8382-1976-9

77 Viktoriia Grivina
Kharkiv—A War City
A Collection of Essays from
2022–23
ISBN 978-3-8382-1988-2

78 Hjørdis Clemmensen,
Viktoriia Grivina, Vasylysa
Shchogoleva
Kharkiv Is a Dream
Public Art and Activism 2013–
2023
With a foreword by Bohdan
Volynskyi
ISBN 978-3-8382-2005-5

79 Olga Khomenko
The Faraway Sky of Kyiv
Ukrainians in the War
With a foreword by Hiroaki
Kuromiya
ISBN 978-3-8382-2006-2

80 Daria Mattingly, Jonathon
Vsetecka (eds.)
The Holodomor in Global
Perspective
How the Famine in Ukraine
Shaped the World
With a foreword by Anne
Applebaum
ISBN 978-3-8382-1953-0

81 Olga Khomenko
Ukrainians beyond Borders
Nine Life Journeys Through the
History of Eastern Europe
With a foreword by Zbigniew
Wojnowski
ISBN 978-3-8382-2007-9

82 Mykhailo Minakov
From Servant to Leader
Chronicles of Ukraine under the
Zelensky Presidency, 2019–2024
With a foreword by John Lloyd
ISBN 978-3-8382-2002-4

83 Volodymyr Hromov (ed.)
A Ruined Home
Sketches of War, 2022–2023
ISBN 978-3-8382-2008-6

84 Olha Tatokhina (ed.)
Why Do They Kill Our People?
Russia's War Against Ukraine as
Told by Ukrainians
With a foreword by Volodymyr
Yermolenko
ISBN 978-3-8382-2056-7

Book series "Ukrainian Voices"

Coordinator
Andreas Umland, National University of Kyiv-Mohyla Academy

Editorial Board
Lesia Bidochko, National University of Kyiv-Mohyla Academy
Svitlana Biedarieva, George Washington University, DC, USA
Ivan Gomza, Kyiv School of Economics, Ukraine
Natalie Jaresko, Aspen Institute, Kyiv/Washington
Olena Lennon, University of New Haven, West Haven, USA
Kateryna Yushchenko, First Lady of Ukraine 2005-2010, Kyiv
Oleksandr Zabirko, University of Regensburg, Germany

Advisory Board
Iuliia Bentia, National Academy of Arts of Ukraine, Kyiv
Natalya Belitser, Pylyp Orlyk Institute for Democracy, Kyiv
Oleksandra Bienert, Humboldt University of Berlin, Germany
Sergiy Bilenky, Canadian Institute of Ukrainian Studies, Toronto
Tymofii Brik, Kyiv School of Economics, Ukraine
Olga Brusylovska, Mechnikov National University, Odesa
Mariana Budjeryn, Harvard University, Cambridge, USA
Volodymyr Bugrov, Shevchenko National University, Kyiv
Olga Burlyuk, University of Amsterdam, The Netherlands
Yevhen Bystrytsky, NAS Institute of Philosophy, Kyiv
Andrii Danylenko, Pace University, New York, USA
Vladislav Davidzon, Atlantic Council, Washington/Paris
Mykola Davydiuk, Think Tank "Polityka," Kyiv
Andrii Demartino, National Security and Defense Council, Kyiv
Vadym Denisenko, Ukrainian Institute for the Future, Kyiv
Oleksandr Donii, Center for Political Values Studies, Kyiv
Volodymyr Dubovyk, Mechnikov National University, Odesa
Volodymyr Dubrovskiy, CASE Ukraine, Kyiv
Diana Dutsyk, National University of Kyiv-Mohyla Academy
Marta Dyczok, Western University, Ontario, Canada
Yevhen Fedchenko, National University of Kyiv-Mohyla Academy
Sofiya Filonenko, State Pedagogical University of Berdyansk
Oleksandr Fisun, Karazin National University, Kharkiv
Oksana Forostyna, Webjournal "Ukraina Moderna," Kyiv
Roman Goncharenko, Broadcaster "Deutsche Welle," Bonn
George Grabowicz, Harvard University, Cambridge, USA
Gelinada Grinchenko, Karazin National University, Kharkiv
Kateryna Härtel, Federal Union of European Nationalities, Brussels
Nataliia Hendel, University of Geneva, Switzerland
Anton Herashchenko, Kyiv School of Public Administration
John-Paul Himka, University of Alberta, Edmonton
Ola Hnatiuk, National University of Kyiv-Mohyla Academy
Oleksandr Holubov, Broadcaster "Deutsche Welle," Bonn
Yaroslav Hrytsak, Ukrainian Catholic University, Lviv
Oleksandra Humenna, National University of Kyiv-Mohyla Academy
Tamara Hundorova, NAS Institute of Literature, Kyiv
Oksana Huss, University of Bologna, Italy
Oleksandra Iwaniuk, University of Warsaw, Poland
Mykola Kapitonenko, Shevchenko National University, Kyiv
Georgiy Kasianov, Marie Curie-Skłodowska University, Lublin
Vakhtang Kebuladze, Shevchenko National University, Kyiv
Natalia Khanenko-Friesen, University of Alberta, Edmonton
Victoria Khiterer, Millersville University of Pennsylvania, USA
Oksana Kis, NAS Institute of Ethnology, Lviv
Pavlo Klimkin, Center for National Resilience and Development, Kyiv
Oleksandra Kolomiiets, Center for Economic Strategy, Kyiv

- Sergiy Korsunsky, Kobe Gakuin University, Japan
- Nadiia Koval, Kyiv School of Economics, Ukraine
- Volodymyr Kravchenko, University of Alberta, Edmonton
- Oleksiy Kresin, NAS Koretskiy Institute of State and Law, Kyiv
- Anatoliy Kruglashov, Fedkovych National University, Chernivtsi
- Andrey Kurkov, PEN Ukraine, Kyiv
- Ostap Kushnir, Lazarski University, Warsaw
- Taras Kuzio, National University of Kyiv-Mohyla Academy
- Serhii Kvit, National University of Kyiv-Mohyla Academy
- Yuliya Ladygina, The Pennsylvania State University, USA
- Yevhen Mahda, Institute of World Policy, Kyiv
- Victoria Malko, California State University, Fresno, USA
- Yulia Marushevska, Security and Defense Center (SAND), Kyiv
- Myroslav Marynovych, Ukrainian Catholic University, Lviv
- Oleksandra Matviichuk, Center for Civil Liberties, Kyiv
- Mykhailo Minakov, Kennan Institute, Washington, USA
- Anton Moiseienko, The Australian National University, Canberra
- Alexander Motyl, Rutgers University-Newark, USA
- Vlad Mykhnenko, University of Oxford, United Kingdom
- Vitalii Ogiienko, Ukrainian Institute of National Remembrance, Kyiv
- Olga Onuch, University of Manchester, United Kingdom
- Olesya Ostrovska, Museum "Mystetskyi Arsenal," Kyiv
- Anna Osypchuk, National University of Kyiv-Mohyla Academy
- Oleksandr Pankieiev, University of Alberta, Edmonton
- Oleksiy Panych, Publishing House "Dukh i Litera," Kyiv
- Valerii Pekar, Kyiv-Mohyla Business School, Ukraine
- Yohanan Petrovsky-Shtern, Northwestern University, Chicago
- Serhii Plokhy, Harvard University, Cambridge, USA
- Andrii Portnov, Viadrina University, Frankfurt-Oder, Germany
- Maryna Rabinovych, Kyiv School of Economics, Ukraine
- Valentyna Romanova, Institute of Developing Economies, Tokyo
- Natalya Ryabinska, Collegium Civitas, Warsaw, Poland
- Darya Tsymbalyk, University of Oxford, United Kingdom
- Vsevolod Samokhvalov, University of Liege, Belgium
- Orest Semotiuk, Franko National University, Lviv
- Viktoriya Sereda, NAS Institute of Ethnology, Lviv
- Anton Shekhovtsov, University of Vienna, Austria
- Andriy Shevchenko, Media Center Ukraine, Kyiv
- Oxana Shevel, Tufts University, Medford, USA
- Pavlo Shopin, National Pedagogical Dragomanov University, Kyiv
- Karina Shyrokykh, Stockholm University, Sweden
- Nadja Simon, freelance interpreter, Cologne, Germany
- Olena Snigova, NAS Institute for Economics and Forecasting, Kyiv
- Ilona Solohub, Analytical Platform "VoxUkraine," Kyiv
- Iryna Solonenko, LibMod - Center for Liberal Modernity, Berlin
- Galyna Solovei, National University of Kyiv-Mohyla Academy
- Sergiy Stelmakh, NAS Institute of World History, Kyiv
- Olena Stiazhkina, NAS Institute of the History of Ukraine, Kyiv
- Dmitri Stratievski, Osteuropa Zentrum (OEZB), Berlin
- Dmytro Stus, National Taras Shevchenko Museum, Kyiv
- Frank Sysyn, University of Toronto, Canada
- Olha Tokariuk, Center for European Policy Analysis, Washington
- Olena Tregub, Independent Anti-Corruption Commission, Kyiv
- Hlib Vyshlinsky, Centre for Economic Strategy, Kyiv
- Mychailo Wynnyckyj, National University of Kyiv-Mohyla Academy
- Yelyzaveta Yasko, NGO "Yellow Blue Strategy," Kyiv
- Serhy Yekelchyk, University of Victoria, Canada
- Victor Yushchenko, President of Ukraine 2005-2010, Kyiv
- Oleksandr Zaitsev, Ukrainian Catholic University, Lviv
- Kateryna Zarembo, National University of Kyiv-Mohyla Academy
- Yaroslav Zhalilo, National Institute for Strategic Studies, Kyiv
- Sergei Zhuk, Ball State University at Muncie, USA
- Alina Zubkovych, Nordic Ukraine Forum, Stockholm
- Liudmyla Zubrytska, National University of Kyiv-Mohyla Academy

Friends of the Series

Ana Maria Abulescu, University of Bucharest, Romania
Łukasz Adamski, Centrum Mieroszewskiego, Warsaw
Marieluise Beck, LibMod—Center for Liberal Modernity, Berlin
Marc Berensen, King's College London, United Kingdom
Johannes Bohnen, BOHNEN Public Affairs, Berlin
Karsten Brüggemann, University of Tallinn, Estonia
Ulf Brunnbauer, Leibniz Institute (IOS), Regensburg
Martin Dietze, German-Ukrainian Culture Society, Hamburg
Gergana Dimova, Florida State University, Tallahassee/London
Caroline von Gall, Goethe University, Frankfurt-Main
Zaur Gasimov, Rhenish Friedrich Wilhelm University, Bonn
Armand Gosu, University of Bucharest, Romania
Thomas Grant, University of Cambridge, United Kingdom
Gustav Gressel, European Council on Foreign Relations, Berlin
Rebecca Harms, European Centre for Press & Media Freedom, Leipzig
André Härtel, Stiftung Wissenschaft und Politik, Berlin/Brussels
Marcel Van Herpen, The Cicero Foundation, Maastricht
Richard Herzinger, freelance analyst, Berlin
Mieste Hotopp-Riecke, ICATAT, Magdeburg
Nico Lange, Munich Security Conference, Berlin
Martin Malek, freelance analyst, Vienna
Ingo Mannteufel, Broadcaster "Deutsche Welle," Bonn
Carlo Masala, Bundeswehr University, Munich
Wolfgang Mueller, University of Vienna, Austria
Dietmar Neutatz, Albert Ludwigs University, Freiburg
Torsten Oppelland, Friedrich Schiller University, Jena
Niccolò Pianciola, University of Padua, Italy
Gerald Praschl, German-Ukrainian Forum (DUF), Berlin
Felix Riefer, Think Tank Ideenagentur-Ost, Düsseldorf
Stefan Rohdewald, University of Leipzig, Germany
Sebastian Schäffer, Institute for the Danube Region (IDM), Vienna
Felix Schimansky-Geier, Friedrich Schiller University, Jena
Ulrich Schneckener, University of Osnabrück, Germany

Winfried Schneider-Deters, freelance analyst, Heidelberg/Kyiv
Gerhard Simon, University of Cologne, Germany
Kai Struve, Martin Luther University, Halle/Wittenberg
David Stulik, European Values Center for Security Policy, Prague
Andrzej Szeptycki, University of Warsaw, Poland
Philipp Ther, University of Vienna, Austria
Stefan Troebst, University of Leipzig, Germany

[Please send requests for changes in, corrections of, and additions to, this list to andreas.umland@stanforalumni.org.]

ibidem.eu